GERMAN MADE SIMPLE

Revised Edition

BY

EUGENE JACKSON

AND

ADOLPH GEIGER

REVISED BY

ROBERT D. VANDERSLICE

AND

ARNOLD LEITNER

THREE RIVERS PRESS

NEW YORK

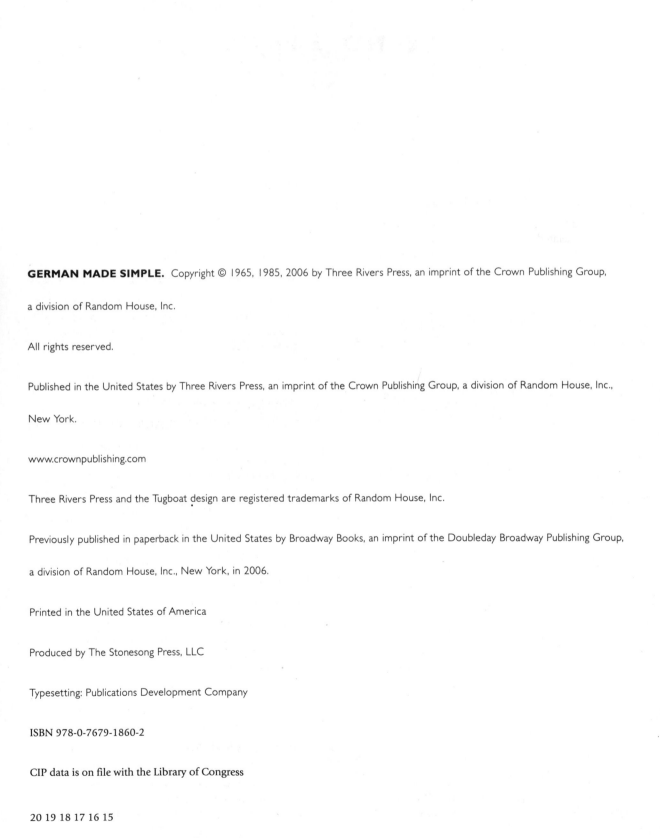

GERMAN MADE SIMPLE. Copyright © 1965, 1985, 2006 by Three Rivers Press, an imprint of the Crown Publishing Group,

a division of Random House, Inc.

Published in the United States by Three Rivers Press, an imprint of the Crown Publishing Group, a division of Random House, Inc.,

New York.

www.crownpublishing.com

Three Rivers Press and the Tugboat design are registered trademarks of Random House, Inc.

Previously published in paperback in the United States by Broadway Books, an imprint of the Doubleday Broadway Publishing Group,

a division of Random House, Inc., New York, in 2006.

Printed in the United States of America

Produced by The Stonesong Press, LLC

Typesetting: Publications Development Company

ISBN 978-0-7679-1860-2

CIP data is on file with the Library of Congress

20 19 18 17 16 15

CONTENTS

CHAPTER 1
MEET THE GERMAN LANGUAGE 1

German and English belong to the same family of languages—Related German and English words—German is not difficult to pronounce and spell—A preview of some interesting features of German.

CHAPTER 2
GERMAN LETTERS AND SOUNDS IN WORDS AND SENTENCES 5

The vowels **a**, **e**, **i**, **o**, **u**—The consonants—The vowel combinations **au**, **ei**, **eu**—The modified vowels **ä**, **ö**, **ü**—Front **ch**, back **ch**—Final **g**—The German alphabet—The German letter **ß**—Summary of letters and sounds.

CHAPTER 3
Die Familie Clark
THE CLARK FAMILY 14

The family (**die Familie**)—Gender of nouns—Definite article and noun in the nominative case—Agreement of third-person pronouns—Asking somebody's name.

CHAPTER 4
Herr Clark Ist Hungrig
MR. CLARK IS HUNGRY 19

The indefinite article **ein**, **kein**—Some German verb endings—The negative **nicht**—The formation of questions.

CHAPTER 5
Wer Ist Herr Clark?
WHO IS MR. CLARK? 23

Noun plurals—Common professions—Present tense of **gehen**—Three ways of saying **you**—Familiar verbs like **gehen** in the present tense—Question words—Asking somebody's age.

CHAPTER 6
Frau Clark Geht Einkaufen
MRS. CLARK GOES SHOPPING 30

Imperative (command) forms—Accusative case of nouns, definite and indefinite articles, **kein**, **wer** and **was**—Feminine nouns with the ending –**in**—Asking for the price.

CHAPTER 7
Das Haus der Familie Clark
THE HOME OF THE CLARK FAMILY 36

The one-family house (**das Einfamilienhaus**)—More noun plurals—Present tense of **sein** and **haben**—Accusative case, third-person pronouns—Some prepositions with the accusative case—Looking for a new home.

CHAPTER 8
Warum Lernt Herr Clark Deutsch?
WHY IS MR. CLARK LEARNING GERMAN? 41

Compound nouns—Opposites—Present tense of **antworten**, **reden**, **sprechen**—Modal verb **wollen**—Word order: normal and inverted word order—Position of infinitives.

CHAPTER 9
Eine Deutschstunde
A GERMAN LESSON 47

Modal verb **müssen**—Dative or "to" case of nouns, articles and **kein**—Some common verbs that may take indirect objects—Dative of third person pronouns and of **wer**—Dative prepositions.

CHAPTER 10
Wo Wohnt die Familie Clark?

WHERE DOES THE CLARK FAMILY LIVE?　54

Expressions of "liking" with **gern** and **lieber**—**Es gibt** there is, there are—Present tense of **laufen, fahren**—Prepositions with the dative or accusative—**Da(r)** and **wo(r)** combinations—What a mess!

CHAPTER 11
Das Geheimnis des Herrn Clark

THE SECRET OF MR. CLARK　61

Genitive case—The use of von in place of the genitive—The interrogative **wessen**—Prepositions with the genitive case—Present tense of **kennen** and of **wissen**.

CHAPTER 12
REVIEW OF CHAPTERS 1–11　67

Summary: Nouns, verbs, prepositions (dative, dative or accusative, accusative, genitive)—German expressions—Vocabulary exercises—Grammar review and exercises: noun declensions, all cases; masculine nouns with -n or -en endings—Compound nouns—Dialogues: 1. Wo ist die Thomasstraße? 2. Wo hält der Bus an?—Lesestücke: 1. Herr Clark lernt Deutsch. 2. Die Deutschsprachigen Länder: Deutschland, Österreich und Schweiz.

CHAPTER 13
Ein Freund Besucht Herrn Clark

A FRIEND VISITS MR. CLARK　76

Present tense of **lesen, treten**—Possessive adjectives (**ein**-words)—Packing a suitcase.

CHAPTER 14
Herr Clark Telefoniert

MR. CLARK MAKES A PHONE CALL　83

Infinitives used as nouns—Numerals 1 to 100—Present tense of **können, tun**—Der-words: **dieser, jener, jeder, welcher, aller**—Making phone calls.

CHAPTER 15
Dollar und Euro

DOLLARS AND EUROS　90

The European currency—Numerals over 100—Arithmetic—Subordinate word order—Subordinating conjunctions **dass, wenn**—Coordinating conjunctions **und, aber, oder, denn**—Talking about prices.

CHAPTER 16
Frau Clark geht mit ihren Kindern einkaufen

MRS. CLARK GOES SHOPPING WITH HER CHILDREN　96

Clothes—The "Do-er"—Present tense of **tragen, lassen**—About adjective endings—Adjectives preceded by a **der**-word—Adjectives preceded by an **ein**-word—Adjectives preceded by neither a **der**-word nor an **ein**-word—Colors.

CHAPTER 17
Wie Spät Ist Es?

WHAT TIME IS IT?　102

Travelling—Expressions of satisfaction or approval—**Dieser** the latter, **jener** the former—Travel expressions—Time of day—The 24-hour clock—Separable verbs, present tense—First and second person pronouns (nominative, dative, accusative).

CHAPTER 18
REVIEW OF CHAPTERS 13–17　108

Summary: Nouns, verbs, German expressions—Vocabulary exercises—Grammar review and exercises: Summary of adjective endings; summary of first-, second- and third-person pronouns (nominative, dative and accusative)—Dialogues: 1. Ihre Uhr geht nach. 2. Wo muss ich aussteigen?—Lesestück: Karl lernt nicht gern Mathematik.

CHAPTER 19
Der Arbeitstag des Herrn Clark

MR. CLARK'S WORKING DAY　115

Some foods—The present tense of **nehmen, dürfen**—Reflexive verbs, present tense of **sich setzen**—Some common reflexive verbs—

Reflexive pronouns in the dative—Separable verbs in subordinate clauses.

CHAPTER 20

Die kleine Anna war krank

LITTLE ANNE WAS SICK 123

Present tense of **schlafen, sollen**—Regular and irregular verbs in English—The past tense of weak (regular) verbs in German—Some familiar weak verbs, present and past—Past tense of strong (irregular) verbs—Some familiar strong verbs, present and past—Some expressions referring to past time—A fairy tale: **Rotkäppchen.**

CHAPTER 21

Was für ein Schreckliches Wetter!

WHAT HORRIBLE WEATHER! 129

Expressions of weather—Some familiar separable verbs (present and past)—The position of the separable prefix of verbs (present and past) in simple sentences and main clauses—Position of separable verbs in subordinate clauses—**Hin** and **her**—More subordinating conjunctions—**Wann, wenn, als.**

CHAPTER 22

Der April Macht Was Er Will

APRIL DOES WHAT IT WANTS 136

The seasons—The months of the year—**Gern, lieber, am liebsten**—Present tense of **werden, mögen**—Inseparable verbs—Verbs that take a dative object.

CHAPTER 23

Ein Besuch für Herrn Clark

A VISIT FOR MR. CLARK 143

Present and past tense of **essen**—The relative pronouns—**Wo(r)** combinations used for relative pronouns with prepositions—**Wer** and **was** as relative pronouns—Call My Bluff.

CHAPTER 24

REVIEW OF CHAPTERS 19–23 149

Summary: Verbs (present and past)—German expressions—Vocabulary exercises—Grammar review and exercises: modal auxiliaries, present tense; modal auxiliaries, past tense; subordinate word order; expressions of definite time and duration of time—Dialogues: **1. Zwei Freunde begegnen sich auf der Straße. 2. Ich habe Hunger**—Lesestück: Herr Clark war krank.

CHAPTER 25

Familie Clark Geht ins Kino

THE CLARK FAMILY GOES TO THE MOVIES 158

Cinema expressions—Ordinal numerals—Dates.

CHAPTER 26

Die Wiedervereinigung Deutschlands

THE REUNIFICATION OF THE TWO GERMANIES 163

The present perfect tense ("**Perfekt**")—Formation of the past participle—The principal parts of verbs—Use of the past and present perfect tenses.

CHAPTER 27

Ein typisches Wochenende bei den Clarks

A TYPICAL WEEKEND AT THE CLARKS' 169

Imperative of **sein**—The past perfect tense—Past participle of verbs ending in **-ieren**—Verbs with the auxiliary **sein**—The principal parts of some **sein**-verbs.

CHAPTER 28

Herr Müller Erzählt von Sich Selbst

MR. MÜLLER TELLS ABOUT HIMSELF 176

Some very special verbs with the auxiliary **sein**—Indirect questions with **wie, wo, wann, wer, was, warum**—The present and past perfect tenses in subordinate clauses.

CHAPTER 29

Herr Clark Schreibt einen Brief an Seinen Geschäftspartner in München

MR. CLARK WRITES A LETTER TO HIS BUSINESS PARTNER IN MUNICH 181

Formal letters: date, beginning, closing—The future tense—The present tense with future meaning—The future tense in subordinate clauses—Hobbies.

CHAPTER 30
REVIEW OF CHAPTERS 25–29   186

Summary: Verbs, German expressions—Vocabulary exercises—Grammar review and exercises: Present, past, present perfect, past perfect and future tenses; the subordinate word order of verbs in the present perfect, past perfect, and future; summary of subordinating conjunctions—Vier Dialoge—Lesestücke: 1. Frau Clark hat Geburtstag. 2. Ein toller Film im Kino.

CHAPTER 31
Herr Clark Erhält eine Antwort auf Seinen Brief

MR. CLARK RECEIVES AN ANSWER TO HIS LETTER   191

Related words—Mixed verbs—The infinitive with **zu**—The infinitive without **zu**.

CHAPTER 32
Die Geographie von Deutschland, Österreich und der Schweiz

THE GEOGRAPHY OF GERMANY, AUSTRIA AND SWITZERLAND   197

Expressions of geography—Imperative in the first-person plural—Comparison of adjectives—Some adjectives irregular in comparison—Case endings in the comparative and superlative—Sights in Germany, Austria, and Switzerland.

CHAPTER 33
Die Deutsche Küche

GERMAN COOKING   203

The **am -sten** form of the superlative of adjectives—Comparison of adverbs—A recipe: **Apfelkuchen.**

CHAPTER 34
Welche Städte Werden Sie Besuchen, Herr Clark?

WHAT CITIES WILL YOU VISIT, MR. CLARK?   209

The future tense of modal auxiliaries—The future perfect tense—Making predictions.

CHAPTER 35
Herr Clark Reist Nach Deutschland Ab

MR. CLARK SETS OUT FOR GERMANY   214

Two word families—About the verbs **lassen** and **verlassen**—Map of Germany.

CHAPTER 36
REVIEW OF CHAPTERS 31–35   219

Summary: Verbs (principal parts), German expressions—Vocabulary exercises—Grammar review and exercises: Case endings for the comparative and superlative of adjectives—Five tenses of verbs—Dialogues: 1. **Deutsche oder amerikanische Filme? 2. Im Restaurant**—Modernes Lesestück: **Frau Clark shoppt im Internet.**

CHAPTER 37
Ankunft in München

ARRIVAL IN MUNICH   224

Am Flughafen At the Airport—**Willkommen in Deutschland** Welcome to Germany—The present participle used as an adjective—More **sein**-verbs.

CHAPTER 38
Herr Clark Besucht die Familie Schiller

MR. CLARK VISITS THE SCHILLER FAMILY   230

Ein Telefongespräch A Telephone Conversation—**Eine Vorstellung** An Introduction—Prepositions with special meanings after certain verbs.

CHAPTER 39
Ein Ausflug an den Ammersee

AN EXCURSION TO THE AMMERSEE   236

Automobile terms—Informal letters: beginnings, endings—More strong verbs, principal parts—Principal parts of modals—The double infinitive—The double infinitive with **lassen, sehen, hören.**

CHAPTER 40
Herr Clark Verlässt Deutschland

MR. CLARK LEAVES GERMANY   242

Summary of German word order in simple sentences and main clauses—Summary of word order in subordinate clauses.

CHAPTER 41
REVIEW OF CHAPTERS 37–40   247

Summary: Verbs, German expressions—Vocabulary exercises—Dialogue: **An der Tankstelle** At the Gas Station—**Lesestücke: 1. Das deutsche Fernsehen. 2. Herrn Clarks Rheinreise.**

CHAPTER 42
Brief an einen Freund in Chicago

LETTER TO A FRIEND IN CHICAGO   252

About the subjunctive—The present subjunctive—The past subjunctive—The present perfect and past perfect subjunctive—The **würde**-form—Use of the subjunctive in conditional sentences—Word order in conditional sentences—Omission of **wenn**—Daydreaming: **Wenn ich . . .**

CHAPTER 43
Bericht eines Gesprächs zwischen Herrn Clark und Herrn Müller

REPORT OF A CONVERSATION BETWEEN MR. CLARK AND MR. MÜLLER   259

The subjunctive in indirect discourse.

CHAPTER 44
Was Geschieht im Hotel?

WHAT HAPPENS IN THE HOTEL?   264

CHAPTER 45
ANSWER SECTION   269

CHAPTER 46
GERMAN-ENGLISH VOCABULARY   287

CHAPTER 47
ENGLISH-GERMAN VOCABULARY   299

CHAPTER 48
COMMUNICATION GAMES   306

CHAPTER 1

MEET THE GERMAN LANGUAGE

1. GERMAN AND ENGLISH BELONG TO THE SAME FAMILY OF LANGUAGES

As you proceed in your study of the German language you will note many resemblances to your native English in vocabulary, idioms and grammatical structure. This is not strange, for German and English belong to the great Germanic family of languages. They are in fact language cousins. The many resemblances between German and English will be a great help to you in acquiring a good German vocabulary and in other phases of your language study.

2. RELATED GERMAN AND ENGLISH WORDS

Some of the most common German words, often repeated in everyday speech, closely resemble English words of the same meaning. The pronunciation differs, of course, but this will offer few difficulties, as you will see when you make a thorough study of German pronunciation in Chapters 2, 3, 4.

a. Some common nouns. Note that all nouns are capitalized in German.

Mann	Gras	Ball	Park	Hand	Hut	Haus	Wind	Sohn
man	grass	ball	park	hand	hat	house	wind	son

Garten	Sommer	Winter	Butter	Mutter	Vater	Onkel	Schule	Finger
garden	summer	winter	butter	mother	father	uncle	school	finger

b. Some frequently used adjectives

warm	kalt	alt	neu	gut	blau	braun	lang	voll	rund
warm	cold	old	new	good	blue	brown	long	full	round

c. Some frequently used verbs

The infinitive of all German verbs ends in **-en** or **-n.** Remove these endings from the following German verbs and note the remarkable resemblance to English verbs of the same meaning.

singen	finden	springen	bringen	sehen	helfen	kommen
to sing	to find	to spring	to bring	to see	to help	to come

senden	fallen	binden	beginnen	waschen	haben	wundern
to send	to fall	to bind	to begin	to wash	to have	to wonder, be surprised

3. GERMAN IS NOT DIFFICULT TO PRONOUNCE AND SPELL

German is a phonetic language. This means that words are generally pronounced as they are spelled and spelled as they are pronounced. There are no silent letters except **e** in the combination **ie,** and

h, which is silent when used after a vowel to indicate that it has a long sound. This is so much simpler than in English, where such words as *height, weight, cough, rough, dough, knight, could,* etc., make English spelling and pronunciation a difficult task for the foreigner.

Each German vowel has a long and a short sound. Thus: German **a** is either long, like *a* in *father,* or short, like *a* in *what.* German **a** is never like *a* in *hate, a* in *tall, a* in *mare,* or *a* in *back.*

Most German words are stressed (accented) on the first syllable. Thus: **Gar**-ten, **On**-kel. When the first syllable is not stressed, an accent mark will be used in the vocabularies to show the stressed syllable. Thus: *Papíer* (pa-*peer) paper.*

In Chapter 2 the German sounds and their spelling are explained in detail, with suitable exercises for practice in words and sentences. These should enable you to pronounce quite well. If possible you should get some German-speaking person to help you with your pronunciation, for it is important for you to hear the sounds correctly spoken and to have your own pronunciation checked.

You can improve your pronunciation and understanding of the spoken word by listening to German radio broadcasts and CDs, by attending German movies wherever possible, and by watching German DVDs.

LIP POSITION OF THE GERMAN VOWEL SOUNDS
(Description in Chapters 2 and 3)

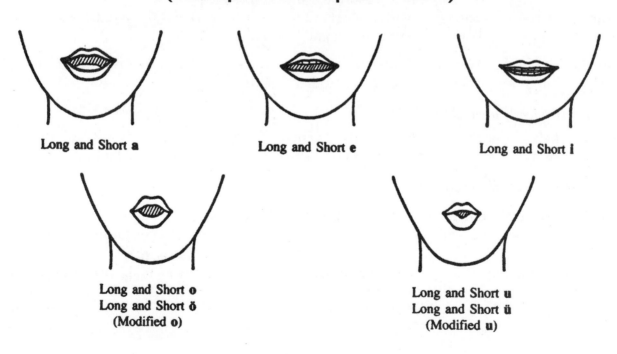

Long and Short **a**   Long and Short **e**   Long and Short **i**

Long and Short **o**
Long and Short **ö**
(Modified **o**)

Long and Short **u**
Long and Short **ü**
(Modified **u**)

THE GERMAN CONSONANTS L, R, and CH
(Description in Chapters 2 and 3)

The top of the tongue rounds upward for German l, not downward as for English *l*.

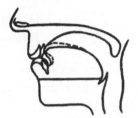

Tip-tongue **r**

The dotted line shows the vibration of the tip of the tongue for the tip-tongue *r*.

Uvular **r** and Back **ch**

The position of the tongue is the same for uvular **r** and back **ch**. The dotted line shows the vibration of the uvula for **r**.

Front **ch**

The front of the tongue is raised for front **ch**. Compare this with the position of the tongue for back **ch**.

4. A PREVIEW OF SOME INTERESTING FEATURES OF GERMAN

a. *German grammatical gender*

In English a male person is masculine in grammatical gender, and we refer to the person as *he*; a female person is feminine in gender and we refer to the person as *she*. All things are neuter and we refer to each thing as *it*. However, we do sometimes personify things such as cars, ships, etc., and refer to each such thing as *she*. Thus: She (the car) goes beautifully. She (the ship) is a beauty.

In German the matter of grammatical gender is quite different. Gender does not depend entirely on sex. The noun for a male is generally (not always) masculine in gender, the noun for a female is generally (not always) feminine in gender. Nouns for things are not always neuter. Some are masculine, some are feminine and some are neuter.

b. "the" and "a (an)" in German

The German word for the definite article "the" is very intriguing. The English word for "the" never changes. The German word for "the" has six forms, depending on its use in the sentence. Thus: **der** is used with masculine nouns, **die** with feminine nouns and **das** with neuter nouns in the nominative case. Here are a few samples to whet your appetite.

Der Mann ist gut.	**Die Frau** ist gut.	**Das Haus** ist alt.
The man is good.	The woman is good.	The house is old.

You will learn all about the forms and uses of the definite article in subsequent chapters.

The German word for the indefinite article "a (an)" is **ein.** It also, as you will see, has various forms according to its use in the sentence.

c. The plural of German nouns

German nouns do not form their plurals by adding **-s** or **-es** as is the case with most nouns in English. In general the German nouns form their plurals in one of four ways which you will learn later. **Kindergarten,** a word borrowed from the German, is made up of the German word **Kinder,** plural of **Kind** (child), plus **Garten** (garden).

d. Verb forms

German verbs have endings which correspond to the subject pronoun. English verbs also once had endings, which have long since disappeared. However, you may still see a few of them in poetry and in the Bible, which you will note are similar to German verb endings of the present day. Thus:

Old English	Modern German	Old English	Modern German
thou hast	**du hast**	thou comest	**du kommst**
he hath	**er hat**	he cometh	**er kommt**

A striking similarity between English and German verbs is the manner in which some very common verbs form their past tense. Thus:

Infinitive	**singen** sing	**trinken** drink	**beginnen** begin	**sehen** see
Past Tense	**sang** sang	**trank** drank	**begann** began	**sah** saw

There are many other interesting features of German which you will discover and master as you proceed in your study of the language. Those that have been mentioned will serve as a slight introduction to the really exciting experience which lies before you.

CHAPTER 2

GERMAN LETTERS AND SOUNDS IN WORDS AND SENTENCES

1. THE VOWELS a, e, i, o, u. THE CONSONANTS

Each German vowel has a long and a short sound. The sign ‾ will be used to indicate long; the sign ˘ to indicate short. These signs are not part of the spelling.

The German consonants **b, d, f, g, h, k, m, n, p, q, t, x** have approximately the same sound as the corresponding English consonants. Those consonants that differ will be given special attention.

Most German words are stressed (accented) on the first syllable. The accent mark (´) is used in the vocabularies of this book only when some other syllable is stressed. It is not part of the spelling.

Nearly all examples given to illustrate German sounds and letters consist of German words which closely resemble English words of the same meaning. As you practice these examples, you will be making a good start in building your German vocabulary. Practice all examples aloud. The description of the sounds and the pronunciation key will enable you to pronounce the words quite accurately.

Long and Short a (See Diagram in Chapter 1)

Long ā is like *a in father.* Key *ah*

Plān	**Glās**	**Jahr**	**kām**	**jā**	**klār**
plahn	*glahs*	*yahr*	*kahm*	*yah*	*klahr*
plan	glass	year	came	yes	clear

Short ă is like *a in what.* Key *ă*

Mănn	**Băll**	**hăt**	**ălt**	**kălt**	**wăs**	**dăs**
mănn	*băll*	*hăt*	*ălt*	*kălt*	*văs*	*dăs*
man	ball	has	old	cold	what	the

Long and Short e (See Diagram in Chapter 1)

Long ē (ee) is like *ay*[1] in *gay.* Key *ay*

dēr	**wēr**	**ēr**	**geht**	**zehn**	**Tee**	**See**
dayr	*vayr*	*ayr*	*gayt*	*tsayn*	*tay*	*zay*
the	who	he	goes	ten	tea	sea

Short ĕ is like *e in bet.* Key *ĕ*

Bĕtt	**Wĕlt**	**wĕnn**	**ĕs**	**lĕrnt**	**jĕtzt**
bĕt	*vĕlt*	*vĕnn*	*ĕs*	*lĕrnt*	*yĕtst*
bed	world	when	it	learns	now

In a few words long **ē** is spelled **ee (Tee, See)**. The silent **h** after **e** is a sign of length.

NOTE I. Prolong English *ay* and note that it has two parts. The second or off-glide is the sound *ee*. German long **ē** is the first part of the combination and should not glide off into *ee*.

Unstressed e

Unstressed **e** is like English *e* in *garden* and *father*. This sound is very common in unstressed syllables in both English and German. Key *e*. In the pronunciation key the stressed syllable is in heavy type.

Garten	Wasser	Vater	Lehrer	Klasse	Jahre	lernen	haben
găr-ten	*văs-ser*	*fah-ter*	*lay-rer*	*klăs-se*	*yah-re*	*ler-nen*	*hah-ben*
garden	water	father	teacher	class	years	to learn	to have

Long and Short i (See Diagram in Chapter I)

Long **ī** is like *ee* in *meet*. Key *ee*

wir	mir	Bier	die	sie	hier	vier
veer	*meer*	*beer*	*dee*	*zee*	*heer*	*feer*
we	to me	beer	the	she	here	four

Short **ĭ** is like *i* in *bit*. Key **ĭ**

Ding	Wind	Kind	Winter	ist	frisch
dĭng	*vĭnt*	*kĭnt*	*vĭn-ter*	*ĭst*	*frĭsh*
thing	wind	child	winter	is	fresh

Long **ō** is like *o*[1] in *wrote*. Key *oh*
Round the lips as in diagram

Brōt	Rōse	Sohn	Mōnat	rōt
broht	*rroh-ze*	*zohn*	*moh-năt*	*roht*
bread	rose	son	month	red

Short **ŏ** is like *o* in *other*. Key **ŏ**
Round the lips as in diagram

Önkel	Stŏck	kŏmmt	vŏll	dŏrt
ŏn-kel	*shtŏck*	*kŏmmt*	*fŏll*	*dŏrt*
uncle	stick	comes	full	there

Long and Short o (See Diagram in Chapter I)

NOTE I. Prolong English *o* and note that it has two parts. The second part is *ōō*. German long **ō** is the first part of the combination and should not glide off into *ōō*.

Long and Short u (See Diagram in Chapter I)

Long **ū** is like *oo* in *root*. Key *ōō*
Round the lips as in diagram

Füss	Schūle	Brüder	Hūt	Stūhl
fōols	*shōō-le*	*brōō-der*	*hōōt*	*shtōōl*
foot	school	brother	hat	chair

Short **ŭ** is like *oo* in *foot*. Key *ōō*
Round the lips as in diagram

Mŭtter	Bŭtter	Sŭppe	ŭnter	ŭnd
mōōt-ter	*bōōt-ter*	*zōōp-pe*	*ōōn-ter*	*ōōnt*
mother	butter	soup	under	and

The Consonant d (Final)

At the end of a word or syllable **d** is pronounced like *t*. **Kind** (*kĭnt*); **Wind** (*vĭnt*)

The Consonants h, j, w, l, r

h before a vowel, is like *h* in *home*. **hat** (*hăt*)

h after a vowel, is silent. It is a sign of length. **Jahr** (*yahr*)

j is like *y* in *year*. **jā** (*yah*) **Jahr** (*yahr*)

w is like *v* in *van*. **wăs** (*văs*)

l is like *l* in *lip*. For description of German **l**, see Diagram.

r is trilled as in *thrrree*. The trill may be produced by the tip of the tongue (see Diagram) or by the uvula (see Diagram). The tip-tongue **r** and the uvular **r** are both acceptable. Use whichever is easier for you.

The Consonants sp and st

sp is pronounced *shp* only at the beginning of a syllable. **Sport** (*shpŏrt*); **spielen** (*shpee-len*) to play

st is pronounced *sht* only at the beginning of a syllable. **Stŏck** (*shtŏck*) stick; **stehen** (*shtay-en*) to stand

The Consonants s, sch, ss, v, z

s before a vowel, is like *z* in *zone*. **See** (*zay*) sea; **seh-en** (*zay-en*) to see

s at the end of a syllable, is like *s* in *house*. **Glās** (*glahs*); **ĕs; dăs; wăs** (*văs*)

sch is like *sh* in *shoot*. **Schwĕster** (*shvĕst-er*) sister; **wăschen** (*vă-shen*) to wash

ss is like *ss* in *class*. **Klăsse** (*klăs-se*); **Wăsser** (*văs-ser*) water

v is like *f* in *fat*. Some German words are spelled with **v** instead of **f**. **Vater** (*fah-ter*) father

z is like *ts* in *its*. **zehn** (*tsayn*) ten; **Dezĕmber** (*de-tsĕm-ber*) December

Exercise I

Read the following sentences aloud and guess their meaning. The answers to all exercises are given in the "Answer Section" in the Appendix. Check all your answers!

1. **Hier īst dăs Glās. Es īst vŏll Wăsser. Dăs Wăsser īst frīsch ŭnd klār. Hier īst dăs Kind. Dăs Kīnd trīnkt Wăsser.**
2. **Dăs Kīnd spielt Băll. Dĕr Băll īst rŏt. Dĕr Băll rŏllt ŭnter dăs Bĕtt.**
3. **Hier īst dĕr Tēē. Dŏrt īst dĕr Kăffée.[1] Dĕr Tēē īst wărm. Dĕr Kăffée īst kălt. Dĕr Vāter trīnkt Kăffée. Die Mŭtter trīnkt Tēē.**
4. **Dĕr Mōnăt Jūnī[2] īst wărm. Dĕr Wīnter īst kălt īn Kănădă. Dĕr Sŏmmer īst wărm hier.**

5. Ist dĕr Kăffée kălt? Ist dĕr Tēē wărm? Ist dăs Bier kalt? Ist die Sŭppe wărm? Wĕr trīnkt Tēē? Wĕr trīnkt Kăffée?

6. Kărl[3] īst vier Jahre ălt. Mărie[4] īst sieben Jahre ălt. Wie[5] ălt īst Hăns?[6] Wie ălt īst dĕr Vāter? Wie ălt īst die Mŭtter? Wie ălt īst dăs Kīnd?

NOTES: 1. **Kăffée** (kăf-*fay*) coffee. 2. **Jūni** (**yoō-**nee) June. 3. **Karl** Charles. 4. **Mărie** (ma-**ree**) Mary. 5. **wie** (vee) how. 6. **Hans** Jack.

2. THE VOWEL COMBINATIONS *au, ei, eu.* **THE MODIFIED VOWELS** *ä, ö, ä.* **THE** *ch* **SOUND. FINAL** *g*

Practice each sound aloud, first in the words on the left, then in the sentences on the right.

The Vowel Combinations au, ei, eu

au, like *ow* in *how.* Key *ow*

Auto	Haus	Frau	blau	braun	kauft
ow-toh	*hows*	*frow*	*blow*	*brown*	*kowft*
car	house	woman	blue	brown	buys

Das Auto ist blau.

Der Mann kauft das Auto.

Die Frau kauft Kaffée und Tee.

Das Haus ist sehr (very) alt.

ei, like *ei* in *height.* Key *ei*

Eisen	ein	eine	heiß[1]	nein	weiß[1]
ei-zen	*ein*	*ei-ne*	*heiss*	*nein*	*veiss*
iron	a (an)	a (an)	hot	no	white

Ist der Hut braun? Nein, er ist weiß.

Ein Mann kauft ein Auto. Es ist rot.

Eine Frau kauft Kaffée und Tee.

Das Eisen ist heiß.

eu, like *oi* in *oil.* Key *oi*

Freund	Deutsch	heute	neu	neun
froint	*doitsh*	*hoi-te*	*noi*	*noin*
friend	German	today	new	nine

Wer lernt jetzt Deutsch?

Der Freund lernt jetzt Deutsch.

Karl ist heute neun Jahre alt.

Ist die Schule hier neu?

NOTE 1. The letter **ß** is another spelling for **ss.** For further explanation see page 11.

The Modified Vowels ä, ö, ü

Long **ā̈,** like *ay* in *day.* The letter **ā̈** is another way of spelling German long **ē.**

Bā̈r	zählen	zählt	wäscht	spät
bayr	*tsay-len*	*tsaylt*	*vaysht*	*shpayt*
bear	to count	counts	washes	late

Das Kind zählt bis zehn.

Ist der Bā̈r ein Tier (animal)?

Ja, der Bā̈r ist ein Tier.

Der Lehrer kommt heute spät.

Der Mann wäscht das Auto.

Short ă is like *e* in *bet*. The letter ă is just another way of spelling German short ĕ.

Mărz	Băcker	băckt	ălter	wărmer
mĕrtz	*bĕck-er*	*bĕckt*	*ĕl-ter*	*vĕr-mer*
March	baker	bakes	older	warmer

Der Băcker băckt Brot.

Karl ist ălter als (than) Maríe.

Florida ist wărmer als New York.

Der Monat Mărz ist oft (often) kalt.

Hier ist es wărmer als in Kanada.

Long ȫ. No equivalent sound in English. To make long ȫ, hold the lips firmly in the position for long ō (*oh*) and try to say ē (*ay*). The result will be long ȫ. (See Diagram in Chapter 1.)

Ȫl	schȫn	hȫren	wir hȫren	er hȫrt
oil	beautiful	to hear	we hear	he hears

Die Schwester ist sehr schȫn.

Das Ȫl ist heiß.

Wir hȫren Musík (*mōō-zeek*).

Er hȫrt Musík.

Die Musík ist sehr schȫn.

Short ŏ̈. No equivalent sound in English. Short ŏ̈ is like long ȫ, but shorter in length. (See Diagram in Chapter 1.)

Kŏ̈ln	Lŏ̈ffel	zwŏ̈lf	wir ŏ̈ffnen
Cologne	spoon	twelve	we open

Kŏ̈ln ist in Deutschland (*doitsh-lant*).

Wir ŏ̈ffnen jetzt die Tȫr.

Der Lŏ̈ffel ist groß.

Das Kind zählt von eins bis zwŏ̈lf.

von (*fŏn*) from, bis to

Long ǖ. No equivalent sound in English. It is like the French *u*. To make long ǖ, hold lips firmly in the position for ū (*ōō*) and try to say ī (*eel*). The result will be long ǖ. (See Diagram in Chapter 1.)

Tǖr	kǖhl	grǖn	fǖhlt	fǖr	Schǖler
door	cool	green	feels	for	pupil

Eine Tǖr ist ŏ̈ffen (open).

Das Wetter ist kǖhl.

Das Gras ist grǖn.

Die Rose ist fǖr die Mutter.

Der Ball ist fǖr das Kind.

Der Schǖler lernt Deutsch.

Er fǖhlt das Wasser. Es ist warm.

Short ŭ. No equivalent sound in English. Short ŭ
is like long ū, but shorter in length. (See Diagram in Chapter 1.)

dŭnn	fŭnf	fŭllt	kŭssen	wŭnschen
thin	five	fills	to kiss	to wish

Das Kind ist fŭnf Jahre alt.

Die Mutter kŭsst das Kind.

Wer wŭnscht ein Glas Wasser?

Maríe fŭllt das Glas voll Wasser.

Das Glas ist dŭnn.

Modified vowels are called **umlaut** vowels. The dots above the letter indicate the modification.

Front ch

Front **ch.** No equivalent in English. To make
front **ch** press the tip of the tongue firmly against
the lower teeth and try to say ĭsh, ĕsh. The result
will be front **ch** in ĭch and ĕch. (See Diagram in
Chapter 1.)

ĭch bin	ĭch lĕrne	ĭch gehe	ĭch hābe
I am	I learn	I go	I have

sprĕchen	ĭch sprĕche	er sprĭcht
shprĕ-chen	*ĭch shprĕ-che*	*ayr shprĭcht*
to speak	I speak	he speaks

Ich sprĕche Deutsch.

Er sprĭcht kein Deutsch.

Ich stehe hier.

Er steht nĭcht hier.

Ich bin Studént.

Er ist kein (no) Studént (*shtoo-dĕnt*).

Ist die Frau reich?

Nein, sie ist nĭcht reich.

Ich habe kein (no) Auto.

Ich trinke Mĭlch.

Ich habe das Lĭcht.

Wir sprechen nĭcht Englisch.

Back ch

Back **ch.** No equivalent sound in English. It is
used after the vowels **a, o, u.** To create back **ch**
place the tongue in position for **k,** and breathe
out strongly as for **h.** This makes a sound like an
outgoing snore. (See Diagram in Chapter 1.)

ăcht	Būch	Kū-chen	Tŏch-ter	sūcht
eight	book	cake	daughter	looks for

Wer hat das Būch?

Ich habe das Būch.

Wie alt ist die Tŏchter?

Sie ist ăcht Jahre alt.

Ist der Kūchen warm?

Nein, er ist nĭcht warm.

Wer sūcht (*zōōcht*) mĭch?

Die Mutter sūcht dĭch (you).

Final g

At the end of a word **g** is pronounced like **k**. In many regions of Germany the **g** after **i** and **e** is pronounced like front **ch**, after **a, o** and **u** like back **ch**.

richtig right
(*rĭch-tĭch, rĭch-tĭk*)

fertig finished
(*fĕr-tĭch, fĕr-tĭk*)

Tag day
(*tāch, tāk*)

Weg way
(*vaych, vayk*)

3. THE GERMAN ALPHABET. SUMMARY OF LETTERS AND SOUNDS

You have learned the German letters and their sounds, and have practiced them in words and sentences. In practicing these letters and their sounds, you have learned a small vocabulary of commonly used words.

This part starts with the complete German alphabet and the names of the letters.

It is most important to memorize the German alphabet by practicing it aloud, since the names of the letters, with one exception (y), illustrate their sounds.

The alphabet is followed by a summary of vowel and consonant sounds with pronunciation key.

Das Deutsche A B C The German A B C

A a *(ah)*	**H h** *(hah)*	**O o** *(oh)*	**U u** *(ōō)*
B b *(bay)*	**I i** *(ee)*	**P p** *(pay)*	**V v** *(fow)*
C c *(tsay)*	**J j** *(yŏt)* (o as in short)	**Q q** *(kōō)*	**W w** *(vay)*
D d *(day)*	**K k** *(kah)*	**R r** *(ĕrr)*	**X x** *(ĭx)*
E e *(ay)*	**L l** *(ĕll)*	**S s** *(ĕss)*	**Y y** *(ĭpsĭlon)*
F f *(ĕff)*	**M m** *(ĕm)*	**T t** *(tay)*	**Z z** *(tsĕt)*
G g *(gay)*	**N n** *(ĕn)*	**ä** *(a-Umlaut)*	**ü** *(u-Umlaut)* **ö** *(o-Umlaut)*

Qu appears in a few words, and is pronounced *kv*. Thus: **Quartier** *(kvahr-teer)* quarters.

y is found only in a few proper names. Thus: **Meyer** (also spelled **Meier** and **Mayer**) and **Bayern** *(bei-ern)* Bavaria.

The German Letters s, ss and ß

German orthography knows three different kinds of "s": "s," "ss" and "ß." It is extremely important to know the difference between these three kinds of "s."

"ss" stands after short vowel sounds and is not voiced: Fluss, essen, dass

"ß" stands after diphthongs (au, eu, äu, ai) and after long vowels. It is also not voiced: heißen, groß, weiß "s" is usually voiced and stands between two vowels: leise, Wiese, Riese. It can, however, be also not voiced and be found at the beginning, the middle and end of German words: das, bis, super.

Summary of Vowel Sounds

Long

Ger. Vowel ā ē ī ō ū

Pron. Key ah ay ee oh ōō

ā **Vater** (*fah-ter*) father

ē **zehn** (*tsayn*) ten

ī **wir** (*veer*) we; **die** (*dee*) the

ō **Brot** (*broht*) bread

ū **Schule** (*shōō-le*) school

ǟ **zählen** (*tsay-len*) to count

ȫ **hören** (*hȫ-ren*) to hear

ǖ **fühlen** (*füh-len*) to feel

Short

ă ĕ ĭ ŏ ŭ

ă ĕ ĭ ŏ ōō

ă **Mann** (*mănn*) man; **was** (*văs*) what

ĕ **Wetter** (*vĕt-ter*) weather

ĭ **Winter** (*vĭn-ter*) winter

ŏ **Onkel** (*ŏn-kel*) uncle

ŭ **Butter** (*boo-ter*) butter

ä̆ **März** (*mĕrtz*) March

ŏ̈ **zwölf** (*tsvŏlf*) twelve

ŭ̈ **füllen** (*fŭl-len*) to fill

Indefinite **e**	**Rose** *(rroh-se)*	**Garten** *(găr-ten)*	**Mutter** *(mōōt-ter)*

Summary of Consonant Sounds Needing Special Attention

v = f **voll** (*fŏll*)

j jung (*yōōng*)

w Wetter (*vĕt-ter*)

l lieben (*lee-ben*)

qu Quartíer (*kvahr-teer*)

r rot (*roht*)

z zehn (*tsayn*)

s (before a vowel) **Sohn** (*zohn*)

Glas (*glahs*)

ss Wasser (*văs-ser*)

ß Fuß (*fōōss*) foot

sch Schuh (*shōō*) shoe

sp (*initial*) **spielen** (*shpee-len*)

st (*initial*) **stehen** (*shtay-en*)

ch (*front*) **ĭch, nĭcht**

ch (*back*) **ăcht, Buch** (*bōōch*)

Final b d g

At the end of a word:

d > t Kind (*kint*) child
b > p Jakob (*ya-kop*) Jacob
g > k, *regional variety: front* **ch,** *back* **ch**

-ig > -ik, -ich fertig (*fĕr-tĭk fĕr-tĭch*) finished
-ag > -ak, -ach Tag (*tāk, tāch*) day
-eg > -ek, -ech Weg (*wēk, wēch*) way

Exercise 2

Practice these words aloud.

ja	**Jahr**	**Jahre**	**jung**	**Juni**	**Vater**	**voll**	**vier**	**von**
yah	*yahr*	*yah-re*	*yŏong*	*yōō-nee*	*vah-ter*	*fŏll*	*feer*	*fŏn*

Wasser	**Winter**	**Wind**	**Welt**	**was**	**wenn**	**wir**	**wie**	**warm**
văs-ser	*vīn-ter*	*vĭnt*	*vĕlt*	*văs*	*vĕnn*	*veer*	*vee*	*vărm*

zehn	**zwölf**	**März**	**Dezember**	**zählen**	**Zigarétte**
tsayn	*tsvŏf*	*mĕrtz*	*dĕ-tsĕm-ber*	*tsay-len*	*tsĭ-gă-rĕt-te*

Sohn	**September**	**Rose**	**Musík**	**sagen**	**singen**	**sitzen**	**sehen**
zohn	*zĕp-tĕm-ber*	*rroh-ze*	*mōō-zeek*	*zah-gen*	*zīng-en*	*zĭ-tsen*	*zay-en*

Schule	**Schwester**	**Deutsch**	**Englisch**	**wünschen**	**frisch**	**Studént**
shōō-le	*shvĕs-ter*	*doitsh*	*ĕng-lish*	*vün-shen*	*frĭsh*	*shtōō-dĕnt*

Sport	**spielen**	**sprechen**	**er spricht**	**Stock**	**Stuhl**	**stehen**
shpŏrt	*shpee-len*	*shprĕ-chen*	*ayr shprĭcht*	*shtŏck*	*shtōōl*	*shtay-en*

DIE FAMILIE CLARK
THE CLARK FAMILY

You have acquired a good working knowledge of German pronunciation and are familiar with a considerable number of words and expressions. You are now ready for a closer study of the German language. Follow all directions for study, reading aloud and speaking. Remember: The only way to learn to speak a language is by speaking it.

This chapter will introduce you to Mr. Clark, a New York businessman who is as eager as you are to learn German. You will also meet his family and his teacher, Mr. Müller, a German by birth but now an American citizen. As he teaches Mr. Clark, he will also teach you in a pleasant and interesting way.

So, **Viel Glück** (Good Luck) and **Gute Reise** (Happy Voyage) as you accompany Mr. Clark on the road which leads to a practical knowledge of the German language.

How to Study Each Chapter

Read the German text silently, referring to the English when necessary to get the meaning. Cover up the English text and read the German text silently. Practice aloud the words and expressions under **Wortschatz** (vocabulary).

Then read the German text aloud, pronouncing carefully. Finally, study "Grammar Notes and Practical Exercises."

Check your answers to each exercise in the "Answer Section."

Die Familie Clark

1. **Vater heißt Robert Clark.**
2. **Die Mutter heißt Helene Clark.**
3. **Das erste Kind heißt Karl.**
4. **Das zweite Kind heißt Wilhelm.**
5. **Das dritte Kind heißt Marie.**
6. **Das vierte Kind heißt Anna.**
7. **Dies ist die Familie Clark.**

The Clark Family

1. The father is called Robert Clark.
2. The mother is called Helen Clark.
3. The first child is called Charles.
4. The second child is called William.
5. The third child is called Mary.
6. The fourth child is called Anne.
7. This is the Clark family.

WORTSCHATZ *(VŎRT-SHĂTZ)* VOCABULARY

der Vater *(fah-ter)* father
die Mutter *(moo-ter)* mother
das Kind *(kint)* child
erste *(ayr-ste)* first
zweite *(tsvei-te)* second

dritte third
vierte *(feer-te)* fourth
heißt *(heisst)* is called
die Familie *(fa-mee-lye)* family
dies *(dees)* this

DIE FAMILIE **(FĂ-MEE-LYE)** THE FAMILY

der Vater	father
der Sohn	son
der Bruder	brother
der Onkel	uncle
der Großvater	grandfather
die Mutter	mother
die Tochter	daughter
die Schwester	sister
die Tante	aunt
die Eltern	parents
der Mann	man, husband
die Frau	woman, wife
die Kinder	children
die Großmutter	grandmother

WICHTIGE REDEMITTEL WORDS AND EXPRESSIONS FROM DAILY LIFE

Guten Tag *(gōō-ten tăk)* Good day
Guten Morgen *(gōō-ten mŏr-gen)* Good morning
Guten Abend *(gōō-ten ah-bent)* Good evening
Gute Nacht Good night
Wie heißen Sie? What is your name?

Ich heiße Engel. My name is Engel.
Ich heiße Thomas. My name is Tom.
Wie heißt er? What is his name?
Er heißt Müller. His name is Müller.
Auf Wiedersehen! Good-bye.

Grammar Notes and Practical Exercises

1. GENDER OF NOUNS

Most (not all) nouns denoting male beings are masculine in gender and take the definite article **der.** Thus, **der Mann** the man, **der Vater** the father, **der Sohn** the son.

Most (not all) nouns denoting female beings are feminine and take the definite article **die.** Thus, **die Mutter** the mother, **die Schwester** the sister, **die Tante** the aunt.

Not all nouns denoting objects are neuter. Some are masculine, some are feminine. Neuter nouns take the definite article **das.** Thus:

masculine	*feminine*	*neuter*
der Ball the ball	**die Schule** the school	**das Glas** the glass

Learn each noun with the definite article, as if the article and noun were one word. Start by memorizing the following nouns with their articles.

2. DEFINITE ARTICLE AND NOUN IN THE NOMINATIVE CASE

The nominative case is the case of the subject of the sentence.

In the nominative case the definite article is **der** with masculine nouns, **die** with feminine nouns, and **das** with neuter nouns.

masculine	*feminine*	*neuter*
Der Vater ist gross.	**Die Mutter** ist jung.	**Das Kind** ist gut.
The father is tall.	The mother is young.	The child is good.
Der Ball ist rot.	**Die Schule** ist alt.	**Das Glas** ist voll.
The ball is red.	The school is old.	The glass is full.
Dies ist **der Ball.**	Das ist **die Schule.**	Das ist **das Glas.**
This is the ball.	That is the school.	That is the glass.

Note that **dies,** meaning *this,* and **das,** meaning *that,* may point out nouns of any gender.

3. AGREEMENT OF THIRD-PERSON PRONOUNS

Third-person pronouns agree in gender and number with the nouns for which they stand.

a. Ist **der Vater** groß? Ja, **er** ist groß.	Is *the father* tall? Yes, *he* is tall.
b. Ist **der Ball** rot? Ja, **er** ist rot.	Is *the ball* red? Yes, *it*[1] is red.
c. Ist **die Mutter** jung? Ja, **sie** ist jung.	Is *the mother* young? Yes, *she* is young.
d. Ist **die Schule** alt? Ja, **sie** ist alt.	Is *the school* old? Yes, *it*[1] is old.
e. Ist **das Kind** gut? Ja, **es** ist gut.	Is *the child* good? Yes, *it* is good.
f. Ist **das Glas** voll? Ja, **es** ist voll.	Is *the glass* full? Yes, *it* is full.

	masculine	*feminine*	*neuter*
Definite Article	**der** Vater, **der** Ball	**die** Mutter, **die** Schule	**das** Kind, **das** Glas
Third-Person Pron.	**er** he, it	**sie** she, it	**es** it, it

NOTE: 1. When **er** stands for a masculine thing and **sie** for a feminine thing, both are translated by *it* and not by *he* and *she*, since in English things cannot be masculine or feminine.

Exercise 3

Complete each sentence with the correct pronoun. Check all your answers in the "Answer Section."

Example 1. **Sie** ist warm.

1. Das ist **die Suppe.** _____ ist warm.

2. Das ist **der Lehrer.** _____ ist gut.

3. Das ist **die Schule.** _____ ist alt.

4. Das ist **der Doktor.** _____ ist hier.

5. Das ist **das Wasser.** _____ ist klar.

6. Das ist **das Bier.** _____ ist kalt.

7. Das ist **die Butter.** _____ ist frisch.

8. Das ist **die Mutter.** _____ ist jung.

9. Das ist **der Hut.** _____ ist rot.

10. Das ist **der Ball.** _____ ist rund.

Exercise 4

Complete the answer to each question by placing the correct form of the definite article (der, die, das) before each noun.

1. **Wer ist das? Das ist** _____ **Vater;** _____ **Schwester;** _____ **Lehrer;** _____ **Doktor;** _____ **Onkel;** _____ **Mutter;** _____ **Bruder;** _____ **Mann;** _____ **Kind;** _____ **Tante.**
2. **Was ist das? Das ist** _____ **Schule;** _____ **Ball;** _____ **Hut;** _____ **Butter;** _____ **Glas;** _____ **Wasser;** _____ **Tee;** _____ **Kaffee;** _____ **Klasse;** _____ **Brot;** _____ **Schuh;** _____ **Hut.**

Exercise 5

Complete the following dialogue with the words and expressions from the box.

> Guten Tag!—heiße—Robert Clark—Auf Wiedersehen!—Angelika Müller—wie—heißen

- _____.

- _____ heißen Sie?

- Ich heiße _____.

- Wie _____ Sie?

- Ich _____.

- Auf Wiedersehen!

- _____!

HERR CLARK IST HUNGRIG
MR. CLARK IS HUNGRY

Herr Clark Ist Hungrig

1. Herr Clark ist hungrig.
2. Er geht in die Küche.
3. Kein Brot ist da.
4. Keine Butter ist da.
5. Kein Kaffee ist da.
6. Ist Frau Clark nicht da?
7. Frau Clark kommt und sagt:
8. "Hier ist ein Laib Brot."
9. "Hier ist ein Stück Butter."
10. "Hier ist eine Tasse Kaffee."
11. Nun ist Herr Clark nicht mehr hungrig.

Mr. Clark Is Hungry

1. Mr. Clark is hungry.
2. He goes into the kitchen.
3. There is no bread.
4. There is no butter.
5. There is no coffee.
6. Is Mrs. Clark not here?
7. Mrs. Clark comes and says:
8. "Here is a loaf of bread."
9. "Here is a piece of butter."
10. "Here is a cup of coffee."
11. Now Mr. Clark is not hungry any more.

Wortschatz

das Brot bread
die Butter butter
der Kaffee coffee
die Küche kitchen
der Laib loaf
das Stück piece
die Tasse cup

kommen to come, to go
sagen to say
hungrig hungry
kein no, not a
nicht not, **nicht mehr** not . . . any more
nun now

Grammar Notes and Practical Exercises

1. THE INDEFINITE ARTICLE *ein* (a, an), *kein* (not a, no)

Compare the forms of **der** with those of **ein**.

Der Ball ist hier.
The ball is here.
Ein Ball ist hier.
A ball is here.

Die Tür ist offen.
The door is open.
Eine Tür ist offen.
A door is open.

Das Glas ist voll.
The glass is full.
Ein Glas ist voll.
A glass is full.

Grammar Notes and Practical Exercises

	masculine	*feminine*	*neuter*
Nom.	**der, ein**	**die, eine**	**das, ein**

Ein has no ending in the nominative masculine and neuter. In the feminine the ending is **e**. **Kein** (not a, no) has the same case forms as **ein**.

Kein Ball ist hier.	**Keine Tür** ist offen.	**Kein Glas** ist voll.
No (not a) ball is here.	No (not a) door is open.	No (not a) glass is full.

Exercise 6

In each sentence substitute the correct form of the indefinite article for the definite article, then, in each sentence, use the proper form of **kein**.

Beispiel (*bei-shpeel*): Example: **Das Kind** spielt Ball. **Ein (kein) Kind** spielt Ball.

1. **Der Plan** ist gut.
2. **Das Bett** ist neu.
3. **Das Auto** ist blau.
4. **Die Tochter** ist hier.
5. **Die Frau** kauft Tee.
6. **Der Bruder** lernt Deutsch.
7. **Die Schwester** lernt Englisch.
8. **Die Tür** ist hier.
9. **Das Glas** ist dort.
10. **Die Schule** ist neu.
11. **Das Haus** ist grün.
12. **Die Tochter** ist zwölf Jahre alt.

2. SOME GERMAN VERB ENDINGS

a.

gehen	kommen	lernen	kaufen	zählen	spielen	wundern
to go	to come	to learn	to buy	to count	to play	to wonder

In the infinitive most German verbs end in **-en**. A few end in **-n**. That part of the verb to which the ending is added is called the *stem.* **geh-, komm-, lern-,** etc., are the stems of **gehen, kommen, lernen,** etc.

b.

ich gehe	I go	ich lerne	I learn	ich zähle	I count
ich komme	I come	ich kaufe	I buy	ich spiele	I play

When the subject is **ich** most German verbs end in -e.

c.

| er geht | he goes | er lernt | he learns | Hans zählt | Jack counts |
| sie kommt | she comes | wer kauft | who buys | Anna spielt | Anna plays |

When the subject is **er, sie** or **es**; a singular noun; **wer** or **was**—most German verbs end in -t.

d.

| wir gehen | we go | wir lernen | we learn | wir zählen | we count |
| wir kommen | we come | wir kaufen | we buy | wir spielen | we play |

When the subject is **wir**, all German verbs end in -en or -n, like the infinitive.

NOTE: The German verb has no special emphatic or progressive forms. Thus: **ich lerne** = I learn, I do learn, I am learning; **er kauft** = he buys, he is buying, he does buy; etc.

Exercise 7

Complete the verb in each sentence with the correct ending.

Beispiel: 1. Der Bruder lernt Deutsch.

1. Der Bruder lern _____ Deutsch.
2. Wir lern _____ Englisch.
3. Sie kauf _____ ein Buch.
4. Der Stuhl steh _____ dort.
5. Ich spiel _____ nicht Tennis.
6. Das Kind ha _____ Brot und Butter.
7. Der Doktor komm _____ heute.
8. Wer trink _____ Kaffee?
9. Er trink _____ Bier.
10. Der Schüler lern ____ gut.
11. Wir spiel _____ Ball.
12. Es steh _____ dort.
13. Marie sing _____ schön.
14. Sie sing _____ sehr schön.
15. Wir hab _____ kein Buch.
16. Er zähl _____ von eins bis zehn.
17. Wer spiel _____ Ball?
18. Was steh _____ dort?

3. THE NEGATIVE *nicht*

Der Mann ist **nicht** reich.	The man is *not* rich.
Ich gehe **nicht** nach Hause.	I am *not* going home.
Wir spielen **nicht** Tennis.	We do *not* play tennis.

nicht corresponds to the English *not*.

4. THE FORMATION OF QUESTIONS

Lernt **der Schüler** Deutsch?	Is the pupil learning German?
Ja, er lernt Deutsch.	Yes, he is learning German.
Spricht **die Frau** Englisch?	Does the woman speak English?
Nein, sie spricht nicht Englisch.	No, she does not speak English.

In questions that require a **ja** (yes) or a **nein** (no) answer, the subject stands after the verb.

Exercise 8

Find the questions to the following answers.

Beispiel: 1. <u>Heißen Sie Peter?</u> Ja, ich heiße Peter.

1. _____? **Ja, ich heiße Peter.**
2. _____? Nein, Herr Clark ist nicht hungrig.
3. _____? Ja, das Brot ist da.
4. _____? Nein, sie heißt Helene.
5. _____? Ja, sie kommt in die Küche.

Exercise 9

Answer these questions in the negative.

Beispiel: 1. Spielt das Kind Ball? Nein, es spielt nicht Ball.

1. Spielt das Kind Ball?
2. Geht der Schüler nach Hause?
3. Ist der Bruder zwölf Jahre alt?
4. Ist das Wetter kühl?
5. Kauft der Mann das Auto?
6. Ist er älter als die Schwester?
7. Ist das Haus sehr alt?
8. Singt Marie schön?
9. Kommt der Doktor heute?
10. Kommt Anna spät nach Hause?

WER IST HERR CLARK?
WHO IS MR. CLARK?

Wer Ist Herr Clark?

1. Robert Clark ist Geschäftsmann.
2. Er ist vierzig Jahre alt.
3. Er ist Amerikaner.
4. Er ist kein Deutscher.
5. Sein Büro ist in New York.
6. Er wohnt aber nicht in New York.
7. Die Familie Clark wohnt in einem Vorort von New York.
8. Herr Clark ist verheiratet.
9. Seine Frau Helene ist vierunddreißig Jahre alt.
10. Herr und Frau Clark haben vier Kinder, zwei Jungen und zwei Mädchen.
11. Karl ist zwölf Jahre alt.
12. Wilhelm ist zehn Jahre alt.
13. Marie ist acht Jahre alt.
14. Anna ist fünf Jahre alt.
15. Karl, Wilhelm und Marie gehen zur Schule.
16. Anna geht nicht zur Schule.
17. Sie ist noch zu jung für die Schule.

Who Is Mr. Clark?

1. Robert Clark is a businessman.
2. He is forty years old.
3. He is an American.
4. He is not a German.
5. His office is in New York.
6. However, he does not live in New York.
7. The Clark family lives in a suburb of New York.
8. Mr. Clark is married.
9. His wife Helen is thirty-four years old.
10. Mr. and Mrs. Clark have four children, two boys and two girls.
11. Charles is twelve years old.
12. William is ten years old.
13. Mary is eight years old.
14. Anne is five years old.
15. Charles, William and Mary go to school.
16. Anne does not go to school.
17. She is still too young for school.

Wortschatz (*vŏrt-shătz*) Vocabulary

der Amerikáner (*ă-may-ree-kah-ner*) American; **Amérika** America

das Büró office

der Herr gentleman, sir, Mr.

das Kind (*kint*) child

der Junge (*yoon-ge*) boy

das Mädchen (*mayt-chen*) girl

das Jahr (*yahr*) year

wohnen (*voh-nen*) to live, to reside

jung young; **alt** old

verheíratet (*fer-hei-rah-tet*) married

noch still; **noch nicht** not yet

zu (*tsōō*) too; **zu viel** too much

für for; **von** from

aber but; **und** (*ōōnt*) and

sein his (like **ein** and **kein**)

alle (*al-le*) all; **viele** many

Wichtige Redemittel Words and Expressions from Daily Life

Was sind Sie von Berúf? What are you by profession? What is your occupation (trade)

Ich bin Lehrer. I am a teacher.

Er ist Anwalt. He is a lawyer.

Herr B. ist Arzt. Mr. B. is a doctor.

Herr C. ist Geschäftsmann. Mr. C. is a businessman.

Frau C. ist Hausfrau. Mrs. C. is a housewife.

Herr K. ist Student. Mr. K. is a student.

zur Schule gehen to go to school

Wir gehen zur Schule. We go to school.

Grammar Notes and Practical Exercises

1. NOUN PLURALS

Only a few German nouns form their plurals by adding **-s**, as is the case with most English nouns. Here are some familiar nouns arranged in groups according to the way they form their plurals. Most German nouns form their plurals in one of the ways indicated below.

	Singular	*Plural*	*Type of Plural*
Group I	**der Lehrer** teacher	**die Lehrer** teachers	-
	der Bruder brother	**die Brüder** brothers	¨-
	das Mädchen girl	**die Mädchen** girls	-
	das Fräulein Miss, young lady	**die Fräulein** young ladies	-
Group II	**der Hut** hat	**die Hüte** hats	¨-e
	der Sohn son	**die Söhne** sons	¨-e
	das Jahr year	**die Jahre** years	-e
Group III	**der Mann** man	**die Männer** men	¨-er
	das Buch book	**die Bücher** books	¨-er
	das Kind child	**die Kinder** children	-er
Group IV	**der Junge** boy	**die Jungen** boys	-n
	die Lampe lamp	**die Lampen** lamps	-n
	der Herr gentleman	**die Herren** gentlemen	-en
Group V	**das Auto** car	**die Autos** cars	-s
	das Taxi taxi	**die Taxis** taxis	-s
	der Opa grandpa	**die Opas** grandpas	-s

Nouns of Group I add no ending to form the plural. They generally add an **umlaut** to **a**, **o** or **u** within the word. Nouns that end in -**er**, -**en**, -**el**, -**chen** or –**lein** typically belong to Group I.

Nouns of Group II add -**e.** They generally add an **umlaut** to **a**, **o** or **u** within the word. Almost 90% of all masculine nouns belong to this group, as well as many monosyllabic feminine and neuter nouns.

Nouns of Group III add -**er.** They always add an **umlaut** to **a**, **o** or **u** within the word. Mostly mono-syllabic neuter nouns belong to Group III.

Nouns of Group IV add -**n** or -**en.** They never add an **umlaut.** All nouns that end in -**heit**, -**keit**, -**schaft** belong to this group, as well as a large number of feminine nouns.

Nouns of Group V add –**s.** They never add an **umlaut.** Nouns of Group V end in –**a**, -**i** or –**o.**

The best way to learn noun plurals is to repeat aloud and write both singular and plural of nouns as they occur.

The definite article in the plural is **die** for all genders. The indefinite article **ein** has no plural, and the plural of **kein** is **keine.**

Die Knaben und **die Mädchen** sind dort.   The boys and the girls are there.
Keine Knaben und **keine Mädchen** sind dort.   No boys and no girls are there.

Exercise 10

Read the first sentence in each pair aloud. Read the second sentence in each pair, inserting the plural of the noun in heavy type.

Beispiel: 1. **Die Kinder** zählen von eins bis zehn.
1. **Das Kind** zählt von eins bis zehn.
   Die _____ zählen von eins bis zehn.
2. **Der Junge** wohnt nicht hier.
   Die _____ wohnen nicht hier.
3. **Das Buch** ist nicht neu.
   Die _____ sind nicht neu.
4. **Das Mädchen** singt schön.
   Die _____ singen schön.
5. **Der Lehrer** lehrt Deutsch und Englisch.
   Die _____ lehren Deutsch und Englisch.
6. Wo ist **die Lampe**?
   Wo sind die _____ ?
7. **Der Herr** spielt sehr gut Tennis.
   Die _____ spielen sehr gut Tennis.

8. **Der Hut** ist blau und weiß.
   Die _____ sind blau und weiß.
9. **Der Sohn** kommt heute nicht.
   Die _____ kommen heute nicht.
10. Wohnt **der Bruder** weit von hier?
    Wohnen die _____ weit von hier?
11. **Der Mann** hat ein Büro in New York.
    Die _____ haben ein Büro in New York.

2. THE PRESENT TENSE of *gehen* to go

Singular	*Plural*
ich gehe I go	**wir gehen** we go
du gehst you go	**ihr geht** you go
er, sie, es geht he, she, it goes	**sie gehen** they go

Polite form (P.F.), singular and plural: **Sie gehen** you go.

a. The endings of nearly all German verbs in the present tense are like those of **gehen**.

*b. **du gehst, ihr geht, Sie gehen** are all translated "you go."*

We say **du** (familiar singular) in addressing a relative, a close friend or a child.

We say **ihr** (familiar plural) in addressing more than one relative, close friend or child.

We say **Sie** to all others, whether singular or plural. This is called the polite form (P.F.) and is always capitalized.

Karl, **du gehst** zu schnell.	Charles, you are going too fast.
Kinder, **ihr geht** zu langsam.	Children, you are going too slowly.
Herr Braun, **Sie gehen** zu früh.	Mr. Braun, you are going too early.
Wohin **gehen Sie,** meine Herren?	Where are you going, (my) gentlemen?

c. The present tense may be translated in three ways.

ich gehe I go, do go, am going, **du gehst** you go, do go, are going; etc.

d. To form a question, invert subject and verb.

Wohin gehen Sie? Where are you going?

Gehen die Kinder zur Schule? Are the children going to school?

e. **To form the negative, use** nicht *(not).*

Sie geht **nicht** zur Schule. She does not go to school.

Gehen Sie **nicht** in die Stadt? Are you not going to the city?

3. FAMILIAR VERBS LIKE *gehen* IN THE PRESENT TENSE

singen	**lernen**	**lehren**	**trinken**	**kommen**	**kaufen**
to sing	to learn	to teach	to drink	to come	to buy
zählen	**wohnen**	**hören**	**spielen**	**stehen**	**wünschen**
to count	to live	to hear	to play	to stand	to wish

Exercise 11

Fill in the grids.

Infinitiv	ich	du	er, sie, es
wohnen			
			singt
	zähle		
			spielt
stehen			
		hörst	

	wir	ihr	sie, Sie (P.F.)
			trinken
	lernen		
		wünscht	
kommen			
	kaufen		
		geht	

Exercise 12

Complete the verbs with the correct personal endings.

1. Was kauf _____ Sie, Fräulein Braun? Ich kauf _____ Bücher.
2. Was kauf _____ Herr Braun? Er kauf _____ Hüte.
3. Komm _____ die Mädchen heute? Nein, sie komm _____ heute nicht.
4. Sing _____ die Mädchen und die Jungen schön? Ja, sie sing _____ sehr schön.
5. Spiel _____ ihr heute Ball, Kinder? Nein, wir spiel _____ heute Tennis.
6. Lern _____ du Englisch, Anna? Ja, ich lern _____ Englisch.
7. Wo wohn _____ der Geschäftsmann? Er wohn _____ nicht weit von hier.
8. Ich hör _____ Musik. Wer spiel _____?
9. Wo steh _____ die Stühle? Sie steh _____ dort.
10. Was trink _____ du, Fritz? Ich trink _____ Milch.

Exercise 13

Fragen Questions

Reread the text **Wer ist Herr Clark?** Then answer the following questions orally and in writing, referring to the text if necessary. Check your written answers in the "Answer Section." Follow this procedure with all **Fragen** exercises.

1. Was ist Herr Clark von Beruf?
2. Ist er ein Deutscher?
3. Wo ist sein Büro?
4. Wohnt er in New York?
5. Wie alt ist der Geschäftsmann?
6. Wie heißt seine Frau?
7. Wie alt ist sie?
8. Wie viele Kinder haben Herr und Frau Clark?
9. Wie heißen die zwei Jungen?
10. Wie alt sind sie?
11. Wie heißen die zwei Mädchen?

Question Words

wer	was	wie	wie viele	warum	wo
who	what	how	how many	why	where

Exercise 14

Bilden Sie Fragen! (Form questions.)

1. _____. Das Mädchen heißt Maria.
2. _____. Er ist Geschäftsmann von Beruf.
3. _____. Ich bin vierzig Jahre alt.
4. _____. Nein, sie wohnen nicht in New York.
5. _____. Karl geht zur Schule.
6. _____. Nein, Herr Clark ist Amerikaner.

Zwei Dialoge

- Guten Tag!
- Guten Tag!
- Wie alt sind Sie?
- Ich bin 34 Jahre alt. Und Sie?
- Ich bin 42 Jahre alt.
- Auf Wiedersehen.
- Auf Wiedersehen.
- Hallo!
- Hallo!
- Wie alt bist du?
- Ich bin 17. Und du?
- Ich bin 15.
- Tschüss.
- Tschüss.

FRAU CLARK GEHT EINKAUFEN
MRS. CLARK GOES SHOPPING

Frau Clark Geht Einkaufen

1. **Sie geht in einen kleinen Supermarkt.**
2. **Sie sieht eine Verkäuferin und fragt: „Wie viel kostet das Brot?"**
3. **„Wie viel kosten die Eier?"**
4. **„Wie viel kostet der Aufschnitt?"**
5. **„Wie viel kosten die Steaks?"**
6. **Die Verkäuferin antwortet geduldig auf alle Fragen.**
7. **Schließlich sagt Frau Clark:**
8. **„Geben Sie mir einen Laib Brot, zweihundert Gramm Aufschnitt, fünf Steaks und ein Dutzend Eier."**
9. **„Ich möchte bitte auch noch eine Flasche Wein."**
10. **Frau Clark zahlt an der Kasse und geht wieder nach Hause.**

Mrs. Clark Goes Shopping

1. She goes to a small supermarket.
2. She sees a salesclerk and asks: "How much is the bread?"
3. "How much are the eggs?"
4. "How much are the cold cuts?"
5. "How much are the steaks?"
6. The salesclerk replies patiently to all questions.
7. Finally Mrs. Clark says:
8. "Give me a loaf of bread, two hundred grams of cold cuts, five steaks and a dozen eggs."
9. "I would also like one bottle of wine."
10. Mrs. Clark pays at the cash counter and goes home again.

Wortschatz

der Aufschnitt cold cuts
das Ei egg
die Flasche bottle
die Frage question
die Kasse cash counter
die Verkäuferin sales clerk (fem.)
der Wein wine
antworten to reply, to answer
einkaufen to shop
fragen to ask
geben to give

kosten to cost, **wie viel kostet . . .** how much is . . .
sehen to see
zahlen to pay
geduldig patient, patiently
klein small
schließlich finally
wieder again
nach Hause home, **nach Hause gehen** to go home

Most Germans shop in modern shopping malls.

Wichtige Redemittel Words and Expressions from Daily Life

Bitte (*bīt-te*) Please

Danke (*dănk-e*) Thanks

Vielen Dank (*fee-len dănk*) Many thanks

Bitte schön (*bīt-te shȫn*) You're welcome

Verzeihen Sie (*věr-tsei-en zee*) Pardon

Ich möchte (*mȫch-te*) I should like

Wie viel kostet . . . (*vee-feel kŏs-tet*) How much does . . . cost?, How much is . . .

Grammar Notes and Practical Exercises

1. THE IMPERATIVE (COMMAND FORM)

Fam. Sing. **Gehe** nach Hause, Kind! Go home, child.

Fam. Plur. **Geht** nach Hause, Kinder! Go home, children.

P.F. Sing. **Gehen Sie** nach Hause, Herr Schmidt! Go home, Mr. Schmidt.

P.F. Plur. **Gehen Sie** nach Hause, meine Damen und Herren! Go home, ladies and gentlemen.

The *imperative singular, familiar* (**du** understood), ends in **-e**, which is often dropped.

The *imperative plural, familiar* (**ihr** understood), is like the verb form with **ihr** in the present tense.

The imperative polite form, singular *and* plural, is like the polite form in the present tense with **Sie** following the verb.

There are a few irregular imperative forms which you will learn as you progress.

Exercise 15

Complete each sentence with the correct imperative form of the given verb.

Beispiel: 1. Lerne Deutsch, Karl!

1. (Lernen) _____ Deutsch, Karl!
2. (Gehen) _____ langsam, Kinder!
3. (Spielen) _____ nicht Ball hier, Jungs!
4. (Trinken) _____ die Milch, Anna!
5. (Singen) _____ nicht so laut, Fräulein!
6. (Kommen) _____ nicht spät, meine Herren!
7. (Antworten) _____ Karl und Anna!
8. (Kaufen) Bitte _____ das Auto, Papa!
9. (Zählen) _____ von eins bis zehn, Maria!
10. (Kaufen) _____ die Bücher, Herr Braun!

2. THE PRESENT TENSE OF *geben* TO GIVE AND *sehen* TO SEE

Singular	*Plural*
ich gebe I give	**wir geben** we give
du gibst you give	**ihr gebt** you give
er, sie, es gibt he, she, it gives	**sie geben** they give

Polite form (P.F.), singular and plural: **Sie geben** you give.

Imperative forms: Fam. Sing. **Gib!**
Fam. Plur. **Gebt!**
P.F. Sing. and Plur. **Geben Sie!**

Singular	*Plural*
ich sehe I see	**wir sehen** we see
du siehst you see	**ihr seht** you see
er, sie, es sieht he, she, it sees	**sie sehen** they see

Polite form (P.F.), singular and plural: **Sie sehen** you see.

Imperative forms: Fam. Sing. **Sieh!**
Fam. Plur. **Seht!**
P.F. Sing. and Plur. **Sehen Sie!**

The endings of **sehen** are like those of **gehen**. Note however the change from **e** to **ie** in the second and third persons singular and in the familiar imperative singular. You will meet other verbs like **sehen**.

Was sehen Sie? Ich sehe			*What do you see? I see*		
den Tisch	**die** Lampe	**das** Buch	the table	the lamp	the book
einen Tisch	**eine** Lampe	**ein** Buch	a table	a lamp	a book
keinen Tisch	**keine** Lampe	**kein** Buch	no table	no lamp	no book
die Tische	**die** Lampen	**die** Bücher	the tables	the lamps	the books
keine Tische	**keine** Lampen	**keine** Bücher	no tables	no lamps	no books

3. THE ACCUSATIVE CASE: NOUNS, DEFINITE AND INDEFINITE ARTICLES; *kein, wer, was*

The accusative case is the case of the direct object. In these examples observe how the noun, the definite and indefinite articles and the interrogative pronoun are expressed in the accusative.

Wen sehen Sie?			*Whom do you see?*		
Ich sehe			*I see*		
den Mann	**die** Frau	**das** Kind	the man	the woman	the child
einen Mann	**eine** Frau	**ein** Kind	a man	a woman	a child
keinen Mann	**keine** Frau	**kein** Kind	no man	no woman	no child
die Männer	**die** Frauen	**die** Kinder	the men	the women	the children
keine Männer	**keine** Frauen	**keine** Kinder	no men	no women	no children

The Definite Article

	Singular			*Plural*
	masculine	*feminine*	*neuter*	*masc. fem. neut.*
Nom.	**der** Mann	**die** Frau	**das** Kind	**die** Männer (Frauen, Kinder)
Acc.	**den** Mann	**die** Frau	**das** Kind	**die** Männer (Frauen, Kinder)

The Indefinite Article and *kein*

Nom.	**ein (kein)**	**eine (keine)**	**ein (kein)**	(No plural of **ein**) **keine**
Acc.	**einen (keinen)**	**eine (keine)**	**ein (kein)**	(No plural of **ein**) **keine**

Note the ending **-en** in the masculine accusative singular of **der, ein** and **kein**.

Nouns are generally identical in the nominative and accusative singular and always identical in the nominative and accusative plural.

Interrogative Pronouns—*wer, was*

Nom.	**Wer** ist hier?	*Who* is here?	**Was** ist hier?	*What* is here?
Acc.	**Wen** sehen Sie?	*Whom* do you see?	**Was** sehen Sie?	*What* do you see?

Exercise 16

Form sentences with the accusative singular.

Wen sehen Sie?

Ich sehe	den	Mädchen
	die	Lehrer
	das	Verkäuferin
		Vater
		Geschäftsmann
		Frau
		Kind

Was sieht er?

Er sieht	einen	Laib Brot
	eine	Geschäft
	ein	Büro
	keinen	Schule
	keine	Flasche
	kein	Haus
		Hut

3. FEMININE NOUNS ENDING IN –in

Masculine nouns denoting persons are often made feminine by adding **–in** (and sometimes an **umlaut**).

der Verkäufer *m.* **die Verkäuferin** *f.*	**der Koch** *m.* **die Köchin** *f.* cook, chef
der Lehrer *m.* **die Lehrerin** *f.* teacher	**der Student** *m.* **die Studentin** *f.* student
der Schüler *m.* **die Schülerin** *f.* pupil	**der Freund** *m.* **die Freundin** *f.* friend

These feminine nouns form a special plural by adding **–nen**.

die Verkäuferin *sing.* **die Verkäuferinnen** *plur.*	**die Köchin** *sing.* **die Köchinnen** *plur.*
die Lehrerin *sing.* **die Lehrerinnen** *plur.*	**die Studentin** *sing.* **die Studentinnen** *plur.*

Exercise 17

Complete the following shopping dialogue with the words from the box.

Laib—Guten Tag—Vielen Dank—kostet—kosten—Dutzend—Aufschnitt—Wie viel—Sie

- Guten Tag.
- _____.
- Wie viel _____ die Eier? Wie viel _____ das Brot? _____ kostet der _____?
- Ein _____ Eier kostet 2 Euro.
- Geben _____ mir bitte Eier und einen _____ Brot.
- Bitte schön.
- _____. Auf Wiedersehen.

CHAPTER 7

DAS HAUS DER FAMILIE CLARK
THE HOME OF THE CLARK FAMILY

Das Haus der Familie Clark

1. Familie Clark wohnt in einem Einfamilienhaus mit Garten.
2. Das Haus ist nicht groß.
3. Es ist aber schön und bequem.
4. Es hat sieben Zimmer: ein Wohnzimmer, ein Esszimmer, eine Küche, drei Schlafzimmer und ein Arbeitszimmer für Herrn Clark.
5. Außerdem hat das Haus zwei Badezimmer.
6. Das Wohnzimmer ist groß, hell und schön möbliert.
7. Es hat zwei Fenster.
8. Durch die Fenster sieht man einen Garten.
9. Das Esszimmer ist nicht so groß wie das Wohnzimmer.
10. Hier sieht man einen Tisch, eine Anrichte und sechs Stühle.
11. Der Tisch ist rund.
12. Die sechs Stühle stehen um den Tisch.
13. Ein Schlafzimmer ist ziemlich groß.
14. Das ist für die Eltern.
15. Zwei Schlafzimmer sind etwas kleiner.
16. Das sind die Kinderschlafzimmer, eins für die zwei Jungen und eins für die zwei Mädchen.
17. Beide Kinderschlafzimmer haben zwei Bettchen, zwei Tischlein, zwei Stühle, einen Kleiderschrank, eine Kommode, und einige Bilder.
18. Ja, das Haus von Familie Clark ist wirklich schön und bequem.

The Clark Family Home

1. The Clark family lives in a one-family house with a garden.
2. The house is not large.
3. It is, however, beautiful and comfortable.
4. It has seven rooms: the living room, the dining room, the kitchen, three bedrooms, and a study for Mr. Clark.
5. In addition, the house has two bathrooms.
6. The living room is large, bright and beautifully furnished.
7. It has two windows.
8. Through the windows one sees a garden.
9. The dining room is not as large as the living room.
10. Here one sees a table, a sideboard, and six chairs.
11. The table is round.
12. The six chairs stand around the table.
13. One bedroom is rather large.
14. That is for the parents.
15. Two bedrooms are somewhat smaller.
16. Those are the children's bedrooms, one for the two boys and one for the two girls.
17. Both children's bedrooms have two little beds, two little tables, two chairs, a wardrobe, a chest of drawers and some pictures.
18. Yes, the house of the Clark family is really beautiful and comfortable.

Wortschatz

die **Anrichte** sideboard, buffet
das **Bett** bed; das **Bettchen**[1] little bed
der **Tisch** table; das **Tischlein**[1] little table
die **Kommóde** dresser, chest of drawers
das **Fenster** window; die **Tür** door
die **Wohnung** dwelling, apartment, home, house
das **Zimmer** room
bequém (*be-kvaym*) comfortable
hell light; **dunkel** dark
klein small; **kleiner** smaller

kennen to know, be acquainted with
möblíert (*mŏ-bleert*) furnished
rund (*rōōnt*) round
wirklich (*vĭrk-lĭch*) really
ziemlich (*tseem-lĭch*) rather
außerdem (*ow-ser-daym*) besides, in addition
beide both; **einige** several
etwas somewhat, something
um around; **mit** with
so groß wie as large as

NOTE: I. **-chen** or **-lein** added to a noun signifies "little," or "fondness for" the person or thing mentioned. Thus: **Brüderlein** little brother or dear brother; **Schwesterchen** little or dear sister.

Das Einfamilienhaus (ein-fa-mee-lyen-hows)
The One-Family House

das **Arbeitszimmer** (*ar-beits-tsim-mer*)
workroom, study
das **Badezimmer** (*bah-de-tsim-mer*), das **Bad**
bathroom
der **Balkon** balcony
das **Esszimmer** (*ess-tsim-mer*) dining room
der **Keller** cellar

die **Garage** garage
das **Schlafzimmer** (*shlahf-tsim-mer*) bedroom
das **Wohnzimmer** (*vohn-tsim-mer*) living room
die **Küche** (*kü-che*) kitchen
der **Hausflur** (*hows-flōōr*) vestibule
WC toilet

Wichtige Redemittel

Hier sieht man viele Häuser. Here one sees
many houses.

Hier lernt man viel Deutsch. Here you learn
much German.
Dort singt man oft. There people often sing.

NOTE: man (one, you, people) is an indefinite pronoun.

Grammar Notes and Practical Exercises

1. MORE NOUN PLURALS. PRACTICE SINGULAR AND PLURAL ALOUD

group I. *Singular*	der **Schüler**	das **Zimmer**	das **Fenster**
Plural: No ending	die **Schüler**	die **Zimmer**	die **Fenster**

group II. *Singular*	der **Stuhl**	der **Tisch**	die **Wand**
Plural: Adds **-e**, plus umlaut with a, o, u	die **Stühle**	die **Tische**	die **Wände**

group III. *Singular*	das Haus	das Buch	das Bild
Plural: Adds **-er**, plus umlaut with a, o, u	die Häuser	die Bücher	die Bilder

group IV. *Singular*	die Tür	die Frau	die Schule
Plural: Adds **-n** or **-en**	die Türen	die Frauen	die Schulen

Exercise 18

Change the subject nouns in these sentences to the plural. Be careful to make any necessary changes in the verbs.

Beispiel: Das Zimmer ist groß. **Die Zimmer** sind groß.

1. **Der Tisch** ist rund.
2. **Das Fenster** ist offen.
3. **Die Tür** ist nicht offen.
4. **Das Bild** ist schön.
5. **Das Fräulein** spielt nicht Tennis.
6. **Der Herr** lernt Englisch.
7. **Die Frau** singt schön.
8. **Der Schüler** spielt Ball.
9. **Der Stuhl** steht dort.
10. **Die Schule** ist nicht weit von hier.

2. PRESENT TENSE OF *sein* to be; *haben* to have

ich bin	wir sind	ich habe	wir haben
du bist	ihr seid	du hast	ihr habt
er, sie, es ist	sie sind	er, sie, es hat	sie haben

P.F. *Sie sind*
Imperative: *sei! seid! seien Sie!*

P.F. *Sie haben*
habe! habt! haben Sie!

3. THE ACCUSATIVE CASE: THIRD-PERSON PRONOUNS

Sehen Sie **den Mann?**
Ich sehe ihn (him).

Sehen Sie **die Frau?**
Ich sehe **sie** (her).

Sehen Sie **das Kind?**
Ich sehe **es** (it).

Sehen Sie **die Männer, die Frauen, die Kinder?**

Ich sehe **sie** (them).

Sehen Sie **den Tisch?**
Ich sehe **ihn** (it).

Sehen Sie **die Füllfeder?**
Ich sehe **sie** (it).

Sehen Sie **das Buch?**
Ich sehe **es** (it).

Sehen Sie **die Tische, die Türen, die Häuser?** Ich sehe **sie** (them).

	masculine	*feminine*	*neuter*	*plural m.f.n.*
Nom.	**er** he, it	**sie** she, it	**es** it	**sie** they
Acc.	**ihn** him, it	**sie** her, it	**es** it	**sie** them

4. PREPOSITIONS WITH THE ACCUSATIVE

für for; **durch** through; **gegen** against, toward; **um** around; and a few other prepositions always take the accusative case.

für die Mutter	durch den Garten	um den Tisch	gegen den Stuhl
für den Vater	durch die Tür	um die Schule	gegen das Fenster
für das Kind	durch das Haus	um das Haus	gegen die Tür
für die Kinder	durch die Gärten	um die Häuser	gegen die Tische

Exercise 19

Practice aloud and add the missing third-person pronouns in the accusative.

Kennen—to know, to be acquainted with a person or thing

- **Kennen Sie den Geschäftsmann, Robert Clark?**
- **Ich kenne _____ sehr gut.**
- **Kennen Sie Frau Clark?**
- **Ja, ich kenne _____.**
- **Kennen Sie die Kinder von Robert Clark?**
- **Nein, ich kenne _____ nicht.**
- **Kennen Sie das Haus, wo er wohnt?**
- **Ich kenne _____. Es ist ein Einfamilienhaus.**

Exercise 20

Complete the answers to each question with the correct third-person pronoun. The pronoun must agree in number and gender with the noun.

Beispiel: 1. Ja, ich sehe **ihn.**

1. **Sehen Sie den Garten dort?** Ja, ich sehe _____.
2. **Sehen Sie das Einfamilienhaus dort?** Ja, wir sehen _____.
3. **Ist der Hut für den Vater?** Ja, er ist für _____.
4. **Sind die Blumen hier für die Kinder?** Ja, sie sind für _____.
5. **Ist das Schlafzimmer für die Kinder?** Ja, es ist für _____.
6. **Zählen die Lehrer die Schüler?** Ja, sie zählen _____.
7. **Suchen Sie das Museum, Fräulein?** Ja, ich suche _____.
8. **Stehen die Kinder um den Lehrer herum?** Nein, sie stehen nicht um _____ herum.
9. **Wünschen Sie die Zeitung, mein Herr?** Nein, ich wünsche _____ nicht.
10. **Kauft der Herr den Tisch und die Stühle?** Nein, er kauft _____ nicht.

Exercise 21

Strike out the word which does not fit.

a. Schlafzimmer—Hausflur—Wohnzimmer—Esszimmer
b. Vater—Mutter—Lehrer—Tochter
c. Lehrerin—Verkäuferin—Studentin—Koch
d. Wein—Brot—Butter—Aufschnitt
e. der—die—keine—das
f. ein—er—sie—es
g. gehen—fragen—bitte—sehen

Exercise 22

Have a look at the drawing and decide where the following rooms could be: **Schlafzimmer, 2 Kinderzimmer, Badezimmer, Wohnzimmer, Küche, WC, Hausflur**

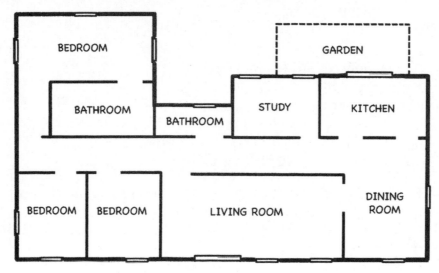

Exercise 23

Familie König sucht eine neue Wohnung. Mr. and Mrs. König and their three children are looking for an apartment in Munich. Help them in deciding which of the following apartments would be best for them.

München, ruhige[1] 3-Zimmerwohnung, mit Bad / WC, 82 m², keine Haustiere,[2] 790 €, Tel.: 34-456-721. Vorort von München, ca. 20 km bis zum Zentrum, Wohnzimmer, 2 Schlafzimmer, 2 Badezimmer, Balkon, 680 €,

Tel.: 453-987-21. Luxuswohnung in München, 5 Zimmer, ca. 110 m², Keller, Tiefgarage,[3] 1200 €, Tel.: 0660-263-263. Nähe Flugplatz[4] München, 4 Zimmer, 2 Balkone, nur 550 €, Tel.: 823-451-223

NOTES: I. ruhig **quiet. 2.** Haustier **pet. 3.** Tiefgarage **underground garage. 4.** Flugplatz **airport.**

WARUM LERNT HERR CLARK DEUTSCH? WHY IS MR. CLARK LEARNING GERMAN?

Warum lernt Herr Clark Deutsch?

1. **Wir wissen schon, Robert Clark ist ein Geschäftsmann in New York.**
2. **Er hat Geschäftspartner in ganz Europa.**
3. **Sein Geschäftspartner in München heißt Heinrich Schiller.**
4. **Im Sommer will Herr Clark eine Reise nach Deutschland machen.**
5. **Er will seinen Geschäftspartner besuchen.**
6. **Er will mit ihm über Geschäftssachen reden.**
7. **Er will auch interessante Plätze in Deutschland besuchen.**
8. **Leider spricht Herr Clark kein Deutsch.**
9. **Aber er will die Menschen in Deutschland verstehen.**
10. **Deswegen lernt Herr Clark Deutsch.**
11. **Herr Clark hat einen Deutschlehrer.**
12. **Er heißt Karl Müller. Er ist fünfzig Jahre alt.**
13. **Er spricht fließend Deutsch.**
14. **Er wohnt nicht weit von Herrn Clark.**
15. **Jeden Dienstag und jeden Donnerstag hat Herr Clark eine Deutschstunde.**
16. **Die Deutschstunde ist fast immer bei Herrn Clark.**
17. **Herr Clark ist intelligent und fleißig.**
18. **Schnell lernt er viele deutsche Wörter und Ausdrücke.**
19. **Herr Clark liebt die Konversation auf Deutsch:**

    „Guten Tag. Wie geht es Ihnen?"
    „Danke, sehr gut. Und Ihnen?"
    „Es geht."
    „Auf Wiedersehen."
    „Auf Wiedersehen."

Why Is Mr. Clark Learning German?

1. We already know Robert Clark is a businessman in New York.
2. He has business partners all over Europe.
3. His partner in Munich is Heinrich Schiller.
4. In the summer Mr. Clark wants to take a trip to Germany.
5. He wants to visit his business partner.
6. He wants to talk with him about business matters.
7. He also wants to visit interesting places in Germany.
8. Unfortunately, Mr. Clark speaks no German.
9. But he wants to understand the people in Germany.
10. Therefore, Mr. Clark is learning German.
11. Mr. Clark has a German teacher.
12. His name is Karl Müller. He is fifty years old.
13. He speaks German fluently.
14. He lives not far from Mr. Clark.
15. Every Tuesday and Thursday Mr. Clark has a German lesson.
16. The German lesson is almost always at Mr. Clark's home.
17. Mr. Clark is intelligent and diligent.
18. He learns quickly many German words and expressions.
19. Mr. Clark loves conversation in German:

    "Good day. How are you?"
    "Thanks, very well. And you?"
    "I am all right."
    "Good-bye."
    "Good-bye."

Wortschatz

Beginning with this vocabulary, the plural of all nouns is indicated.

der Geschäftspartner *pl.* - the business partner
die Sache *pl.* -n the thing, matter; **die Geschäftssache** business matter
der Mensch *pl.* -en the person, human being
der Platz *pl.* ¨-e the place
die Reise *pl.* -en the trip, voyage, journey
der Sommer *pl.* - the summer
die Stunde *pl.* -n the hour, the lesson
die Deutschstunde the German lesson
besúchen (*be-zōō-chen*) to visit
fragen to ask; **antworten** to answer
lernen to learn, to study
lieben to love
machen to do, to make
sprechen to speak

verstehen to understand
wissen to know (facts)
wohnen to live, to stay
wollen to want
fleißig industrious
intelligént (*een-tĕl-lĭ-gĕnt*) (hard g) intelligent
interessánt (*een-te-res-sănt*) interesting
fast almost
fließend fluent, fluently
immer always; **nie** never
leider unfortunately
schnell quick, quickly
schon already
deswegen (*dĕs-vay-gen*) therefore
bei at the house (home) of
es geht it is all right, it is OK

Gegenteile (gay-gen-tei-le) the opposites
Das Gegenteil von **fleißig** ist **faul.**
The opposite of *industrious* is *lazy.*
Das Gegenteil von **immer** ist **nie.**
The opposite of *always* is *never.*

Karl ist nicht **faul,** sondern[1] **fleißig.**
Charles is not *lazy,* but *industrious.*
Die Schule ist nicht **groß,** sondern **klein.**
The school is not *large,* but *small.*

NOTE: I. Use **sondern** (but) in the sense of *but on the contrary.* Otherwise use **aber.** Thus:

Die Wohnung ist nicht groß, **aber** sie ist bequem.

The apartment is not large, *but* it is comfortable.

Compound Nouns

German consists of a high amount of compound nouns. You have met a number of them in Chapter 7: **das Badezimmer, das Esszimmer, das Einfamilienhaus,** etc. If you know the meaning of each part of the compound, you can usually get the meaning of the whole. The gender of the last noun in the compound is the gender of the whole word. Thus:

das Haus + <u>die</u> **Tür** → <u>die</u> **Haustür**

das Haus + **die Tür** +<u>der</u> **Schlüssel** → <u>der</u> **Haustürschlüssel**

Practice the following by reading aloud:

die Deutschstunde *pl.* **-n**	**die Geschäftssache** *pl.* **-n**	**der Deutschlehrer** *pl.* **¨-**
(*doitsh-shtoon-de*)	(*ge-shäfts-za-che*)	the German teacher
the German lesson	the business matter	

Wichtige Redemittel

eine Reise machen to take (make) a trip
Wann machen Sie eine Reise nach Berlin?
Wie heißt das auf Deutsch =
Wie sagt man das auf Deutsch? =
How do you say that in German?
auf Deutsch in German; **auf Englisch** in
English; **auf Französisch** in French
usw. = **und so weiter** = and so forth

jeden Dienstag every Tuesday
jeden Donnerstag every Thursday
bei Herrn Clark at Mr. Clark's house
Wie geht's (dir)? How are you?
(Used in addressing a friend, child or relative.)
Wie geht es Ihnen? How are you?
(Used in addressing anyone else.)

Grammar Notes and Practical Exercises

1. PRESENT TENSE OF *antworten, reden, sprechen*

antworten	reden	sprechen
to answer	to talk	to speak
ich antworte	ich rede	ich spreche
du antwortest	du redest	du sprichst
er, sie, es antwortet	er, sie, es redet	er, sie, es spricht
wir antworten	wir reden	wir sprechen
ihr antwortet	ihr redet	ihr sprecht
sie antworten	sie reden	sie sprechen
P.F. Sie antworten	*P.F.* Sie reden	*P.F.* Sie sprechen

a. *When the stem of a verb ends in* -t *or* -d (antwort-en, red-en) *the letter* -e *is inserted before* -st *and* -t *for ease of pronunciation.*

b. *Short* -ĕ *in the stem of some verbs becomes* ī *in the* du *and* er, sie, es *forms* (du sprichst, er spricht), *and in the imperative familiar singular* (sprich!).

2. THE MODAL VERB *wollen* (PRESENT TENSE)

ich will	**wir wollen**
du willst	**ihr wollt**
er, sie, es will	**sie wollen**
	P.F. **Sie wollen**

NOTE: The German modal verbs add the infinitive without **zu** (to). **Er will alles verstehen.** He wants to understand everything.

Exercise 24

Practice by reading aloud.

Ich will Deutsch lernen.

Willst du eine Reise machen?

Er will seinen Freund besuchen.

Sie will ein Kleid kaufen.

Was wollen Sie tun?

Wir wollen ins Theater gehen.

Wollt ihr das Buch lesen?

Die Kinder wollen ins Kino gehen.

Sie wollen jetzt nicht spielen.

Wollen Sie mit uns gehen?

Exercise 25

Kurze Dialóge Brief Dialogues. Read aloud.

1. **Was heißt „to speak" auf Deutsch?**
   —Das heißt „sprechen."
   —Vielen Dank.
   —Bitte.

2. **Sprechen Sie Deutsch?**
   —Ja, ich spreche Deutsch.
   —Spricht das Fräulein auch Deutsch?
   —Nein, sie spricht nur[1] Englisch.
   —Wie geht's dir?
   —Gut, danke. Und dir?
   —Auch gut.

3. **Ist Herr Clark Lehrer oder Arzt?**[2]
   —Er ist weder[3] Lehrer noch[3] Arzt.
   —Was ist er denn?[4]
   —Er ist Geschäftsmann.

3. WORD ORDER—NORMAL AND INVERTED

In normal word order the verb follows the subject: *Subject—Verb.*

Herr Clark **lernt** schnell. **Er hat** einen Geschäftspartner in München.

In inverted word order the subject follows the verb. *Verb—Subject.*

In German, inverted word order is very common. It is used:

a. In questions.

Lernt Herr Clark schnell? **Hat er** einen Geschäftspartner in München?

NOTES: 1. **nur** only. 2. **Arzt** (*ărtst*) physician. 3. **weder** (**vay**-*der*) . . . **noch,** neither . . . nor. 4. **denn** then (often used for emphasis). The word for *then* (time) is **dann. Dann** geht er nach Hause. *Then* he goes home.

b. In the polite form of the imperative.

Bitte, **antworten Sie** auf Deutsch! Please answer in German.

c. When a simple sentence or independent clause begins with some word or words other than the subject.

Schnell lernt Herr Clark Deutsch. **In München** hat er einen Vertreter. **Jeden Donnerstag** hat er eine Deutschstunde. **Hier** spricht man Deutsch.

The words: **und** (and), **aber** (but), **oder** (or), which are called coordinating conjunctions, do not cause inverted word order.

Ich lerne Deutsch, und er lernt Französisch. Herr Clark ist Geschäftsmann, aber Herr Braun ist Lehrer.

4. WORD ORDER—POSITION OF INFINITIVES

The infinitive is placed at the end of a simple sentence or independent clause.

Er will seinen Vertreter **besuchen**.   He wants to visit his agent.
Er will eine Reise **machen**.   He wants to make a trip.

Exercise 26

Read the following sentences, putting the words in bold first.

Beispiel: In München hat der Geschäftsmann einen Partner.

1. Der Geschäftsmann hat einen Partner **in München**.
2. Er lernt **deswegen** Deutsch.
3. Herr Clark hat **jeden Dienstag** eine Deutschstunde.
4. Der Lehrer wohnt **nicht weit von hier**.
5. Man spricht **hier** Deutsch.
6. Wir sehen einen Garten **durch die Fenster**.
7. Sechs Stühle stehen **um den Tisch**.
8. Die Kinder gehen **heute** nicht zur Schule.

Exercise 27

Form sentences using the correct form of **wollen**.

Ich	wollen	den Lehrer	sein.
Du		Deutsch	fragen.
Er, sie, es		die Mutter	lernen.
Wir		fleißig	besuchen.
Ihr		Brot	kaufen.
Sie		Deutschland	sehen.

Exercise 28

Übersetzen Sie!

1. Who speaks German? Mr. M. speaks German. _____
2. Do you (**Sie**) speak German? No, I do not speak German. _____
3. Who asks: What is this? And what is that?_____
4. Does Mr. C. answer well? Is he intelligent and industrious? _____
5. Whom does Mr. C. want to visit? He wants to visit his business partner in Munich._____
6. I want to take a trip to Germany. Therefore I am learning German._____
7. Mr. C. is neither (**weder**) a teacher nor (**noch**) a doctor. He is a businessman. _____
8. The boys are not lazy but (**sondern**) industrious. _____

EINE DEUTSCHSTUNDE
A GERMAN LESSON

1. **Heute sind wir im Arbeitszimmer von Herrn Clark.**

2. **Das Zimmer ist nicht groß.**

3. **Im Zimmer sehen wir einen Schreibtisch, einen Stuhl vor dem Schreibtisch, einen Lehnstuhl, ein Sofa und viele Bücherregale mit Büchern.**

4. **An der Wand sehen wir eine Landkarte von Deutschland.**

5. **Der Deutschlehrer, Herr Müller, ist bei Herrn Clark. Der Lehrer sitzt auf dem Sofa. Der Schüler, Herr Clark, sitzt im Lehnstuhl.**

1. Today we are in the study of Mr. Clark.

2. The room is not big.

3. In the room we see a desk, a chair in front of the desk, an easy chair, a sofa and many bookshelves with books.

4. On the wall we see a map of Germany.

5. The teacher, Mr. Müller, is again at the home of Mr. Clark. The teacher is sitting on the sofa. The pupil, Mr. Clark, is sitting in the easy chair.

6. Herr Müller spricht mit seinem Schüler.

7. M.: Hier in Amerika spricht man Englisch und nennt die Dinge auf Englisch; in Frankreich nennt man die Dinge auf Französisch; in Spanien nennt man die Dinge auf Spanisch; in Italien nennt man die Dinge auf Italienisch; und . . .

8. C.: Jawohl, und in Deutschland spricht man Deutsch, und man muss die Dinge auf Deutsch nennen!

9. M.: Richtig! Sagen Sie mir nun auf Deutsch, was Sie hier im Zimmer sehen.

10. C.: Das ist ja leicht. Dies ist ein Lehnstuhl; das ist ein Sofa; das sind Bücherregale; das ist ein Schreibtisch; und . . .

11. M.: Gut. Nun sagen Sie mir, bitte: Was liegt auf dem Schreibtisch?

12. C.: Ein Bleistift, eine Füllfeder, einige Briefe und Papiere liegen dort.

13. Dann reicht der Lehrer dem Schüler ein Buch und fragt: „Was für ein Buch ist dies?"

14. Herr Clark antwortet: „Das ist ein Wörterbuch."

15. Der Lehrer gibt dem Herrn Clark andere Dinge und fragt immer wieder: Was ist dies? Und was ist das? Und Herr Clark antwortet immer schnell und richtig.

16. Endlich sagt der Lehrer zum Geschäftsmann: „Das ist für heute Abend genug. Ich muss jetzt gehen. Wir haben am Donnerstag wieder eine Stunde, nicht wahr?"

17. „Stimmt," antwortet Herr Clark.

18. Beide Herren gehen aus dem Zimmer. Herr Clark geht mit Herrn Müller zur Tür, gibt ihm die Hand und sagt zu ihm: „Bis Donnerstag, auf Wiedersehen!"

6. The teacher, Mr. Müller, is speaking with his pupil:

7. M.: Here in America one speaks English and gives the names of things in English; in France one gives the names of things in French; in Spain one gives the names of things in Spanish; in Italy one gives the names of things in Italian; and . . .

8. C.: Yes indeed, and in Germany one speaks German and one must give the names of things in German.

9. M.: Exactly. Now tell me in German what you can see in this room.

10. C.: That is indeed easy. This is an easy chair; that is a sofa; those are bookshelves; that is a desk; and . . .

11. M.: Good. Now tell me, please: What is lying on the desk?

12. C.: A pencil, a fountain pen, a few letters and papers are lying there.

13. Then the teacher hands the pupil a book and asks: "What kind of a book is this?"

14. Mr. Clark answers: "That is a dictionary."

15. The teacher gives other things to Mr. Clark and asks again and again: What is this? and what is that? And Mr. Clark always answers quickly and correctly.

16. Finally the teacher says to the businessman: "That is enough for this evening. I must go now. On Thursday we again have a lesson, don't we?"

17. "That's right," answers Mr. Clark.

18. Both gentlemen go out of the room. Mr. Clark goes with Mr. Müller to the door, shakes hands with him, and says to him: "Till Thursday, good-bye."

Wortschatz

der **Brief** *pl.* -e the letter

das **Papíer** (*pa-peer*) paper; *pl.* **Papiere** means documents, papers

der **Lehnstuhl** *pl.* ¨-e easy chair

der **Schreibtisch** *pl.* -e desk; das **Sofa** *pl.* -s sofa

die **Landkarte** *pl.* -n map

das **Bücherregal** *pl.* -e bookcase

geben to give; **reichen** to hand

nennen to name, tell the name of

leicht easy; **schwer** difficult

da there; **dann** then

endlich (*ent-lich*) finally

nun now; **jetzt** now

überáll (*über-ăll*) everywhere

wieder again; **immer wieder** again and again

jedesmal every time

mir me, to me, for me (*dat. of* **ich**)

bis until

damit with it, with them

Einige Länder and Sprachen von Europa (*oi-roh-pă*)
Some Countries and Languages of Europe

das Land	Deutschland	Frankreich	Spanien	Italien
	doitsh-lant	*frănk-reich*	*shpah-nyen*	*ee-tah-lyen*
die Sprache	Deutsch	Französisch	Spanisch	Italienisch
	doitsh	*frăn-tsȫ-zish*	*shpah-nish*	*ee-tă-lyay-nish*

Wichtige Redemittel

heute Abend this evening

heute Morgen this morning

ja indeed (*for emphasis*)

Das ist ja leicht. That is indeed easy.

Stimmt! (*shtimmt*) That's correct.

Was für ein what kind of

Was für ein Mann ist er?

What kind of man is he?

Er gibt ihm die Hand.

He shakes hands with him.

Nicht wahr? Isn't it true?

Er kommt heute, nicht wahr?

He is coming today, isn't he?

Er spricht Deutsch, nicht wahr?

He speaks German, doesn't he?

Grammar Notes and Practical Exercises

1. PRESENT TENSE OF THE MODAL VERB *müssen* to have to, must

ich **muss**	wir **müssen**
du **musst**	ihr **müsst**
er, sie, es **muss**	sie (Sie) **müssen**

Note the irregular of **müssen,** with no -e ending in the first and third persons, singular.

2. THE DATIVE OR "to" CASE: NOUNS, DEFINITE AND INDEFINITE ARTICLES

In the sentence: I give the man the book, the direct object is *the book* and the indirect object is *the man*, with "to" understood. Another way of saying this sentence is: I give the book *to* the man.

In German the indirect object is in the *dative* or "to" case. The direct object is of course in the *accusative* case. In the following sentences note the formation of articles and nouns in the dative case, singular and plural.

Ich gebe **dem Mann** das Buch.	I give *the man* the book.
Ich gebe **der Frau** die CD.	I give *the woman* the CD.
Ich gebe **dem Kind** den Ball.	I give *the child* the ball.
Ich gebe **den Frauen** die Bücher.	I give *the women* the books.
den Kindern	*the children*
den Männern	*the men*

Definite Article

	masc.	fem.	neut.	m.f.n.
	Singular			*Plural*
Nom.	der Mann	die Frau	das Kind	die Männer, Frauen, Kinder
Dat.	dem Mann	der Frau	dem Kind	den Männern, Frauen, Kindern
Acc.	den Mann	die Frau	das Kind	die Männer, Frauen, Kinder

Indefinite Article and *kein*

	masc.	fem.	neut.	m.f.n.
	Singular			*Plural*
Nom.	ein (kein)	eine (keine)	ein (kein)	keine
Dat.	einem (keinem)	einer (keiner)	einem (keinem)	keinen
Acc.	einen (keinen)	eine (keine)	ein (kein)	keine
			(no plural of *ein*)	

a. *The dative case endings of the definite and indefinite articles (and* kein*) in the singular are: masculine and neuter, -em; feminine, -er; in the plural, -en.*

b. *Nouns usually show no change in the dative singular. Most masculine and all neuter monosyllables <u>may</u> add -e. This form, however, is considered more and more old fashioned.*

c. *The dative plural of nouns always ends in -n. If the nom. plur. ends in -n, of course no -n is added. Exceptions are nouns whose plural ends in -s. Thus:*

Plur. Nom.	die Schüler	die Kinder	die Söhne	die Mädchen	die Autos
Plur. Dat.	den Schülern	den Kindern	den Söhnen	den Mädchen	den Autos

d. *The indirect (dative) object must always precede the direct object noun.*

3. SOME COMMON VERBS THAT MAY TAKE INDIRECT OBJECTS

geben to give	**bringen** to bring	**reichen** to hand	**schreiben** to write
zeigen to show	**schicken** to send	**kaufen** to buy	**schenken** to present

Exercise 29

Complete the answer to each question with the dative of the noun in parentheses.

Beispiel: 1. Er reicht **dem Lehrer** das Buch.

1. Wem reicht er das Buch?
2. Wem geben Sie einen Ball?
3. Wem gibt er die Hand?
4. Wem schenkt die Mutter eine Uhr?
5. Wem schreiben die Kinder einen Brief?
6. Wem bringt der Vater Bilder?
7. Wem zeigt er die Landkarte?
8. Wem kauft[1] die Mutter die Hüte?

Er reicht _____ das Buch. (der Lehrer)
Wir geben _____ einen Ball. (das Kind)
Er gibt _____ die Hand. (der Freund)
Sie schenkt _____ eine Uhr. (die Tochter)
Sie schreiben _____ einen Brief. (die Mutter)
Er bringt _____ Bilder. (die Kinder)
Er zeigt _____ die Landkarte. (die Schüler)
Sie kauft _____ die Hüte. (die Mädchen)

NOTE: 1. kaufen to buy (something, *accusative;* for somebody, *dative*).

4. DATIVE: THIRD PERSON PRONOUNS; INTERROGATIVE *wem?* to whom?

Wem geben Sie die Bücher?
Ich gebe **ihm (dem Mann)** die Bücher.
Ich gebe **ihr (der Frau)** die Bücher.
Ich gebe **ihm (dem Kind)** die Bücher.
Ich gebe **ihnen (den Frauen)** die Bücher.
    den Kindern
    den Männern

To whom are you giving the books?
I am giving *him (the man)* the books.
I am giving *her (the woman)* the books.
I am giving *him (the child)* the books.
I am giving *them (the women)* the books.
    the children
    the men

The Interrogative *wer*

Nom.	**wer**	who
Dat.	**wem**	(to) whom
Acc.	**wen**	whom

Third Person Pronouns

	Singular			*Plural*
Nom.	er	sie	es	sie
Dat.	ihm	ihr	ihm	ihnen
Acc.	ihn	sie	es	sie

Exercise 30

Complete the answer to each question with the dative case of the correct third-person pronoun.

Beispiel: 1. Ja, ich gebe **ihnen** den Ball.

1. Gibst du **den Kindern** den Ball?   Ja, ich gebe _____ den Ball.
2. Schicken Sie **den Frauen** die Blumen?   Ja, wir schicken _____ die Blumen.
3. Kaufen Sie **der Tochter** ein Kleid?   Ja, ich kaufe _____ ein Kleid.
4. Schreibt er **dem Lehrer** einen Brief?   Nein, er schreibt _____ keinen Brief.
5. Zeigt er **den Schülern** die Bilder?   Ja, er zeigt _____ die Bilder.
6. Schenkst du **dem Vater** eine Uhr?   Ja, ich schenke _____ eine Uhr.
7. Bringt sie **der Schwester** das Kleid?   Ja, sie bringt _____ das Kleid.
8. Schickt er **der Mutter** den Hut?   Nein, er schickt _____ den Hut nicht.

5. PREPOSITIONS WITH THE DATIVE

The following prepositions *always* take the dative case. Memorize them!

aus out of   **nach** after, to, toward
außer except, outside of   **seit** since, for
bei by, at, at the house of, with   **von** from, about, of
mit with   **zu** to (usually with persons)

These contractions are very common:

bei dem = beim   **von dem = vom**   **zu dem = zum**   **zu der = zur**

The prepositions **an** at, on, up against; **auf** on, upon, on top of; **in** in; and **vor** before, in front of, are used in this chapter with the dative case.

an der Wand on the wall   **vor dem Pult** in front of the desk
auf dem Pult on the desk   **in dem Zimmer** in the room
auf der Straße on the street   **in dem Lehnstuhl** in the armchair
auf dem Sofa on the sofa   **in der Schule** in the school

In Chapter 10 you will learn more about these prepositions and others like them, which *sometimes* take the dative and *sometimes* the accusative.

Exercise 31

Complete the dialogue with the words in the box.

ihnen—wem—ihm—der—den—ihr—einem—ihr

Geschenke[1]

„Was schenkt ihr Karl?" "Wir schenken _____ eine Uhr."

„Und Maria?" „Wir schenken _____ ein Kleid."

„_____ schenkt ihr den Ball?" „Den Ball geben wir _____ Mädchen."

„Kauft ihr auch _____ Lehrerin etwas?" „Nein, aber wir bringen _____ einen Kuchen."

„Schickt ihr _____ Kindern etwas?" „Ja, wir schicken _____ einen Brief."

NOTE: presents.

Exercise 32

Complete these phrases with the correct dative case endings.

1. aus d _____ Haus
2. bei d _____ Lehrer
3. mit ein _____ Buch
4. von d _____ Schule
5. nach ein _____ Stunde
6. mit ein _____ Füllfeder
7. zu d _____ Geschäftsmann
8. von d _____ Mutter
9. bei d _____ Arzt
10. mit d _____ Schüler _____ (*pl.*)
11. von d _____ Bilder _____ (*pl.*)
12. zu d _____ Kinder _____ (*pl.*)
13. von d _____ Herr _____ (*pl.*)
14. seit zwei Jahr _____ (*pl.*)
15. seit zwei Monat _____ (*pl.*)

CHAPTER 10

WO WOHNT DIE FAMILIE CLARK? WHERE DOES THE CLARK FAMILY LIVE?

Wo Wohnt die Familie Clark?

1. Herr Clark und Herr Müller gehen in das Arbeitszimmer. Herr Müller setzt sich auf das Sofa. Herr Clark setzt sich in den Lehnstuhl. Auf einem kleinen Tisch steht eine Flasche Rotwein. Neben der Weinflasche sind zwei Gläser.

2. Herr Müller nimmt sein Glas in die Hand und beginnt zu reden.

3. M.: Sie wohnen in der Vorstadt, aber Ihr Geschäft und Ihr Büro sind in der Stadt. Jeden Tag fahren Sie in die Stadt, um das Geschäft zu führen. Sagen Sie doch mal: Wohnen Sie gern in der Vorstadt?

4. C.: Ich wohne gern in der Vorstadt. Aber ich habe die Stadt auch gern.

5. M.: Warum haben Sie die Stadt gern?

6. C.: In der Stadt gibt es Bibliotheken, Theater, Museen, Universitäten, usw.

7. M.: Aber es gibt auch viel Verkehr, Lärm, Verbrechen und auf den Straßen Menschenmassen, die hin und her laufen.

8. C.: Sehr richtig! Deswegen wohne ich lieber in der Vorstadt. Hier ist das Leben ruhig und gemütlich.

9. M.: Hat Frau Clark das Leben in der Vorstadt auch gern?

10. C.: Sie hat es sehr gern. Manchmal fährt sie in die Stadt, um Freunde zu besuchen, oder in ein Konzert zu gehen.

11 M.: Gibt es auch gute Schulen in der Vorstadt?

Where Does the Clark Family Live?

1. Mr. Clark and Mr. Müller go into the study. Mr. Müller sits down on the sofa. Mr. Clark seats himself in an easy chair. On a little table is a bottle of red wine. Next to the bottle are two glasses.

2. Mr. Müller takes his glass into his hand and begins to talk.

3. M.: You live in the suburbs, but your business and your office are in the city. Every weekday you drive into the city in order to do business. Tell me then: Do you like to live in the suburbs?

4. C.: I like to live in the suburbs. But I also like the city.

5. M.: Why do you like the city?

6. C.: In the city there are libraries, theaters, museums, universities, etc.

7. M.: There is also a lot of traffic, noise, crime, and on the streets crowds of people who are running back and forth.

8. C.: Very correct. Therefore I prefer to live in the suburbs. Here life is quiet and comfortable.

9. M.: Does Mrs. Clark also like life in the suburbs?

10. C.: She likes it very much. Sometimes she drives into the city in order to visit friends or to go to a concert.

11. M.: Are there also good schools in the suburbs?

Wo Wohnt die Familie Clark?	*Where Does the Clark Family Live?*

12. C.: Die Schulen sind viel besser als in der Stadt, und die Kinder lieben ihre Lehrer und Lehrerinnen.

12. C.: The schools are much better than in the city, and the children love their teachers.

13. M.: Das Leben in der Vorstadt scheint recht schön zu sein!

13. M.: Life in the suburbs seems to be really beautiful.

14. C.: Da haben Sie Recht, Herr Müller.

14. C.: There you are right, Mr. Müller.

15. M.: Ich muss Sie loben, Herr Clark. Sie machen ja große Fortschritte im Deutschen.

15. M.: I must praise you, Mr. Clark. You are indeed making great progress in German.

16. C.: Es ist sehr nett von Ihnen,[1] das zu sagen.

16. C.: It's very nice of you to say that.

NOTE: 1. Ihnen dative case of **Sie.** It is like the dative of **sie** (they), but always capitalized.

Wortschatz

die Stadt *pl.* ¨-e city

das Geschäft *pl.* -e business

der Mensch *pl.* -en human being, man

die Menschenmasse *pl.* -n crowd of people

das Leben *pl.* - life; **die Zeit** *pl.* -en time

der Lärm noise

das Verbrechen *pl.* - crime

das Muséum *pl.* **Muséen** museum

die Universität (*ōō-nee-vĕr-zee-tēt*) *pl.* -en university

der Verkehr traffic

der Wein wine; **Rotwein, Weißwein** red wine, white wine

die Bibliothék (*bee-blee-oh-tēk*) *pl.* -en library

das Theáter (*tay-ah-ter*) *pl.* - theater

ins Theater gehen to go to the theater

beginnen to begin; **scheinen** to seem

führen to lead; **das Geschäft führen** to carry on (do) business

legen to put, to lay; **loben** to praise

besser better, **besser als** better than

gemütlich pleasant, comfortable

nett nice; **nett von Ihnen** nice of you

hin und her back and forth

manchmal sometimes

gern gladly **lieber** more gladly, preferably
A verb + **gern** indicates *liking* for a particular thing or action.

A verb + **lieber** indicates *preference* for a particular thing or action.

Ich habe die Stadt gern, aber ich habe die Vorstadt lieber.

I like the city, but I prefer the suburbs.

Er geht gern ins Kino, aber er geht lieber ins Theater oder ins Konzert.

He likes to go to the movies, but he prefers to go to the theater or to a concert.

Es gibt there is, there are

Es gibt (*lit.* it gives) + an object means *there is* or *there are,* denoting existence in general or within a wide range.

Es gibt viel Lärm auf der Straße.	There is much noise in the street.
Es gibt viele Theater in der Stadt.	There are many theaters in the city.
Was gibt's Neues? Es gibt nichts Neues.	What's new? There's nothing new.

In the sense of *to be present* (or *absent*), use **es ist** or **es sind.**

Es ist kein Arzt da.	There is no doctor there.
Es sind heute fünf Schüler abwesend.	There are five pupils absent today.

Wichtige Redemittel

Sie haben Recht. You are right.

Sie haben Unrecht. You are wrong.

Er macht Fortschritte. He makes progress.

Sie macht Einkäufe. She shops, goes shopping (makes purchases).

um . . . zu in order to
Sie geht in die Stadt, um Einkäufe zu machen. She goes to the city to shop.
Ich arbeite, um Geld zu verdienen. I work in order to earn money.

Grammar Notes and Practical Exercises

1. PRESENT TENSE OF *laufen* to run; *fahren* to drive, to go by car
    (bus, train . . .)

ich laufe	wir laufen	ich fahre	wir fahren
du läufst	ihr lauft	du fährst	ihr fahrt
er, sie, es läuft	sie (Sie) laufen	er, sie, es fährt	sie (Sie) fahren

Imperative: **laufe!**	**fahre!**
lauft! laufen Sie!	**fahrt! fahren Sie!**

Some verbs add an *Umlaut* to the vowel **a** in the second and third person singular. This *Umlaut* does not appear in the imperative.

2. PREPOSITIONS WITH THE DATIVE OR ACCUSATIVE

You have already learned:

The prepositions **durch, für, gegen, um** always take the accusative case.
The prepositions **aus, außer, bei, mit, nach, seit, von, zu** always take the dative case.

You will now learn nine prepositions, which sometimes take the dative and sometimes the accusative case. They are usually called the "doubtful prepositions." Memorize them!

an on, at, up against	**in** in, into	**unter** under, among
auf on, upon, on top of	**neben** next to, near	**vor** before, in front of
hinter behind	**über** over, above	**zwischen** between

Some common contractions are:

an dem = am   **an das = ans**   **auf das = aufs**   **in dem = im**   **in das = ins**

Study the following sentences and you will easily discover the rule which will tell you when to use the dative and when the accusative after the doubtful prepositions.

Wo? Where (place where) Dative

1. Das Bild ist **an der Wand.**
   The picture is on the wall.
2. Herr M. sitzt **auf dem Stuhl.**
   Mr. M. is sitting on the chair.
3. Der Garten ist **hinter dem Haus.**
   The garden is behind the house.
4. Das Büro ist **in der Stadt.**
   The office is in the city.
5. Das Tischlein ist **neben dem Sofa.**
   The little table is next to the sofa.
6. Das Porträt hängt **über dem Klavier.**
   The portrait hangs over the piano.
7. Der Ball liegt **unter dem Bett.**
   The ball is lying under the bed.
8. Das Kind steht **vor der Tür.**
   The child stands before the door.
9. Der Stuhl steht **zwischen den Fenstern.**
   The chair stands between the windows.

Wohin? Where (place to which) Accusative

1. Er hängt das Bild **an die Wand.**
   He hangs the picture on the wall.
2. Herr C. setzt sich **auf den Stuhl.**
   Mr. C. seats himself on the chair.
3. Hans läuft **hinter das Haus.**
   Hans runs behind the house.
4. Jeden Tag fährt er **in die Stadt.**
   Every day he rides into the city.
5. Er stellt das Tischlein **neben das Sofa.**
   He puts the little table next to the sofa.
6. Er hängt es **über das Klavier.**
   He hangs it over the piano.
7. Der Ball rollt **unter das Bett.**
   The ball rolls under the bed.
8. Das Kind springt **vor die Tür.**
   The child jumps in front of the door.
9. Er stellt ihn **zwischen die Fenster.**
   He puts it between the windows.

The doubtful prepositions take the dative case when they indicate *place where.* They answer the question **wo? Wo** steht der Stuhl? Where is the chair standing?

They take the accusative when they indicate *place to which.* They answer the question **wohin. Wohin** stellt er den Stuhl? Where is he putting the chair?

Exercise 33

Practice aloud.

Wo ist der Geschäftsmann? Er ist im (in dem) Arbeitszimmer (im Büro; im Theater; im Konzert; im Geschäft; in der Vorstadt; im Garten).

Wohin geht der Geschäftsmann? Er geht ins (in das) Arbeitszimmer (ins Büro; ins Theater; ins Konzert; in das Geschäft; in die Vorstadt; in den Garten).

Wo ist der Junge? Er ist im (in dem) Hause (im Park; im Garten; im Wasser; in der Schule; auf dem Gras).

Wohin läuft der Junge? Er läuft ins (in das) Haus (in den Park; in den Garten; ins Wasser; in die Schule; auf das Gras).

Wo liegt der Ball? Er liegt unter dem Bett (neben dem Klavier; hinter der Tür; zwischen den Fenstern; vor dem Mädchen; auf der Straße).

Wohin rollt der Ball? Er rollt unter das Bett (neben das Klavier; hinter die Tür; zwischen die Fenster; vor das Mädchen; auf die Straße).

Exercise 34

Fill in the missing dative or accusative endings.

Beispiel: 1. Das Auto fährt vor **die** Schule.

1. Das Auto fährt vor d _____ Schule.
2. Die Herren sitzen oben in d _____ Arbeitszimmer.
3. Hängen Sie das Bild dort an d _____ Wand!
4. In d _____ Stadt gibt es viele Bibliotheken.
5. Er muss jeden Tag in d _____ Stadt fahren.
6. Der Schüler setzt sich neben d _____ Lehrer.
7. Die Kinder spielen nicht auf d _____ Straße.
8. Die Papiere liegen hier unter d _____ Bücher _____.
9. Er stellt das Glas auf d _____ Tisch.
10. Was steht dort hinter d _____ Tür?
11. Er hängt den Hut hinter d _____ Tür.
12. Das Bild hängt zwischen d _____ Fenster _____ (*pl.*).

Exercise 35

Was für eine Unordnung! What a mess! Describe the picture. First write at least ten sentences where the things in the room are. **Beispiel: Der Apfel ist auf dem Bett.**

Then write at least ten sentences where the things in the room should be. **Beispiel: Der Apfel gehört[1] in die Küche.**

NOTE: 1. gehören to belong.

3. DA(R) AND *WO(R)* COMBINED WITH PREPOSITIONS

Liegt das Buch auf dem Tisch?	Is the book lying on the table?
Ja, es liegt **darauf.**	Yes, it is lying *on it.*
Schreiben sie **mit den Füllfedern?**	Are they writing with the fountain pens?
Ja, sie schreiben **damit.**	Yes, they are writing *with them.*
Worauf liegt das Buch?	*On what* is the book lying?
Es liegt auf dem Tisch.	It is lying on the table.

4. SOME COMMON COMBINATIONS OF *DA(R)* AND *WO(R)* + A PREPOSITION

damit with it, with them	**darin** in it, in them	**worauf** on what
darauf on it, on them	**womit** with what	**wofür** for what
dafür for it, for them	**davon** from, of, about it (them)	**worin** in what
	wovon from, of, about what	

Compare the above forms with the old English words *therewith, wherewith, therein, wherein,* etc.

da(r) and **wo(r)** + *a preposition* refer only to things, never to persons. When prepositions are used with persons, personal pronouns must be used. Thus:

mit wem with whom	**womit** with what
mit ihm (ihr, etc.) with him (her, etc.)	**damit** with it or them (things)
von wem from whom	**wovon** from what
von ihm (ihr, etc.) from him (her, etc.)	**davon** from it or them (things)

Exercise 36

Fragen

Reread the text: **Stadt und Vorstadt.** Then answer these questions.

1. **Wohin gehen Herr Clark und Herr Müller?**
2. **Wohin setzt sich Herr Müller?**
3. **Wohin setzt sich Herr Clark?**
4. **Was steht auf dem Tisch?**
5. **Was steht neben der Flasche?**

6. Wo wohnt der Geschäftsmann?
7. Wohin fährt er jeden Arbeitstag?
8. Wo ist sein Büro?
9. Wohnt er lieber in der Vorstadt als in der Stadt?
10. Wer fährt manchmal in die Stadt?
11. Wie ist das Leben in der Vorstadt?
12. Wo sind die Schulen besser, in der Stadt oder in der Vorstadt?
13. Wer macht große Fortschritte im Deutschen?

Das Geheimnis des Herrn Clark

1. **Wir wissen schon, jeden Tag fährt Herr Clark in die Stadt zur Arbeit.**
2. **Er geht dann in sein Büro. Dort arbeitet er bis Mittag.**
3. **In der Mittagspause isst er in der Kantine der Firma. Er isst immer das Menü des Tages: Suppe, eine Hauptspeise, Obst und einen Kaffee.**
4. **Heute ist Herr Clark während des Essens nervös. Er isst hastig und verlässt dann die Firma.**
5. **Er geht schnell durch die Straßen der Stadt. Vor einem Geschäft bleibt er stehen. Er tritt ein und begrüßt den Besitzer des Ladens.**
6. **Herr Clark: „Guten Tag."**
   Besitzer: „Guten Tag. Was wünschen Sie?"

   C.: „Ich möchte ein Armband für meine Frau."
   B.: „Anstatt des Armbands kann ich Ihnen Ohrringe empfehlen."
   C.: „Ja, bitte zeigen Sie mir die Ohrringe."
7. **Nach einer Weile kauft Herr Clark die Ohrringe.**
8. **Am Abend fährt er nach Hause und stellt ein kleines Päckchen auf den Tisch.**
9. **Frau Clark fragt: „Wessen Päckchen ist das?"**
10. **Herr Clark: „Es ist für dich. Ich habe es während der Mittagspause gekauft. Heute ist unser Hochzeitstag!"**

The Secret of Mr. Clark

1. We already know every day Mr. Clark drives into the city to work.
2. Then he goes into his office. There he works until midday.
3. In his lunch break he eats in the canteen of the company. He always eats the meal of the day: soup, a main dish, fruit and a coffee.
4. Today Mr. Clark is nervous during his meal. He eats hastily and then leaves the building.
5. He walks quickly through the streets of the city. He stops in front of a shop. He enters and greets the owner of the shop.
6. Mr. Clark: "Good afternoon."
   Owner of the shop: "Good afternoon. What do you wish? (How can I help you?)"
   C.: "I would like a bracelet for my wife."

   O.: "Instead of the bracelet I can recommend earrings."
   C.: "Yes, please show me the earrings."
7. After a while Mr. Clark buys the earrings.
8. In the evening he drives home and puts a small package on the table.
9. Mrs. Clark asks: "Whose package is it?"
10. Mr. Clark: "It is for you. I bought it during my lunch break. Today is our wedding anniversary."

Wortschatz

die Arbeit *pl.* -en work
die Mittagspause *pl.* -n lunch break
das Menü *pl.* -s set meal
die Kantine *pl.* -n canteen
die Firma *pl.* -en company
die Suppe *pl.* -en soup
das Obst fruit
die Hauptspeise *pl.* -en main dish
das Armband *pl.* ¨-er bracelet
der Ohrring *pl.* -e earring
das Päckchen *pl.* - package
der Hochzeitstag *pl.* -e wedding anniversary

gehen to go
essen to eat; **er isst** he eats
empfehlen to recommend
verlassen to leave
stehen bleiben to stop
eintreten to enter
begrüßen to greet
wünschen to wish
zeigen to show
bis until; **bis morgen** until tomorrow
immer always

Wichtige Redemittel

möchte should like, would like
Ich möchte darüber weiter sprechen.
I should like to talk further about it.

Wir möchten ein neues Auto kaufen.
We would like to buy a new car.
leider unfortunately
Ich kann leider nicht gehen.
Unfortunately I cannot go.

Grammar Notes and Practical Exercises

1. PRESENT TENSE OF *kennen* TO KNOW, TO BE ACQUAINTED WITH A PERSON OR A THING; *wissen* TO KNOW (FACTS)

ich kenne	wir kennen	ich weiß	wir wissen
du kennst	ihr kennt	du weißt	ihr wisst
er, sie, es kennt	sie (Sie) kennen	er, sie, es weiß	sie (Sie) wissen

The present of **kennen** is regular. Note carefully the irregular singular of **wissen**.

kennen means *to know* in the sense of to be acquainted with, to be familiar with.

wissen means to know facts.

Ich kenne den Mann.
Wir kennen das Haus.
Ich weiß, wo er wohnt.
Er weiß die Adresse.

I know (am acquainted with) the man.
We know (are acquainted with) the house.
I know where he lives.
He knows the address.

Exercise 37

Practice aloud.

1. —Kennst du den Mann?
   —Ich kenne ihn gut.
   —Weißt du, wo er wohnt?
   —Das weiß ich nicht.

2. Kennst du dieses Haus?
   —Ja, es ist die Wohnung eines Geschäftsmanns.
   —Weißt du vielleicht, wie er heißt?
   —Ja, er heißt Robert Clark.

3. Wissen Sie, was er verkauft?
   —Er verkauft Kunstgegenstände.
   —Wo ist sein Geschäft?
   —Ich weiß es nicht.

4. Kennen Sie dieses Fräulein?
   —Natürlich kenne ich sie.[1]
   —Wissen Sie, wie alt sie ist?
   —Das weiß ich nicht.

NOTE: 1. The pronoun **sie** is commonly used for **das Fräulein** and **das Mädchen**.

2. THE GENITIVE CASE

The genitive case is another name for the possessive case.

In English possession is expressed by *'s* and *s'*, and by the preposition *of*.

The man's house (the house of the man) is new.

The pupils' books (the books of the pupils) are old.

In the following sentences note the formation of the article and noun in the genitive case.

Das Haus **des Mannes** ist neu.	The house *of the man* (the man's house) is new.
Das Kleid **der Frau** ist weiß.	The dress *of the woman* (the woman's dress) is white.
Der Ball **des Kindes** ist rot.	The ball *of the child* (the child's ball) is red.
Die Hüte **der Männer, der Frauen** und **der Kinder** sind schön.	The hats *of the men, women and children* are pretty. (The men's, women's and children's hats are pretty.)

Definite Article

	Singular			Plural
	masc.	*fem.*	*neut.*	*m.f.n.*
Nom.	der	die	das	die
Gen.	des	der	des	der
Dat.	dem	der	dem	den
Acc.	den	die	das	die

Indefinite Article

	Singular			Plural
	masc.	*fem.*	*neut.*	*m.f.n.*
Nom.	ein	eine	ein	keine
Gen.	eines	einer	eines	keiner
Dat.	einem	einer	einem	keinen
Acc.	einen	eine	ein	keine

a. *The genitive case endings of the definite and indefinite articles (and* kein*) in the singular are: masculine and neuter -er; feminine -er; in the plural -er.*

b. *Most masculine and neuter nouns add -s or -es in the genitive singular.*[1] *One-syllable nouns often add -es.*[1]

N.	der Lehrer	das Mädchen	der Hut	der Mann	das Kind
G.	des Lehrers	des Mädchens	des Hutes	des Mannes	des Kindes

c. *Feminine nouns add no endings in the singular.*

N.	die Mutter	die Schwester	die Tochter	die Tür	die Wand
G.	der Mutter	der Schwester	der Tochter	der Tür	der Wand

d. *The nominative plural of the noun remains unchanged in the genitive plural.*

Nom. Plur.	die Lehrer	die Hüte	die Männer	die Schwestern	die Mädchen
Gen. Plur.	der Lehrer	der Hüte	der Männer	der Schwestern	der Mädchen

e. *The noun in the genitive case usually follows the noun it possesses.*

ein Teil des Gesprächs   **die Zimmer des Hauses**   **Das Porträt einer Frau**

f. A phrase with von *is often used instead of a genitive. Thus:*

die Wohnung von Herrn[1] Clark = die Wohnung des Herrn[1] Clark

NOTE: 1. A few masculine and neuter nouns add **-n** or **-en** in the genitive case. Such nouns add **-n** or **-en** in all other cases, singular and plural. Nouns of this type you have met are: **der Junge,** *gen.* **des Jungen,** *pl.* **die Jungen; der Herr,** *gen.* **des Herrn,** *pl.* **die Herren; der Student,** *gen.* **des Studenten,** *pl.* **die Studenten.**

3. THE INTERROGATIVE PRONOUN *wer* IN THE GENITIVE CASE

Wessen Hut ist grau?	Whose hat is gray?
Der Hut des Lehrers ist grau.	The teacher's hat is gray.
Wessen Hüte sind schön?	Whose hats are pretty?
Die Hüte der Frauen sind schön.	The women's hats are pretty.

Nom. **wer** who   *Gen.* **wessen** whose   *Dat.* **wem** to whom   *Acc.* **wen** whom

4. GENITIVE PREPOSITIONS

Very few prepositions take the genitive case. The most common are: **während** during; **wegen** on account of; **anstatt (statt)** instead of. Thus: **während der Nacht** during the night.

Exercise 38

Practice aloud.

1. Wessen Wohnung ist nicht groß? Die Wohnung des Geschäftsmanns (des Lehrers, der Lehrerin, des Arztes, des Schülers, der Schülerin, des Freundes, der Freundin, der Frauen, der Herren) ist nicht groß.
2. Wessen Päckchen steht auf dem Tisch? Das Päckchen des Vaters (der Mutter, des Kindes, des Onkels, der Tante, des Bruders, der Schwester, der Kinder) steht auf dem Tisch.
3. Wessen Hüte liegen auf dem Sofa? Die Hüte der Jungen (der Mädchen, der Kinder, der Schüler, der Schülerinnen, der Lehrer, der Lehrerinnen) liegen auf dem Sofa.

Exercise 39

Complete these sentences with the missing genitive case endings.

1. Wo ist die Wohnung d _____ Geschäftsmann _____ ?
2. Die Farbe d _____ Klavier _____ ist schwarz.
3. Die Farbe d _____ Auto _____ (*sing.*) ist blau.
4. Die Farbe d _____ Kleid _____ (*pl.*) ist grün.
5. Die Farbe d _____ Tinte ist schwarz.
6. Die Farbe d _____ Sofa _____ (*pl.*) ist rot.
7. Dort hängt das Porträt ein _____ Frau.
8. Hier hängt das Porträt ein _____ Mann _____ .

9. Die Farben d _____ Landkarte sind grün, grau und braun.
10. Wo ist die Wohnung d _____ Arzt _____ ?
11. Ich arbeite während d _____ Tag _____ aber er arbeitet während d _____ Nacht.
12. Wegen d _____ Lärm _____ kann ich nicht arbeiten.

Exercise 40

Use the genitive instead of the phrase with **von**.

Beispiel: 1. Das Haus des Mannes

1. Das Haus von dem Mann.
2. Die Bücher von dem Kind.
3. Das Auto von der Frau.
4. Die Bilder von den Mädchen.
5. Das Wohnzimmer von der Familie Clark.
6. Das Glas von dem Lehrer.
7. Die Päckchen von den Jungen.
8. Das Büro von dem Geschäftsmann.
9. Die Wohnung von dem Arzt.
10. Der Garten von dem Onkel.

Summary of Some Common Nouns
(Singular and Plural)

Practice these nouns aloud, in the singular and plural.

Group I No Ending Added, but Sometimes Adds Umlaut

der Vater	die Väter	der Onkel	die Onkel	das Zimmer	die Zimmer
der Bruder	die Brüder	der Garten	die Gärten	das Theater	die Theater
der Lehrer	die Lehrer	das Mädchen	die Mädchen	die Mutter	die Mütter
der Schüler	die Schüler	das Fräulein	die Fräulein	die Tochter	die Töchter

Group II Adds -E, and Sometimes Umlaut

der Sohn	die Söhne	der Bleistift	die Bleistifte	die Stadt	die Städte
der Hut	die Hüte	der Tisch	die Tische	das Ding	die Dinge
der Stuhl	die Stühle	die Hand	die Hände	das Jahr	die Jahre
der Tag	die Tage	die Wand	die Wände	das Papier	die Papiere

Group III Adds -ER, and Sometimes Umlaut

der Mann	die Männer	das Haus	die Häuser	das Buch	die Bücher
das Kind	die Kinder	das Bild	die Bilder	das Land	die Länder

Group IV Adds -N or -EN, Never Adds Umlaut

der Herr	die Herren	die Schule	die Schulen	die Stunde	die Stunden
der Mensch	die Menschen	die Tante	die Tanten	die Schwester	die Schwestern
der Junge	die Jungen	die Straße	die Straßen	die Lehrerin	die Lehrerinnen

Group V Adds -S

das Auto	die Autos	das Baby	die Babys	die Kamera	die Kameras
das Sofa	die Sofas	das Handy	die Handys	das Radio	die Radios
das Taxi	die Taxis	das Foto	die Fotos	der Opa	die Opas

Verbs

1. gehen		1. to go	
2. kommen		2. to come	
3. machen		3. to make	
4. stehen		4. to stand	
5. sitzen		5. to sit	
6. liegen		6. to lie	
7. legen		7. to put	
8. reichen		8. to hand	
9. wohnen		9. to live (dwell)	
10. schicken		10. to send	
11. hängen		11. to hang	
12. besuchen		12. to visit	
13. plaudern		13. to chat	
14. lernen		14. to learn	
15. lehren		15. to teach	
16. hören		16. to hear	
17. spielen		17. to play	
18. schreiben		18. to write	
19. sagen		19. to say	
20. fragen		20. to ask	
21. antworten		21. to answer	
22. kennen		22. to know (persons)	
23. reden		23. to talk	
24. zählen		24. to count	
25. bringen		25. to bring	
26. sehen (er sieht)		26. to see (he sees)	
27. sprechen (er spricht)		27. to speak (he speaks)	
28. geben (er gibt)		28. to give (he gives)	
29. fahren (er fährt)		29. to ride (he rides)	
30. laufen (er läuft)		30. to run (he runs)	
31. haben (er hat)		31. to have (he has)	
32. sein (er ist)		32. to be (he is)	
33. wissen (er weiß)		33. to know (objects and facts) (he knows)	
34. müssen (er muss)		34. to have to (he must)	

Prepositions—Memorize in the Numbered Order

With Dative Only

1. aus	1. out of
2. außer	2. besides, except
3. bei	3. at the house of
4. mit	4. with
5. nach	5. after, to
6. seit	6. since
7. von	7. from, of
8. zu	8. to

With Accusative Only

1. bis	1. until
2. durch	2. through
3. für	3. for
4. gegen	4. against, toward
5. ohne	5. without
6. um	6. around

With Dative (Place Where);
With Accusative (Place to Which)

1. an	1. at, on (up against)
2. auf	2. on, on top of
3. hinter	3. behind
4. in	4. in, into
5. neben	5. near, next to
6. über	6. over, above
7. unter	7. under
8. vor	8. before
9. zwischen	9. between

With Genitive Only

1. während	1. during
2. wegen	2. on account of
3. anstatt (statt)	3. instead of

Expressions

1. Hier spricht man Deutsch.	1. Here one speaks (they, people speak) German.
2. Wie heißen Sie?	2. What is your name?
3. Ich heiße Schmidt.	3. My name is Schmidt.
4. Er macht eine Reise.	4. He is taking a trip.
5. mal = einmal	5. once, just
6. Sagen Sie mal . . .	6. Just tell me . . .
7. Sehen wir uns mal das Haus an!	7. Just let us take a look at the house.
8. Ich wohne gern hier.	8. I like to live here.
9. auf Deutsch (auf Englisch)	9. in German (in English).
10. Er wohnt lieber in der Stadt.	10. He prefers to live in the city.
11. Sie macht Einkäufe.	11. She goes shopping.
12. also	12. so, and so, thus
13. Stimmt!	13. That's correct.
14. Er macht Fortschritte.	14. He makes progress.
15. Jawohl!	15. Yes, indeed.
16. Er gibt ihm die Hand.	16. He shakes hands with him.
17. Sie ist zu Hause.	17. She is at home.
18. Ich gehe nach Hause.	18. I am going home.

Exercise 41

Select the words from Column II which best complete the sentences begun in Column I.

Beispiel: (1d) Ich wohne lieber in der Vorstadt als in der Stadt.

I	*II*
1. Ich wohne lieber	a. ist dort auf dem Tisch.
2. Jeden Dienstag sitzt Herr Müller	b. dort auf den Tisch.
3. Nennt man in Deutschland die Dinge	c. denn da ist es still und gemütlich.
4. Stellen Sie bitte Ihr Glas	d. in der Vorstadt als in der Stadt.
5. Während des Deutschunterrichts	e. mit dem Auto zur Arbeit.
6. Ich wohne lieber in der Vorstadt,	f. auf Deutsch oder auf Englisch?
7. Das Päckchen für Frau Clark	g. im Arbeitszimmer beim Geschäftsmann.
8. Ich fahre jeden Tag	h. eine Reise nach Deutschland machen.
9. Im Sommer möchte ich	i. und das Haus des Geschäftsmanns an!
10. Sehen wir uns nun den Garten	j. trinken die Herren Wein.

Exercise 42

Make compound nouns of the following pairs of nouns. Translate them. Remember: The gender of the compound noun is that of the last noun in the compound. Thus: **die Hand + der Schuh = der Handschuh** glove (*lit. handshoe*)

1. das Haus + die Tür
2. die Wand + die Uhr
3. der Schlaf + das Zimmer
4. die Bilder + das Buch
5. der Garten + das Haus
6. das Deutsch + der Lehrer
7. die Wörter + das Buch
8. das Geschäft(s) + die Reise
9. die Musik + das Instrument
10. der Vater + das Land

Grammar Review and Practical Exercises

1. NOUN DECLENSIONS

You have learned the forms and uses of four cases of nouns with the definite and indefinite article and **kein**.

To decline a noun with its article means to give all four cases in the singular and plural. This is called a declension, and is a handy method for summarizing and remembering the case forms. Here are the declensions of some familiar nouns.

	Singular	*Plural*	*Singular*	*Plural*
Nom.	der (ein) Vater	die (keine) Väter	der (ein) Sohn	die (keine) Söhne
Gen.	des (eines) Vaters	der (keiner) Väter	des (eines) Sohnes	der (keiner) Söhne
Dat.	dem (einem) Vater	den (keinen) Vätern	dem (einem) Sohn	den (keinen) Söhnen
Acc.	den (einen) Vater	die (keine) Väter	den (einen) Sohn	die (keine) Söhne

	Singular	*Plural*	*Singular*	*Plural*
Nom.	das (ein) Kind	die (keine) Kinder	die (eine) Frau	die (keine) Frauen
Gen.	des (eines) Kindes	der (keiner) Kinder	der (einer) Frau	der (keiner) Frauen
Dat.	dem (einem) Kind	den (keinen) Kindern	der (einer) Frau	den (keinen) Frauen
Acc.	das (ein) Kind	die (keine) Kinder	die (eine) Frau	die (keine) Frauen

2. RULES OF NOUN DECLENSION

In the Singular
a. *Feminine nouns take no endings in the singular.*
b. *Most masculine and all neuter nouns add -s or -es in the genitive singular; usually -s with nouns of more than one syllable and -es with one-syllable nouns.*
c. *The nominative and accusative singular are usually alike.*

In the Plural
a. *The nominative plural of nouns must be memorized.*
b. *The genitive and accusative plural are like the nominative.*
c. *The dative plural must add -n unless the nominative plural already ends in -n (den Vätern, den Söhnen, den Kindern, den Frauen).*

Exercise 43

Practice aloud.

Wer ist hier? Who is here?
Nom. Sing. **Der Vater (der Sohn, das Kind, die Frau)** ist hier.
Nom. Plur. **Die Väter (die Söhne, die Kinder, die Frauen)** sind hier.

Wessen Bücher liegen dort? Whose books are lying there?
Gen. Sing. Die Bücher **des Vaters (des Sohnes, des Kindes, der Frau)** liegen dort.
Gen. Plur. Die Bücher **der Väter (der Söhne, der Kinder, der Frauen)** liegen dort.

Wem geben Sie die Bücher? To whom are you giving the books?
Dat. Sing. Ich gebe **dem Vater (dem Sohn, dem Kind[e], der Frau)** die Bücher.
Dat. Plur. Ich gebe **den Vätern (den Söhnen, den Kindern, den Frauen)** die Bücher.

Wen sehen Sie dort? Whom do you see there?
Acc. Sing. Ich sehe **den Vater (den Sohn, das Kind, die Frau)** dort.
Acc. Plur. Ich sehe **die Väter (die Söhne, die Kinder, die Frauen)** dort.

3. MASCULINE NOUNS WITH -n or -en ENDINGS

A few masculine nouns add **-n** (or **-en**) to the nominative to form all other cases, singular and plural. Thus:

	Singular	*Plural*	*Singular*	*Plural*	*Singular*	*Plural*
Nom.	**der** Junge	die Jungen	der Student	die Studenten	der Herr	die Herren
Gen.	**des** Jungen	der Jungen	des Studenten	der Studenten	des Herrn	der Herren
Dat.	**dem** Jungen	den Jungen	dem Studenten	den Studenten	dem Herrn	den Herren
Acc.	**den** Jungen	die Jungen	den Studenten	die Studenten	den Herrn	die Herren

Exercise 44

Complete these sentences with the correct case endings.

Beispiel: 1. Die Wohnung **des Geschäftsmanns** ist nicht groß.

1. D _____ Wohnung d _____ Geschäftsmann _____ ist nicht groß.
2. Herr Clark hat ein _____ Wohnung in d _____ Vorstadt.
3. D _____ Zimmer d _____ Wohnung sind schön möbliert.
4. D _____ Freund _____ d _____ Kinder kommen heute.
5. Sehen wir nun d _____ Wände d _____ Zimmer _____ (*sing.*) an.
6. Einige Bild _____ hängen an d _____ Wänden.
7. In d _____ Esszimmer sehen wir ein _____ Tisch.
8. D _____ Tisch ist rund.
9. Um d _____ Tisch stehen sechs Stühle.
10. D _____ Lehrer sitzt auf ein _____ Stuhl.
11. D _____ Geschäftsmann setzt sich auf d _____ Sofa.
12. Über d _____ Klavier hängt das Porträt ein _____ Frau.
13. Herr Clark hat ein _____ Geschäftspartner in München.
14. Er will d _____ Partner besuchen.
15. München ist ein _____ Stadt in Deutschland.

Exercise 45

Answer each question using the proper case of the noun in parentheses. Use plural of noun where indicated.

Beispiel: 1. Der Lehrer hat eine Wohnung in der Stadt.

1. Wer hat eine Wohnung in der Stadt? (der Lehrer)
2. Wessen Kinder spielen im Garten? (der Geschäftsmann)
3. Wem bringst du den Hut? (die Schwester)
4. Wen lieben die Kinder? (die Lehrerin, *pl.*)
5. Was suchen die Jungen? (der Ball)
6. Zu wem spricht der Lehrer? (der Schüler, *pl.*)
7. Wessen Porträt hängt im Wohnzimmer? (die Frau)
8. Womit schreibt der Junge? (der Bleistift)
9. Womit schreibt das Mädchen? (die Füllfeder)
10. Wen fragt der Vater? (das Kind, *pl.*)
11. Wem geben Sie die Briefe? (die Mutter)

Zwei Dialoge

Read each dialogue silently several times and make certain of its meaning. Practice the German text aloud many times. Follow this procedure with all dialogues.

WO IST DIE THOMASSTRASSE?[1]

—Entschuldigen Sie bitte, können Sie mir sagen, wo die Thomasstraße ist?

—Gehen Sie immer gerade aus.

—Ist es weit?

—Nein, es ist nur eine kurze Strecke.

—Danke vielmals.

—Bitte schön.

NOTE: I. There is no "ß" in capital letters. "SS" is used instead.

WO HÄLT DER BUS AN?

—Können Sie mir bitte sagen, wo der Bus anhält?

—Er hält dort an der Ecke an.

—Ich danke Ihnen sehr.

—Bitte sehr.

Exercise 46

Das erste Lesestück (The first reading selection)

How to Read the Lesestück

Read the passage silently from beginning to end to get the meaning as a whole. Reread the passage. Most of the new words are given in the footnotes. Look up the meaning of any other words you may not know in the German-English vocabulary at the end of this book.

Read the passage silently a third time. A translation is given in the "Answer Section."

Follow this procedure in all other reading selections.

HERR CLARK LERNT DEUTSCH

Herr Clark ist ein Geschäftsmann. Sein Büro ist in einem Wolkenkratzer in der Stadt New York. Seine Wohnung aber ist nicht in der Stadt, sondern[1] in einem Vorort nicht weit davon.[2] Jeden Wochentag fährt Herr Clark in die Stadt und führt dort sein Geschäft.

Die Firma des Herrn Clark hat einen Geschäftspartner in Deutschland. Er heißt Heinrich Schiller und wohnt in der Stadt München. Im Frühling dieses[3] Jahres macht Herr Clark eine Reise nach Deutschland, um Herrn Schiller zu besuchen.[4] Er will mit seinem Partner über wichtige[5] Geschäftssachen reden. Herr Clark will auch die Menschen in Deutschland verstehen. Deswegen beginnt Herr Clark, Deutsch zu lernen.

Herr Clark hat einen guten Lehrer, Karl Müller. Jeden Dienstag und Donnerstag kommt der Lehrer in die Wohnung seines Schülers, um ihm eine Deutschstunde zu geben.[6] Herr Clark ist fleißig und intelligent und lernt schnell. Während der ersten Stunde lernt er diese deutschen

Ausdrücke auswendig:[7] Guten Tag; Wie geht es Ihnen?; Vielen Dank; Bitte schön; Auf Wiedersehen; usw (und so weiter). Er weiß schon die deutschen Namen für viele Dinge in seinem Wohnzimmer und kann auf diese Fragen richtig antworten: Was ist dies? Was ist das? Wo ist das? Warum ist das?

Herr Müller ist mit dem Fortschritt[8] seines Schülers sehr zufrieden,[9] und er sagt: „Sehr gut. Das ist genug für heute. Ich komme Donnerstag wieder. Auf Wiedersehen.“

NOTES: **1.** but rather. **2. davon** from it. **3.** of this. **4. um . . . zu besuchen** in order to visit. **5.** important. **6. um . . . geben** in order to give. **7.** by heart. **8.** progress. **9.** satisfied.

Exercise 47

Das zweite Lesestück (The Second Reading Selection)

DIE DEUTSCHSPRACHIGEN LÄNDER

In Deutschland spricht man natürlich Deutsch. Aber auch in Österreich und in der Schweiz spricht man Deutsch. Alle drei Länder liegen in Mitteleuropa.[1] Nach dem Ende des Zweiten Weltkriegs[2] war[3] Deutschland in zwei Teilen geteilt,[4] Westdeutschland[5] und Ostdeutschland.[6] Die Elbe trennte[7] die zwei Teile Deutschlands. Jetzt sind Westdeutschland und Ostdeutschland wieder vereint.

Die Hauptstadt[8] von Deutschland ist Berlin. Unter[9] den großen Städten im Westen[10] sind Köln, München, Stuttgart, Frankfurt, Düsseldorf und die großen Hafenstädte,[11] Hamburg und Bremen. Unter den großen Städten im Osten[12] sind Leipzig, Dresden und Chemnitz.

Die Hauptstadt von Österreich ist Wien. Viele Touristen kommen auch nach Salzburg, um die Geburtsstadt[13] von Wolfgang Amadeus Mozart zu besuchen, oder um in den Bergen Ski zu fahren.

Auch in der Schweiz gibt es viele hohe Berge. In der Schweiz spricht man nicht nur Deutsch, sondern auch Französisch und Italienisch.

NOTES: **1.** Central Europe. **2.** the Second World War. **3.** was. **4.** divided. **5.** West Germany. **6.** East Germany. **7.** separated. **8.** capital. **9.** among. **10.** west. **11.** seaport cities. **12.** east. **13.** birthplace.

CHAPTER 13

EIN FREUND BESUCHT HERRN CLARK

Wilhelm Engel ist ein Freund von Herrn Clark. Sein Büro ist im selben Gebäude wie das Büro des Herrn Clark.

William Engel is a friend of Mr. Clark. His office is in the same building as the office of Mr. Clark.

Herr Engel spricht fließend Deutsch. Er weiß, sein Freund lernt seit einigen Monaten Deutsch, und er will erfahren, was für Fortschritte er macht.

Mr. Engel speaks German fluently. He knows his friend has been studying German for some months and he wants to find out what progress he is making.

Eines Tages sitzt Herr Clark an seinem Schreibtisch und liest Briefe. Plötzlich öffnet jemand die Tür und tritt ins Büro.

One day Mr. Clark is sitting at his desk and reading letters. Suddenly someone opens the door and steps into the office.

Es ist sein Freund Wilhelm Engel.

It is his friend William Engel.

Herr Engel beginnt sofort Deutsch zu sprechen, und Herr Clark antwortet ihm[1] auf Deutsch.

Mr. Engel begins immediately to speak German, and Mr. Clark answers him in German.

E.: Wie geht's, mein Freund?

E.: How are you, my friend?

C.: Sehr gut, danke. Und dir?

C.: Very well, thanks. And you?

E.: Sehr gut. Ich höre, du[2] lernst seit einigen Monaten Deutsch.

E.: Very well. I hear you have been studying German for several months.

C.: Das ist wahr. Ich will nämlich im Sommer eine Reise nach Deutschland machen.

C.: That is true. I want, you know, to take a trip to Germany in the summer.

E.: Eine Geschäftsreise oder eine Vergnügungsreise?

E.: A business trip or a pleasure trip?

C.: Beides. Ich will den Geschäftspartner unserer Firma in München besuchen und mit ihm unsere Geschäftsangelegenheiten besprechen. Dann hoffe ich, andere Städte in Deutschland, in Österreich und in der Schweiz zu besuchen.

C.: Both. I want to visit the business partner of our firm in Munich and discuss our business matters with him. Then I hope to visit other cities in Germany, in Austria and in Switzerland.

E.: Wann fliegst du?

E.: When are you flying?

C.: Ich fliege Anfang Juli.

C.: At the beginning of July.

E.: Hast du schon das Flugticket gekauft?

C.: Noch nicht. Aber morgen gehe ich ins Reisebüro, um mich über Einzelheiten des Fluges zu erkundigen.

E.: Donnerwetter! Du sprichst ja wunderbar Deutsch!

C.: Es ist sehr nett von dir,[3] das zu sagen. Ich hoffe, noch besser zu werden.

E.: Nun, gute Reise!

Sie geben sich die Hand. Herr Engel verlässt das Büro.

E.: Have you already bought the flight ticket?

C.: Not yet. But tomorrow I am going to the travel agency to find out details about the flight.

E.: Wow! You speak German splendidly.

C.: It is very nice of you to say that. I hope to speak even better.

E.: Well, happy voyage!

They shake hands. Mr. Engel leaves the office.

NOTES: 1. Antworten and a number of other verbs take a dative object. **2.** As Mr. Clark and Mr. Engel are very good friends, they use the familiar **du. Sie duzen** (*doo*-tsen) **sich.** They say **du** to each other. **3. dir** is the dative case of **du.**

Wortschatz

der Anfang *pl.* ¨-e beginning

das Gebäude *pl.* - building

die Einzelheit *pl.* -en detail

das Reisebüro *pl.* -s travel agency

die Stadt *pl.* ¨-e city

bespréchen to discuss

erkundigen to find out, to enquire

fliegen to fly; **hoffen** to hope

lesen to read; **lernen** to study

treten to step; **er tritt ins Zimmer** he steps into the room

verlássen to leave, to go away from

noch still, yet; **noch nicht** not yet

wunderbar wonderful

plötzlich suddenly

sofort immediately, at once

selb same; **im selben Gebäude** in the same building

jemand somebody; **niemand** nobody

dir you, to you (*dative of du*)

mir me, to me (*dative of ich*)

Practice Aloud

das Reisebüro
travel agency

das Flugticket
flight ticket

die Fluglinie
flōok-lee-nye
airline

die Vergnügungsreise
fer-gnü-gŏongs-rei-ze
pleasure trip

die Geschäftsreise
ge-shäfts-rei-se
business trip

die Geschäftsangelegenheit
ge-shäfts-ăn-ge-lay-gen-heit
business matter

Wichtige Redemittel

eines Tages, eines Morgens, eines Nachmittags, eines Abends one day, one morning, one afternoon, one evening

Gute Reise! Happy voyage! Have a good trip!

Karl antwortet ihm (ihr, mir, dir, Ihnen) auf Deutsch. Charles answers him (her, me, you *fam.*, you *pol.*) in German.

The verb **antworten** takes a dative object.

Donnerwetter! (*dŏn-ner-vĕt-ter*) Wow!

seit wann? since when? **wie lange?** how long?

Seit wann (wie lange) lernt er Deutsch? Er lernt Deutsch seit einem Jahr. Since when has he been studying German? He has been studying German since (for) a year.

An action begun in the past and continuing in the present is expressed in German by the *present tense*, in English by the present perfect.

Grammar Notes and Practical Exercises

1. **PRESENT TENSE OF** *lesen* **to read,** *treten* **to step**

ich lese	wir lesen	ich trete	wir treten
du liest	ihr lest	du trittst	ihr tretet
er liest	sie (Sie) lesen	er tritt	sie (Sie) treten

Imperative: **lies! lest! lesen Sie!**   **tritt! tretet! treten Sie!**

a. **lesen** *is like* **sehen** (ich sehe, du siehst, *etc.*), *and* **treten** *is like* **sprechen** (ich spreche, du sprichst, *etc.*).

2. **POSSESSIVE ADJECTIVES (*ein*-words)**

For every personal pronoun there is a corresponding possessive adjective.

Pers. Pron.		Possessive Adjective				Pers. Pron.		Possessive Adjective			
		masc.	*fem.*	*neut.*				*masc.*	*fem.*	*neut.*	
ich	I	mein	meine	mein	my	wir	we	unser	uns(e)re	unser	our
du	you	dein	deine	dein	your	ihr	you	euer	eu(e)re	euer	your
er	he	sein	seine	sein	his	sie	they	ihr	ihre	ihr	their
sie	she	ihr	ihre	ihr	her	Sie	you	Ihr	Ihre	Ihr	your
es	it	sein	seine	sein	its						

The possessive adjectives agree in number, gender and case with the nouns they possess. In these sentences compare the endings of the possessive adjective with those of **ein** and **kein**.

1. **Ein** Bleistift liegt auf dem Pult.
   Mein Bleistift liegt auf dem Pult.
2. **Ein** Füller liegt auf dem Tisch.
   Dein Füller liegt auf dem Tisch.

3. **Ein** Buch liegt auf dem Stuhl.
   Sein Buch liegt auf dem Stuhl.
4. **Keine** Bilder sind an der Wand.
   Uns(e)re Bilder sind an der Wand.
5. Seht ihr **einen** Lehrer, Kinder?
   Seht ihr **eu(e)ren** Lehrer, Kinder?
6. Die Farbe **eines** Bleistifts ist schwarz.
   Die Farbe **meines** Bleistifts ist schwarz.
7. Die Farbe **einer** Feder[1] ist rot.
   Die Farbe **ihrer** Feder ist rot.
8. Karl spielt mit **keinen** Kindern.
   Karl spielt mit **uns(e)ren** Kindern.
9. Haben Sie **einen** Hut, Herr Schmidt?
   Haben Sie **Ihren** Hut, Herr Schmidt?
10. **Keine** Mädchen lernen Französisch.
    Uns(e)re Mädchen lernen Französisch.

a. *The endings of the possessive adjectives are exactly like those of* ein *and* kein. *Possessive adjectives and* kein *are called* ein-*words.*

NOTE: 1. **die Feder** *pl.* **–n** feather.

		ein, kein						*ein-word unser*		
		Singular		*Plural*				*Singular*		*Plural*
	masc.	*fem.*	*neut.*	*m.f.n.*			*masc.*	*fem.*	*neut.*	*m.f.n.*
N.	ein	eine	ein	keine		N.	unser	uns(e)re[1]	unser	uns(e)re
G.	eines	einer	eines	keiner		G.	uns(e)res	uns(e)rer	uns(e)res	uns(e)rer
D.	einem	einer	einem	keinen		D.	uns(e)rem	uns(e)rer	uns(e)rem	uns(e)ren
A.	einen	eine	ein	keine		A.	uns(e)ren	uns(e)re	unser	uns(e)re

NOTE: 1. **(e)** means that the letter **e** may be omitted.

b. *Note carefully that* ein, kein *and all* ein-*words have no endings in the nominative masculine singular, and in the nominative and accusative neuter singular. The other endings are like those of* der.

c. *Just as there are three words for you (*du, ihr, Sie*), so there are three words for your (*dein, euer, Ihr*). Use a form of* dein *(your) in speaking to a person whom you would address with* du *(you).*

d. *Use a form of* euer *(your) in speaking to persons whom you would address with* ihr *(you). Use a form of* Ihr *(your), always capitalized, in speaking to one or more persons whom you would address with* Sie *(you).*

Hast du deine Bücher, Karl?	Have you your books, Charles?
Habt ihr eure Bücher, Kinder?	Have you your books, children?
Haben Sie Ihre Bücher, mein Herr?	Have you your books, Sir?
Haben Sie Ihre Bücher, meine Damen und Herren?	Have you your books, ladies and gentlemen?

Exercise 48

Practice aloud.

1. Wo wohnt der Geschäftspartner Ihrer Firma?
   —Der Geschäftspartner unsrer Firma wohnt in München.
   —Seit wann wohnt er dort?
   —Er wohnt seit einem Jahr dort.

2. Wessen Porträt ist das?
   —Es ist das Portät meiner Frau.
   —Ist dies das Foto Ihrer Kinder?
   —Ja, dies ist das Foto unsrer vier Kinder.

3. Ist deine Wohnung in der Stadt?
   —Nein, meine Wohnung ist in der Vorstadt.
   —Und wo ist dein Büro?
   —Mein Büro ist in der Stadt.

4. Wo ist eure Schule, Kinder?
   —Unsre Schule ist in der Karlstraße.
   —Geht ihr dahin[1] zu Fuß?[2]
   —Nein, wir fahren mit dem Autobus.

NOTES: I. **dahin** there (to that place). **2. zu Fuß gehen** to go on foot, to walk.

Exercise 49

Complete these sentences by adding the words in the box.

eure—Ihren—ihrer—deines—Ihr—seines—unserem—ihre —ihres—unseren—Ihrer—mein

1. Wo ist die Wohnung _____ Freundes, Karl?
2. Wo sind _____ Eltern, Kinder?
3. Wo ist _____ Büro, Herr Clark?
4. Die Farbe _____ Kleider ist blau.
5. Die Farbe _____ Hutes ist grau.
6. Die Farbe _____ Hauses ist weiß.
7. Wir gehen mit _____ Eltern ins Kino.
8. Das Bild _____ Kinder ist sehr schön, Frau Clark.
9. Er will _____ Auto kaufen.
10. Sie will _____ Freundinnen besuchen.
11. Wir wollen mit _____ Lehrer sprechen.
12. Wollen Sie mir _____ Hut geben?

Exercise 50

Was gehört Karl? Was gehört Marie? Was gehört Herrn und Frau Clark?

der Ball—der Bleistift—die Füllfeder—das Porträt—das Foto—der Hut—das Auto—der Lehrer—die Bücher—das Flugticket—das Büro—die Freundin—die Firma—die Schule—das Glas—der Wein—das Haus

DRAWING Karl	DRAWING Marie	DRAWING Mr./Mrs. Clark
Das ist sein Ball.	Das ist ihre Freundin.	

Exercise 51

Charles and William are packing their suitcases. Mrs. Clark is worried and asks: „**Habt ihr eure Pullover?**" Charles and William answer: „**Ja, wir haben unsere Pullover.**"

Continue: **die Pullover, die Bücher, der Ball, das Flugticket, das Geld, die Füllern, das Deutschbuch, die Fotos, die Hüte, die Landkarte.**

Exercise 52

Fragen

Reread the text: **Ein Freund besucht Herrn Clark.** Then answer these questions.
  1. **Wer ist Herr Engel?**
  2. **Wo ist sein Büro?**
  3. **Spricht er Deutsch?**
  4. **Was will er erfahren?**
  5. **Wo sitzt Herr Clark eines Tages?**
  6. **Was liest er?**
  7. **Wer tritt plötzlich in sein Büro?**

8. Beginnt Herr Engel sofort, auf Deutsch zu sprechen?
9. Antwortet Herr Clark seinem Freund auf Englisch?
10. Wie lange studiert Herr Clark schon Deutsch?
11. Wann beabsichtigt Herr Clark, eine Reise nach Deutschland zu machen?
12. Wohin geht er morgen?
13. Was tun[1] die Herren am Ende[2] des Gesprächs?

NOTES: 1. **tun** to do—**ich tue, du tust, er tut, wir tun, ihr tut, sie tun.** 2. **das Ende** the end; **am Ende** at the end.

1. Herr Clark muss in seinem Beruf viel telefonieren. Zum Telefonieren hat er in seinem Büro ein Telefon und natürlich auch ein Mobiltelefon.
2. So kann Herr Clark jederzeit alle Personen anrufen, die für seine Arbeit wichtig sind.
3. Heute sitzt Herr Clark in seinem Büro und will arbeiten. Das plötzliche Klingeln seines Telefons stört ihn beim Arbeiten.
4. Hallo? Hier spricht Robert Clark. Wer spricht, bitte?
5. Hier spricht Julia Graf. Kann ich bitte Ihre Frau sprechen, Herr Clark?
6. Meine Frau ist nicht hier in meinem Büro. Sie können aber bei mir zu Hause anrufen.
7. Das ist sehr freundlich von Ihnen. Können Sie mir bitte die Telefonnummer geben?
8. Selbstverständlich, Frau Graf. Unsere Privatnummer ist 34 02 78 26.
9. Vielen Dank. Auf Wiedersehen.
10. Auf Wiedersehen, Frau Graf.
11. Nach einer Weile greift Herr Clark erneut zum Telefonhörer. Er muss in Deutschland anrufen. Während er wählt, spricht Herr Clark die Telefonnummer laut mit:
12. 00 41 63 87 42 45 12
13. Hallo?
14. Hier spricht Robert Clark aus New York. Kann ich bitte mit meinem Geschäftspartner Heinrich Schiller sprechen?
15. Herr Schiller ist leider momentan nicht hier. Aber Sie können gerne eine Nachricht hinterlassen.

1. Mr. Clark has to make many phone calls in his job. In order to make phone calls he has a telephone in his office and of course also a mobile phone.
2. Like this he can call anytime all the persons who are important for his work.
3. Today Mr. Clark is sitting in his office and he wants to work. The sudden ringing of his phone disturbs him in his work.
4. Hello? Robert Clark is speaking. Who is this, please?
5. Hello, this is Julia Graf speaking. Could I please speak to your wife, Mr. Clark?
6. My wife is not here in my office. But you can call at my home.
7. That is very nice of you. Could you please give me the telephone number?
8. Certainly, Mrs. Graf. Our private phone number is 34 02 78 26.
9. Thank you. Good-bye.
10. Good-bye.
11. After a while Mr. Clark picks up the receiver again. He has to phone Germany. While he is dialing he says the telephone number out loud.
12. 00 41 63 87 42 45 12
13. Hello?
14. This is Robert Clark from New York speaking. Could I please speak with my partner Heinrich Schiller?
15. Unfortunately Mr. Schiller isn't in at the moment. But you can leave a message.

16. Das ist nicht notwendig. Aber ich will Herrn Schiller einen Brief schreiben und habe seine Privatadresse nicht.

17. Das ist kein Problem. Herr Schiller wohnt in der Abtenaustraße 47.

18. Können Sie mir auch die Postleitzahl mitteilen?

19. Natürlich. Die Postleitzahl ist 53012.

20. Vielen Dank.

21. Nichts zu danken. Auf Wiedersehen.

16. That is not necessary. But I want to write a letter to Mr. Schiller and I don't have his private address.

17. That is no problem. Mr. Schiller lives in Abtenau Street 47.

18. Could you also tell me the ZIP code?

19. Certainly. The ZIP Code is 53012.

20. Thank you very much.

21. Don't mention it. Good-bye.

Wortschatz

der Beruf *pl.* **-e** job
das Mobiltelefon *pl.* **-e**; also: **das Handy** *pl.* **-ys** mobile phone
die Nachricht *pl.* **-en** message
die Persón *pl.* **-en** person
die Postleitzahl *pl.* **-en** ZIP code
die Privatadresse *pl.* **-en** home address
der Telefonhörer *pl.* **-** receiver
die Telefonnummer *pl.* **-en** telephone number
die Weile a while; **nach einer Weile** after a while
anrufen to phone, to call
greifen to seize, to take
hinterlassen to leave
klingeln to ring

mitteilen to tell, to inform
stören to disturb
wählen to dial
erneut again
freundlich nice, friendly
laut loud, aloud
jederzeit all the time
momentan at the moment
natürlich certainly, of course
plötzlich (*adj.*, *adv.*) sudden, suddenly
während while
viel much; **nichts** nothing
wichtig important; **unwichtig** unimportant

Infinitives Used as Nouns

Infinitives may be used as nouns. Such nouns are always neuter.

kaufen to buy
das Kaufen the buying

verkaufen to sell
das Verkaufen the selling

telefonieren to telephone
das Telefonieren the telephoning

zum Kaufen for buying
Zum Kaufen braucht man Geld.
For buying one needs money.

zum Verkaufen for selling

zum Telefonieren for telephoning

Wichtige Redemittel

Hier spricht . . . This is . . . . speaking
Vielen Dank Many thanks, thank you very much
Nichts zu danken. Don't mention it.

Kann ich mit . . . . sprechen? Can I speak with . . . ?
Selbstverständlich Of course, it goes without saying.

Grammar Notes and Practical Exercises

1. DIE ZAHLEN VON 1 BIS 100. THE NUMERALS FROM 1 TO 100

1	eins	22	zweiundzwanzig
2	zwei	23	dreiundzwanzig
3	drei	24	vierundzwanzig
4	vier	25	fünfundzwanzig
5	fünf	30	dreißig
6	sechs	31	einunddreißig
7	sieben	40	vierzig
8	acht	42	zweiundvierzig
9	neun	50	fünfzig
10	zehn	53	dreiundfünfzig
11	elf	60	sechzig
12	zwölf	64	vierundsechzig
13	dreizehn	70	siebzig
14	vierzehn	75	fünfundsiebzig
15	fünfzehn	80	achtzig
16	sechzehn	86	sechsundachtzig
17	siebzehn	90	neunzig
18	achtzehn	97	siebenundneunzig
19	neunzehn	100	hundert
20	zwanzig		
21	einundzwanzig		

Exercise 53

Read each expression aloud. Then write out the numbers in German.

a. 30 Stühle
b. 10 Bücher
c. 50 Studenten
d. 12 Häuser

e. 7 Städte

f. 60 Schüler

g. 70 Schülerinnen

h. 19 Jungen

i. 14 Mädchen

j. 31 Bilder

k. 25 Freunde

l. 43 Freundinnen

m. 89 Männer

n. 90 Kinder

o. 100 Menschen

p. 39 Briefe

q. 28 Lehrer

r. 36 Lehrerinnen

s. 15 Straßen

t. 12 Wörter

Exercise 54

Read each sentence aloud. Then answer in a complete sentence, giving the number in German.

Beispiel: 1. Die Woche hat sieben Tage.

1. **Wie viele[1] Tage hat die Woche?**
2. **Wie viele Monate hat das Jahr?**
3. **Wie viele Stunden hat der Tag?**
4. **Wie viele Minuten hat die Stunde?**
5. **Wie viele Sekunden hat die Minute?**
6. **Wie viele Tage hat der Monat September?**
7. **Wie viele Tage hat der Monat Juli?**
8. **Wie viele Staaten[2] sind in den Vereinigten Staaten?**
9. **Wie alt ist der Vater? (40 Jahre)**
10. **Wie alt ist die Mutter? (36 Jahre)**
11. **Wie viel ist ein Dutzend?[3]**
12. **Wie viele Finger hat die Hand?**

NOTES: I. wie viel, wie veile how much, how many. **2. der Staat** (*shtaht*) *pl.* **die Staaten** state; **die Vereinigten Staaten** the United States. **3. das Dutzend** ($\overline{oo}$*t-tsent*) dozen.

2. PRESENT TENSE OF *können* to be able, can; *tun* to do

ich kann	wir können	ich tue	wir tun
du kannst	ihr könnt	du tust	ihr tut
er, sie, es kann	sie (Sie) können	er, sie, es tut	sie (Sie) tun

Note the irregular singular of **können**. Compare with the singular of **müssen**, **wissen** and **wollen**.

Exercise 55

Fill in the gaps with the correct form of **können**.

Ich _____ das nicht schreiben.

_____ die Eltern heute kommen?

Er _____ das nicht kaufen.

Sie _____ das nicht finden.

Ihr _____ das nicht bringen.

_____ Sie morgen kommen?

Wir _____ das nicht glauben.

Du _____ das nicht lernen.

Exercise 56

Practice aloud.

—Was tun Sie?

—Ich schreibe einen Brief.

—Was tut Hans?

—Er spielt Klavier.

—Was tust du, mein Kind?

—Ich höre Radio.

—Was tut Marie?

—Sie spielt mit ihrer Puppe (doll).

3. THE der-WORDS, *dieser, jener, jeder, welcher, aller*

A number of words take almost the same endings as **der** and are called **der**-words. Five of these are: **dieser** this (*pl.* these); **jener** that (*pl.* those); **jeder** each, every; **welcher** which, what; and **aller** all. In the following sentences compare the endings of **dieser** with those of **der**.

Der Bleistift ist rot.
Dieser Bleistift ist rot.
Die Feder ist schwarz.
Diese Feder ist schwarz.
Das Buch ist neu.
Dieses Buch ist neu.
Sehen Sie **das** Buch?
Sehen Sie **dieses** Buch?

Ich gebe **dem** Lehrer das Papier.
Ich gebe **diesem** Lehrer das Papier.
Die Farbe **des** Bleistifts ist rot.
Die Farbe **dieses** Bleistifts ist rot.
Die Lehrer sind meine Freunde.
Diese Lehrer sind meine Freunde.
Karl spielt mit **den** Knaben.
Karl spielt mit **diesen** Knaben.

The Definite Article—Der

	Singular masc.	*fem.*	*Plural* neut.	*m.f.n*		*Singular* masc.	*fem.*	*Plural* neut.	*m.f.n.*
N.	der	die	das	die	*N.*	dieser	diese	dieses	diese
G.	des	der	des	der	*G.*	dieses	dieser	dieses	dieser
D.	dem	der	dem	den	*D.*	diesem	dieser	diesem	diesen
A.	den	die	das	die	*A.*	diesen	diese	dieses	diese

The endings of **dieser** are like those of **der** except in the neuter nominative and accusative, where -**es** takes the place of -**as**.

The endings of other **der**-words (**jener, jeder, welcher, aller**) are exactly like those of **dieser**.

Like **der**, the **der**-words agree in number, gender and case with their nouns: **dieses Buch, jenes Buch, jeder Junge, welche Frau, alle Menschen.**

Exercise 57

Substitute the correct form of **dieser** and **jener** for the definite article in heavy type.

Beispiel: 1. Dieser (jener) Geschäftsmann wohnt in der Vorstadt.

1. **Der** Geschäftsmann wohnt in der Vorstadt.
2. Die Wohnung **des** Geschäftsmanns ist nicht groß.
3. Sein Büro ist in **dem** Wolkenkratzer.
4. Sehen Sie **die** Landkarte von Deutschland?
5. Hinter **dem** Hause ist ein Garten.
6. Wir müssen **die** Wörter schreiben.
7. Geben Sie **den** Mädchen die Hüte!
8. Ich verstehe **das** Wort nicht.
9. Die Eltern **der** Kinder sind heute in der Schule.
10. Der Vater **der** Frau ist Arzt.

Exercise 58

Make a question of each statement using the correct form of **welcher** in place of the form of **dieser**.

Beispiel: 1. Welches Haus hat keinen Garten?

1. **Dieses** Haus hat keinen Garten.
2. **Dieser** Mann hat die Vorstadt nicht gern.
3. **Dieser** Lehrer hat zwanzig Schüler in seiner Klasse.
4. **Dieses** Schlafzimmer ist für die Mädchen.
5. Alle Schüler können **diese** Bücher lesen.
6. Der Schüler weiß **diese** Wörter.
7. Wir kennen **diese** Herren nicht.
8. Sie muss **diese** Wörter schreiben.

Exercise 59

Mr. Clark is packing his suitcase. He is undecided which things to take to Germany and asks his wife for advice. Make short dialogues.

- Welche Hose soll ich einpacken?
- Diese finde ich nicht so schön.
- Und jene?
- Die ist besser.

die Hose—der Pullover—das Hemd—der Hut—der Mantel—die Schuhe—das T-Shirt

Exercise 60

Sie sind falsch verbunden. . . . I am afraid you have the wrong number. . . .

Make dialogues giving the numbers in German.

- Hallo?
- Kann ich bitte mit Helene sprechen?
- Da sind Sie falsch verbunden. Hier ist 93 55 46.
- Entschuldigen Sie bitte.[1]
- Das macht doch nichts.[2]

a.	Helene	93 55 46
b.	Günther	88 12 45
c.	Sophie	81 46 21
d.	Herr Heiß	45 31 15
e.	Frau Scheidl	64 74 11
f.	Frau Noll	38 76 51
g.	Werner	75 06 66

NOTES: 1. I am sorry. **2.** It doesn't matter.

DOLLAR UND EURO

1. Heute hat Herr Clark wieder eine Deutschstunde. Er freut sich, dass Herr Müller bei ihm im Wohnzimmer sitzt. Herr Müller und Herr Clark sprechen über das Geldsystem in Europa und Deutschland.
2. Sie wissen sicher, Herr Clark, dass man fast in der ganzen Europäischen Union nun mit dem Euro zahlen kann.
3. Natürlich. Das macht viele Sachen einfach. Wenn ich von Deutschland nach Österreich reise, brauche ich nicht mehr Geld zu wechseln.
4. Das stimmt. Aber wenn Sie nun in die Schweiz reisen wollen?
5. Wenn ich in die Schweiz reise, muss ich Euro in Schweizer Franken wechseln.
6. Wissen Sie auch, wie viele Dollar ein Euro wert ist?
7. Ja, ein Euro ist ungefähr einen Dollar und dreißig Cent wert. Das bedeutet, dass ein Dollar circa 0,75 Euro oder fünfundsiebzig Cent wert ist.
8. Wenn Sie zehn Dollar in Euro wechseln, wie viele Euro bekommen Sie?
9. Ich bekomme ungefähr sieben Euro und fünfzig Cent.
10. Wenn Sie zweihundert Dollar in Euro wechseln, wie viele Euro bekommen Sie dann?
11. Ich bekomme ungefähr hundertfünfzig Euro.

1. Today Mr. Clark has again a German lesson. He is pleased that Mr. Müller is sitting with him in his living room. Mr. Müller and Mr. Clark are talking about the monetary system in Europe and Germany.
2. You certainly know, Mr. Clark, that you can pay with euros almost in the entire European Union.
3. Of course. That makes many things easy. If I travel from Germany to Austria, I don't need to change money.
4. That is correct. But what if you want to travel to Switzerland?
5. If I travel to Switzerland, I have to change euros for Swiss francs.
6. Do you also know how many dollars a euro is worth?
7. Yes, a euro is worth about one dollar thirty cents. That means that a dollar is worth about 0.75 euros or seventy-five cents.
8. If you change ten dollars for euros, how many euros do you get?
9. I get about seven euros and fifty cents.
10. If you change two hundred dollars into euros, how many euros do you get then?
11. I get about one hundred fifty euros.

12. Richtig! Und nun weiter: Sie gehen zum Bahnhof. Sie wollen zwei Fahrkarten kaufen. Jede Karte kostet sechzehn Euro, und Sie geben dem Beamten am Kartenschalter einen Fünfzigeuroschein. Wie viele Euro gibt er Ihnen zurück?

13. Zweimal sechzehn macht zweiunddreißig. Fünfzig minus zweiunddreißig macht achtzehn. Er gibt mir achtzehn Euro zurück.

14. Sehr gut. Nächstes Mal sprechen wir weiter über diese wichtige Sache. Sie kennen ja das deutsche Sprichwort: Übung macht den Meister.

15. Jawohl. Das englische Sprichwort heißt: Practice makes perfect.

12. Right. And now to continue: You go to the railroad station. You want to buy two tickets. Each ticket costs sixteen euros, and you give the employee at the ticket window a fifty-euro bill. How many euros does he give you back?

13. Two times sixteen makes thirty-two. Fifty minus thirty-two makes eighteen. He gives me back eighteen euros.

14. Very good. Next time we will speak further about this important matter. You know of course the German proverb: Practice makes the master.

15. Yes, indeed. The English proverb is: Practice makes perfect.

Wortschatz

der Bahnhof *pl.* ¨-e railroad station
der Kartenschalter *pl.* - ticket window
der Béamte *pl.* -n employee (civil service)
die Fahrkarte *pl.* -n ticket
der Reisende *pl.* -n traveler
das Geld money; **das Geldsystem** monetary system
der Zehneuroschein *pl.* -e ten-euro bill
die Sache *pl.* -n thing
bekommen to receive, to get

brauchen to need
stimmen to be true, to be correct
wechseln (*věk-seln*) to change
einfach easy
fast almost
ungefähr about, approximately
weit far; **weiter** further

Ein Sprichwort

Übung macht den Meister.

Practice makes perfect (*lit.* makes the master).

Das europäische Geldsystem

The European Monetary System

The monetary unit in Europe and Germany is the euro. The **Euro, € = 100 Cents.** The U.S. $1.00 equals about 0.75 cents.

Wichtige Redemittel

nächstes Mal next time
voriges Mal last time
diesmal this time
das stimmt that is true

Geld wechseln to change money
Ich will hundert Dollar in Euro wechseln.
I want to change one hundred dollars into euros.
Ich brauche 10 Euro. I need 10 euros.

Grammar Notes and Practical Exercises

1. DIE ZAHLEN ÜBER HUNDERT. READ ALL NUMBERS ALOUD.

100 hundert	1000 tausend	eine Million
200 zweihundert	2000 zweitausend	zwei Millionen
300 dreihundert	3000 dreitausend	drei Millionen
900 neunhundert	100 000 hunderttausend	hundert Millionen

156 hundertsechsundfünfzig	1265 tausendzweihundertfünfundsechzig
529 fünfhundertneunundzwanzig	1929 tausendneunhundertneunundzwanzig
875 achthundertfünfundsiebzig	5697 fünftausendsechshundertsiebenundneunzig

Im jahre In the year

1492 vierzehnhundertzweiundneunzig	1776 siebzehnhundertsechsundsiebzig
1809 achtzehnhundertneun	1964 neunzehnhundertvierundsechzig

Exercise 61

Write out these numbers in German.

a. 500
b. 625
c. 746
d. 247
e. 136
f. 999
g. 1640
h. 5320
i. im Jahre 1620
j. im Jahre 1970

2. SUBORDINATE WORD ORDER—THE SUBORDINATING CONJUNCTIONS *dass, wenn*

You are familiar with normal and inverted word order. (See Chapter 7, Grammar Note 2.)

Normal: Subject—Verb. **Frau Clark fährt heute** in die Stadt.

Inverted: Verb—Subject. Heute **fährt Frau Clark** in die Stadt.

Normal and inverted word order are found in simple sentences and main clauses.

Subordinate word order, as the name indicates, is found only in subordinate clauses.

Compare the position of the verb in the simple sentences, paragraph A, with the position of the verb when these sentences are changed to subordinate clauses, paragraph B.

A. 1. Die Wohnung des Geschäftsmanns **ist** nicht groß.
   2. Ein Porträt **hängt** über dem Klavier.
   3. Sie **fährt** mit dem Auto in die Stadt.
   4. Wir **machen** eine Reise.

B. 1. Ich weiß, dass die Wohnung des Geschäftsmanns nicht groß **ist**.
   2. Wir wissen, dass ein Porträt über dem Klavier **hängt**.
   3. Frau Clark besucht ihre Freundinnen, wenn sie mit dem Auto in die Stadt **fährt**.
   4. Wir brauchen Geld, wenn wir eine Reise **machen**.
   5. Wenn wir eine Reise **machen, brauchen wir** viel Geld.

In subordinate clauses the verb must stand last. This is called subordinate or transposed word order.

The conjunctions **dass** (that) and **wenn** (when, if) are called subordinating conjunctions. They introduce subordinate clauses.

The subordinate clause may precede the main clause. In that case the main clause has inverted word order (Sentence 5).

3. THE COORDINATING CONJUNCTIONS *und, aber, oder, denn*

The conjunctions **und** *and;* **aber** *but, however;* **oder** *or;* and **denn** *for, because;* have no effect on word order. They are called coordinating conjunctions.

Karl lernt Englisch **und** Wilhelm lernt Französisch.

Das Haus des Herrn Clark ist nicht groß, **aber** es ist sehr bequem.

Er hat die Vorstadt sehr gern, **denn** es ist still und gemütlich dort.

Exercise 62

Read each sentence to yourself. Read it aloud several times. By such repetition you will get a "feeling" for the correct word order.

1. Jeder Schüler weiß, dass die Verben und Hauptwörter wichtig sind.
2. Wir wissen, dass Herr Clark ein Geschäftsmann ist.
3. Wenn er nach Hause kommt, spielt er mit seinen Kindern.
4. Herr Müller sagt, dass sein Schüler große Fortschritte macht.
5. Man kann nicht reisen, wenn man kein Geld hat.
6. Wenn die Kinder in der Schule sind, ist es im Hause sehr still.
7. Sie gehen zu Fuß zur Schule, wenn das Wetter schön ist.
8. Wenn das Wetter schön ist, gehen sie zu Fuß zur Schule.
9. Ich glaube, dass dieser Hut zehn Euro kostet.
10. Sie wissen ja, dass unsre Firma einen Geschäftspartner in München hat.
11. Jeder Reisende weiß, dass wir auf einer Reise Geld gebrauchen.

12. Wenn man hundert Dollar in Euro wechselt, bekommt man ungefähr 75 Euro.
13. Wir wissen, dass der Dollar ungefähr 75 Cent wert ist.
14. Anna geht in den Kindergarten, denn sie ist zu jung für die Schule.
15. Ich möchte eine Reise nach Europa machen, aber ich habe nicht genug Geld.

Exercise 63

Combine each of the sentences using the conjunctions **wenn**, **dass**, **denn**, **aber** and **und**. Make any necessary changes in word order. Subordinate clauses are always set off by commas.

Beispiel: **1.** Die Schüler sitzen sehr still, **wenn** der Lehrer ins Zimmer **kommt.**

1. Die Schüler sitzen sehr still. Der Lehrer kommt ins Zimmer.
2. Die Kinder gehen zu Fuß zur Schule. Das Wetter ist schön.
3. Wir wissen es.[1] Dieser Geschäftsmann hat einen Partner in München.
4. Mein Freund lernt schnell. Er ist intelligent und fleißig.
5. Ich bin in München. Ich will mit diesem Mann reden.
6. Ich weiß es.[2] Sie machen im Sommer eine Reise nach Deutschland.
7. Wir möchten dieses Auto kaufen. Es ist viel zu teuer.
8. Man muss die Dinge auf Deutsch nennen. Man ist in Deutschland.
9. Ich kann heute nicht kommen. Ich habe viel zu tun.
10. Unsere Freunde gehen ins Kino. Wir müssen zu Hause bleiben.[3]

NOTES: 1. Omit **es** in the combined sentence. 2. See Grammar Note 2B. 3. **bleiben** to remain.

Exercise 64

Fragen

Review the numbers 1–1000. Then answer these questions in complete sentences.

1. Wie viel Cent hat ein Euro?
2. Wie viel Euro ist der Dollar wert?
3. Etwas kostet 150 Euro. Wenn Sie dem Verkäufer einen 500 Euroschein (Fünfhunderteuroschein) geben, wie viel Geld bekommen Sie zurück?
4. Ein Auto kostet 15 790 Euro. Wenn Sie dem Autohändler[1] einen Scheck über sechzehntausend Euro geben, wie viel Geld gibt er Ihnen zurück?
5. Sie haben in Ihrer Geldtasche[2] zwei Fünfhunderteuroscheine; einen 100 Euroschein (Hunderteuroschein); drei Fünfzigeuroscheine; 3,50 Euro (drei Euro fünfzig Cent). Wie viel Geld haben Sie im Ganzen?[3]
6. Ein Anzug kostet 210 (zweihundertzehn) Euro. Wenn Sie dem Verkäufer dreihundert Euro geben, wie viel bekommen Sie zurück?
7. Wie viel ist eine Million geteilt durch zehn?

NOTES: 1. **der Autohändler** car dealer. 2. **die Geldtasche** purse. 3. **im Ganzen** in all.

Exercise 65

- Wie viel kostet . . . ?
- Wie viel kostet das Auto?
- Ich glaube, dass das Auto 21 999 € kostet.

das Auto	9, 99 €
der Hut	27, 50 €
der Bleistift	21 999 €
die Fahrkarte	0,65 €
das Kleid	178 000 €
die Wohnung	2, 20 €

1. Heute begleiten wir Frau Clark auf einem langen Einkaufsbummel. Frau Clark geht nicht allein einkaufen, sondern mit ihren braven Kindern.
2. Wilhelm braucht eine schwarze Hose, Karl sucht ein graues Hemd, Marie will einen schicken Hut und Anna wünscht sich eine neue Puppe.
3. Gemeinsam betreten sie ein großes Warenhaus. Zuerst gehen sie in den dritten Stock, denn dort ist die Abteilung für Bekleidung. Marie entdeckt gleich eine große Auswahl von Hüten. Sie sagt zu einer Verkäuferin:
4. Entschuldigen Sie, bitte. Ich will diesen grünen Hut probieren. Wie viel kostet er denn?
5. Dieser grüne Hut ist der letzte Modeschrei. Er kostet 65 Dollar.
6. Das ist zu teuer. Haben Sie auch günstige Hüte?
7. Ja, dieser rote Hut ist im Sonderangebot. Er kostet nur 39,99 Dollar.
8. Gut, dann nehme ich diesen roten Hut.
9. Auch Wilhelm und Karl bringen ihre Kleidungsstücke zur Kasse. Die schwarze Hose kostet 69,99 Dollar und das graue Hemd kostet genau 45 Dollar. Frau Clark muss also 154,98 Dollar bezahlen.
10. Danach gehen alle in die Spielwarenabteilung. Anna sieht sogleich eine schöne Puppe mit blauen Augen.

1. Today we accompany Mrs. Clark on a long shopping spree. Mrs. Clark doesn't go shopping alone but together with her good children.
2. William needs black pants, Charles is looking for a grey shirt, Mary wants a stylish hat and Ann wishes to have a new doll.
3. Together they enter a big department store. First they go to the fourth floor, because there is the clothes department. Mary discovers immediately a huge selection of hats. She says to a shop assistant:
4. Excuse me, please. I want to try on this green hat. How much does it cost?
5. This green hat is the latest thing in fashion. It costs 65 dollars.
6. That is too much. Do you also have inexpensive hats?
7. Yes, this blue hat is on special offer. It costs only 39.99 dollars.
8. Good, then I'll take this red hat.
9. Also William and Charles bring their clothes to the cash desk. The black trousers cost 69.99 dollars and the grey shirt costs exactly 45 dollars. Thus Mrs. Clark has to pay 154.98 dollars.
10. After that they all go to the toy department. Ann discovers immediately a beautiful doll with blue eyes.

11. Bitte Mama, darf ich diese Puppe haben?
12. Du hast doch schon so viele Puppen zu Hause!
13. Bitte Mama, ich liebe Puppen!
14. Also kauft Frau Clark auch noch eine Puppe für Anna. Die neue Puppe kostet 25,50 Dollar.
15. Frau Clark zahlt und geht mit ihren glücklichen Kindern wieder nach Hause.

11. Please, Mom, may I have this doll?
12. But you already have so many dolls at home!
13. But Mom, I love dolls!
14. So Mrs. Clark buys also a doll for Ann. The new doll costs 25 dollars and 50 cents.
15. Mrs. Clark pays and goes home with her happy children.

NOTE: In Germany the first floor is called **Erdgeschoß** (ground floor). Thus the second floor is called **erster Stock,** the third floor **zweiter Stock** etc.

Wortschatz

die Bekleidung clothing
der Einkaufsbummel *pl.* - shopping spree
die Hose *pl.* -n pants
das Hemd *pl.* -en shirt
die Puppe *pl.* -en doll
der Schrei *pl.* -e cry, shout; **der letzte Schrei** the latest thing
die Spielwarenabteilung *pl.* -en toy department
das Sonderangebot *pl.* -e special offer
der Stock *pl.* ¨-e floor; **im ersten Stock** on the second floor
das Warenhaus *pl.* ¨-er department store

einkaufen to go shopping
lieben to love
probieren to try
suchen to search, to look for
wünschen to wish, to want
brav good
glücklich happy
grau grey; **schwarz** black; **blau** blue; **rot** red
schick elegant, stylish
teuer expensive; **billig** cheap
gemeinsam together
gleich immediately

The Doer

The word for the *doer* in German is often formed by adding **-er** to the verb stem. Sometimes an **Umlaut** is also added.

arbeiten to work	**lehren** to teach	**lesen** to read	**verkaufen** to sell
Arbeiter worker	**Lehrer** teacher	**Leser** reader	**Verkäufer** seller

Wichtige Redemittel

ein Paar (*noun*) a pair. **Ich kaufe ein Paar Schuhe, ein Paar Handschuhe, ein Paar Strümpfe, ein Paar Socken.** I am buying a pair of shoes, a pair of gloves, a pair of stockings, a pair of socks.

ein paar (*adj.*) a few (like **einige** a few). **Ich habe ein paar (einige) alte Anzüge.** I have a couple of (a few) old suits.

Grammar Notes and Practical Exercises

1. PRESENT TENSE OF *tragen* to carry, *lassen* to leave

ich trage	wir tragen	ich lasse	wir lassen
du trägst	ihr tragt	du lässt	ihr lasst
er, sie, es trägt	sie (Sie) tragen	er, sie, es lässt	sie (Sie) lassen

Imperative: **trage! tragt! tragen Sie!**   **lasse! lasst! lassen Sie!**

Note the vowel change of **a** to **ä** in second- and third-person singular.

2. ABOUT ADJECTIVE ENDINGS

Predicate adjectives have no endings. Thus: Der Mann ist **groß**. Die Frau ist **jung**. Das Kind ist **klein**. When adjectives *precede* nouns they always have endings. The pattern of endings depends upon:

a. Whether the adjective is preceded by a **der**-word (**der, dieser, jener, jeder, welcher, aller**).
b. Whether the adjective is preceded by an **ein**-word (**ein, kein, mein, dein, sein, unser, euer, ihr, Ihr**).
c. Whether no **der**-word or **ein**-word precedes the adjective.

Der (Dieser) junge Mann ist mein Bruder.   Ich kenne den (diesen) jungen Mann.
Die (Diese) junge Frau ist meine Schwester.   Ich kenne die (diese) junge Frau.
Das (Dieses) gute Kind ist acht Jahre alt.   Ich kenne das (dieses) gute Kind.

Note well! When any **der**-word precedes an adjective, the adjective ends in **-e** in the nominative (m.f.n.) and in the accusative (f.n.). In all other cases singular and plural the ending is **-en**. Thus:

Singular

N.	der (dieser) gut**e** Mann	die (jene)	jung**e** Frau	das (jenes)	gut**e** Kind
G.	des (dieses) gut**en** Mannes	der (jener)	jung**en** Frau	des (jenes)	gut**en** Kindes
D.	dem (diesem) gut**en** Mann	der (jener)	jung**en** Frau	dem (jenem)	gut**en** Kind
A.	den (diesen) gut**en** Mann	die (jene)	jung**e** Frau	das (jenes)	gut**e** Kind

Plural

N.	die (diese) gut**en** Männer	die (jene)	jung**en** Frauen	die (jene)	gut**en** Kinder
G.	der (dieser) gut**en** Männer	der (jener)	jung**en** Frauen	der (jener)	gut**en** Kinder
D.	den (diesen) gut**en** Männern	den (jenen)	jung**en** Frauen	den (jenen)	gut**en** Kindern
A.	die (diese) gut**en** Männer	die (jene)	jung**en** Frauen	die (jene)	gut**en** Kinder

Exercise 66

Complete these sentences with the correct adjective endings.

Beispiel: 1. Der kleine Mann trägt den schweren Koffer.

1. Der klein_____ Mann trägt den schweren Koffer.
2. Das Gewicht des schwer_____ Koffers ist 25 Kilo.
3. Was ist in diesem schwer_____ Koffer?
4. Die schwer_____ Koffer stehen im großen Wartesaal des Bahnhofs.
5. Der rund_____ Tisch steht in dem Esszimmer.
6. Um diesen rund_____ Tisch stehen sechs Stühle.
7. Ich schreibe mit dem rot_____ Bleistift.
8. Haben Sie die neu_____ Hefte?
9. Jene deutsch_____ Bücher sind sehr interessant.
10. Nennen Sie die Farben dieser deutschen Landkarte!
11. Welche englisch_____ Bücher lesen Sie?

b. *Adjectives preceded by* ein-*words* (ein, kein, mein, dein, sein, unser, euer, ihr, Ihr).

Singular

N.	ein (kein)	gut**er** Sohn	eine (unsere)	gut**e** Tochter	ein (Ihr)	gut**es** Buch
G.	eines (keines)	gut**en** Sohnes	einer (unserer)	gut**en** Tochter	eines (Ihres)	gut**en** Buches
D.	einem (keinem)	gut**en** Sohn	einer (unserer)	gut**en** Tochter	einem (Ihrem)	gut**en** Buch
A.	einen (keinen)	gut**en** Sohn	eine (unsere)	gut**e** Tochter	ein (Ihr)	gut**es** Buch

Plural

N.	keine	gut**en** Söhne	unsere	gut**en** Töchter	Ihre	gut**en** Bücher
G.	keiner	gut**en** Söhne	unserer	gut**en** Töchter	Ihrer	gut**en** Bücher
D.	keinen	gut**en** Söhnen	unseren	gut**en** Töchtern	Ihren	gut**en** Büchern
A.	keine	gut**en** Söhne	unsere	gut**en** Töchter	Ihre	gut**en** Bücher

Note well! In the dative plural: **der**-words, **ein**-words, adjectives and nouns all end in the letter -**n**.

After any **ein**-word the endings of the adjective are exactly like the adjective endings after a **der**-word, except in the *singular nominative masculine,* and in the *singular nominative and accusative neuter.* In these cases the adjective must have the endings which the **ein**-word lacks.

dies**er** gute Mann
ein gut**er** Mann

dies**es** gute Kind
ein gut**es** Kind

Exercise 67

Complete these sentences with the correct adjective endings.

1. Herr Clark ist ein amerikanisch_____ Geschäftsmann.
2. Sein Büro ist in der Stadt, aber seine Wohnung ist in einem klein_____ Vorort.[1]
3. Er wohnt in einem schön_____ Einfamilienhaus.
4. Hinter dem Haus ist ein klein_____ Garten.
5. Die Kinder des Geschäftsmanns spielen gern in ihrem klein_____ Garten.
6. Herr Clark hat in der groß_____ Stadt München einen tüchtig _____[2] Geschäftspartner.
7. Im Sommer will Herr Clark eine kurz_____ Reise nach Deutschland machen.
8. Er will seinen deutsch_____ Geschäftspartner in München besuchen.
9. Jeden Monat sendet dieser Partner eine groß_____ Bestellung[3] an die Firma von Herrn Clark.
10. Ein schwer_____ Koffer steht im Wartesaal.

NOTES: 1. der Vorort suburb. **2. tüchtig** able, diligent. **3. die Bestellung** order.

c. Adjectives not preceded by **ein-***words or* **der-***words.*

In these sentences compare the endings of the adjectives with those of **dieser.**

Dieser Kaffee ist teuer.	**Diese** Milch ist gut.	**Dieses** Wasser ist klar.
Guter Kaffee ist teuer.	**Frische** Milch ist gut.	**Frisches** Wasser ist klar.
Ich habe **diesen** Kaffee gern.	Ich trinke **diese** Milch.	Trinken Sie **dieses** Wasser?
Ich habe **guten** Kaffee gern.	Ich trinke **frische** Milch.	Trinken Sie **frisches** Wasser?

When an adjective is not preceded by an **ein**-word or **der**-word it has the same endings as **dieser,** except in the genitive singular, masculine and neuter, where **-en** takes the place of **-es.**

die Farbe **dieses Weines (dieses Bieres)**	the color of this wine (of this beer)
die Farbe **guten Weines (guten Bieres)**	the color of good wine (of good beer)

3. COLORS

rot	red	**grün**	green	**blau**	blue	**gelb**	yellow
orange	orange	**schwarz**	black	**grau**	gray	**lila**	purple
weiß	white	**braun**	brown	**rosa**	rose	**türkis**	turquoise

Use the adjectives **hell-** and **dunkel-** (light and dark) in order to express the different shades of colors. Thus: **hellblau, dunkelrot,** etc.

Exercise 68

What shall I wear? Make at least seven different sentences.

Ich ziehe	ein	rot	Jacke	an.
	eine	grün	Hemd	
	einen	dunkelblau	Pullover	
		gelb	Hose	
		türkis	Rock	
		hellrot	Kleid	
		schwarz	Sakko	
		grün	T-Shirt	
		hellgrau		
		weiß		
		orange		
		dunkelgelb		
		lila		
		hellbraun		
		rosa		
		hellgrün		

CHAPTER 17

WIE SPÄT IST ES?

1. Herr Müller und Herr Clark haben heute wieder eine Deutschstunde. Diesmal reden sie über die Uhrzeit.

2. Herr Müller sagt: „Die Uhrzeit! Jedermann will wissen: Wie spät ist es? Um wie viel Uhr kommt das Flugzeug an? Um wie viel Uhr fährt der Zug ab? Um wie viel Uhr beginnt die Prüfung? Um wie viel Uhr fängt die Vorstellung an?"

3. Herr Müller und Herr Clark machen ein Rollenspiel. Herr Müller spielt die Rolle des Beamten am Kartenschalter auf dem Bahnhof von Frankfurt. Herr Clark spielt die Rolle des Reisenden. Er will eine Fahrkarte kaufen.

4. Eine Fahrkarte zweiter Klasse nach Köln, bitte.

   —Einfach oder Rückfahrkarte?

   —Geben Sie mir eine Rückfahrkarte, bitte. Wie viel kostet das?

   —Achtunddreißig Euro.

   —(Der Beamte gibt dem Reisenden die Fahrkarte. Dieser[1] zahlt.)

   —Um wie viel Uhr fährt der Zug von Frankfurt ab, und wann kommt er in Köln an?

   —Es gibt einige Züge täglich nach Köln. Ein Zug fährt um 14 (vierzehn) Uhr ab und kommt um 16.50 Uhr (sechzehn Uhr fünfzig) in Köln an.

   —Ich danke Ihnen[2] sehr.

   —Bitte schön.

5. Herr Müller: Großartig, Herr Clark! Sie spielen Ihre Rolle wunderbar.
   Jetzt spiele ich die Rolle des Angestellten an der Kasse im Kino. Sie spielen die Rolle des Touristen. Sie wünschen Auskunft über die Vorstellung. Bitte fangen Sie an!

1. Today Mr. Müller and Mr. Clark have again a German lesson. This time they talk about the time of the day.

2. Mr. Müller says: "The time of day! Everybody wants to know: What time is it? At what time does the plane arrive? At what time does the train leave? At what time does the examination begin? At what time does the performance begin?"

3. Mr. Müller and Mr. Clark are doing a role play. Mr. Müller plays the role of the employee in the ticket office at the railroad station in Frankfurt. Mr. Clark plays the role of the traveler. He wants to buy a ticket.

4. A second-class ticket for Cologne, please.

   —One-way or round-trip?

   —Give me a round-trip ticket, please. How much does that cost?

   —Thirty-eight euros.

   —(The employee gives the traveler the ticket. The latter pays.)

   —At what time does the train leave Frankfurt, and at what time does it arrive in Cologne?

   —There are several trains daily for Cologne. One train leaves at 2 o'clock and arrives in Cologne at 4:50 P.M.

   —I thank you very much.

   —Don't mention it.

5. Mr. Müller: Splendid, Mr. Clark! You play your role wonderfully.
   Now I shall play the role of the employee in the cashier's booth at the movies. You will play the role of the tourist. You wish information about the performance. Please, begin.

6. Bitte, sagen Sie mir: Um wie viel Uhr fängt die Vorstellung an?
   —Wir haben drei Vorstellungen. Die erste beginnt um 4.20 (vier Uhr zwanzig) nachmittags; die zweite um 6.50 (sechs Uhr fünfzig); und die dritte um 9.10 (neun Uhr zehn) abends.
   —Wie viel kostet eine Eintrittskarte?
   —Die Karte kostet sieben Euro.
   —Bitte, geben Sie mir zwei Karten für die dritte Vorstellung.
   (Der Angestellte gibt dem Touristen die Eintrittskarten. Dieser[1] zahlt.)
7. Herr M.: Ausgezeichnet! Ich muss es wieder sagen. Sie spielen Ihre Rolle wunderbar.
8. Herr C.: Danke bestens. Es war für mich eine interessante und wertvolle Übung.

6. Please tell me at what time the performance begins.
   —We have three performances. The first begins at 4:20 P.M.; the second at 6:50; and the third at 9:10 in the evening.

   —What is the price of a ticket?
   —A ticket costs seven euros.
   —Please give me two tickets for the third performance.
   (The employee gives the tourist the tickets. The latter pays.)
7. Mr. M.: Excellent! I must say it again, you play your role wonderfully.
8. Mr. C.: Thanks a lot. It was an interesting and valuable exercise for me.

NOTES: 1. Dieser (the latter) refers to the last one mentioned, i.e. **der Tourist.** The first one mentioned, **der Angestellte,** would be referred to as **jener** (the former). **2. Ihnen,** dative of **Sie.** The verb **danken** takes a dative object. You will meet other verbs that take a dative object.

Wortschatz

der Reisende *pl.* **-n** traveler
der Béamte *pl.* **-n** employee (civil service)
der Angestellte *pl.* **-n** employee
die Eintrittskarte pl. **-en** ticket
der Preis *pl.* **-e** price, cost
der Film *pl.* **-e** film, movie
die Rolle *pl.* **-n** role
die Übung *pl.* **-en** practice, exercise

die Prüfung *pl.* **-en** test, examination
ab-fahren to leave, to ride off, depart
an-fangen to begin
an-kommen to arrive
auf-stehen to get up
wünschen to wish; **zahlen** to pay
als as; **als Übung** as (for) practice
wertvoll valuable
jedermann everyone, everybody

Words Dealing with Travel

der Bahnhof *pl,* **¨-e** railroad station **auf dem Bahnhof** at the railroad station
der Flughafen *pl.* **¨-** airport
das Flugzeug *pl.* **-e** airplane
der Zug *pl.* **¨-e** train
der Wartesaal *pl.* **-säle** waiting room
Ich reise mit dem Zug (dem Autobus, dem Flugzeug). I travel by train (bus, plane).
Ich fliege morgen nach Frankfurt. I fly to Frankfurt tomorrow.

eine Fahrkarte erster (zweiter, dritter) Klasse a first (second, third) class ticket
eine einfache Fahrkarte, eine Rückfahrkarte a one-way ticket, a round-trip ticket
Wann kommt der Zug von Köln an? When does the train from Cologne arrive?
Wann fährt der Zug von Köln ab? When does the train leave Cologne?
Der Zug von Hamburg hat fünf Minuten Verspätung. The train from Hamburg is five minutes late.

Wichtige Redemittel

Bitte please (stands for **ich bitte** I ask, I request)
bitten um to ask for, to request; **Ich bitte um eine Antwort.** I ask for an answer.
Bitte schön. Don't mention it.

Ich wünsche Auskunft. I want information.
Ausgezeichnet! Excellent!
Großartig! Splendid!
Wunderbar! Wonderful!

Grammar Notes and Practical Exercises

1. TIME OF DAY

Wie viel Uhr ist es? *or* **Wie spät ist es?**	What time is it?
1.00 Es ist ein Uhr *or* **Es ist eins.**	It is one o'clock.
2.00 Es ist zwei Uhr *or* **Es ist zwei.**	It is two o'clock.
3.00 drei Uhr; 4.00 vier Uhr; usw.	three o'clock; four o'clock; etc.
3.10 zehn Minuten nach drei	ten minutes after three
3.15 Viertel nach drei	a quarter past three
3.30 halb vier	half past three
3.45 Viertel vor vier	a quarter to four
3.50 zehn Minuten vor vier	ten minutes to four
Um wie viel Uhr? Um eins; um Viertel nach zehn; usw.	At what time? At one; at a quarter past ten; etc.

In general, the method of expressing clock time is the same in English and German. **vor** = to and **nach** = after, past. But watch for the half hours! They are figured with reference to the next hour. Thus: 9:30 = **halb zehn** (half an hour toward ten); 12:30 = **halb eins;**[1] etc.

NOTE: 1. The quarter hours may also be figured in the same way. Thus 3:15 = **(ein) Viertel** (toward) **vier; 3:45 = drei Viertel vier;** etc.

In train and plane timetables, also in theater announcements, time is usually indicated by the 24-hour clock beginning with midnight (24.00). This eliminates the need for A.M. and P.M. and for the German expressions: **morgens** in the morning, **nachmittags** in the afternoon, and **abends** in the evening. Thus:

6.30 (sechs Uhr dreißig) = 6:30 A.M.   14.00 (vierzehn Uhr) = 2:00 P.M.
10.15 (zehn Uhr fünfzehn) = 10:15 A.M.   17.20 (siebzehn Uhr zwanzig) = 5:20 P.M.
12.00 (zwölf Uhr) = 12:00 noon   23.10 (dreiundzwanzig Uhr zehn) =11:10 P.M.

Exercise 69

Say and write the German for these time expressions, using the 12-hour clock.

Beispiel: 10.15 = Viertel nach zehn; 4:55 = fünf Minuten vor fünf.

a. 1.15   e. 3.20   i. 12.30
b. 5.10   f. 3.55   j. 7.30
c. 8.15   g. 11.00   k. 9.45
d. 2.45   h. 4.20   l. 10.23

Exercise 70

Read these sentences, giving the time according to the 24-hour clock.

Beispiel: 1. Ein guter Zug fährt **um einundzwanzig Uhr zehn ab.**

1. **Ein guter Zug fährt um 21.10 ab.**
2. **Dieser Zug kommt um 17.25 in Köln an.**
3. **Der Schnellzug nach Bremen fährt um 15.14 ab.**
4. **Der Zug von Hamburg hat zehn Minuten Verspätung. Er kommt gegen 8.25 an.**
5. **Es gibt Züge nach Bonn um 6.25 und 18.50.**
6. **Das Flugzeug verlässt den Flughafen in New York um 19.00 Uhr. Es kommt um 10.10 am Flughafen in München an.**
7. **Die Opernvorstellung beginnt heute abend um 19.30.**
8. **Die erste Vorstellung im Kino beginnt um 14.30.**
9. **Die letzte Vorstellung fängt um 22.30 an.**

2. SEPARABLE VERBS. PRESENT TENSE OF *aufstehen* to stand up, to get up

I get up early every day. You get up early every day, etc.

Ich stehe jeden Tag früh **auf.**   **Wir stehen** jeden Tag früh **auf.**
Du stehst jeden Tag früh **auf.**   **Ihr steht** jeden Tag früh **auf.**
Er steht jeden Tag früh **auf.**   **Sie stehen** jeden Tag früh **auf.**

Imperative:
Stehe jeden Tag früh **auf!**   **Steht** jeden Tag früh **auf!**   **Stehen Sie** jeden Tag früh **auf!**

a. Verbs often have prefixes which may separate from the verb itself. Such prefixes are called separable prefixes *and the verbs to which they are attached are called* separable verbs. *The most important separable prefixes are:*

ab-	bei-	hin-	weg-
an-	ein-	los-	zu-
auf-	fest-	mit-	zurück-
aus-	her-	vor-	zusammen-

The stress in separable verbs is always on the prefix. The meaning of a separable verb is usually the meaning of the simple verb plus the meaning of the prefix. Thus: **auf-stehen** to stand up, to get up; **ab-fahren** to go (ride) away, to leave; **zurück-geben** to give back; **zurück-kommen** to come back; **an-fangen** to begin. A hyphen is used in the vocabularies to indicate separable prefixes.

b. The separable prefix goes to the end of a simple sentence or main clause in the present tense and in the imperative.

Sie gibt uns fünf Mark **zurück.**	She gives us back five marks.
Wann **fährt** der Schnellzug **ab?**	When does the express train leave?
Steht um sieben Uhr **auf,** Kinder!	Get up at seven o'clock, children.

Exercise 71

Complete these sentences with the present tense of the verbs in parentheses or with the imperative (*impv.*) if so indicated.

Beispiel: 1. Um 8 Uhr **fangen wir** die Prüfung **an.**

1. (anfangen) Um 8 Uhr _____ wir die Prüfung _____.
2. (zurückgeben) Er _____ uns fünf Mark _____.
3. (abfahren) Wer _____ morgen früh um 6 Uhr _____?
4. (aufstehen) Warum _____ Sie so früh _____?
5. (zurückkommen) Wann _____ du vom Kino _____?
6. (anfangen) Wir _____ die Arbeit um 9 Uhr _____.
7. (ankommen) Wann _____ der Zug von Köln _____?
8. (anfangen, *impv.*) _____ Sie die Arbeit jetzt _____!
9. (aufstehen, *impv.*) _____ sofort _____, Kinder!
10. (zurückkommen, *impv.*) _____ bald _____, Marie!

Exercise 72

Fill in the blanks with the correct prefixes from the box.

aus—mit—weg—an—auf—ein—zu—ab

1. Thomas macht mir die Türe _____.
2. Morgen gehe ich mit ihm _____.
3. Zuerst kaufe ich in dem Supermarkt _____.
4. Wenn du willst, dann gehe ich _____.
5. Es ist kalt. Bitte mach das Fenster _____.
6. Maria holt ihren Freund vom Bahnhof _____.
7. Der Zug kommt um 12.30 _____.
8. Yvonne fährt am Sonntag wieder _____.

3. FIRST- AND SECOND-PERSON PRONOUNS (NOMINATIVE, DATIVE AND ACCUSATIVE)

	Singular		*Plural*		*Polite:* *Sing. & Plural*
N.	**ich** I	**du** you	**wir** we	**ihr** you	**Sie** you
D.	**mir** (to) me	**dir** (to) you	**uns** (to) us	**euch** (to) you	**Ihnen** (to) you
A.	**mich** me	**dich** you	**uns** us	**euch** you	**Sie** you

NOTE: The polite form is like the third person plural: *N.* **sie,** *D.* **ihnen,** *A.* **sie;** but all cases of the polite form must be capitalized.

Exercise 73

Complete the sentences by translating the pronouns in parentheses.
1. Diese Eintrittskarte ist für (me).
2. Bitte, bringen Sie (me) den Koffer.
3. Ist dieser Brief für (you), Herr Braun?
4. Bitte, sagen Sie (us), was Sie wollen!
5. Ich möchte (you) diese neuen Bilder zeigen, Herr Braun.
6. Wir können (you) nicht alles sagen, Kinder.
7. Wir sprechen eben von (you), Karl.
8. Die Mutter sucht (you), Wilhelm.
9. Verstehen Sie (me)?
10. Wir verstehen (you, *pol.*) nicht.
11. Geben Sie (me) die Fahrkarte zurück!

REVIEW OF CHAPTERS 13–17

Summary of Nouns (Singular and Plural)

Practice the following nouns aloud, singular and plural. Thus: **der Kellner, die Kellner; der Preis, die Preise.**

der Kellner	*pl.* -	der Markt	*pl.* ¨-e	das Trinkgeld	*pl.* -er	die Wahrheit	*pl.* -en
der Verkäufer	*pl.* -	das Ding	*pl.* -e	das Taschentuch	*pl.* ¨-er	die Prüfung	*pl.* -en
der Schalter	*pl.* -	der Bleistift	*pl.* -e	die Sache	*pl.* -n	die Rechnung	*pl.* -en
der Preis	*pl.* -e	das Flugzeug	*pl.* -e	die Meile	*pl.* -n	die Übung	*pl.* -en
der Zug	*pl.* ¨-e	das Problem	*pl.* -e	die Summe	*pl.* -n	die Vorstellung	*pl.* -en
der Film	*pl.* -e	der Bahnhof	*pl.* ¨-e	die Fahrkarte	*pl.* -n	die Verkäuferin	*pl.* -nen
das Paar	*pl.* -e	das Wort	*pl.* ¨-er	die Person	*pl.* -en	die Mahlzeit	*pl.* -en
das Stück	*pl.* -e	das Ei	*pl.* -er	die Nummer	*pl.* –n	die Gelegenheit	*pl.* -en

Some Rules for Gender

All nouns ending in **-chen** or **-lein** are neuter (**das Mädchen, das Fräulein**).

All nouns ending in **-heit, -ung, -in** are feminine (**die Wahrheit, die Übung, die Lehrerin**).

Nearly all nouns ending in **-e,** denoting objects, are feminine (**die Schule, die Sache, die Meile**).

Some rules for plurals:

Nouns in **-chen** and **-lein** do not change in the plural (**das Mädchen** *pl.* -; **das Fräulein** *pl.* -).

Feminine nouns of more than one syllable add **-n** or **-en** (**die Schwester** *pl.* -n, **die Übung** *pl.* -en). Exceptions—only two (**die Mutter** *pl.* -; **die Tochter** *pl.* [¨]-). Nouns with **-in** double the **-n** in the plural (**die Lehrerin, die Lehrerinnen**).

Verbs

1. fliegen	1. to fly
2. glauben	2. to believe
3. hoffen	3. to hope
4. brauchen	4. to need
5. zahlen	5. to pay
6. wünschen	6. to wish
7. bleiben	7. to remain
8. reservieren	8. to reserve
9. studieren	9. to study
10. speisen	10. to dine
11. rechnen	11. to figure
12. denken (an) + *acc.*	12. to think (of)
13. verlassen	13. to leave
14. gebrauchen	14. to use
15. bekommen	15. to receive
16. verstehen	16. to understand
17. erwarten	17. to await
18. wollen	18. to want
19. er will	19. he wants
20. können	20. to be able
21. er kann	21. he can

Verbs with stem change (**e > ie, e > i,** and **a > ä**) in second- and third-person singular.

sehen	lesen	sprechen	treten	geben	zurückgeben
to see	to read	to speak	to step	to give	to give back
ich sehe	lese	spreche	trete	gebe	gebe zurück
du siehst	liest	sprichst	trittst	gibst	gibst zurück
er sieht	liest	spricht	tritt	gibt	gibt zurück

fahren	tragen	fallen	verlassen[1]	laufen	anfangen
to ride	to carry	to fall	to leave	to run	to begin
ich fahre	trage	falle	verlasse	laufe	fange an
du fährst	trägst	fällst	verlässt	läufst	fängst an
er fährt	trägt	fällt	verlässt	läuft	fängt an

NOTE: 1. Er verlässt die Stadt. He leaves (goes away from) the city.

Redemittel

1. **Gute Reise!** Safe journey!
2. **Donnerwetter!** Wow!
3. **eines Tages** one day
4. **eines Morgens** one morning

5. **eines Abends** one evening
6. **Es freut mich** I am glad
7. **Es freut uns** We are glad
8. **denken (an)** + *acc.* to think (of)
9. **zu Fuß gehen** to go on foot (walk)
10. **Wir gehen zu Fuß** We go on foot (walk)
11. **Fangen wir an!** Let's begin!
12. **Dollar in Euro wechseln** to change dollars for euros
13. **Sie geben sich die Hand** They shake hands
14. **alles, was möglich ist** everything that is possible
15. **Seit wann sind Sie hier?** Since when have you been here?
16. **Es ist nicht viel wert.** It is not worth much.

Exercise 74

Complete these sentences by translating the words in parentheses.

1. **Ich möchte** (to change euros for dollars).
2. **Sein alter Freund wünscht ihm eine** (safe journey).
3. **Herr Clark** (is making great progress), **denn er ist fleißig und intelligent.**
4. **Was wünschen Sie? Ich wünsche** (information) **über die Vorstellungen.**
5. **Wir gehen zur Station** (on foot), **wenn das Wetter schön ist.**
6. **An wen denken Sie?** (I am thinking of) **meinen alten Schulfreund.**
7. (One evening) **sitzen wir im Arbeitszimmer und sprechen über die Tageszeit.**
8. (Since when) **lernen Sie Deutsch?**
9. (I have been studying) **seit zwei Jahren Deutsch.**
10. (I shake hands with him) **und sage: Auf Wiedersehen.**
11. (I am glad), **dich zu sehen.**
12. (Let's begin). **Es ist schon spät.**

Exercise 75

Kurze Gespräche

Practice these short conversations aloud. Translate them.

1. —**Was lesen Sie?** —**Ich lese eine deutsche Zeitung.**[1] —**Was liest er?** —**Er liest eine englische Zeitung.**
2. —**Was schenkst du der Mutter zum Geburtstag?**[2] —**Ich schenke ihr ein seidenes**[3] **Taschentuch.** —**Was schenkt Karl ihr?** —**Er schenkt ihr ein hübsches Halstuch.**[4]
3. —**Spricht Herr Kurz Englisch und Französisch?** —**Er spricht weder Englisch noch Französisch. Er spricht nur Deutsch.**
4. —**Welchen Anzug trägt**[5] **er heute?** —**Er trägt seinen neuen, braunen Anzug.**
5. —**Um wie viel Uhr verlässt er jeden Tag das Haus?** —**Er verlässt das Haus um Punkt sieben Uhr.**

6. —Wie lange bleiben Sie hier in dieser Stadt? —Ich bleibe ein ganzes[6] Jahr hier.
7. —Haben Sie einen großen Koffer? —Ich habe einen großen und einen kleinen. —Leihen[7] Sie mir bitte den großen. —Gerne.[8]
8. Was für ein[9] hübsches Kleid! —Was für ein schöner Garten! —Was für eine schöne Frau!

NOTES: 1. die Zeitung the newspaper. **2. der Geburtstag** birthday; **zum Geburtstag** for (her) birthday. **3. seiden** silk. **4. das Halstuch** scarf. **5. tragen** to carry or to wear. **6. ganz** whole. **7. leihen** to lend. **8. gerne** gladly. **9. Was für ein . . . !** What a . . . !

Exercise 76

Select the words from Column II which best complete the sentences in Column I.

I	*II*
1. Frau Clark geht in den großen Laden	a. Geschäftsreise nach Europa zu machen.
2. In Deutschland rechnet man das	b. um Punkt halb sieben auf.
3. Ich beabsichtige, im Sommer eine	c. und jetzt will ich einen grauen kaufen.
4. Jedermann weiß, dass man ohne	d. wenn sie immer fleißig sind.
5. Ich stehe jeden Tag außer Sonntag	e. und kauft neue Kleider für die Kinder.
6. Wenn Sie im Juni nach Europa reisen,	f. Gewicht nicht in Pfund sondern in Kilo.
7. Wissen Sie, um wie viel Uhr	g. dass Sie eine ganze Woche hier bleiben.
8. Ich habe einen blauen Anzug,	h. Geld nicht auskommen kann.
9. Es freut uns zu erfahren,	i. der Zug von Hamburg ankommt?
10. Alle Schüler können Deutsch lernen,	j. müssen Sie sofort einen Platz reservieren.

Grammar Review and Practical Exercises

1. REVIEW ADJECTIVE ENDINGS

Exercise 77

Complete these sentences with the correct case of the adjective expression in parentheses.

Beispiel: 1. Wir kaufen der Mutter **ein seidenes Halstuch.**

1. Wir kaufen der Mutter (ein seidenes Halstuch).
2. Ich schreibe mit (der rote Bleistift).
3. Er trägt (ein schwerer Koffer).
4. Er trägt (der schwere Koffer in den Wartesaal).
5. Das Porträt (eine schöne Frau) hängt über dem Klavier.
6. Herr Müller ist der Geschäftspartner (dieser amerikanische Geschäftsmann).
7. Die Zigaretten liegen auf (jener kleine Tisch).
8. Die Stühle stehen um (der runde Tisch).

9. Was für (ein schönes Mädchen)!
10. Deutschland ist auf (der europäische Kontinent).
11. Der Partner (diese große Firma) heißt Müller.
12. Die Herren sitzen in (das gemütliche Zimmer) des Geschäftsmanns.
13. Ich will (kein altes Auto) kaufen.
14. Das Gewicht (unser schwerer Koffer) ist 26 Kilo.
15. Er will (sein deutscher Geschäftspartner) in München besuchen.

Exercise 78

Change the adjective expressions in heavy type to the plural. Change the verb whenever necessary.

Beispiel: 1. Die jungen Männer sitzen in dem Arbeitszimmer.

1. **Der junge Mann** sitzt in dem Arbeitszimmer.
2. **Dieses schöne Bild** kostet 100 Euro.
3. Wir sprechen soeben von **unsrem deutschen Lehrer.**
4. Kennen Sie **dieses kleine Mädchen?**
5. Wo ist die Wohnung **deiner neuen Freundin?**
6. **Die deutsche Übung** ist nicht schwer.
7. Wo ist **das neue Heft?**
8. Ich habe **kein deutsches Buch.**
9. Wo wohnen die Eltern **jenes hübschen Kindes?**
10. Das können Sie in **der deutschen Zeitung lesen.**
11. **Lieber** (dear) **Freund.**
12. **Liebe Freundin.**

2. SUMMARY OF FIRST, SECOND, AND THIRD PERSON PRONOUNS—NOMINATIVE, DATIVE, ACCUSATIVE

	Singular						*Plural*			*Sing. & Plur.* *Polite*
	1st	*2nd*		*3rd*			*1st*	*2nd*	*3rd*	
N.	ich	du	er	sie	es	*N.*	wir	ihr	sie	Sie
D.	mir	dir	ihm	ihr	ihm	*D.*	uns	euch	ihnen	Ihnen
A.	mich	dich	ihn	sie	es	*A.*	uns	euch	sie	Sie

Exercise 79

Read each question. Complete each answer with the correct pronoun.

Beispiel: 1. Herr Müller lehrt uns Deutsch.

1. Wer lehrt euch Deutsch?
2. Kennen Sie Herrn Braun?
3. Wo erwartet mich der Professor?

4. Ist Doktor Schulz bei Ihnen (*pl.*)?
5. Schreibst du dem Onkel einen Brief?

6. Was schenkt ihr der Mutter zum Geburtstag?

7. Für wen ist dieser neue Anzug?
8. Kannst du mir zehn Euro leihen?

9. Haben Sie meine deutsche Zeitung?
10. Wo ist der Aschenbecher?
11. Wo ist die Füllfeder?
12. Wo ist mein Deutschheft?

1. Herr Müller lehrt _____ Deutsch.
2. Wir kennen _____ sehr gut.
3. Er erwartet _____ (*pol.*) im Arbeitszimmer.
4. Ja, er ist bei _____.
5. Ja, ich schreibe _____ einen langen Brief.
6. Wir schenken _____ eine goldene Uhr.
7. Er ist für _____ , Herr Engel.
8. Ich kann _____ (*fam.*) nur fünf Euro leihen.
9. Nein, ich habe _____ nicht.
10. _____ ist auf dem kleinen Tisch.
11. _____ ist auf dem großen Schreibtisch.
12. _____ (It) ist in diesem Schlafzimmer.

Der erste Dialog
Ihre Uhr Geht Nach

—Sie kommen ja zu spät. Die Vorstellung fängt schon an.
—Entschuldigen Sie, dass ich spät komme. Wegen des Verkehrs musste mein Taxi sehr langsam fahren.

—Wie spät ist es auf Ihrer Uhr?
—Halb neun.
—Ihre Uhr geht nach. Es ist schon zwanzig Minuten vor neun.
—Ich glaube, Ihre Uhr geht ein bisschen vor. Auf der Uhr da drüben ist es erst fünfundzwanzig Minuten vor neun.

The First Dialogue
Your Watch Is Slow

—Why, you're late. The performance is already beginning.
—Excuse me for being late. On account of the traffic my taxi had to go very slowly.

—What time is it by your watch?
—Half past eight.
—Your watch is slow. It is already twenty minutes to nine.
—I believe that your watch is a little fast. On the clock over there it is only twenty-five minutes to nine.

Der zweite Dialog	*The Second Dialogue*
Im Autobus—Wo Muss Ich Aussteigen?	*In the Bus—Where Must One Get Off?*

—Entschuldigen Sie, bitte. Wo muss ich aussteigen, um zu dem Hauptpostamt zu kommen? (zum Bahnhof, zur Frauenkirche, zur amerikanischen Botschaft, usw.)

—Excuse me, please. Where must I get off for the main post office? (the railroad station, the Church of Our Lady, the American Embassy, etc.)

—Sie müssen am Odeonsplatz aussteigen.

—You must get off at Odeon Place.

—Ist es weit von hier?

—Is it far from here?

—Nein, nicht sehr weit. Ich werde die Haltestelle ausrufen.

—No, not very far. I will call out the stop.

Exercise 80

Lesestück

KARL LERNT NICHT GERN MATHEMATIK

Karl kommt eines Tages aus der Schule nach Hause und sagt zu seiner Mutter: „Ich lerne nicht gern Mathematik. Sie ist zu schwer. Warum müssen wir so viele Übungen und Aufgaben[1] machen? Wir haben doch Taschenrechner[2] und Computer, nicht wahr?"

Die Mutter sieht ihren Sohn an und sagt: „Du hast Unrecht, mein Kind. Man kann nichts tun ohne Mathematik. Man gebraucht Mathematik nicht nur[3] auf allen Gebieten[4] der Wissenschaft, sondern auch[3] im täglichen Leben." Die Mutter hört auf[5] zu sprechen, denn sie sieht, ihr Sohn gibt nicht acht[6] auf das, was sie sagt.

„Sage einmal, lieber Junge, interessiert dich Baseball nicht?" „Natürlich interessiert mich Baseball!" „Nun also, wenn die Dodgers achtzig Spiele gewinnen[7] und dreißig verlieren,[8] weißt du welchen Prozentsatz[9] der Spiele sie gewinnen?" Karl antwortet: „Für den Prozentsatz der Spiele brauche ich keine Mathematik. Ich finde doch alles ausgerechnet[10] in der Zeitung. Du hast aber Recht, Mutter. Ich muss mehr lernen. Ich hoffe eines Tages auf eine Universität zu gehen,[11] und deswegen muss ich die Schulprüfungen gut bestehen,[12] nicht nur in Mathematik, sondern auch in den anderen Fächern."[13]

NOTES: 1. **die Aufgabe** task, assignment. 2. calculator. 3. **nicht nur . . . sondern auch** not only . . . but also. 4. **auf . . . Wissenschaft** in all fields of science. 5. **auf-hören** to stop. 6. **achtgeben auf** to pay attention to. 7. win. 8. lose. 9. percentage. 10. figured out. 11. **auf . . . gehen** to go to a university. 12. **eine Prüfung bestehen** to pass an examination. 13. **das Fach** subject.

CHAPTER 19

DER ARBEITSTAG DES HERRN CLARK

1. Herr Clark, darf ich Sie fragen, wie Sie einen typischen Arbeitstag verbringen?
2. Gewiss. Wenn ich in mein Büro gehe, muss ich um sechs Uhr aufstehen. Ich wasche mich, rasiere mich und ziehe mich an. Das dauert ungefähr eine halbe Stunde. Gegen sieben setze ich mich an den Tisch im Esszimmer zum Frühstück.
3. Und Ihre Frau steht auch so früh auf?
4. Ja, meine Frau steht früh auf, und wir frühstücken zusammen. Ich habe das natürlich sehr gern. So haben wir eine gute Gelegenheit, uns zu unterhalten.
5. Was essen Sie zum Frühstück?
6. Gewöhnlich habe ich Orangensaft, Semmeln, Eier und Kaffee.
7. Wie ich sehe, essen Sie ein ausgiebiges Frühstück. Und dann nach dem Frühstück?
8. Um halb acht fahre ich mit dem Auto zur U-Bahnstation, wo ich die U-Bahn nehme.
9. Um wie viel Uhr erreichen Sie Ihr Büro?
10. Ich erreiche das Büro um neun Uhr. Im Büro lese ich zuerst die Post, dann diktiere ich meiner Sekretärin einige Briefe und führe Telefongespräche mit verschiedenen Kunden. Ich tue im allgemeinen alles, was ein Geschäftsmann zu tun hat.
11. Wann essen Sie Ihr Mittagessen?
12. Fast immer um ein Uhr. Ich brauche nur ungefähr zwanzig Minuten zum Essen.

1. Mr. Clark, may I ask you how you spend a typical working day?
2. Certainly. When I go to my office I must get up at six o'clock. I wash myself, shave and dress. That takes about half an hour. Toward seven o'clock I sit down at the table in the dining room for breakfast.
3. And your wife also gets up so early?
4. Yes. My wife gets up early and we breakfast together. Naturally I like that very much. Thus we have a good opportunity to talk.
5. What do you eat for breakfast?
6. Usually I have orange juice, rolls and eggs and coffee.
7. As I see, you eat a substantial breakfast. And then after breakfast?
8. At half past seven I drive to the subway station in my car, where I take the subway.
9. At what time do you reach your office?
10. I reach the office at nine o'clock. In the office I read the mail first of all, then I dictate some letters to my secretary and carry on telephone conversations with various customers. In general I do everything that a businessman has to do.
11. When do you have lunch? (*Lit.* midday meal.)
12. Almost always at one o'clock. I take only twenty minutes for lunch.

13. Das ist sehr wenig! In Deutschland macht man es anders mit dem Essen. Die Deutschen verbringen viel Zeit bei den Mahlzeiten, besonders beim Mittagessen. Das ist für sie die Hauptmahlzeit. Aber davon sprechen wir ein anderes Mal. Was tun Sie nach dem Mittagessen?

13. That is very little! In Germany they do it differently in the matter of eating. The Germans spend much time at meals, especially at the midday meal (dinner). That is for them the main meal. But we'll speak about that another time. What do you do after lunch?

14. Oft besuchen mich Kunden. Von Zeit zu Zeit gehe ich zu den Kunden.

14. Often customers come to visit me. From time to time I go to the customers.

15. Um wie viel Uhr beenden Sie Ihren Arbeitstag?

15. At what time do you finish your day's work?

16. Ich verlasse Punkt fünf mein Büro. Ich komme um Viertel nach sechs nach Hause. Ich spiele ein wenig mit den Kindern, bevor wir uns an den Tisch zum Abendessen setzen.

16. I leave my office at five o'clock sharp. I get home at a quarter past six. I play with the children a little, before we sit down at the table for dinner.

17. Nach einem solchen Tag sind Sie wohl etwas müde.

17. After such a day you surely are somewhat tired.

18. Jawohl, Herr Müller. Und ich freue mich immer sehr, zu Hause zu sein.

18. Yes indeed, Mr. Müller. And I am always very happy to be at home.

Wortschatz

die Hauptmahlzeit *pl.* **-en** chief meal
das Frühstück *pl.* **-e** breakfast
das Mittagessen *pl.* **-** dinner, noon meal
das Abendessen *pl.* **-** supper, evening meal
die Post mail; der Kunde *pl.* **-n** customer
die Sekretärin *pl.* **-nen** secretary
die Zeit *pl.* **-en** time; das Mal time (*See* „Wichtige Redemittel" on next page.)
beénden to finish, to complete
dauern to last, to take (time)
diktíeren to dictate
erréichen to reach
essen (ich esse, du isst, er isst) to eat

telefoníeren to telephone
verbríngen to spend (time)
weg-gehen to go away; er geht heute weg
beréit ready; müde tired
halb (*halp*) half; eine halbe Stunde
verschíeden various; nur only
natürlich naturally, of course
besónders especially; anders otherwise
sowíe and also, as well as
solch such
bevór = ehe (*subordinate conj.*) before; Er küsst die Kinder, bevor (ehe) er morgens weggeht.

Einige Lebensmittel Some Foods

das Brot bread
das Brötchen *pl.* - roll
die Semmel *pl.* -n roll
die Butter butter

die Milch milk
die Sahne cream
das Ei *pl.* -er egg
der Kuchen *pl.*- cake
der Orangensaft (*oh-răn-zhen-zăft*) orange juice

das Fleisch meat
das Gemüse vegetable
das Obst fruit
der Fisch *pl.* -e fish

Wichtige Redemittel

das Mal time; **das erste Mal, das zweite Mal** the first time, the second time

-mal is used in many compounds to express "number of times" or "definite point of time." Thus: **einmal** one time, once; **zweimal** two times, twice; **dreimal** three times; **manchmal** sometimes; **keinmal** no time; **diesmal** this time; **letztesmal** last time.

zum Frühstück for breakfast

zum Abendessen for supper

zum Mittagessen for dinner

wohl indeed, surely, is used for emphasis. **Sie sind wohl müde nach einem solchen Tag.** You are surely tired after such a day.

dauern to last, to take (time) **Die Prüfung dauert zwei Stunden.** The examination lasts two hours.

Grammar Notes and Practical Exercises

1. PRESENT TENSE OF *nehmen* to take; *dürfen* to be permitted, may

ich nehme	wir nehmen	ich darf	wir dürfen
du nimmst	ihr nehmt	du darfst	ihr dürft
er, sie, es nimmt	sie (Sie) nehmen	er, sie, es darf	sie (Sie) dürfen

Imperative: **nimm! nehmt! nehmen Sie!**

Exercise 81

Read aloud and translate the following sentences.

1. **Darf ich Sie fragen, wie alt Sie sind?**
2. **Darf ich Sie um Ihren Namen bitten?**
3. **Darf ich das Zimmer verlassen?**
4. **Darf ich Ihnen das Brot reichen?**
5. **Darf ich Sie um Feuer[1] bitten?**
6. **Darf ich Ihnen meine Freundin vorstellen?[2]**
7. **Dürfen wir hereinkommen?[3]**

8. Um halb drei dürfen sie die Schule verlassen.
9. Die Kinder dürfen nicht auf der Straße spielen.
10. Es darf niemand[4] in dieses Zimmer eintreten.[5]
11. Darf ich Ihnen eine Zigarette anbieten?[6]
12. Keiner[7] darf hereinkommen.

NOTES: 1. das Feuer fire, a light for smoking. **2. vor-stellen** to introduce. **3. herein-kommen** to come in. **4. niemand** nobody. **5. ein-treten** to step into. **6. an-bieten** to offer. **7. keiner = niemand.**

1. REFLEXIVE VERBS. PRESENT TENSE OF *sich setzen* to seat oneself, to sit down

ich setze **mich** I seat *myself*

du setzt **dich** you seat *yourself*

er setzt **sich** he seats *himself*

sie setzt **sich** she seats *herself*

es setzt **sich** it seats *itself*

wir setzen **uns** we seat *ourselves*

ihr setzt **euch** you seat *yourselves*

sie setzen **sich** they seat *themselves*

Sie setzen **sich** you seat *yourself*

you seat *yourselves*

Imperative: Setze **dich**, Hans! Setzt **euch**, Kinder! Setzen **Sie sich**, meine Herren!

The reflexive pronouns in the first and second person are like the accusative of the personal pronouns (**mich, dich, uns, euch**).

For the third person and the polite form, the reflexive pronoun is **sich** in both the singular and plural. Thus **sich** may mean *oneself, himself, herself, itself, themselves, yourself* (*pol.*), *yourselves* (*pol.*). The polite **sich** is not capitalized.

2. SOME COMMON REFLEXIVE VERBS

Note that German reflexive verbs are not always translated by English reflexive verbs.

sich waschen	to wash oneself	ich wasche mich	du wäschst dich
sich rasiéren	to shave oneself	ich rasiere mich	er rasiert sich
sich anziehen	to dress oneself	ich ziehe mich an	sie zieht sich an
sich freuen	to be glad (happy)	ich freue mich	wir freuen uns
sich unterhálten	to converse	ich unterhalte mich	sie unterhalten sich
sich amüsiéren	to amuse (enjoy) oneself, to have a good time	ich amüsiere mich	Sie amüsieren sich

Exercise 83

Read the following questions and answer them accordingly.

1. **Um wie viel Uhr stehst du auf?**
2. **Ziehst du dich schnell an?**
3. **Sind Sie müde am Ende des Tages?**
4. **Amüsieren sich die Kinder im Park?**
5. **Worüber unterhalten Sie sich beim Frühstück?**
6. **Um wie viel Uhr setzen Sie sich zum Frühstück?**
7. **Rasieren Sie sich jeden Morgen?**

Exercise 84

Complete each German sentence with the correct reflexive pronoun.

Beispiel: 1. Ziehe dich an, Karl! Zieht euch an, Kinder!

1. Get dressed, Charles. Get dressed, children.

2. How will you enjoy yourselves this evening?

3. I don't feel well today.
4. The boy is already shaving himself.
5. They are conversing about the weather.

6. We must dress quickly.
7. At ten o'clock we sit down at the table.

8. Why don't you sit down?
9. William, wash and dress yourself.

10. Please sit down in the dining room.

11. We are glad when papa arrives.

1. Ziehe _____ an, Karl! Zieht _____ an, Kinder!
2. Wie amüsieren Sie _____ heute abend?
3. Ich fühle _____ heute nicht wohl.
4. Der Junge rasiert _____ schon.
5. Sie unterhalten _____ über das Wetter.
6. Wir müssen _____ schnell anziehen.
7. Um zehn Uhr setzen wir _____ an den Tisch.
8. Warum setzen Sie _____ nicht?
9. Wilhelm, wasch _____ und zieh _____ an!
10. Bitte, setzen Sie _____ in das Esszimmer!
11. Wir freuen _____ , wenn Papa ankommt.

4. REFLEXIVE PRONOUNS IN THE DATIVE

The reflexive pronoun stands in the accusative (**mich, dich, sich, uns, euch, sich**), if it is the only object in the sentence. (e.g., **Ich ziehe mich an.**) Some reflexive verbs, however, can also have two (or more) objects. In that case the second object stands in the accusative while the reflexive pronoun has to be in the dative:

Ich ziehe <u>mir</u> das Hemd an.
Du ziehst <u>dir</u> das Hemd an.

Luckily only the first and second persons in the singular differ from the reflexive pronouns in the accusative.

Exercise 85

Fill in the correct reflexive pronoun.

1. Ich wasche _____ die Haare.
2. Ihr zieht _____ eine Jacke an.
3. Sie amüsieren _____ auf der Party.
4. Ich muss _____ jetzt verabschieden.
5. Darf ich _____ mit Ihnen unterhalten?
6. Herr Müller setzt _____ auf den Sessel.
7. Wasch _____ bitte die Hände!
8. Zieh _____ bitte um.

5. SEPARABLE VERBS IN SUBORDINATE CLAUSES

In subordinate clauses separable verbs, like simple verbs, must stand last. However, note that the prefix does *not* separate from the verb in subordinate word order.

Normal word order. **Der Zug fährt um 7.45 ab. Herr Clark geht morgens weg.**

Subordinate word order: **Ich weiß, dass der Zug um 7.45 abfährt. Herr Clark küsst die Kinder, bevor er morgens weggeht.**

Exercise 86

Read aloud and translate.

1. **Herr Clark steht jeden Werktag früh auf.**
2. **Er wäscht sich und rasiert sich sehr schnell.**
3. **Er zieht sich schnell an.**

4. Herr Clark und seine Frau frühstücken zusammen.
5. Er fährt zur U-Bahnstation mit dem Auto.
6. Der Zug kommt bald[1] an.
7. Herr Clark steigt mit vielen anderen Leuten in den Zug ein.
8. Der Zug fährt in einigen Minuten ab.
9. Der Zug kommt in einer halben[2] Stunde in New York an.
10. Alle Passagiere steigen aus.
11. Herr Clark geht zu Fuß in sein Büro.
12. Er arbeitet tüchtig[3] den ganzen Tag.[4]

NOTES: 1. bald (*bălt*) soon. **2. halb** (*hălp*) half. **3. tüchtig** (*tǔch-tǐch*) diligently. **4.** Duration of time and definite time are expressed by the accusative: **den ganzen Tag** all day, **jeden Tag** every day.

Exercise 87

Make a subordinate clause out of each sentence in Exercise 86 by beginning with **Wir wissen, dass . . .**

Beispiel: Wir wissen, (1) dass Herr Clark jeden Werktag früh aufsteht; (2) dass er sich sehr schnell wäscht und rasiert; usw.

Exercise 88

Fragen

Reread the text: **Der Arbeitstag des Herrn Clark.** Then answer these questions.

1. Um wie viel Uhr muss Herr Clark aufstehen, wenn er in sein Büro geht?
2. Wie viel Zeit braucht er, um sich zu waschen, zu rasieren und anzuziehen?
3. Um wie viel Uhr setzt er sich zum Frühstück?
4. Frühstückt er allein oder mit seiner Frau?
5. Unterhalten sie sich während des Frühstücks über die Kinder?
6. Was hat Herr Clark gewöhnlich zum Frühstück?
7. Fährt er zu der U-Bahnstation mit dem Auto oder geht er zu Fuß?
8. Was liest er, sobald[1] er im Büro ankommt?

9. Mit wem telefoniert er?
10. Wie viel Zeit braucht er zum Mittagessen?
11. Um wie viel Uhr verlässt er sein Büro?
12. Um wie viel Uhr kommt er nach Hause?
13. Ist er müde am Ende des Tages?
14. Freut er sich, zu Hause zu sein?

NOTE: 1. **sobald** (*subordinate conjunction*) as soon as. Note the subordinate word order.

DIE KLEINE ANNA WAR KRANK

1. Es war im Monat Februar. Es schneite, und das Wetter war sehr kalt, als Herr Müller zur Wohnung des Herrn Clark kam und klingelte. Karl, der ältere Sohn des Geschäftsmanns, kam zur Tür und öffnete sie.

2. Er sagte: „Guten Abend, Herr Müller, Kommen Sie herein! Geben Sie mir bitte Ihren Hut und Ihren Mantel! Papa wartet auf Sie im Arbeitszimmer."

3. Herr Müller erwiderte: „Danke schön"; gab ihm Hut und Mantel und ging ins Arbeitszimmer, wo Herr Clark ihn erwartete.

4. Sie begannen sofort zu plaudern.

5. Wie geht es Ihnen heute, Herr Müller?

6. Sehr gut, danke. Und Ihnen? Und was macht Ihre Familie?

7. Mir geht's gut, danke. Aber unsere kleine Anna ist krank.

8. Das tut mir sehr leid. Was fehlt ihr?

9. Sie hat Halsschmerzen und Fieber. Der Doktor sagt, Anna hat die Grippe. Sie soll so viel wie möglich ruhen und viel Fruchtsaft trinken. Er verschrieb ihr auch eine Medizin. Heute abend geht es ihr ein wenig besser. Sie schläft jetzt ruhig.

10. Es freut mich, das zu hören. Sagen Sie mir, bitte, geht Anna zur Schule?

11. Sie geht in den Kindergarten, denn sie ist noch zu jung für die Schule. Sie ist erst fünf Jahre alt.

12. Die Herren redeten noch eine Weile über Herrn Clarks Familie, über die Schulen in der Vorstadt und über andere Dinge.

13. Endlich sagte Herr Müller: „Es ist Zeit, dass ich gehe. Hoffentlich fühlt sich die kleine Anna bald besser und munter."

---

1. It was in the month of February. It was snowing and the weather was very cold when Mr. Müller came to the home of Mr. Clark and rang the doorbell. Charles, the older son of the businessman, came to the door and opened it.

2. He said: "Good evening, Mr. Müller. Come in! Please give me your hat and coat. Papa is waiting for you in the study."

3. Mr. Müller answered: "Thank you kindly," gave him his hat and coat and went into the study, where Mr. Clark was waiting for him.

4. They began to chat immediately.

5. How are you today, Mr. Müller?

6. Very well, thank you. And you? And how is your family?

7. I'm fine, thank you. But our little Anne is sick.

8. I'm very sorry. What is wrong with her?

9. She has a sore throat and fever. The doctor says Anne has the flu. She is to rest as much as possible and drink a lot of fruit juice. He also prescribed a medicine for her. This evening she feels a little better. She is now sleeping quietly.

10. I am glad to hear that. Tell me, please, does Anne go to school?

11. She goes to kindergarten, because she is still too young for school. She is only five years old.

12. The men talked a while longer about Mr. Clark's family, about the schools in the suburbs and other things.

13. Finally Mr. Müller said: "It is time for me to go. I hope little Anne will soon feel well and lively."

14. Herr Clark dankte ihm, ging mit ihm zur Tür und half ihm mit dem Mantel.

14. Mr. Clark thanked him, went with him to the door, and helped him with his coat.

15. Sie gaben sich die Hand und sagten: „Auf Wiedersehen!"

15. They shook hands and said "Good-bye."

Wortschatz

der Mantel *pl.* ¨- coat
die Medizín *pl.* -en medicine
eine Weile a while
danken + *dat. object* to thank
erwarten to await, expect
helfen + *dat. object* to help
warten auf + *acc.* to wait for
heréin-kommen to come in
klingeln to ring a bell
ruhen to rest
verschreiben (*past* verschrieb) to prescribe

alt old; älter older
krank sick; die Krankheit *pl.* -en sickness
gesúnd well; die Gesúndheit health
ruhig still, quiet, quietly
munter cheerful, lively; traurig sad
hoffentlich I hope
als when (*subordinate conj., used with past tense*).
Als er ins Haus hereinkam, grüßte ihn Karl.
When he came into the house, Charles greeted him.

Sprichwort

Es geht nichts über die Gesundheit.

Nothing is better than health.

Wichtige Redemittel

Was fehlt ihm? —Er hat Zahnweh (Kopfweh). What is the matter with him? —He has a toothache (a headache).

Was fehlt ihr? —Sie hat die Grippe. What is the matter with her? —She has the flu.

Was fehlt Ihnen? —Ich habe einen Schnupfen. What is the matter with you? —I have a cold.

Das tut mir leid. I am sorry.

Das tut uns leid. We are sorry.

Er war krank. Jetzt geht es ihm besser. He was sick. Now he is feeling better.

Ich war krank. Jetzt geht es mir besser. I was sick. Now I am feeling better.

Wir rufen den Arzt. We call the doctor.

Er verschrieb eine Medizin. He prescribed a medicine.

Grammar Notes and Practical Exercises

1. PRESENT TENSE OF *schlafen* to sleep, *sollen* shall, to be supposed to, to be said to

ich schlafe	wir schlafen	ich soll	wir sollen
du schläfst	ihr schlaft	du sollst	ihr sollt
er, sie, es schläft	sie (Sie) schlafen	er, sie, es soll	sie (Sie) sollen

Imperative: schlafe! schlaft! schlafen Sie!

Note the irregular singular of sollen.

Exercise 89

Repeat each German sentence aloud several times.

1. **Anna soll viel Fruchtsaft trinken.**	1. Anne is to drink much fruit juice.
2. **Wir sollen auf den Arzt warten.**	2. We are to wait for the doctor.
3. **Sollen wir diese Aufgabe machen?**	3. Shall we do this assignment?
4. **Sie sollen sehr reich sein.**	4. They are said to be very rich.
5. **Sollen wir fahren oder zu Fuß gehen?**	5. Shall we ride or go on foot?
6. **Was soll ich damit machen?**	6. What shall I do with it?
7. **Du darfst gehen, aber um vier Uhr sollst du zurück sein.**	7. You may go, but you must be back at four o'clock.
8. **„Du sollst nicht stehlen!"**[1]	8. "Thou shalt not steal!"

NOTE: 1. **sollen** may be used in place of the imperative, as in the Ten Commandments.

2. REGULAR AND IRREGULAR VERBS IN ENGLISH

Regular verbs form their past tense by adding **-ed** to the verb stem. Irregular verbs form their past tense by changing the stem vowel. Thus:

	Regular				*Irregular*		
Infinitive	to learn	to work	to talk	*Infinitive*	to come	to give	to see
Past	I learned	I worked	I talked	*Past*	I came	I gave	I saw

In German there are likewise regular verbs, called **weak verbs,** and irregular verbs, called **strong verbs.**

3. THE PAST TENSE OF WEAK (REGULAR) VERBS IN GERMAN

lernen to learn		**antworten** to answer	
I learned, you learned, etc.		I answered, you answered, etc.	
ich lernte	**wir lernten**	**Ich antwortete**	**wir antworteten**
du lerntest	**ihr lerntet**	**du antwortetest**	**ihr antwortetet**
er, sie, es lernte	**sie (Sie) lernten**	**er, sie, es antwortete**	**sie (Sie) antworteten**

A weak verb forms its past tense (in German called **Präteritum** and sometimes also **Imperfekt**) by adding **-te** or **-ete** to the infinitive stem, without any vowel change in the stem. The ending **-ete** is necessary for reasons of pronunciation when the stem ends in **-d, -t** or **-fn.** Thus:

antworten   antwortete   reden   redete   öffnen   öffnete

The personal endings of the past tense of weak verbs are like those of the present, except that the third-person singular, like the first person, ends in **-e.**

The past tense may be translated in three ways. Thus: **ich lernte:** I learned, I was learning, I did learn; you learned, etc.

4. SOME FAMILIAR WEAK VERBS, PRESENT AND PAST

Infinitive	Present	Past	Infinitive	Present	Past
sagen	ich sage	ich sagte	arbeiten	ich arbeite	ich arbeitete
fragen	ich frage	ich fragte	reden	ich rede	ich redete
machen	ich mache	ich machte	öffnen	ich öffne	ich öffnete
danken	ich danke	ich dankte	kaufen	ich kaufe	ich kaufte
wohnen	ich wohne	ich wohnte	sich setzen	ich setze mich	ich setzte mich
warten	ich warte	ich wartete	haben	ich habe	ich hatte[1]

NOTE: 1. The past tense of **haben** drops **-b** from the stem and doubles the **-t.** Thus: **ich hatte, du hattest; er hatte, wir hatten; ihr hattet, sie hatten.**

Exercise 90

Change these sentences to the past tense.

Beispiel: 1. Der ältere Sohn des Geschäftsmanns öffnete die Tür.

1. Der ältere Sohn des Geschäftsmanns öffnet die Tür.
2. Was sagt der Junge?
3. Was antwortet Herr Müller?
4. Sein Vater wartet auf Herrn Müller im Arbeitszimmer.
5. Sie reden über das Wetter.
6. Ich mache große Fortschritte.
7. Ich lerne Deutsch.
8. Wir setzen uns um acht Uhr an den Tisch im Esszimmer.
9. Sie kauft ein Paar Handschuhe.
10. Wohnst du in der Vorstadt?
11. Ich wohne in der Stadt.
12. Habt ihr einen guten Lehrer?
13. Wir haben eine gute Lehrerin.
14. Was fragt der Tourist?
15. Diese Leute arbeiten in der Fabrik.

5. THE PAST TENSE OF STRONG (IRREGULAR) VERBS

kommen to come		**gehen** to go	
I came, was coming, did come, etc.		I went, was going, did go, etc.	
ich kam	wir kamen	ich ging	wir gingen
du kamst	ihr kamt	du gingst	ihr gingt
er, sie, es kam	sie (Sie) kamen	er, sie, es ging	sie (Sie) gingen

A strong verb forms its past tense by changing the stem vowel, sometimes along with consonant changes. You must learn **kommen—kam, gehen—ging, stehen—stand,** just as little schoolchildren must learn *come—came, go—went, stand—stood,* etc.

The personal endings of the past tense of a strong verb are like those of the present, except that the first- and third-persons singular have no endings.

6. SOME FAMILIAR STRONG VERBS, PRESENT AND PAST

Infinitive	*Present*	*Past*	*Infinitive*	*Present*	*Past*
schreiben	er schreibt	er schrieb	sprechen	er spricht[1]	er sprach
beginnen	er beginnt	er begann	geben	er gibt	er gab
stehen	er steht	er stand	nehmen	er nimmt	er nahm
sitzen	er sitzt	er saß	fahren	er fährt[1]	er fuhr
sehen	er sieht[1]	er sah	tragen	er trägt	er trug
lesen	er liest	er las	laufen	er läuft	er lief
helfen	er hilft[1]	er half	sein	er ist	er war[2]

NOTES: 1. Only strong verbs have the vowel changes **e > ie, e > i** and **a > ä** in the present tense, second- and third-person singular. **2.** The complete past of **sein** to be: **ich war, du warst, er war; wir waren, ihr wart, sie waren.**

7. EXPRESSIONS REFERRING TO PAST TIME

gestern yesterday

gestern Abend last night

gestern früh yesterday morning

vorgestern the day before yesterday

vor einer Woche a week ago

vor einem Monat a month ago

vor zwei Jahren two years ago

vor + *the dative* of a noun of time = ago

Exercise 91

Change these sentences to the past tense.

Beispiel: 1. Ich stand um sieben Uhr auf.

1. Ich stehe um sieben Uhr auf.
2. Die Kinder stehen manchmal früh auf.
3. Wann essen Sie das Mittagessen?
4. Wir fahren in die Stadt mit dem Auto.
5. Es gibt jeden Tag drei Vorstellungen.
6. Um wie viel Uhr kommt der Zug in Bonn an?
7. Um wie viel Uhr fährt der Zug von Hamburg ab?
8. Er trägt den Koffer in den Wartesaal.
9. Viele Leute stehen auf dem Bahnsteig.
10. Die Herren sitzen den ganzen Tag im Arbeitszimmer.
11. In der Deutschstunde sprechen wir immer Deutsch.
12. Schreibst du einen Brief an Frau Braun?

Exercise 92

Read Germany's most famous fairy tale and add the missing words (strong and weak verbs) in the **Präteritum**.

ROTKÄPPCHEN

> sein—wohnen—sagen—gehen—kommen—sehen—laufen—fressen—legen—kommen—
> denken—fragen—antworten—springen—schlucken—legen—schlafen—vorbeikommen—
> hören—treten—sehen—schneiden—springen—geben—nähen—fallen—müssen

Es _____ einmal ein junges Mädchen, das bei seiner Mutter _____ . Eines Tages _____ die Mutter: "Geh zur Großmutter und bring ihr einen Kuchen und eine Flasche Wein, denn sie ist krank." Das Mädchen _____ sogleich los. Als es zu einem dunklen Wald _____ , _____ es der Wolf. Der Wolf _____ zum Haus der Groß-mutter, _____ diese mit einem Bissen[1] auf und _____ sich ins Bett der Großmut-ter. Als das Mädchen zum Haus ihrer Großmutter _____ , _____ sie, ihre Großmutter ist im Bett.Sie _____ : "Großmutter, warum hast du so große Augen? Groß-mutter, warum hast du einen so großen Mund?" Der Wolf _____ : "Damit ich dich besser fressen kann!" Er _____ aus dem Bett und _____ das Mädchen mit einem Bissen herunter. Dann _____ er sich in das Bett und _____ ein. Ein Jäger, der an dem Häuschen _____ ,_____ das Schnarchen[2] des Wolfes und _____ in das Haus ein. Dort _____ er den Wolf. Er _____ ihm den Bauch auf und das Mädchen und seine Großmutter _____ unverletzt aus dem Wolfsbauch heraus. Dann _____ sie Steine in den Bauch des Wolfes und _____ ihn wieder zu. Der Wolf wegen der schweren Steine in seinem Bauch in einen Brunnen und _____ ertrinken.

NOTES: 1. der Bissen bite. **2. das Schnarchen** snoring.

WAS FÜR EIN SCHRECKLICHES WETTER!

1. Es war im Monat März. Es regnete in Strömen, als Herr Müller das Haus des Herrn Clark erreichte. Er klingelte und Wilhelm, der jüngere Sohn, öffnete die Tür. Herr Müller trat ein.

2. Wilhelm sagte zu ihm: „Guten Abend, Herr Müller. Was für ein schreckliches Wetter! Kommen Sie herein, kommen Sie ins Haus. Sie sind durch und durch nass. Bitte geben Sie mir Ihren Regenmantel und Ihren Hut. Stellen Sie Ihren Regenschirm in den Schirmständer."

3. Herr Müller gab ihm seinen Hut und seinen Regenmantel und antwortete: „Danke schön. Es regnet sehr stark, aber kalt ist es nicht. Ich erkälte mich sicher nicht. Ist dein Papa zu Hause?"

4. „Ja. Er wartet auf Sie im Wohnzimmer. Da ist er schon!"

5. „Guten Abend, Herr Müller. Es freut mich, Sie zu sehen, aber es ist nicht gut, bei solch schrecklichem Wetter auszugehen. Kommen Sie doch ins Esszimmer und trinken Sie eine Tasse Tee mit Rum, um sich ein wenig zu wärmen."

6. „Danke, danke vielmals, Herr Clark. Eigentlich ist mir wirklich etwas kalt. Trinken wir eine Tasse Tee! Und während wir den Tee trinken, können wir über das Wetter sprechen. Das ist ein wichtiges Thema und ist besonders passend für diesen Abend."

1. It was the month of March. It was absolutely pouring when Mr. Müller reached Mr. Clark's house. He rang the doorbell, and William, the younger son, opened the door. Mr. Müller entered.

2. William said to him: "Good evening, Mr. Müller. What terrible weather! Come in, come into the house. You are wet through and through. Please give me your raincoat and your hat. Put your umbrella into the umbrella stand."

3. Mr. Müller gave him his hat and raincoat, and answered: "Thank you. It is raining very hard, but it is not cold. I'll surely not catch cold. Is your father at home?"

4. "Yes, indeed. He is waiting for you in the living room. Here he is now!"

5. "Good evening, Mr. Müller. I am glad to see you, but it is not good to go out in such terrible weather. Do come into the dining room and drink a cup of tea with rum in order to warm yourself a bit."

6. "Thanks, many thanks, Mr. Clark. I really feel somewhat cold. Let's drink a cup of tea. And while we drink the tea, we can speak about the weather. That is a very important topic, and it is especially fitting for this evening."

7. Die Herren gingen ins Esszimmer und begannen, lebhaft zu sprechen. Sie setzten sich, und Frau Clark brachte ihnen auf einem Serviertablett zwei Tassen mit Untertassen, eine Teekanne, eine Zuckerdose, einige Teelöffel und eine Torte. Sie stellte alles auf den Tisch. Sie nahm eine Flasche Rum aus dem Schrank und stellte sie neben die Teekanne. Dann verließ sie das Esszimmer.

8. „Bitte, Herr Müller, ich schenke Ihnen ein,"sagte Herr Clark. Er goss den Tee in die Tassen ein und dazu für jeden eine kräftige Portion Rum.

9. Während sie den Tee mit Rum tranken, sprachen sie lebhaft weiter.

10. Draußen regnete es noch immer weiter.

7. The men went into the dining room and began to talk in a lively way. They sat down and Mrs. Clark brought them a tray, two cups and saucers, a teapot, a sugar bowl, some teaspoons, and a cake. She put everything on the table. She took down a bottle of rum from the buffet and put it next to the teapot. Then she left the dining room.

8. "Please, Mr. Müller, let me serve you," said Mr. Clark. He poured the tea into the cups and along with it a goodly portion of rum for each.

9. While they were drinking the tea with rum, they continued to speak in a lively manner.

10. Outside it continued to rain.

Wortschatz

die Flasche *pl.* -n the bottle
der Regenmantel *pl.* ¨- the raincoat
der Regenschirm *pl.* -e the (rain) umbrella
der Schirmständer *pl.* - the umbrella stand
die Torte *pl.* -n the cake, the tart
das Serviertablett *pl.* -s the tray
aus-gehen to go out
ein-schenken to serve
sich erkälten to catch cold
stellen to put
sich wärmen to warm oneself

bringen (*past* brachte) to bring
jung young; jünger younger
kräftig strong, goodly; schwach weak
lebhaft lively
nass wet; trocken dry
stark strong; es regnet stark it is raining heavily
passend suitable, fitting
schrecklich terrible
dazu in addition, along with it
während (*sub. conj.*) while

Das Tischgeschirr Tableware

das Messer *pl.* - the knife
die Gabel *pl.* -n the fork; der Löffel *pl.* - the spoon
der Teelöffel *pl.* - the teaspoon
der Esslöffel *pl.* - the tablespoon
die Tasse *pl.* -n the cup

die Untertasse *pl.* -n the saucer
die Zuckerdose *pl.* -n the sugar bowl
die Teekanne *pl.* -n the teapot
der Krug *pl.* ¨-e the pitcher
der Teller *pl.*- the dish, the plate

Das Wetter

Wie ist das Wetter? How is the weather?

Es ist schön; warm; kalt; kühl; windig; stürmisch, neblig, bewölkt. The weather is nice; warm; cold; cool; windy; stormy, foggy, cloudy.

Die Sonne scheint. The sun is shining.

Es regnet heute. Es regnete gestern. It is raining today. It rained yesterday.

Es schneit. Es schneite gestern. It is snowing. It snowed yesterday.

Es regnet in Strömen. Es gießt. It is raining in streams. It is pouring.

Es regnete immer weiter. It continued to rain.

Ist dir (Ihnen) kalt? Mir ist kalt. Are you cold? I am cold.

Ist ihm warm? Ihm ist warm. Is he warm? He is warm.

Ist ihr kalt? Ihr ist nicht kalt. Is she cold? She is not cold.

Note carefully! In German we do not say: I am cold (warm); You are cold (warm), etc.; but *literally:* To me (to you, to him, to her, etc.) it is cold (warm).

Grammar Notes and Practical Exercises

1. SOME FAMILIAR SEPARABLE VERBS, INFINITIVE, PRESENT AND PAST

Infinitive		*Present (er)*	*Past (er)*
auf-stehen	to get up, stand up	er steht . . . auf	er stand . . . auf
an-kommen	to arrive	er kommt . . . an	er kam . . . an
ab-fahren	to ride off, leave	er fährt . . . ab	er fuhr . . . ab
an-fangen	to begin	er fängt . . . an	er fing . . . an
ein-treten	to step in, enter	er tritt . . . ein	er trat . . . ein
ein-steigen	to get on (train)	er steigt . . . ein	er stieg . . . ein
aus-steigen	to get off (train)	er steigt . . . aus	er stieg . . . aus
sich an-ziehen	to dress oneself	er zieht sich . . . an	er zog sich . . . an
weiter-sprechen	to go on speaking	er spricht . . . weiter	er sprach . . . weiter
zurück-gehen	to go back	er geht . . . zurück	er ging . . . zurück
zurück-geben	to give back	er gibt . . . zurück	er gab . . . zurück
ein-gießen	to pour in	er gießt . . . ein	er goss . . . ein
herab-nehmen	to take down	er nimmt . . . herab	er nahm . . . herab

a. *The separable prefix of a verb stands at the end of a simple sentence or main clause in the present and past tenses.*

Ich ziehe mich schnell an. I dress (myself) quickly. **Ich zog mich schnell an.** I dressed (myself) quickly.

b. *In subordinate clauses, the separable verb stands last in the present and past tenses, but the prefix does not separate from the verb.*

Wir steigen aus, sobald der Zug **ankommt.**   We get off as soon as the train arrives.

Wir stiegen aus, sobald der Zug **ankam.**   We got off as soon as the train arrived.

Exercise 93

Complete the sentences from Column I with the appropriate words from Column II.

I	II
1. Herr Clark stand gestern	a. seine schöne Jacke an.
2. Dann zog er sich	b. um 9 Uhr in München an.
3. Herr Müller läutete an der Tür	c. müssen wir aussteigen.
4. Er trat schnell	d. erst um 8.30 auf.
5. Herr Clark schenkte seinem Gast	e. Tee mit Rum ein.
6. Der Zug kommt	f. als der Regen anfing.
7. Von Frankfurt fährt er	g. um 13.15 ab.
8. Wenn der Zug stehenbleibt	h. in das Arbeitszimmer ein.

2. *hin-* **and** *her-*

hin- and **her-** are often attached to separable prefixes.

hin- shows that the action is *away* from the observer or *away* from some given point.

her- shows that the action is *toward* the observer or *toward* some given point. Thus:

Someone outside the house says:
    Der Doktor geht ins Haus hinein. (away from the observer)
    Der Doktor kommt aus dem Haus heraus. (toward the observer)

Someone inside the house says:
    Kommen Sie herein! Come in! (toward the speaker)
    Gehen Sie hinaus! Go out! (away from the speaker)

Exercise 94

Change these sentences from the present to the past tense.

Beispiel: 1. Sei sprachen lebhaft weiter.

1. **Sie sprechen lebhaft weiter.**
2. **Stehen Sie früh auf?**
3. **Um wie viel Uhr kommt der Zug von Bonn an?**
4. **Um wie viel Uhr fährt der Zug nach Frankfurt ab?**

5. Die dritte Vorstellung fängt um neun Uhr an.
6. Viele Passagiere steigen aus.
7. Andere Passagiere steigen ein.
8. Wir ziehen uns die neuen Anzüge an.
9. Ich gebe Ihnen zehn Euro zurück.
10. Ich nehme die Flasche vom Schrank herab.
11. Er tritt eben ein.
12. Wir gehen ins Museum hinein.

3. MORE SUBORDINATING CONJUNCTIONS

bevor, ehe before; **während** while; **sobald** as soon as; **ob** whether, **weil** because; **bis** until

Practice these German sentences aloud.

Herr Clark küsste die Kinder, bevor er wegging.	Mr. Clark kissed the children before he left.
Während wir den Tee trinken, können wir über das Wetter sprechen.	While we are drinking tea, we can talk about the weather.
Er liest die Post, sobald er im Büro ankommt.	He reads the mail as soon as he arrives at the office.
Weißt du, ob er meinen Füller hat?	Do you know whether he has my fountain pen?
Er lernt Deutsch, weil er Deutschland besuchen will.	He is learning German, because he wants to visit Germany.
Alle warteten, bis er nach Hause kam.	All waited until he came home.

Exercise 95

Combine each pair of sentences using the conjunction in parentheses. Warning: In subordinate clauses the verb stands last!

Beispiel: 1. **Sie kauften die Eintrittskarten, während wir draußen warteten.**

1. **Sie kauften die Eintrittskarten. (während) Wir warteten draußen.**
2. **Die Familie setzte sich zum Abendessen. (sobald) Herr Clark kam nach Hause.**
3. **Am Abend ist er sehr müde. (weil) Er arbeitet fleißig den ganzen Tag.**
4. **Wissen Sie? (ob) Der Zug kommt pünktlich an.**
5. **Ein Freund trat ins Zimmer. (als) Herr Clark diktierte seiner Sekretärin Briefe.**
6. **(Als) Herr Müller erreichte Herrn Clarks Wohnung. Es regnete[1] in Strömen.**
7. **Wir können dieses Auto nicht kaufen. (weil) Es kostet zu viel.**
8. **Alle Passagiere steigen aus. (wenn) Der Zug kommt in Hamburg an.**
9. **(Wenn) Papa kommt nach Hause. Die Kinder freuen sich.[1]**
10. **(Während) du spielst. Ich muss[1] arbeiten.**

NOTE: 1. Remember: when the subordinate clause comes first, the main clause must have inverted word order.

4. **wann, als, wenn**

wann (when) is used in direct and indirect questions.

Wann kommt er? Weißt du wann er kommt? When is he coming? Do you know when he is coming?

Als (when) is used with verbs in any past tense.

Als er das Haus erreichte, regnete es. When he reached the house, it was raining.

Wenn (when) is used with verbs in the present or future.

Wenn Sie kommen, dann gehe ich. When you come, then I'll go.

wenn (whenever, if) is used with any tense of the verb.

Wenn ich ihn sah, war er immer müde. Whenever I saw him, he was always tired.

Wenn man Geld hat, kann man reisen. If one has money, one can travel.

Exercise 96

Sprechen Sie über das Wetter!

. . . die Sonne scheint.

. . . es in Strömen regnet.

. . . es neblig ist.

Ich mag es, <u>wenn</u> . . .   . . . es heiß ist.

Ich mag es nicht, <u>wenn</u> . . .   . . . es schneit.

. . . mir kalt ist.

. . . es stürmisch ist.

. . . mir warm ist.

Exercise 97

Fragen

Reread the text: **Was für ein schreckliches Wetter!** Then answer these questions.

1. **Was ist der Titel dieses Kapitels?**
2. **Wie war das Wetter, als Herr Müller die Wohnung des Geschäftsmanns erreichte?**
3. **Wer öffnete ihm die Tür?**
4. **Was gab der Lehrer dem Jungen?**
5. **Wer erschien,[1] als Wilhelm mit dem Lehrer sprach?**

6. Was sollte² Herr Müller trinken, um sich zu wärmen?
7. Welches Thema war besonders passend für diesen Abend?
8. In welches Zimmer gingen die zwei Herren?
9. Wer brachte Ihnen zwei Tassen mit Untertassen, eine Teekanne, usw.?
10. Was nahm sie vom Schrank herunter?
11. Wohin stellte sie die Flasche Rum?
12. Blieb³ Frau Clark im Esszimmer?
13. Worüber sprachen die Herren, als sie den Tee mit Rum tranken?

NOTES: **1. erscheinen** to appear (*past* **erschien**). **2.** should, ought. **3. bleiben** to remain (*past* **blieb**).

DER APRIL MACHT WAS ER WILL

1. Die beiden Herren saßen immer noch im Esszimmer. Sie redeten weiter, während sie Tee mit Rum tranken. Draußen regnete es noch. Herr Müller fühlte sich wohl. Es war ihm nicht mehr kalt.

2. Er sagte zu seinem Schüler: „Hier in New York geht das Klima von einem Extrém zum anderen."

3. „Das stimmt, Herr Müller. Im Sommer ist es heiß. Manchmal sehr heiß. Im Winter ist es kalt. Es wird manchmal sogar sehr kalt. Von Zeit zu Zeit bekommen wir auch Schnee."

4. „Aber der Frühling ist schön, nicht wahr, Herr Clark?"

5. „Gewiss. Im Frühling wird das Wetter recht schön. Der Monat März ist zwar oft stürmisch, so wie heute Abend, aber im April fällt ein warmer Regen. Im Mai werden die Wiesen und Felder grün. Im Juni ist der Himmel blau, und die Sonne scheint hell und klar. Wie der amerikanische Dichter Lowell schrieb:

   Und was ist so schön wie ein Tag im Juni?"

6. „Auch in Deutschland gibt es ein Sprichwort über das Wetter. Man sagt: Der April macht was er will."

7. „Was soll das bedeuten?"

8. „Das bedeutet, dass sich das Wetter im April sehr schnell verändern kann. Erst scheint die Sonne, dann fängt es plötzlich zu regnen an, dann kommt ein starker Wind, es schneit vielleicht kurz und dann kommt wieder die Sonne hinter den Wolken hervor."

9. „Das muss ich mir merken. Aber der Winter ist kalt in Deutschland, nicht wahr?"

1. The two gentlemen were still seated in the dining room. They continued to speak while they were drinking tea and rum. Outside it was still raining. Mr. Müller was feeling fine. He did not feel cold anymore.

2. He said to his pupil: "Here in New York the climate goes from one extreme to another."

3. That's right, Mr. Müller. In summer it is hot. Sometimes it is very hot. In winter it is cold. Sometimes it even becomes very cold. From time to time we also get snow.

4. But spring is beautiful, isn't it, Mr. Clark?

5. Certainly. In the spring the weather becomes really beautiful. The month of March is often stormy to be sure, just as this evening; but in April a warm rain falls. In May the meadows and fields become green. In June the sky is blue and the sun shines bright and clear. As the American poet Lowell wrote:

   And what is so rare as a day in June?

6. Also in Germany there is a proverb about the weather. People say: "April does whatever he wants."

7. What does it mean?

8. It means that the weather in April can change very quickly. First the sun is shining, then suddenly it begins to rain, then a strong wind comes, it might snow a bit and then the sun appears again behind the clouds.

9. I have to remember that. But the winter is cold in Germany, isn't it?

10. „Der Winter ist wohl kalt, besonders in den Bergen. In Österreich gibt es im Winter auch viel Schnee in den Bergen. Viele Touristen kommen deshalb zum Skifahren nach Österreich."

10. The winter is cold to be sure, especially in the mountains. In Austria in winter there is much snow on the mountains. Therefore many tourists come to Austria to go skiing.

11. „Und im Sommer? Wie ist es im Sommer in Deutschland?"

11. And in summer? What is it like in summer in Germany?

12. „Im Sommer ist es beinahe überall in Deutschland sehr angenehm warm. Aber am schönsten ist gewöhnlich der Frühling. Dann gehen viele Deutsche spazieren. Ein berühmtes Kinderlied geht so:

    Kuckuck! Kuckuck! ruft's¹ durch den Wald;

    Lasset² uns singen, tanzen und springen,

    Frühling, Frühling, wird³ es nun bald."

12. In summer it is very comfortable nearly everywhere in Germany. But spring is usually most beautiful. Then many Germans go for a walk. A famous children's song goes like this:

    Cuckoo! Cuckoo! resounds through the woods.

    Let us sing, dance and leap;

    Spring, spring is coming soon.

13. „Das ist ein schönes Lied, Herr Müller."

13. That is a beautiful song, Mr. Müller.

14. „Ja, und der Frühling ist eine schöne Jahreszeit, Herr Clark."

14. Yes, and spring is a beautiful season, Mr. Clark.

NOTES: 1. **ruft's** short for **ruft es.** 2. **lasset,** poetic form of **lasst.** 3. **es wird** = it is becoming.

Wortschatz

die **Kälte** cold; die **Hitze** heat
der **Schnee** snow; der **Regen** rain
die **Luft** air; der **Himmel** sky
das **Feld** *pl.* -er field
das **Sprichwort** *pl.* -̈er proverb, saying
der **Wald** *pl.* ["]-er forest
die **Wiese** *pl.* -n meadow
die **Wolke** *pl.* -n cloud
der **Unterschied** *pl.* -e difference
gefállen + *dat. object* (*past* **gefiel**) to please

singen (*past* **sang**) to sing
sich verändern to change
tanzen to dance
spaziéren gehen to take a walk
angenehm pleasant
beináhe = **fast** almost
berühmt famous
sogár even
am schönsten most beautiful
am besten best

Die Jahreszeiten The Seasons

der **Frühling**	der **Sommer**	der **Herbst**	der **Winter**
im **Frühling**	im **Sommer**	im **Herbst**	im **Winter**

Die Monate des Jahres

(der) Januar (*yă-nōō-ār*)   (der) Mai (*mai*)   (der) September (*zĕp-tĕm-ber*)
(der) Februar (*fay-brōō-ār*)   (der) Juni (*yōō-nee*)   (der) Oktober (*ŏk-toh-ber*)
(der) März (*mĕrtz*)   (der) Juli (*yōō-lee*)   (der) November (*noh-vĕm-ber*)
(der) April (*ă-preel*)   (der) August (*ow-gōōst*)   (der) Dezember (*day-tsĕm-ber*)

Wichtige Redemittel

You have learned that a verb plus **gern** means to like a thing or action; a verb plus **lieber** means to prefer a thing or action. Note now that a verb plus **am liebsten** means to like a thing or action best of all.

Ich habe den Herbst gern. Er hat den Sommer lieber. Sie hat den Frühling am liebsten. I like autumn. He prefers summer. She likes spring best of all.

Sie geht gern spazieren. Ich spiele lieber Tennis. Er spielt am liebsten Fußball. She likes to go walking. I prefer to play tennis. He likes best of all to play football.

spazíeren-gehen to go for a walk

Grammar Notes and Practical Exercises

1. PRESENT TENSE OF *werden* to become, to get; *mögen* to like, to care to, may

I become, you become, etc.   *I like, you like, etc.*

ich werde   wir werden   ich mag   wir mögen
du wirst   ihr werdet   du magst   ihr mögt
er, sie, es wird   sie (Sie) werden   er, sie, es mag   sie (Sie) mögen

Exercise 98

a. Make sentences using the correct form of werden.

Ich		hungrig
Du		müde
Er		ungeduldig[1]
Sie	werden	laut
Es		böse[2]
Wir		kalt
Ihr		dunkel
Sie		gesund

NOTES: 1. geduldig patient; **ungeduldig** impatient. **2. böse** angry.

b. *Make sentences using the correct form of* mögen *(to like).*

Ich		dich nicht.
Du		das warme Wetter.
Er		unseren Deutschlehrer.
Sie	mögen	den Regen nicht.
Wir		Eiscreme.
Ihr		den Monat Juni am liebsten.
Sie		nicht gern spielen.[1]

1. Note that **mögen** (to like) is equivalent to the expression of *verbs* + **gern(e)**. **Gern(e)** can also be used with **mögen**.

   Ich mag diesen Lehrer. = **Ich habe diesen Lehrer gern.** = I like this teacher.
   Ich mag nicht (gern) spielen. = **Ich spiele nicht gern.** = I don't like to play.

2. Note the meaning of **mögen** = *may* in the following sentences:
   Es mag sein, dass er kein Geld hat. It may be, that he doesn't have any money.
   Er mag sagen was er will, wir glauben ihm nicht. He may say what he wants, we don't believe him.

2. **INSEPARABLE VERBS. PRESENT TENSE OF** *bekommen* **to receive and** *erfahren* **to find out**

I receive, you receive, etc.		*I find out, you find out, etc.*	
ich bekomme	wir bekommen	ich erfahre	wir erfahren
du bekommst	ihr bekommt	du erfährst	ihr erfahrt
er, sie, es bekommt	sie (Sie) bekommen	er, sie, es erfährt	sie (Sie) erfahren

Simple verbs may add prefixes which *do not* separate from the verb as do the separable prefixes. Such prefixes are called *inseparable prefixes,* and the verbs to which they are attached are called *inseparable verbs.* The prefixes **be-, emp-, ent-, er-, ge-, miss-, ver-, zer-** are always inseparable. Here are examples of inseparable verbs, most of which you already know. The stress is always on the verb, never on the inseparable prefix.

Simple Verbs	*Inseparable Verbs*	*Simple Verbs*	*Inseparable Verbs*
suchen to seek	**besúchen** to visit	**warten** to wait	**erwárten** to await
kommen to come	**bekómmen** to receive	**zählen** to count	**erzählen** to tell, relate
sprechen to speak	**bespréchen** to discuss	**fallen** to fall	**gefállen** to please
tragen to carry	**betrágen** to amount to	**kaufen** to buy	**verkáufen** to sell
stehen to stand	**entstéhen** to arise	**schreiben** to write	**verschréiben** to prescribe
billigen to approve	**missbilligen** to disapprove		
		stehen to stand	**verstéhen** to understand
fahren to ride	**erfáhren** to find out		
lassen to leave (something), to let, to relinquish	**verlássen** to leave (to go away from)	**brechen** to break	**zerbréchen** to break to pieces

The meaning of the inseparable prefix is generally not obvious, as is the case with the separable prefixes. However, **zer-** clearly indicates "to pieces" and **miss-** has the same meaning as the English prefix *dis-*.

The past tense of inseparable verbs is formed in the same way as that of the simple verbs. Thus:

| *Infin.* | besuchen | bekommen | besprechen | betragen | entstehen | erfahren |
| *Past.* | besuchte | bekam | besprach | betrug | entstand | erfuhr |

| *Infin.* | erwarten | gefallen | verkaufen | verschreiben | verstehen | zerbrechen |
| *Past* | erwartete | gefiel | verkaufte | verschrieb | verstand | zerbrach |

Exercise 99

Change these sentences to the past tense.

Beispiel: 1. Ich besuchte Herrn Clark in seinem Büro.

1. **Ich besuche Herrn Clark in seinem Büro.**
2. **Er erwartet mich dort um elf Uhr.**
3. **Wir beginnen sofort Deutsch zu sprechen.**
4. **Er versteht mich, und ich verstehe ihn.**
5. **Wir besprechen wichtige Geschäftssachen.**
6. **Ich erfahre, dass er große Fortschritte im Deutschen macht.**
7. **Um zwölf Uhr gehen wir in ein Restaurant zum Mittagessen.**
8. **Die Rechnung für die zwei Mahlzeiten beträgt $11,50 (elf Dollar fünfzig Cent).**
9. **Während wir die Rechnung bezahlen,[1] entsteht ein großer Lärm auf der Straße.**
10. **Wir gehen auf die Straße hinaus, um zu sehen, was los ist.[2]**

NOTES: 1. bezahlen to pay (*past*, **bezahlte**). **2. Was ist los?** What's the matter?

Exercise 100

Which verbs are separable and which are not?

1. **Er _____ keinen Spaß _____ . (verstehen)**
2. **Sandra _____ ein Baby _____ . (bekommen)**
3. **Wir _____ um 7.30 _____ . (aufstehen)**
4. **Du _____ natürlich mit uns _____ . (mitfahren)**
5. **Der Lehrer _____ die Aufgabe _____ . (zerreißen)**
6. **Erich _____ im Supermarkt _____ . (einkaufen)**
7. **Ich _____ dir eine gute Suppe _____ . (empfehlen)**
8. **Peter _____ immer lustige Geschichten _____ . (erzählen)**

3. VERBS THAT TAKE A DATIVE OBJECT

Certain German verbs take a dative object.

antworten:	Er antwortete *mir* nicht.	He did not answer *me*.
danken:	Ich danke *Ihnen* für die Bücher.	I thank *you* for the books.
helfen:	Wir halfen *ihr* mit der Aufgabe.	We helped *her* with the assignment.
glauben:	Ich kann *ihm* nicht glauben.	I cannot believe *him*.
verzeihen:	Verzeihen Sie (*mir*).	Pardon (*me*).
gehören:	Dieses Buch gehört *dem Lehrer*.	This book belongs *to the teacher*.
fehlen:	Was fehlte *dem Kind*?	What was the matter with *the child*? (*Lit.* What was lacking *to the child*?)
gefallen:	Das gefällt *dir* nicht.	That doesn't please *you*.

The verb **gefallen** + *a dat.* to please, is another way of expressing "liking."

Das gefällt *uns* am besten. = That pleases *us* best. = *We* like that best.

Exercise 101

Complete these sentences by translating the English words.

1. **Warum antworteten Sie** (her) **nicht?**
2. **Was fehlt** (your *fam.* father)**?**
3. **Diese schöne Wohnung gehört** (him)**.**
4. **Helfen Sie** (them) **bitte mit ihren Aufgaben!**
5. (Pardon me)**, dass ich spät komme!**
6. **Ich danke** (you *pol.*) **vielmals.**
7. **Er sagt, dass es wahr ist, aber wir** (don't believe him)**.**
8. (To whom) **gehört dieses neue Auto?**
9. **Es gehört** (us)**.**
10. **Der neue Mantel gefällt** (my sister) **nicht.**
11. (We like) **unser neues Zimmer.** Translate: Our new room pleases us.
12. **Gefallen** (them) **diese Kleider?**

Exercise 102

Verbinden Sie die Satzteile zu sinnvollen Sätzen! (*Form meaningful sentences!*)

Guten Tag! Ich möchte	dir	nicht?
Das Kleid gefällt	ihm	sehr gut.
Agnes, ich helfe	ihr	für Ihr Kommen herzlich danken!
Warum antwortet ihr	Ihnen	doch immer gern.
Gerhard glaubt	mir	alles, was er sagt.

Exercise 103

Fragen

Reread the text: **Der April macht was er will.** Then answer these questions.

1. Was taten die Herren, während sie Tee mit Rum tranken?
2. Wie fühlte sich Herr Müller?
3. War es ihm noch kalt?
4. Wie ist der Winter in New York?
5. Bekommt man oft Schnee?
6. Wie wird das Wetter im Frühling?
7. Was für ein Regen fällt?
8. Wie ist der Winter in Deutschland und in Österreich?
9. Warum kommen viele Touristen im Winter nach Österreich?
10. Wie ist es im Sommer in Deutschland?
11. Welche Jahreszeit ist am schönsten in Deutschland?
12. Was tun die Deutschen am liebsten im Frühling?
13. Nennen Sie die vier Jahreszeiten!

1. Herr Clark saß in seinem Büro und war im Begriff, einen Brief zu schreiben, den er nach Deutschland schicken wollte.
2. Plötzlich klopfte es an seiner Tür, die wie immer geschlossen war. Als Herr Clark "Herein!" rief, traten Frau Clark und die vier Kinder in das Büro.
3. Die Kinder begrüßten ihren Vater, der sie sogleich in den Arm nahm.
4. Im Büro bewunderten die Kinder alle die Dinge, die sie zum ersten Mal sahen: den großen Schreibtisch, auf dem viele Briefe und Akten lagen; den Computer, der auf dem letzten Stand der Technik war, und das schöne Gemälde, das über dem Schreibtisch ihres Vaters hing.
5. Karl deutete auf eine Ansichtskarte, die auf dem Schreibtisch lag, und fragte: "Wo ist diese Karte her, Papa?"
6. "Diese Karte, die ich soeben bekam, ist aus Deutschland. Sie ist von Herrn Schiller, den ich im Sommer in Deutschland besuche."
7. Die kleine Anna, die erst fünf Jahre alt ist, blickte aus dem Fenster des Büros, das sich im einunddreißigsten Stock eines Wolkenkratzers befand. "Schau her, Mama, die Autos, die auf der Straße vorbeifahren, sind ganz klein!"
8. "Ja, Anna, und die Menschen, die unten gehen, sehen wie Ameisen aus."
9. Als der Besuch zu Ende war, gingen alle in ein Restaurant, das sich nicht weit von Herrn Clarks Büro befand. So endete der Tag, der mit einer Überraschung für Herrn Clark begonnen hatte, für alle sehr angenehm.

---

1. Mr. Clark was sitting in his office and was about to write a letter which he wanted to send to Germany.
2. Suddenly someone knocked at his door, which was closed as usual. When Mr. Clark called "Come in!" his wife and his four children stepped into the office.
3. The children greeted their father, who embraced them at once.
4. In the office the children admired all the things which they saw for the first time: the big desk, on which many letters and files were lying; the computer which was state-of-the-art, and the beautiful painting which was hanging on the wall over their father's desk.
5. Charles pointed at a picture postcard that was lying on the desk and asked: "Where does the card come from, dad?"
6. "This card, which I received just now, is from Germany. It is from Mr. Schiller, whom I visit in Germany this summer."
7. Little Anne, who is only five years old, looked out of the window of the office, which was on the thirty-first story of a skyscraper. "Look, Mom, the cars which ride past on the street, are very small!"
8. "Yes, Anne, and the people who walk down there look like ants."
9. When the visit was at an end, all went to a restaurant which was located not far from Mr. Clark's office. Thus the day which had begun with a pleasant surprise for Mr. Clark ended pleasantly for everyone.

Wortschatz

die Überráschung *pl.* -en surprise	klopfen to knock
der Wolkenkratzer *pl.* - skyscraper	bewúndern to admire
der Stock *pl.* ¨-e floor (story of building); stick	hängen to hang
der Besuch *pl.* -e visit	hináus-schauen, hinaus-blicken to look out
das Gemälde *pl.* - painting	geschlossen closed
die Akte *pl.* -n file	unten below, down there
die Ansichtskarte *pl.* -n picture postcard	angenehm pleasant
liegen (*past* lag) to lie	weit far
essen (*past* ass) to eat	
vorbéi-fahren (*past* fuhr . . . vorbei) to ride past	

Wichtige Redemittel

im Begriff sein to be about to
Ich war im Begriff, einen Brief zu schreiben. I was about to write a letter.
Ich habe Appetít. I have an appetite.
Ich habe Hunger (Ich bin hungrig). I am hungry.
Ich habe Durst (Ich bin durstig). I am thirsty.

Das macht mir Freude. That gives me pleasure.
sich befinden to be located Wo befindet sich das Büro? Where is the office located? Es befindet sich in einem Wolkenkratzer. It is (located) in a skyscraper.

Sprichwörter

Der Appetit kommt mit dem Essen.	Appetite comes with eating.
Der Mensch ist, was er isst.	Man is what he eats.

1. PRESENT AND PAST OF *essen* to eat

Present		Past	
ich esse	wir essen	ich aß	wir aßen
du isst	ihr esst	du aßest	ihr aßt
er, sie, es isst	sie (Sie) essen	er, sie, es aß	sie (Sie) aßen

Imperative: iss! esst! essen Sie!

2. THE RELATIVE PRONOUNS *der, welcher*

Der Mann, *der* dort steht, ist mein Bruder.	The man *who* stands there is my brother.
Die Frau, *die* dort steht, ist meine Schwester.	The woman *who* stands there is my sister.
Das Bild, *das* dort hängt, ist sehr alt.	The picture *which* hangs there is very old.
Der Mann, *den* Sie dort sehen, ist ein Arzt.	The man *whom* you see there is a doctor.
Die Frau, *die* Sie dort sehen, ist Lehrerin.	The woman *whom* you see there is a teacher.
Das Bild, *das* Sie dort sehen, ist teuer.	The picture *that* you see there is expensive.
Die Füllfeder, mit *der* ich schrieb, war nicht gut.	The pen with *which* I wrote was not good.
Das Kind, *dessen* Mutter aus Österreich kommt, heißt Sophie.	The child *whose* mother is from Austria is called Sophie.

The relative pronouns in English are: *who (whom), that, which.*

The relative pronouns in German are **der** and **welcher.** The forms of **der** are preferable.

The antecedent of a relative pronoun is the noun (or pronoun) to which it refers.

The relative pronoun agrees in number and gender with its antecedent, but it gets its case from its use in the relative clause; if it is the subject of the clause, it is nominative; if it is the object it is accusative; if it is the indirect object it is dative; if it shows possession it is genitive; if it is after a preposition it has the case the preposition requires.

All relative clauses are subordinate clauses, and therefore they must have subordinate word order, i.e. the verb stands at the end of the clause. A relative pronoun may never be omitted in German. A relative clause must be set off by commas.

Forms of the Relative Pronoun *der*

	masc.	*fem.*	*neut.*	*m.f.n.*	*Meaning*
		Singular		*Plural*	
Nom.	der	die	das	die	who, which
Gen.	dessen	deren	dessen	deren	whose, of which
Dat.	dem	der	dem	denen	(to) whom, which
Acc.	den	die	das	die	whom, that, which

The Relative Pronoun *welcher*

	Singular			Plural	
	masc.	*fem.*	*neut.*	*m.f.n.*	*Meaning*
Nom.	welcher	welche	welches	welche	who, that, which
Dat.	welchem	welcher	welchem	welchen	(to) whom, which
Acc.	welchen	welche	welches	welche	whom, that, which

The relative pronoun **der** is like the definite article **der**, except in the genitive case singular and plural, and in the dative plural—these cases add a syllable.

The relative pronoun **welcher** (who, that, which) is like the **der**-word **welcher**, except that it is never used in the genitive case.

Exercise 104

Complete these sentences with the correct form of the relative pronoun (**der, die, das**).

Beispiel: 1. Wo ist der Student, **dessen** Bücher und Hefte hier liegen?

1. **Wo ist der Student, (whose) Bücher und Hefte hier liegen?**
2. **Die kleine Anna, (who) erst fünf Jahre alt ist, bewunderte alles.**
3. **Hier ist der Bleistift, (which) Sie suchten.**
4. **Wo sind die Leute, mit (whom) Sie sprachen?**
5. **Die Kinder sahen den blauen Himmel, (that) wolkenlos war.**
6. **Das Restaurant, (which) sie besuchten, war nicht weit vom Büro.**
7. **Das war wirklich eine angenehme Überraschung, (which) wir heute hatten.**
8. **Die Kinder, (who) sehr hungrig waren, aßen mit gutem Appetit.**
9. **Wo wohnt der Junge, (to whom) du die Bilder schickst?**
10. **Der Herr, für (whom) er arbeitete, heißt Schmidt.**

Exercise 105

Fill in the gaps with the correct form of the relative pronoun.

The **welcher** form is allowable, but the **der** form is preferable.

1. **Die Kinder bewunderten alle Dinge, _____ sie im Büro sahen.**
2. **Das Büro, _____ Herr Clark seit zwei Jahren bewohnt, befindet sich in einem großen Wolkenkratzer.**
3. **Die Autos, _____ unten auf der Straße vorbeifuhren, schienen sehr klein zu sein.**

4. Herr Clark hatte heute eine angenehme Überraschung, von _____ er seinem Lehrer erzählen will.
5. Kennen Sie den Herrn, _____ gestern ins Büro hereinkam?
6. Ja, er ist der deutsche Freund, von _____ Herr Clark uns erzählte.
7. Dieser Freund wohnt in einem Vorort, _____ Einwohner meistens[1] in der Stadt arbeiten.
8. Die Bilder, von _____ wir gestern sprachen, sind sehr teuer.
9. Gefällt dir der Mantel, _____ ich gestern kaufte?
10. Frau Clark, _____ Tochter krank ist, lässt den Doktor kommen.[2]
11. Die Schüler, _____ Bücher und Hefte hier liegen, sollen sie sofort wegnehmen.
12. Die kleine Anna, _____ erst fünf Jahre alt ist, hatte die Grippe.

NOTES: **1.** for the most part. **2.** sends for the doctor.

Exercise 106

Stellen Sie in die richtige Reihenfolge! Beginnen Sie jeweils mit dem unterstrichenen Wort. (*Reorder the words in the sentences! Start with the underlined word.*)

1. Kinder—Dinge—bewunderten—Meine—alle—Büro—die—sahen—sie—im.
2. gestern—Bilder—von—Die—denen—teuer—sehr—wir—sprachen—sind.
3. Mantel—den—kaufen—dir—der—ich—Gefällt—gestern—wollte?
4. rot—Das—das—fährt—Herr Clark—Auto—ist.
5. mit—schreibt—der—Die – er—Füller—grün—ist.

3. wo(r) + A PREPOSITION USED IN PLACE OF A RELATIVE PRONOUN WITH A PREPOSITION

Relative pronouns preceded by a preposition may be replaced by **wo(r)** plus a preposition if the antecedent is <u>a pronoun which refers to a thing or things</u>. These combinations cannot be used if the antecedent pronoun refers to persons.

The **wo(r)**-form can also be used if it refers to a <u>whole sentence</u>. Thus:

Ich mache <u>vieles</u>, **worüber** (= über das) sich meine Kinder freuen.

I do much about which my children are pleased.

<u>Thomas kam am Samstag nach München</u>, **worüber** ich mich sehr freute.

Thomas came to Munich on Saturday, which pleased me very much.

but: Der Herr, **mit dem** ich sprach, ist mein Deutschlehrer.

The man with whom I was speaking is my German teacher.

Exercise 107

Wovon or **von dem?** Complete the following sentences with the correct relative pronoun.

Beispiel: 1. **Die Leute, von denen ich sprach, sind aus Stuttgart.**

1. **Die Leute, _____ ich sprach, sind aus Stuttgart.**
2. **Das Restaurant, _____ ich Ihnen erzählte, befindet sich fünf Strassen von hier.**
3. **Das Telefon klingelte endlich, _____ ich schon lange wartete.**
4. **Der Autobus _____ wir in die Stadt fuhren, war groß und bequem.**
5. **Er sagte einiges, _____ ich mich ärgerte.**
6. **Kennen Sie alle die Bücher, _____ er sprach?**
7. **Wir besuchten den Eifelturm, _____ ich mich schon gefreut hatte.**
8. **Der Vorort, _____ wir fuhren, war sehr schön.**

4. *Wer* AND *was* AS RELATIVE PRONOUNS

a. **wer** *is used as a relative pronoun in the sense of* **he who** *or* **whoever.**

Wer viele Freunde hat, ist glücklich.	*He who* has many friends is happy.
Wer jetzt gehen will, kann gehen.	*Whoever* wants to go now may go.

b. **was** *is used as a relative pronoun in the sense of* **what, that which, whatever.** *It is also used after such antecedents as* **alles** *all,* **nichts** *nothing,* **etwas** *something,* **viel** *or* **vieles** *much.*

Alles, **was** sie sahen, war ihnen neu.	*All that* they saw was new to them.
Was er auch sagt, ich glaube ihm nicht.	*Whatever* he says, I don't believe him.

Memorize these proverbs (**Sprichwörter**).

Nicht alles was glänzt ist Gold	Not all that glitters is gold.
Wer A sagt, muss auch B sagen.	He who says A must also say B.
Wer zuletzt lacht, lacht am besten.	He who laughs last, laughs best.

Exercise 108

Play "Call My Bluff" in German: Use relative clauses to suggest three definitions (only one is correct) for the following words (you might have to use a dictionary).

Beispiel: 1.

a. **Ein Dummkopf ist eine Person, mit der man sich gut unterhalten kann.**
b. **Ein Dummkopf ist eine Person, die nicht sehr intelligent ist?** ☑
c. **Ein Dummkopf ist eine Person, die einen großen Kopf hat.**

1. **Dummkopf**	6. **Schraubenzieher**
2. **Schultasche**	7. **Postkasten**
3. **Papierkorb**	8. **Kleiderhaken**
4. **Langläufer**	9. **Tintenpatrone**
5. **Wörterbuch**	10. **Jahreszeit**

Weak (Regular) Verbs. No Vowel Change

Infinitive		*Past Tense*
1. dauern	to last	es dauerte
2. machen	to make	ich (er) machte
3. spielen	to play	ich (er) spielte
4. brauchen	to need	ich (er) brauchte
5. stellen	to put	ich (er) stellte
6. fragen	to ask	ich (er) fragte
7. sagen	to say	ich (er) sagte
8. wohnen	to live	ich (er) wohnte
9. danken	to thank	ich (er) dankte
10. lernen	to learn	ich (cr) lernte
11. lehren	to teach	ich (er) lehrte
12. ruhen	to rest	ich (er) ruhte
13. regnen	to rain	es regnete
14. schneien	to snow	es schneite
15. kaufen	to buy	ich (er) kaufte
16. öffnen	to open	ich (er) öffnete
17. reden	to talk	ich (er) redete
18. antworten	to answer	ich (er) antwortete
19. besuchen	to visit	ich (er) besuchte
20. erzählen	to relate	ich (er) erzählte
21. arbeiten	to work	ich (er) arbeitete
22. plaudern	to chat	ich (er) plauderte
23. verkaufen	to sell	ich (er) verkaufte
24. bewohnen	to occupy	ich (er) bewohnte
25. verdienen	to earn	ich (er) verdiente
26. erwarten	to await	ich (er) erwartete

Strong (Irregular) Verbs. Vowel Changes

Infinitive		*Present*	*Past*
1. gehen	to go	er geht	er ging
2. kommen	to come	er kommt	er kam
3. stehen	to stand	er steht	er stand
4. sehen	to see	er sieht	er sah
5. lesen	to read	er liest	er las
6. nehmen	to take	er nimmt	er nahm
7. geben	to give	er gibt	er gab
8. sitzen	to sit	er sitzt	er saß
9. sprechen	to speak	er spricht	er sprach
10. treten	to step	er tritt	er trat
11. essen	to eat	er isst	er aß
12. liegen	to lie	er liegt	er lag
13. trinken	to drink	er trinkt	er trank
14. beginnen	to begin	er beginnt	er begann
15. finden	to find	er findet	er fand
16. scheinen	to shine	er scheint	er schien
17. schreiben	to write	er schreibt	er schrieb
18. tragen	to carry	er trägt	er trug
19. fahren	to ride	er fährt	er fuhr
20. waschen	to wash	er wäscht	er wusch
21. laufen	to run	er läuft	er lief
22. tun	to do	er tut	er tat

Past Tense of **sein** *and* **haben**

ich war	wir waren	ich hatte	wir hatten
du warst	ihr wart	du hattest	ihr hattet
er, sie, es war	sie (Sie) waren	er, sie, es hatte	sie (Sie) hatten

Redemittel

1. **im Allgemeinen** in general
2. **vor einem Monat (einem Jahr, einer Woche, sechs Jahren)** a month (a year, a week, six years) ago
3. **Er war im Begriff zu gehen.** He was about to go.
4. **Was macht Ihre (deine) Familie?** How is your family?
5. **Es freut mich, das zu hören.** I am glad to hear that.
6. **Das macht mir viel Freude.** That gives me much pleasure. That makes me very happy.
7. **Sie war krank. Jetzt geht es ihr besser.** She was sick. Now she is feeling better.
8. **Was fehlt dir (ihm, ihr, Ihnen)?** What is the matter with you (him, her, you *pol.*)?
9. **Ich habe Kopfschmerzen.** I have a headache.

10. **Das tut mir lied.** I am sorry.
11. **Wo befindet sich das Büro?** Where is the office located?
12. **Ich habe den Sommer gern.** I like summer.
13. **Er hat den Herbst lieber.** He prefers autumn.
14. **Sie hat den Frühling am liebsten.** She likes spring best.
15. **den Doktor kommen lassen** to send for the doctor **Ich lasse den Doktor kommen.**
16. **zum Frühstück (Mittagessen, Abendessen)** for breakfast (dinner, supper)
17. **Was ist los?** What's the matter? What's up?

Exercise 109

Complete these sentences by translating the words in parentheses.

1. (I am sorry to hear), **dass Ihr Bruder krank ist.**
2. **Sagen Sie mir:** (What is the matter with him?)
3. **Er hat** (a headache and fever).
4. **Sie war krank,** (but now she is feeling better).
5. (Five years ago) **wohnten wir in einem kleinen Vorort.**
6. **Ich habe Tee gern, aber** (I prefer coffee).
7. **Mein Büro** (is located) **in einem großen Wolkenkratzer.**
8. (It gave me great pleasure) **zu erfahren, dass Sie Deutsch lernen.**
9. **Wir mussten** (to send for the doctor).
10. **Was essen Sie gewöhnlich** (for supper)?
11. (We are sorry), **dass Sie nicht kommen können.**

Exercise 110

From Group II select the opposite of each word in Group I.

Group I	*Group II*
1. **Gesundheit**	a. **hereinkommen**
2. **weggehen**	b. **nichts**
3. **hinausgehen**	c. **zurückkommen**
4. **immer**	d. **alles**
5. **jemand**	e. **her**
6. **sich setzen**	f. **niemand, keiner**
7. **es tut mir leid**	g. **nie**
8. **nichts**	h. **mir ist kalt**
9. **hin**	i. **Krankheit**
10. **etwas**	j. **es macht mir Freude**
11. **das gefällt mir nicht**	k. **Ich habe das gern**
12. **mir ist warm**	l. **aufstehen**

Exercise III

Select the group of words in Column II which best complete each of the sentences begun in Column I.

Beispiel: (1c) Das Wetter ist gar nicht kalt, aber mir ist kalt.

<table>
<tr><td>I</td><td>II</td></tr>
<tr><td>1. Das Wetter ist gar nicht[1] kalt,</td><td>a. stand Herr Clark auf und begrüßte ihn.</td></tr>
<tr><td>2. Nehmen Sie meinen Regenschirm,</td><td>b. dass Herr Clark vier Kinder hat.</td></tr>
<tr><td>3. Während sie über das Wetter sprachen,</td><td>c. aber mir ist kalt.</td></tr>
<tr><td>4. Wir mussten den ganzen Sommer arbeiten,</td><td>d. der Zug von Hamburg pünktlich ankommt?</td></tr>
<tr><td>5. Tee mit Rum ist ein Getränk,[2]</td><td>e. denn es regnet in Strömen.</td></tr>
<tr><td>6. Als der Freund ins Büro trat,</td><td>f. um genug Geld zu verdienen.</td></tr>
<tr><td>7. Die Mutter ließ den Doktor kommen,</td><td>g. das Sie sicherlich erwärmt.</td></tr>
<tr><td>8. Können Sie nur sagen, ob</td><td>h. brachte ihnen Frau Clark Tee mit Rum.</td></tr>
<tr><td>9. Bevor Herr Clark den Zug nahm,</td><td>i. weil Anna Kopfschmerzen hatte.</td></tr>
<tr><td>10. Die Leser dieses Buches wissen,</td><td>j. als der Vater früh heimkam.[3]</td></tr>
<tr><td>11. Die Kinder freuten sich sehr,</td><td>k. kaufte er den Kindern Bonbons.[4]</td></tr>
</table>

NOTES: 1. gar nicht not at all. **2. das Getränk** beverage. **3. heim-kommen = nach Hause kommen. 4.** candy.

Grammar Review and Exercises

1. THE MODAL AUXILIARIES—PRESENT TENSE

You are familiar with the following six verbs, which are called "modal auxiliaries."

dürfen	to be permitted, may	**müssen**	to have to, must
können	to be able, can	**wollen**	to want, to desire
mögen	to like, care to, may	**sollen**	to be supposed to, to be said to, shall

Present Tense of the Modal Auxiliaries

ich darf	kann	mag	muss	soll	will
du darfst	kannst	magst	musst	sollst	willst
er, sie, es darf	kann	mag	muss	soll	will
wir dürfen	können	mögen	müssen	sollen	wollen
ihr dürft	könnt	mögt	müsst	sollt	wollt
sie, Sie dürfen	können	mögen	müssen	sollen	wollen

All six modal auxiliaries are irregular in the singular of the present tense.

Exercise 112

Fill in the correct present-tense form of the verb in parentheses.

Beispiel: 1. Herr Clark muss eine Reise machen.

1. Herr Clark (müssen) eine Reise machen.
2. Ich (wollen) meinen Vertreter besuchen.
3. (Können) er Deutsch sprechen?
4. Wir (müssen) früh aufstehen.
5. Der Zug (sollen) pünktlich um neun Uhr ankommen.
6. Ich (mögen) nicht spielen, denn ich bin müde.
7. (Dürfen) ich hereinkommen?
8. Er (wollen) sich ein paar Schuhe kaufen.
9. (Können) Sie mir zehn Euro leihen?
10. Wann (sollen) ich da sein?
11. (Dürfen) er das Zimmer verlassen?
12. Ich (müssen) einen Brief schreiben.
13. Wir (wollen) ins Kino gehen.
14. (Können) du mitkommen?
15. Wie viel Trinkgeld (sollen) ich geben?
16. (Wollen) du einen Regenmantel kaufen?
17. Was (können) ich für Sie tun?
18. Er (mögen) die kühle, frische Luft.

2. THE MODAL AUXILIARIES—PAST TENSE

ich durfte	konnte	mochte	musste	sollte	wollte
du durftest	konntest	mochtest	musstest	solltest	wolltest
er, sie, es durfte	konnte	mochte	musste	sollte	wollte
wir durften	konnten	mochten	mussten	sollten	wollten
ihr durftet	konntet	mochtet	musstet	solltet	wolltet
sie, Sie durften	konnten	mochten	mussten	sollten	wollten

The modal auxiliaries form their past tense like weak (regular) verbs by adding -**te** to the stem. Note, however, that the four verbs that have an **Umlaut** in the infinitive drop it in the past tense; note also that **mögen** becomes **mochte**.

The meanings of the past tense of the modals are:

ich (er) durfte	I (he) was allowed	**ich (er) musste**	I (he) had to, was compelled to
ich (er) konnte	I (he) was able, could	**ich (er) sollte**	I (he) was to, was supposed to, ought to, should
ich (er) mochte	I (he) liked, cared to	**ich (er) wollte**	I (he) wanted, desired

Note that **ich mochte** = I liked. Don't confuse it with **ich möchte** (I should like) which is an expression you have met many times.

Exercise 113

Translate the verb in parentheses.

Beispiel: 1. Ich wollte nach München fahren.

1. (I wanted) **nach München fahren.**
2. (We were to) **bis Seite[1] 50 (fünfzig) lesen.**
3. (I was able) **ihm nur einen Dollar leihen.**
4. (We did not care to) **ins Kino gehen.**
5. (We could not) **ohne das Wörterbuch auskommen.[2]**
6. **Niemand** (was permitted) **im Theater rauchen.**
7. **Die Jungen** (were not allowed) **auf der Straße Fußball spielen.**
8. (I liked) **die frische, klare Luft des Vororts.**
9. **Alle** (wanted) **das deutsche Museum besuchen.**
10. (We were to) **zu Fuß gehen.**

NOTES: 1. die Seite *pl.* **-n** page. **2. aus-kommen** to get along.

3. SUBORDINATE WORD ORDER

Subordinate conjunctions: **dass** that; **weil** because; **ehe, bevor** before; **sobald** as soon as; **während** while; **bis** until; **wenn** if, or when (*with present tense*); **als** when (*with past tense*); **ob** whether. In subordinate clauses the verb must stand last.

Exercise 114

Combine each pair of sentences with the conjunctions indicated.

Beispiel: 1. Ich muss Ihnen sagen, dass ich nicht gehen kann.

1. **Ich muss es Ihnen sagen.** (dass) **Ich kann nicht gehen.**
2. **Wir können unsere Aufgaben nicht machen.[1]** (wenn) **Die Kinder machen so viel Lärm.**
3. **Niemand durfte reden.** (als) **Wir schrieben eine Prüfung.[2]**

4. Er will nicht warten. (bis) Der Doktor kommt nach Hause.

5. Wir konnten nicht spazieren gehen. (weil) Es regnete in Strömen.

6. Sie mag nicht Tennis spielen. (weil) Sie ist müde.

7. Du darfst nach Hause gehen. (sobald) Du bist mit der Arbeit fertig.

8. Die Kinder sollen sich die Hände waschen.[3] (bevor) Sie setzen sich an den Tisch.

9. Ich musste arbeiten. (während) Alle amüsierten sich.

10. Alle Schüler mussten aufstehen. (als) Der Lehrer trat ins Zimmer herein.

11. Ich weiß nicht, (ob) Der Autobus fährt um sieben Uhr ab.

12. Weißt du? (ob) Wir haben eine Aufgabe für morgen.

NOTES: 1. eine Aufgabe machen to do an assignment. **2. eine Prüfung schreiben** to take an examination. **3.** The children are to wash their hands. (*Lit.* to wash to themselves the hands.)

4. REFLEXIVE VERBS

Reflexive verbs are quite common in German. The reflexive pronoun is normally accusative, e.g. **Ich wasche mich.** However, if the sentence already contains an object, the reflexive pronoun is in the dative case. Thus: **Ich wasche mir die Hände.**

Exercise 115

Fill in the grid with the reflexive pronouns in the accusative and the dative.

	Ich	du	er	sie	es	wir	ihr	sie (Sie)
acc.								
dat.								

Exercise 116

Complete the following sentences with the appropriate reflexive pronouns (accusative or dative).

Beispiel: 1. Anna kann sich schon allein anziehen.

1. Anna kann _____ schon allein anziehen.

2. Ich ziehe _____ heute ein schönes Hemd an.

3. Was zieht ihr _____ ins Theater an?

4. Kommt, wir müssen _____ beeilen.

5. Guten Tag, Herr Müller. Bitte setzen Sie _____.

6. Du musst _____ noch die Haare waschen.

7. Wir waren so müde, dass wir _____ sofort ins Bett legten.

8. Er regte _____ wegen des Unfalls sehr auf.[1]

NOTE: 1. sich aufregen to get upset.

5. PAST TENSE OF WEAK AND STRONG VERBS

Exercise 117

Change this passage to the past tense.

Beispiel: 1. Ich stand jeden Werktag früh auf.

1. Ich stehe jeden Werktag früh auf.
2. Ich wasche und rasiere mich.
3. Ich ziehe mich schnell an.
4. Meine Frau und ich frühstücken zusammen.
5. Nach dem Frühstück fahre ich zu der U-Bahnstation mit dem Auto.
6. Viele Leute warten schon auf dem Bahnsteig.[1]
7. Der Zug kommt bald an.
8. Ich steige mit vielen anderen Passagieren in den Zug ein.
9. Der Zug fährt in einigen Minuten ab.
10. Im Zug versuchen[2] einige Passagiere ein bisschen[3] zu schlafen.
11. Andere lesen Zeitungen, Bücher oder Zeitschriften.
12. In einer halben Stunde kommt der Zug in New York an, und alle Passagiere steigen aus.

NOTES: 1. der Bahnsteig *pl.* **-e** platform. **2. versuchen** to try. **3. ein bisschen** a little, a little bit.

6. EXPRESSIONS OF DEFINITE TIME AND DURATION OF TIME

Nouns used in expressions of definite time or duration of time (*without prepositions*) are in the accusative case.

Jeden Werktag arbeitet er acht Stunden.   He works eight hours every workday.
Er arbeitete nur einen Monat hier.   He worked here only a month.

jeden Tag	every day	**einen Tag**	for one day	**den ganzen Tag**	the whole day
jede Woche	every week	**eine Woche**	for one week	**die ganze Woche**	the whole week
jedes Jahr	every year	**ein Jahr**	for one year	**das ganze Jahr**	the whole year

DER ERSTE DIALOG

THE FIRST DIALOGUE

Zwei Freunde begegnen sich auf der Straße
—Wie geht's, mein Freund?
—Ich fühle mich nicht wohl.
—Was fehlt dir?
—Ich habe Kopfschmerzen.
—Das tut mir leid. Warum nimmst du denn nicht etwas Aspirin?
—Das tue ich, sobald ich nach Hause komme.

Two Friends Meet on the Street
—How are you, my friend?
—I don't feel well.
—What's the matter with you?
—I have a headache.
—I'm sorry to hear that. Well, why don't you take some aspirin?
—I'll do that as soon as I get home.

DER ZWEITE DIALOG

—Wollen wir etwas essen?

—Mit Vergnügen. Ich habe Hunger. Kennen Sie ein gutes Restaurant?

—Nicht weit von hier ist ein Restaurant mit guter deutscher Küche.

—Gut. Gehen wir dahin.

THE SECOND DIALOGUE

—Shall we eat something?

—With pleasure. I'm hungry. Do you know a good restaurant?

—Not far from here there is a restaurant serving good German cooking.

—Fine. Let's go there.

Exercise 118

Lesestück

HERR CLARK WAR KRANK

Am Donnerstag, den zwanzigsten April, um acht Uhr abends erreichte Herr Müller das Haus seines Schülers. Der ältere Sohn, ein Junge von zwölf Jahren, öffnete die Tür und grüßte[1] den Lehrer höflich.[2] Sie gingen in das Wohnzimmer, wo Herr Clark gewöhnlich seinen Lehrer erwartete.

Aber heute Abend war er nicht da. Frau Clark war auch nicht da. Herr Müller wunderte sich[3] sehr und fragte den Jungen: „Wo ist denn dein Papa?" Der Sohn antwortete traurig:[4] „Der Papa ist krank. Er ist im Bett, denn er hat eine Erkältung[5] mit Fieber. Mutter versuchte Sie anzurufen, um Ihnen zu sagen, Sie sollten heute Abend nicht kommen. Aber sie konnte Sie nicht erreichen."

Der Lehrer sagte: „Es tut mir leid, dass dein Vater krank ist. Ich wünsche ihm gute Besserung.[6] Wenn er nächste Woche wieder gesund und munter[7] ist, können wir zwei Stunden nacheinander[8] machen. Also bis zum nächsten Dienstag. Tschüss, Karl." Der Junge erwiderte: „Auf Wiedersehen, Herr Müller."

NOTES: **1.** **grüßen** to greet. **2.** politely. **3.** **sich wundern** to wonder, be surprised. **4.** sadly. **5.** a cold. **6.** recovery. **7.** cheerful. **8.** one after the other, in succession.

FAMILIE CLARK GEHT INS KINO

1. Eines Samstagabends[1] will die Familie Clark gemeinsam ausgehen. Herr und Frau Clark wollen gern ins Theater gehen, doch die Kinder finden das Theater langweilig.

2. „Gehen wir doch ins Kino!," schlägt Wilhelm vor. "Der neueste Film aus Hollywood läuft gerade."

3. Doch Herr Clark bezweifelt, dass dieser Film für die ganze Familie passend ist: „Anna ist noch zu jung für diesen Film. Wir müssen einen Film finden, der auch für sie passt."

4. Die Kinder schlagen vor, einen Zeichentrickfilm anzusehen. Da sind alle einverstanden.

5. Als sie beim Kino ankommen, geht Herr Clark zur Kasse: „Wir möchten gerne zwei Eintrittskarten für Erwachsene und vier Karten für Kinder."
   —„In welcher Reihe wollen Sie sitzen?"
   —„In der 14. Reihe, bitte!"
   —„In der 14. Reihe ist schon alles besetzt. Aber Sie können sich in die 12. oder auch in die 15. Reihe setzen."
   —„Dann bitte sechs Plätze in der 12. Reihe."

6. Herr Clark bezahlt und nimmt die Eintrittskarten. Dann fragt er noch: „In welchem Saal spielt der Zeichentrickfilm?"
   —„Im dritten Saal."
   —„Vielen Dank."

7. Die Kinder kaufen noch Popcorn, bevor sie in den Kinosaal gehen. Vor dem Film gibt es noch lustige Werbung und eine Vorschau auf kommende Filme. Dann wird es dunkel und der Film beginnt.

1. One Saturday evening the Clark family wants to go out together. Mr. and Mrs. Clark want to go to the theater but the children think that the theater is boring.

2. "Let's go to the movies!," William suggests. "The latest movie from Hollywood is on."

3. But Mr. Clark doubts that this movie is suitable for the whole family: "Anne is still too young for this movie. We have to find a movie that is suitable also for her."

4. The children suggest going to see a cartoon. They all agree.

5. When they arrive at the movie theater, Mr. Clark goes to the box office and says: "We would like two tickets for adults and four tickets for children."
   —"In which row would you like to sit?"
   —"In the fourteenth row, please."
   —"In the fourteenth row all the seats are taken. But you can sit in the twelfth or in the fifteenth row."
   —"Then we would like to have six seats in the twelfth row."

6. Mr. Clark pays and takes the tickets. Then he asks something else: "In which theater is the cartoon being shown?"
   —"In the third theater."
   —"Thank you very much."

7. The children buy some popcorn before going into the movie theater. Before the film there are some funny commercials and a preview of forthcoming movies. Then it gets dark and the movie begins.

8. Während des Films lachen die Leute, und am Ende klatschen alle Beifall.

8. During the movie people laugh and at the end they give a round of applause.

9. Als Familie Clark aus dem Kino kommt, ist es draußen schon dunkel. Alle sind sich einig, dass dies ein angenehmer Abend war.

9. When the Clark family leaves the movie theater, it is already dark outside. They all agree that it was a pleasant evening.

NOTE: I. The genitive case may be used to express indefinite time: **eines Tages** one day, **eines Abends** one evening.

Wortschatz

der Beifall applause
der Saal *pl.* **Säle** hall, auditorium
die Eintrittskarte *pl.* **-n** admission ticket
die Vorschau preview
die Werbung *pl.* **-en** commercial, advertisement
der Zeichentrickfilm *pl.* **-e** cartoon
der Platz *pl.* **¨-e** seat, place
die Reihe *pl.* **-en** row

klatschen to applaud, to clap
passen to fit, to be suitable
vorschlagen to suggest
zweifeln to doubt
langweilig boring
besetzt occupied; **frei** vacant, free
sich einig sein to agree
hinten in back; **vorne** in front

Wichtige Redemittel

ohne Zweifel without doubt

nach meinem Geschmack to my taste

Was spielt heute abend (morgen, diese Woche)? What is playing / on this evening (tomorrow, this week)?

Sind noch Plätze für heute abend zu haben? Are there any seats left (to be had) for this evening?

Nur noch in der ersten Reihe. Only in the first row.

Ich möchte zwei Plätze in der zwölften Reihe. I would like two seats in the twelfth row.

Die zwölfte Reihe ist ausverkauft. The twelfth row is sold out.

Die Plätze sind alle besetzt. All the seats are taken.

Es sind keine Plätze frei. No seats are vacant.

Grammar Notes and Practical Exercises

1. THE ORDINAL NUMERALS

The cardinal numerals are 1, 2, 3, 4, etc. The ordinal numerals are the first, second, third, fourth, etc. Learn the ordinals in German.

der erste	1st	der neunte	9th	der vierzigste	40th
der zweite	2nd	der zehnte	10th	der fünfzigste	50th
der dritte	3rd	der elfte	11th	der sechzigste	60th
der vierte	4th	der zwölfte	12th	der siebzigste	70th
der fünfte	5th	der dreizehnte	13th	der achtzigste	80th
der sechste	6th	der neunzehnte	19th	der neunzigste	90th
der siebente (siebte)	7th	der zwanzigste	20th	der hundertste	100th
der achte	8th	der dreißigste	30th	der letzte	last

Ordinal numerals are formed by adding **-te** to the cardinal numerals up to 19, and **-ste** to those above 19. **der erste** and **der dritte** are irregular.

Ordinal numerals are adjectives and take case endings like other adjectives. Thus:

N.	der erste Tag	die zweite Woche	das dritte Jahr
G.	des ersten Tages	der zweiten Woche	des dritten Jahres
D.	dem ersten Tag	der zweiten Woche	dem dritten Jahr
A.	den ersten Tag	die zweite Woche	das dritte Jahr

Exercise 119

Read aloud.

1. Die Woche hat sieben Tage. In Deutschland ist der Montag der erste Tag der Woche und der Sonntag der siebente. In Amerika ist der Sonntag der erste Tag der Woche und der Samstag der siebente.
2. Das Jahr hat vier Jahreszeiten. Die erste Jahreszeit ist der Frühling; die zweite ist der Sommer; die dritte ist der Herbst; die vierte ist der Winter.
3. Das Jahr hat zwölf Monate. Der erste Monat ist der Januar; der elfte ist der November. Der letzte Monat des Jahres ist der Dezember.
4. Wo sitzen Sie am liebsten? Ich sitze am liebsten in der vierten Reihe. Wo sitzt Heinrich am liebsten? Er sitzt am liebsten in der ersten Reihe.

2. *DAS DATUM* — THE DATE

Der wievielte (*vee-f´eel-te*) **ist heute?** — What date is today?

Den wievielten haben wir heute? — What date have we today?

Heute ist der 1. Mai (der erste Mai). — Today is May 1.

Gestern war der 30. April (der dreißigste April). — Yesterday was April 30.

Vorgestern war der 29. April (der neunundzwanzigste April). — The day before yesterday was April 29.

Lincolns Geburtstag ist am 12. Februar (am zwölften Februar). — Lincoln's birthday is on February 12.

A period (.) after a numeral is an abbreviation of the ordinal. Thus: **der 1. Mai = der erste Mai; der 8. Juni = der achte Juni.**

On a certain date = **am** + ordinal + month. Thus: **am 1. Mai (am ersten Mai)** = May 1; **am 31. Dezember (am einunddreißigsten Dezember)** = December 31; **am 12. Februar (am zwölften Februar)** = February 12.

Exercise 120

Read each sentence aloud. Write out in full each date.

Beispiel: 1. am zweiundzwanzigsten Februar.

1. Washingtons[1] Geburtstag ist am 22. Februar.
2. Herrn Clarks Geburtstag ist am 27. August.
3. Karls Geburtstag ist am 19. Juni.
4. Wilhelms Geburtstag ist am 20. Januar.
5. Annas Geburtstag ist am 9. Juli.
6. Maries Geburtstag ist am 10. Mai.
7. Frau Clarks Geburtstag ist am 22. März.
8. Der Frühling beginnt am 21. März.
9. Der 1. Januar ist Neujahrstag.
10. Heute lernen wir das 25. Kapitel.

NOTE: 1. In the case of names the genitive of possession is commonly used *before* the noun. The ending **s** corresponds here to the English 's and is used with both masculine and feminine names. Thus: **Washingtons (Lincolns, Karls, Annas, Frau Clarks, Herrn Clarks) Geburtstag.**

3. *DIE JAHRESZAHLEN.* THE DATE OF THE YEAR

The date of the year is expressed in German very much like in English. Thus:

Neunzehn vierundneunzig (= nineteen ninety-four)

or

Sechzehnhundertdreizehn (= sixteen hundred and thirteen)

Exercise 121

When did the following persons live?

Beispiel: 1. James Joyce: von achtzehn zweiundachtzig bis neunzehn einundvierzig.

1. James Joyce: 1882–1941
2. William Shakespeare: 1564–1616
3. John Steinbeck: 1902–1968

4. Hermann Hesse: 1877–1962
5. Arthur Schnitzler: 1862–1931
6. Hugo von Hofmannsthal: 1874–1929
7. Heinrich Böll: 1917–1985
8. Friedrich Dürrenmatt: 1921–1990

Exercise 122

Fragen

Lesen Sie noch einmal den Text: **Familie Clark geht ins Kino** und beantworten Sie dann diese Fragen!

 1. Wann will die Familie Clark gemeinsam ausgehen?
 2. Was wollen Herr und Frau Clark tun?
 3. Warum wollen dies die Kinder nicht?
 4. Wohin wollen die Kinder gehen?
 5. Warum schlagen die Kinder vor, in einen Zeichentrickfilm zu gehen?
 6. Warum kann sich die Familie Clark nicht in die 14. Reihe setzen?
 7. In welchem Saal findet die Vorstellung statt?
 8. Was kaufen die Kinder vor der Vorstellung?
 9. Was sehen die Zuschauer vor dem Film?
10. Was tun die Zuschauer am Ende des Films?
11. War dies ein angenehmer Abend für die Familie Clark?

CHAPTER 26

DIE WIEDERVEREINIGUNG DEUTSCHLANDS

The Brandenburg Gate was built to commemorate peace. It later was incorporated into the Berlin Wall, but it now stands as a symbol of reunification.

1. Herr Clark und Herr Müller haben wieder eine Deutschstunde. Diesmal erzählt Herr Müller über die Wiedervereinigung Deutschlands. Herr Clark hört gespannt zu.

2. „Sie wissen sicher, Herr Clark, dass Deutschland nach dem Zweiten Weltkrieg in West- und Ostdeutschland geteilt war. Westdeutschland nannte man die BRD (Bundesrepublik Deutschland) und Ostdeutschland die DDR (Deutsche Demokratische Republik)."

3. „Ja, das ist mir natürlich bekannt. Auch Berlin, die heutige Hauptstadt Deutschlands, war eine geteilte Stadt. Eine Mauer trennte Westberlin von Ostberlin. Die Menschen vom Osten durften nicht in den Westen reisen."

1. Mr. Clark and Mr. Müller are having a German lesson again. This time Mr. Müller tells about the reunification of Germany. Mr. Clark is listening in eager anticipation.

2. "I am sure, Mr. Clark, that you know that after the Second World War Germany was divided into West and East Germany. West Germany was called BRD (FRG—Federal Republic of Germany) and East Germany was called DDR (GDR—German Democratic Republic)."

3. "Yes, of course I know that. Also Berlin, today's capital of Germany, was a divided city. A wall separated West Berlin and East Berlin. The people from East Germany were not allowed to travel to the West."

4. „Genauso war es. Aber hören Sie nun, was im November 1989 geschehen ist:
   Ich bin aus beruflichen Gründen in Westberlin gewesen. Am Abend habe ich laute Rufe von der Straße gehört. Ich habe mein Hotel verlassen und bin auf die Straße gegangen. Die Menschen haben getanzt und gesungen, manche haben auch geweint. Ich habe gefragt, was passiert ist. Da hat ein Mann gerufen, dass die Grenze zwischen Ost- und Westberlin nicht mehr geschlossen ist. Ich habe es zuerst nicht geglaubt, doch dann habe ich die Menschen aus Ostberlin gesehen."

5. „Sie haben großes Glück gehabt, dass Sie zu diesem historischen Moment in Berlin gewesen sind, Herr Müller!"

6. „Ja, es war ein großer Zufall."

7. „Was ist denn danach geschehen?"

8. „Tausende Menschen aus Ostberlin sind über die Grenze gekommen. Fremde Leute haben sich herzlich begrüßt und umarmt. Später hat man die Mauer in Berlin niedergerissen und zerstört. Aus BRD und DDR ist dann ein einziges Deutschland geworden."

9. „Herr Müller, ich danke Ihnen vielmals für den lebendigen Geschichteunterricht!"

4. "That was exactly the situation. But listen to what happened in August 1989:
   For professional reasons I was staying in West Berlin. In the evening I heard loud shouts from the streets. I left my hotel and went out on the street. The people were dancing and singing, some were also crying. I asked them what had happened. Then a man shouted that the border between East and West Berlin was not closed anymore. First I didn't believe it, but then I saw people from East Berlin."

5. "You were very lucky to have been in Berlin at such a historic moment, Mr. Müller!"

6. "Yes, it was a big coincidence."

7. "What happened afterwards?"

8. "Thousands of people from East Berlin came across the border. People unknown to each other kindly greeted and hugged one another. Later the wall in Berlin was torn down and destroyed. FRG and GDR became one Germany."

9. "Mr. Müller, I thank you very much for the vivid lesson in history!"

Wortschatz

der Osten east; der Westen west
die Mauer pl. -n wall
der Krieg pl. -e war; der Frieden peace
die Geschichte pl. -n story, history
die Stadt (shtätt) pl. ¨-e city
der Zufall pl. ¨-e coincidence
glauben to believe
passieren to happen

schlagen to hit, beat, defeat
teilen to divide
trennen to separate
umarmen to hug
weinen to cry
zerstören to destroy
herzlich kind, warm, hearty
histórisch historical
lebendig lively, vivid

Wichtige Redemittel

mit Vergnügen with pleasure
es ist mir bekannt, es ist mir klar it is evident (clear) to me
es ist ihm (ihr, Ihnen, etc.) klar it is evident to him (to her, to you, etc.)

aus beruflichen Gründen for professional reasons

aus privaten (persönlichen, finanziellen, zeitlichen) Gründen for personal (private, financial, temporal) reasons

Grammar Notes and Practical Exercises

1. THE PRESENT PERFECT TENSE (= "DAS PERFEKT")

The present perfect tense in English is formed by the auxiliary verb *have* + the past participle of a verb. Thus: *I have learned; you have worked; he has seen; they have spoken.* Observe the present perfect tense in German:

lernen to learn	**sehen** to see
I have learned the numerals well.	*I have not seen the new film.*
You have learned the numerals well; etc.	*You have not seen the new film; etc.*
Ich habe die Zahlen gut **gelernt.**	**Ich habe** den neuen Film nicht **gesehen.**
Du hast die Zahlen gut **gelernt.**	**Du hast** den neuen Film nicht **gesehen.**
Er hat die Zahlen gut **gelernt.**	**Er hat** den neuen Film nicht **gesehen.**
Wir haben die Zahlen gut **gelernt.**	**Wir haben** den neuen Film nicht **gesehen.**
Ihr habt die Zahlen gut **gelernt.**	**Ihr habt** den neuen Film nicht **gesehen.**
Sie haben die Zahlen gut **gelernt.**	**Sie haben** den neuen Film nicht **gesehen.**

a. *The* **Perfekt** *of most verbs in German is formed by the auxiliary* **haben** + *the past participle of the main verb.*

b. *The verb "sein" and all intransitive verbs indicating a* **change of place** *or a* **change of condition** *take the present of the auxiliary* **sein** (ich bin, *etc.*) *in the* **Perfekt.**

An intransitive verb is a verb that does not take an object. Examples from our text are: **Ich bin . . . gegangen; Ich bin . . . gewesen.**

c. *The past participle stands at the end of a simple sentence or main clause.*

2. FORMATION OF THE PAST PARTICIPLE

Weak (Regular) Verbs		*Strong (Irregular) Verbs*	
ich habe **gelernt**	I have *learned*	habe ich **geschrieben?**	have I *written?*
du hast **gearbeitet**	you have *worked*	hast du **gelesen?**	have you *read?*
er hat **gerechnet**	he has *figured*	hat sie **gesprochen?**	has she *spoken?*
wir haben **gekauft**	we have *bought*	haben wir **gestanden?**	have we *stood?*
ihr habt **gemacht**	you have *made*	habt ihr **gesehen?**	have you *seen?*
sie haben **aufgemacht**	they have *opened*	haben sie **angesehen?**	have they *looked at?*
Sie haben **verkauft**	you have *sold*	haben Sie **verstanden?**	have you *understood?*

a. *The past participle of weak verbs is formed by adding* -t *or* -et *to the infinitive stem and prefixing* ge-.

The ending **-et** is used when the stem ends in **-t** or **-d**, and after certain consonant groups, for ease in pronunciation (**ge-arbeit-et, ge-red-et, ge-rechn-et, ge-öffn-et**).

b. *The past participle of strong verbs has the ending* -en *and the prefix* ge-.

c. Verbs with separable prefixes form their past participles like the simple verbs, and the prefix ge-stands between the separable prefix and the verb (aufgemacht, angesehen).

d. Verbs with inseparable prefixes (be-, emp-, ent-, er-, ge-, ver-, zer-) do not add the prefix ge- to the past participle (verkauft, verstanden).

Exercise 123

Find all the past participles of the text "**Die Wiedervereinigung Deutschlands**" and assign them to the correct column in the grid.

ge.......t...	...ge.....t	.........t	ge.......en	...ge.....en	.........en
geweint			geschehen		

Exercise 124

Complete these sentences with the past participle of the verb in parentheses.

Beispiel: 1. Er hat die neuen Wörter gelernt.

1. Er hat die neuen Wörter (lernen).
2. Ich habe ihn heute nicht (sehen).
3. Sie haben gut (antworten).
4. Hat Heinrich schwer (arbeiten)?
5. Er hat gestern einen Brief (schreiben).
6. Hast du das Porträt (ansehen)?
7. Der Tisch ist hier (stehen).
8. Die Schüler haben gut (rechnen).
9. Die Jungen haben zu viel (reden).
10. Niemand hat Deutsch (sprechen).
11. Wann haben Sie das Auto (verkaufen)?
12. Sie hat einen neuen Hut (kaufen).

3. THE PRINCIPAL PARTS OF VERBS

Weak Verbs (Regular). No Vowel Change in Stem Vowel

Infinitive	Present (er, sie, es)	Past (ich, er, sie, es)	Present Perfect (er, sie, es)
lernen	er lernt	lernte	hat gelernt
fragen	er fragt	fragte	hat gefragt
reden	er redet	redete	hat geredet
antworten	er antwortet	antwortete	hat geantwortet
verkaufen	er verkauft	verkaufte	hat verkauft
haben	er hat	hatte	hat gehabt

Strong Verbs (Irregular). The Stem Vowel Changes

schreiben to write	**er schreibt**	schrieb	hat geschrieben
geben to give	**er gibt**	gab	hat gegeben
an-geben to mention	**er gibt . . . an**	gab . . . an	hat angegeben
lesen to read	**er liest**	las	hat gelesen
sehen to see	**er sieht**	sah	hat gesehen
an-sehen to look at	**er sieht . . . an**	sah . . . an	hat angesehen
sprechen to speak	**er spricht**	sprach	hat gesprochen
vergessen to forget	**er vergisst**	vergaß	hat vergessen
nehmen to take	**er nimmt**	nahm	hat genommen
sitzen to sit	**er sitzt**	saß	hat gesessen
liegen to lie	**er liegt**	lag	hat gelegen
stehen to stand	**er steht**	stand	hat gestanden
verstehen to understand	**er versteht**	verstand	hat verstanden
finden to find	**er findet**	fand	hat gefunden
statt-finden to take place	**er findet . . . statt**	fand . . . statt	hat stattgefunden
trinken to drink	**er trinkt**	trank	hat getrunken
schlagen to hit, defeat	**er schlägt**	schlug	hat geschlagen

All weak verbs have a like pattern, so that it is not necessary to memorize the principal parts of each verb separately.

The principal parts of strong verbs have vowel changes and must be memorized. A foreigner learning English has a similar problem. He must learn the irregular verb forms such as: *speak, spoke, spoken; give, gave, given; write, wrote, written; etc.*

4. USE OF THE PAST ("PRÄTERITUM") AND PRESENT PERFECT ("PERFEKT") TENSES

In German both the past and present perfect are used to express *past time*. Thus the German **Perfekt** resembles the English present perfect tense only in the way it is formed, but *not* in its use!

Er kaufte sich gestern einen Hut.	He bought himself a hat yesterday.
Er hat sich gestern einen Hut gekauft.	

In conversation the present perfect is generally used.

Haben Sie Herrn Schiller geschrieben?	Did you write to Mr. Schiller?
Ja, ich habe ihm gestern geschrieben.	Yes, I wrote to him yesterday.

However, to narrate a sequence of events, the past tense is preferable.

Ich stand um sieben Uhr auf.	I got up at seven o'clock.
Ich zog mich schnell an.	I dressed quickly.
Ich frühstückte, usw.	I had breakfast, etc.

Exercise 125

Change these sentences to the **Perfekt**.

Beispiel: 1. Herr Clark **hat** einen Brief an seinen Geschäftspartner **geschrieben.**

1. Herr Clark schreibt einen Brief an seinen Geschäftspartner.
2. Wir schenken dem Vater eine Füllfeder zum Geburtstag.
3. Ich trinke ein Glas Bier zum Mittagessen.
4. Ich lese die Geschichte Deutschlands.
5. Die Kinder sitzen vor dem Fernsehapparat.
6. Sie antwortet richtig auf alle Fragen.
7. Was fragt der Lehrer?
8. Arbeiten Sie den ganzen Tag?
9. Jeden Abend hören wir ein Musikprogramm.
10. Was sehen die Kinder im Büro des Vaters?
11. Ich beantworte alle Fragen.

Exercise 126

Practice these short dialogues aloud.

1. —Hat der Lehrer Heinrich schwere Fragen gestellt? —Jawohl. Er hat ihm einige sehr schwere Fragen gestellt. —Hat Heinrich richtig geantwortet? —Ja, er hat auf alle Fragen richtig geantwortet.
2. —Haben Sie einen Brief an Ihren Freund geschrieben? —Ich habe ihm vor zwei Wochen geschrieben. —Haben Sie schon eine Antwort bekommen? —Eben heute habe ich eine lange Antwort bekommen, aber ich habe sie noch nicht gelesen.

1. —Did the teacher ask Henry difficult questions? —Yes, indeed. He asked him several very difficult questions. —Did Henry answer correctly? —Yes, he answered all the questions correctly.
2. —Have you written a letter to your friend? —I wrote to him two weeks ago. —Have you already received an answer? —Only today I received a long answer, but I haven't read it yet.

EIN TYPISCHES WOCHENENDE BEI DEN CLARKS

—Herr Clark, Sie haben mir schon erzählt, wie Sie einen typischen Arbeitstag verbringen. Seien Sie[1] so gut und erzählen Sie mir jetzt, wie Sie den vorigen Sonntag verbracht haben.

—Mit Vergnügen, Herr Müller.

Vorgestern war Sonntag. Ich bin erst um halb zehn aufgestanden. An Werktagen stehe ich, wie Sie wissen, um sechs Uhr auf. Ich habe mich gewaschen, rasiert und angezogen. Meine Frau und Kinder waren vor mir aufgestanden; aber sie hatten noch nicht gefrühstückt. Um zehn Uhr haben wir uns alle zum Frühstück gesetzt. Am Sonntag freuen wir uns natürlich, dass wir zusammen essen können.

—Und nach dem Frühstück?

—Nach dem Frühstück habe ich die Zeitung gelesen. In der Sonntagszeitung interessiert mich besonders die Geschäftsbeilage, wie Sie sich wohl vorstellen können.

Die Sportnachrichten habe ich gar nicht angeschaut. Ich interessiere mich nicht für Sport. Meine zwei Jungen interessieren sich riesig dafür, besonders für Fußball und Baseball.

—Was taten die Kinder, während Sie die Zeitung lasen?

—Die jüngeren saßen vor dem Fernsehapparat, und die älteren besuchten Freunde in der Nachbarschaft.

Um ein Uhr haben wir uns zum Mittagessen gesetzt. Meine Frau hatte ein schmackhaftes Essen bereitet, und alle ließen es sich gut schmecken.

—Mr. Clark, you have already told me how you spend a typical weekday. Be so kind as to tell me now, how you spent last Sunday.

—With pleasure, Mr. Müller.

The day before yesterday was Sunday. I did not get up until half past nine. On weekdays, as you know, I get up at six o'clock. I washed, shaved and dressed. My wife and children had gotten up before me; but they had not yet had breakfast. At ten o'clock all of us sat down to breakfast. On Sunday we are naturally happy to have our meals together.

—And after breakfast?

—After breakfast I read the newspaper. In the Sunday newspaper I am especially interested in the business section, as you can well imagine.

I did not look at the sports news at all. I am not interested in sports. My two boys are mightily interested in these, especially in soccer and baseball.

—What were the children doing while you were reading the newspaper?

—The younger ones were watching television, and the older ones were visiting friends in the neighborhood.

At one o'clock we sat down to dinner. My wife had prepared a tasty meal and everybody enjoyed eating it.

—Und nach dem Mittagessen?

—Nach dem Mittagessen haben die Kinder gejammert. Sie wollten ins Kino gehen. Wir mussten also mit ihnen ins Kino! Da haben meine Frau und ich uns furchtbar gelangweilt, aber die Kinder haben sich gut amüsiert.

    Vom Kino sind wir nach Hause gegangen. Nach dem Abendessen habe ich einem Freund geschrieben, der neulich eine Reise nach Deutschland gemacht hat. Dann habe ich einige deutsche Kurzgeschichten gelesen.

    Um elf Uhr bin ich zu Bett gegangen.

—Ausgezeichnet, Herr Clark. Sie haben alles sehr schön erzählt. Ihre Aussprache war besonders gut.

—Dafür muss ich Ihnen danken, Herr Müller.

—Danke, Sie sind sehr liebenswürdig.

—And after dinner?

—After dinner the children pestered us. They wanted to go to the movies. So we had to go with them to the movies! There my wife and I were terribly bored, but the children enjoyed themselves very much.

    From the movies we went home. After supper I wrote a letter to a friend who has recently taken a trip to Germany. Then I read a few German short stories.

    At eleven o'clock I went to bed.

—Excellent, Mr. Clark. You have related everything very nicely. Your pronunciation was especially good.

—For this I must thank you, Mr. Müller.

—Thank you, you are very kind.

NOTE: 1. The imperative of **sein: Sei** gut! **Seid** gut! **Seien Sie gut!** Be good.

Wortschatz

die **Aussprache** *pl.* -n pronunciation
die **Beilage** *pl.* -n section, supplement
der **Fernsehapparát** *pl.* -e television set
die **Kurzgeschichte** *pl.* -n short story
die **Nachbarschaft** *pl.* -en neighborhood
die **Zeitschrift** *pl.* -en magazine
bereíten to prepare

sich langweilen to be bored
sich interessíeren für to be interested in
jammern to moan, to pester
verbríngen to spend (time)
sich vorstellen to imagine
furchtbar terrible, terribly
schmackhaft tasty

Strong Verbs. Principal Parts

lassen to let, to leave	er **lässt**	**ließ**	**hat gelassen**
sich waschen to wash oneself	er **wäscht sich**	**wusch sich**	**hat sich gewaschen**
sich an-ziehen to dress oneself	er **zieht sich an**	**zog sich an**	**hat sich angezogen**

Wichtige Redemittel

zu Bett gehen to go to bed
sich interessieren für to be interested in
Wir interessieren uns nicht für Sport. We are not interested in sports.
schmecken to taste (*takes no object*)
versuchen to try, to taste (*takes an object*)

Das Fleisch schmeckt gut. The meat tastes good. **Sie ließen es sich gut schmecken.** They enjoyed eating it (*lit.* They let it taste good to themselves).
Haben Sie diese Suppe versucht? Have you tasted this soup?

Grammar Notes and Practical Exercises

1. THE PAST PERFECT (= PLUSQUAMPERFEKT")

I had learned, you had learned, etc.
Ich hatte Deutsch **gelernt.**
Du hattest Deutsch **gelernt.**
Er, sie, es hatte Deutsch **gelernt.**
Wir hatten Deutsch **gelernt.**
Ihr hattet Deutsch **gelernt.**
Sie hatten Deutsch **gelernt.**

I had not seen him, you had not seen him, etc.
Ich hatte ihn nicht **gesehen.**
Du hattest ihn nicht **gesehen.**
Er, sie, es hatte ihn nicht **gesehen.**
Wir hatten ihn nicht **gesehen.**
Ihr hattet ihn nicht **gesehen.**
Sie hatten ihn nicht **gesehen.**

The past perfect of most German verbs is formed by the past tense of the auxiliary **haben (hatte)** + the past participle of the verb.

The past perfect is used for events which happened in the past before other events happened.

Ich hatte Deutsch gelernt, bevor ich die Reise nach Deutschland machte.

I had learned German before I took the trip to Germany.

Er war sehr müde, denn er hatte eine lange Reise gemacht.

He was very tired, for he had taken a long trip.

2. THE PAST PARTICIPLES OF VERBS ENDING IN *-ieren*

Ich hatte vier Jahre auf der Universität Jena studiert.

I had studied four years at the University of Jena.

Die Kinder haben sich gut amüsiert.

The children have enjoyed themselves greatly.

The past participle of verbs in **-ieren** does not have the prefix **ge-**.

Some **-ieren** verbs you have met are: **studíeren** to study; **reservíeren** to reserve; **sich rasíeren** to shave oneself; **interessíeren** to interest; **sich interessieren für** to be interested in; **sich amüsíeren** to enjoy oneself, to have a good time.

Exercise 128

Change these sentences from the **Perfekt** to the **Plusquamperfekt**.

Beispiel: 1. Sie hatten mir von einem typischen Arbeitstag erzählt.

1. Sie haben mir von einem typischen Arbeitstag erzählt.
2. Er hat sich schnell gewaschen und angezogen.
3. Unsere Familie hat schon gefrühstückt.
4. Der Vater hat die Sonntagszeitung gelesen.
5. Um sieben Uhr haben wir uns zum Abendessen gesetzt.
6. Die Mutter hat immer eine schmackhafte Mahlzeit bereitet.
7. Der Geschäftsmann hat die Geschäftsbeilage gelesen.
8. Die Kinder haben sich im Kino gut amüsiert.
9. Wir aber haben uns furchtbar gelangweilt.
10. Was haben die Kinder getan?[1]

NOTE 1. Principal parts of **tun** to do: **er tut, tat, hat getan.**

3. VERBS WITH AUXILIARY *sein*

In older English (Shakespeare, the Bible, etc.) the use of the auxiliary *to be* instead of *to have* with the perfect tenses of certain verbs was quite common. You still meet some remnants of this usage in such expressions as:

The time is come, meaning The time has come.
The people are gone away, meaning The people have gone away.

This usage of the auxiliary *to be* instead of *to have* is found in quite a large number of German verbs. The verbs **kommen** (to come) and **gehen** (to go) are typical.

Perfect and Past Perfect		*Perfect and Past Perfect*	
I have come, you have come, etc.		*I have gone, you have gone, etc.*	
I had come, you had come, etc.		*I had gone, you had gone, etc.*	
ich bin gekommen	wir sind gekommen	ich bin gegangen	wir sind gegangen
du bist gekommen	ihr seid gekommen	du bist gegangen	ihr seid gegangen
er ist gekommen	sie sind gekommen	er ist gegangen	sie sind gegangen
ich war gekommen	wir waren gekommen	ich war gegangen	wir waren gegangen
du warst gekommen	ihr wart gekommen	du warst gegangen	ihr wart gegangen
er war gekommen	sie waren gekommen	er war gegangen	sie waren gegangen

See also Chapter 26, Grammar Note 1.

4. THE PRINCIPAL PARTS OF A NUMBER OF SEIN-VERBS YOU HAVE ALREADY MET

Infinitive		*Present 3rd Sing.*	*Past*	*Present Perfect*
gehen	to go	**er geht**	**ging**	**ist gegangen**
weg-gehen	to go away	**er geht . . . weg**	**ging . . . weg**	**ist weggegangen**
kommen	to come	**er kommt**	**kam**	**ist gekommen**
an-kommen	to arrive	**er kommt . . . an**	**kam . . . an**	**ist angekommen**
fahren	to ride	**er fährt**	**fuhr**	**ist gefahren**
ab-fahren	to leave	**er fährt . . . ab**	**fuhr . . . ab**	**ist abgefahren**
laufen	to run	**er läuft**	**lief**	**ist gelaufen**
fallen	to fall	**er fällt**	**fiel**	**ist gefallen**
fliegen	to fly	**er fliegt**	**flog**	**ist geflogen**
auf-stehen	to get up	**er steht . . . auf**	**stand . . . auf**	**ist aufgestanden**

Note that the above are intransitive verbs indicating a change of place.

Two important intransitive verbs showing a *change of condition* are:

sterben	to die	**er stirbt**	**starb**	**ist gestorben**
wachsen (*văk-sen*)	to grow	**er wächst** (*vĕkst*)	**wuchs** (*vōoks*)	**ist gewachsen** (*ge-văk-sen*)

Der Patient ist gestern gestorben. The patient died yesterday.
Diese Pflanzen sind schnell gewachsen. These plants have grown quickly.

Exercise 129

Kurze Gespräche (Short Conversation). Practice aloud.

1. —**Wo kommen Sie her?** —**Ich komme aus Hamburg.** —**Sind Sie mit dem Flugzeug gekommen?** —**Nein, ich bin mit dem Schnellzug gekommen.**

1. —Where are you coming from? —I have come from Hamburg. —Did you come by plane? —No, I came on the express train.

2. —**Wo ist Wilhelm?** —**Er ist zur U-Bahnstation gegangen, um den Vater zu erwarten.** —**Ist sein Bruder Karl mitgegangen?** —**Ja, und seine Schwester Marie ist auch mitgegangen.**

2. —Where is William? —He has gone to the subway station to wait for his father. —Did his brother, Charles, go with him? —Yes, and his sister Marie also went with him.

3. —**Wo ist Frau Müller?** —**Sie ist in die Stadt gefahren, um Einkäufe zu machen.** —**Ist sie noch nicht zurückgekommen?** —**Nein, noch nicht.**

3. —Where is Mrs. Müller? —She has gone to the city to shop. —Hasn't she come back yet? —No, not yet.

Exercise 130

Complete the following sentences in the perfect tense with the correct form of the auxiliary **sein** or **haben** as required.

Beispiele: 1. Wir sind früh aufgestanden. 2. Wir haben um acht Uhr gefrühstückt.

1. Wir _____ früh aufgestanden.
2. Wir _____ um acht Uhr gefrühstückt.
3. Die Kinder _____ alle ins Kino gegangen.
4. _____ Sie schon die Fahrkarten gekauft?
5. Welche Geschichte _____ Sie gelesen?
6. Um wieviel Uhr _____ der Vater nach Hause gekommen?
7. _____ der Zug schon angekommen?
8. Die Familie _____ sich zum Frühstück gesetzt.
9. Alle _____ im Auto in die Stadt gefahren.
10. _____ sich die Kinder gut amüsiert?

Exercise 131

Complete the sentences from Exercise 130 in the past perfect tense with the correct form of the auxiliaries **sein** or **haben** as required.

Beispiele: 1. Wir waren früh aufgestanden. 2. Wir hatten um acht Uhr gefrühstückt.

Exercise 132

Complete the following sentences using always the **Plusquamperfekt**.

Beispiel 1. Ich habe den Zug versäumt, weil ich die Fahrkarte vergessen hatte.

1. Ich habe den Zug versäumt, weil _____ .

2. Ich konnte nicht zu deiner Party kommen, weil _____ .

3. Ich war sehr müde, weil _____ .

4. Ich bin um 7 Uhr aufgestanden, weil _____ .

5. Ich ging nicht ins Restaurant, weil _____ .

6. Ich habe viel eingekauft, weil _____ .

7. Ich konnte nicht schnell laufen, weil _____ .

8. Ich hatte große Angst, weil _____ .

Exercise 133

Fragen

Lesen Sie noch einmal den Text: **Wie Herr Clark gewöhnlich den Sonntag verbringt**, und dann beantworten Sie folgende Fragen!

1. Um wie viel Uhr ist Herr Clark am Sonntag aufgestanden?
2. Waren seine Frau und Kinder vor ihm aufgestanden?
3. Hatten sie schon gefrühstückt?
4. Um wie viel Uhr haben alle sich zum Frühstück gesetzt?
5. Was hat Herr Clark nach dem Frühstück getan?
6. Was taten die jüngeren Kinder, als er die Zeitung las?
7. Was taten die älteren?
8. Wer hatte eine schmackhafte Mahlzeit bereitet?
9. Wohin wollten die Kinder nach dem Mittagessen gehen?
10. Was mussten also die Eltern tun?
11. Haben die Eltern sich im Kino gelangweilt oder amüsiert?
12. Wohin sind sie nach dem Kino gegangen?
13. Wem hat Herr Clark nach dem Abendessen geschrieben?
14. Was hat er gelesen?
15. Um wie viel Uhr ist er zu Bett gegangen?

Herr Müller erzählt von sich selbst

1. Herr Clark, vor einigen Tagen haben Sie mir erzählt, wie Sie den Sonntag verbringen und auch anderes mehr über sich selbst und Ihre familie. Heute möchte ich Ihnen etwas von mir selbst erzählen. Mit anderen Worten, ich bin selbst das Thema des Gesprächs.

2. Das ist sicherlich sehr interessant. Darf ich Ihnen einige Fragen stellen?

3. Jawohl, es freut mich immer, Ihre Fragen zu beantworten. Wie Sie schon wissen, bin ich in Deutschland geboren und bin jetzt Bürger der Vereinigten Staaten. Ich bin verheiratet und habe zwei Kinder.

4. Was ist Ihr Beruf?

5. Ich bin Lehrer und unterrichte an einer Sekundarschule, die ungefähr zehn Meilen von hier entfernt ist. Ich lehre Deutsch und Französisch.

6. Ach! Sie können Französisch!

7. Jawohl, ich spreche sehr gut Französisch. Ich habe in Deutschland auf dem Gymnasium Französisch und Englisch gelernt und dann auch auf der Universität studiert. Später habe ich vier Jahre lang in Paris gelebt.

8. Wann sind Sie denn in Paris gewesen?

9. Ich bin vom Jahre 1978 bis zum Jahre 1983 dort gewesen. Ich war damals ein junger Mann.

10. Darf ich fragen, was Sie in Paris getan haben?

Mr. Müller Tells about Himself

1. Mr. Clark, a few days ago you told me how you spend Sunday and also other things about yourself and your family. Today I should like to tell you something about myself. In other words, I myself am the topic of the conversation.

2. That surely is very interesting. May I ask you questions?

3. Of course, I am always glad to answer your questions. As you already know, I was born in Germany and am now a citizen of the United States. I am married and have two children.

4. What is your profession?

5. I am a teacher and teach in a secondary school which is about ten miles distant from here. I teach German and French.

6. Oh! You know French!

7. Yes, I speak French very well. In Germany I studied French and also English in high school and the same also at the university. Later I lived in Paris for four years.

8. When were you in Paris?

9. I was there from the year 1978 to the year 1983. I was then a young man.

10. May I ask what you did in Paris?

11. Ich habe als Zeitungskorrespondent in der Redaktion einer französischen Zeitung gearbeitet.

11. I worked as a newspaper correspondent in the editorial office of a French newspaper.

12. Und wann sind Sie nach Amerika gekommen?

12. And when did you come to America?

13. Ich bin im Jahre 1983 hergekommen. Da ich sowohl Englisch als auch Deutsch und Französisch konnte, ist es mir bald gelungen, eine Stelle als Lehrer für Deutsch und für Französisch zu bekommen, und zwar an der Sekundarschule, an der ich eben jetzt unterrichte.

13. I came here in 1983. Since I knew English as well as German and French, I soon succeeded in obtaining a position as teacher of German and French, and, as a matter of fact, in the secondary school in which I am now teaching.

14. Haben Sie hier geheiratet?

14. Did you marry here?

15. Ganz richtig. Ich habe eine Amerikanerin geheiratet, und wir haben, wie Sie wissen, zwei Kinder.

15. Quite right. I married an American, and as you know we have two children.

16. Ich danke Ihnen, Herr Müller. Hoffentlich habe ich Sie mit meinen Fragen nicht zu sehr belästigt.

16. I thank you, Mr. Müller. I hope I haven't annoyed you too much with my questions.

17. Im Gegenteil. Es ist mir ein Vergnügen gewesen.

17. On the contrary; it was a pleasure for me.

Wortschatz

der Bürger *pl.* - citizen

das Gymnásium (*gĭm-nah-zyoom*)[1] *pl.* -ien German secondary school, high school

die Stelle *pl.* -n position, job

das Wort *pl.* -e or ¨-er[2] word

die Vereínigten Stáaten (*fĕr-ei-nĭk-ten shtah-ten*) the United States

belästigen to annoy

ein-wandern to immigrate

heiraten to marry (someone)

leben to live

unterríchten to teach

entférnt distant

sicherlich surely

sowóhl als auch as well as

selber, selbst self

NOTES: 1. The **g** in **Gymnasium** is hard. **2.** The plural **Worte** is used for words joined to make sense in phrases, expressions, sentences. **Wörter** are words unconnected in sense, as in vocabularies and dictionaries (**Wörterbücher**).

Wichtige Redemittel

jemandem (*dat.*) **Fragen stellen** to ask (put) someone questions. **Der Lehrer stellt den Schülern Fragen** The teacher asks the pupils questions.

Ich kann Deutsch (Französisch, Englisch, usw.). I know German (French, English, etc.). This is short for **Ich kann Deutsch, usw., sprechen, lesen, schreiben.**

Ich bin am 31. Juni 1975 geboren. I was born June 31, 1975.

selber, selbst self. **Ich selber (selbst)** I myself; **der Lehrer selber** the teacher himself; **Sie erzählt von sich selber.** She tells about herself. **Erzählen Sie von sich selber!** Tell about yourself.

Grammar Notes and Practical Exercises

1. SOME VERY SPECIAL VERBS WITH THE AUXILIARY *sein*

sein	to be	er ist	war	ist gewesen
werden	to become, to get	er wird	wurde	ist geworden
bleiben	to remain, to stay	er bleibt	blieb	ist geblieben
gelingen	to succeed	es gelingt	gelang	ist gelungen
geschehen	to happen	es geschieht	geschah	ist geschehen

a. Ich bin vor zwei Jahren in Paris gewesen.	I was in Paris two years ago.
b. Heute ist es sehr kalt geworden.	Today it has become very cold.
c. Wegen des schlechten Wetters sind wir alle zu Hause geblieben.	Because of the bad weather, we all stayed at home.
d. Es ist mir gelungen, nach Amerika auszuwandern.	I succeeded in emigrating to America. (*Lit.* It succeeded to me to emigrate.)

Note that **gelingen** is used impersonally and is followed by a dative object. **Es gelingt mir** = I succeed; **es gelingt Ihnen** = you succeed; **es gelingt uns** = we succeed; **es gelingt meinem Freund** = my friend succeeds, etc.

e. Was ist geschehen? Ein Unglück ist geschehen.	What has happened? A misfortune has happened.

Exercise 134

Kurze Gespräche. Practice aloud.

—Was ist geschehen? —Der kleine Hans ist gefallen und hat sich den Arm verletzt. —Haben Sie den Doktor gerufen? —Ja, natürlich. Er ist schon hier gewesen. Er sagt, es ist nichts Schlimmes.

—What has happened? —Little Hans fell and injured his arm. —Have you called the doctor? —Of course. He has already been here. He says it is nothing serious.

—Wo bist du den ganzen Nachmittag gewesen? —Ich war im Park. —Was hast du dort gemacht? —Ich habe Tennis gespielt.

—Where have you been all afternoon? —I was in the park. —What were you doing there? —I was playing tennis.

—Sie sehen müde aus. Wann sind Sie zu Bett gegangen? —Um halb zwei. —Warum sind Sie so lange aufgeblieben? —Ich musste mich auf eine Prüfung vorbereiten.

—You look tired. When did you go to bed? —At half past one. —Why did you stay up so long? —I had to prepare for an examination.

2. INDIRECT QUESTIONS WITH *wie, wo, wann, wer, was, warum*

Direct Question	*Indirect Question*
Wie verbringen Sie gewöhnlich den Sonntag?	Sagen Sie mir, bitte, wie Sie den Sonntag *verbringen.*
Warum wohnen Sie in diesem kleinen Vorort?	Darf ich fragen, warum Sie in diesem kleinen Vorort *wohnen?*
Wann kommt der Zug von Hamburg an?	Wissen Sie, wann der Zug von Hamburg *ankommt?*
Wo unterrichten Sie jetzt?	Ich möchte fragen, wo Sie jetzt *unterrichten.*
Wer war heute morgen hier?	Weißt du, wer heute morgen *hier war?*
Was taten sie den ganzen Tag?	Er fragt, was sie den ganzen Tag *taten?*

Interrogative words (**wie, wo, was,** etc.) may introduce direct or indirect questions. Indirect questions are subordinate clauses, and, as in all subordinate clauses, the verb stands last.

Exercise 135

Transform the direct questions into indirect ones. Start with: "**Sagen Sie mir bitte, . . .**"

Beispiel: 1. Sagen Sie mir bitte, wo Sie gewesen sind.

1. Wo sind Sie gewesen?
2. Warum sind Sie gestern so spät gekommen?
3. Wieso haben Sie heute keinen Appetit?
4. Was möchten Sie essen?
5. Wie gefällt Ihnen dieses Bild?
6. Wer hat mit Ihnen gesprochen?
7. Wann reisen Sie morgen ab?
8. Wo haben Sie Ihre Frau getroffen?

3. THE PRESENT AND PAST PERFECT TENSES IN SUBORDINATE CLAUSES

In a subordinate clause the verb, as you know, must stand last. If the verb is in the present perfect or past perfect, the *auxiliary part of the verb* preceded by the past participle must stand last.

Simple Sentence

Herr Müller hat vier Jahre in Paris gelebt.
Er ist im Jahre 1983 nach Amerika gekommen.
Haben Sie eine Amerikanerin geheiratet?
Der Zug ist um 18.30 in München angekommen.

Subordinate Clause

Wir wissen schon, dass Herr Müller vier Jahre in Paris *gelebt hat.*

Er sagt, dass er im Jahre 1983 nach Amerika *gekommen ist.*

Darf ich fragen, ob (whether) Sie eine Amerikanerin *geheiratet haben.*

Herr M. erreichte den Bahnhof, bevor der Zug in München *angekommen ist.*

Exercise 136

Join each pair of sentences by means of the subordinate conjunction indicated. Remember: In subordinate clauses the verb stands last. If the tense of the verb has two parts the auxiliary must stand last.

Beispiel: 1. Herr Müller konnte eine Stelle als Lehrer bekommen, weil er Englisch gelernt hatte.

1. Herr Müller konnte eine Stelle als Lehrer bekommen. (weil) Er hatte Englisch gelernt.
2. Darf ich fragen? (warum) Sie haben Frankreich verlassen.
3. Ist es wahr? (dass) Sie sind vier Jahre in Paris gewesen.
4. Ich möchte gern wissen. (wie) Sie verbringen den Sonntag.
5. Es freut mich. (dass) Sie machen große Fortschritte im Studium der deutschen Sprache.
6. Wir mussten ins Kino gehen. (weil) Die Kinder wollten gehen.
7. Wir haben uns gelangweilt. (weil) Der Film war für uns nicht interessant.
8. Was taten die Kinder? (während) Die Mutter bereitete die Mahlzeit?
9. Was tat Herr Clark? (nachdem)[1] Er hatte die Zeitung gelesen.
10. Ich kann Ihnen dafür danken. (dass) Ich habe große Fortschritte im Deutschen gemacht.

NOTE: 1. nachdem *(subordinate conjunction)* after.

Exercise 137

Fragen

Lesen Sie noch einmal den deutschen Text: **Herr Müller erzählt von sich selbst,** und dann beantworten Sie diese Fragen!

1. Wer hat erzählt, wie er den Sonntag verbringt?
2. Wer wollte heute etwas von sich selbst sagen?
3. Wo ist Herr Müller geboren?
4. Ist er verheiratet oder ledig (single)?
5. In welcher Schule unterrichtet er?
6. Was lehrt er?
7. Wo hat Herr Müller Französisch und Englisch gelernt?
8. Wie lange hat er in Frankreich gelebt?
9. Wo hat er als Zeitungskorrespondent gearbeitet?
10. In welchem Jahre kam er in die Vereinigten Staaten?
11. Hat er hier eine Stelle an einer Sekundarschule oder an einer Universität bekommen?
12. Hat er eine amerikanische oder eine französische Frau geheiratet?

HERR CLARK SCHREIBT EINEN BRIEF AN SEINEN GESCHÄFTSPARTNER IN MÜNCHEN

1. Herr Clark denkt schon an seine Reise nach Deutschland. Da er die Vergnügungsreise mit einer Geschäftsreise verbinden will, schreibt er einen Brief an seinen Geschäftspartner in München.

2. Herr Clark hat natürlich auf Deutsch geschrieben, da er in Zukunft mit Herrn Schiller auf Deutsch kommunizieren will.

3. Dies ist also eine gute Gelegenheit für Herrn Clark, Deutsch zu üben.

4. Hier ist also der Brief, den Herr Clark geschrieben hat:

New York, den 4. Mai 2005

Sehr geehrter Herr Schiller!

Ich freue mich, Sie zu benachrichtigen, dass ich beabsichtige, eine Reise nach Deutschland zu machen. Ich werde New York am 31. Mai um 7 Uhr abends per Flugzeug verlassen und werde am 1. Juni um 10.10 morgens am Münchener Flughafen ankommen.

Ich beabsichtige, zwei Monate in Deutschland zu verbringen. Das wird eine Vergnügungsreise und zugleich eine Geschäftsreise sein. Ich werde zwei oder drei Wochen in München bleiben und von dort aus will ich einige Ausflüge machen, um die interessantesten Plätze in der Umgebung von München zu besichtigen.

Ich werde auch andere Teile Deutschlands besuchen, vielleicht auch Österreich und die Schweiz.

Während meines Aufenthaltes in München möchte ich Sie gerne persönlich kennen lernen. Ich hoffe, dass wir einen passenden Termin für ein Treffen finden werden. Ich weiß, dass Sie sehr beschäftigt sind, und dass

1. Mr. Clark is already thinking of his trip to Germany. As he wants to combine the pleasure trip with a business trip, he is writing a letter to his business partner in Munich.

2. Mr. Clark has written in German, because he wants to communicate in the future with Mr. Schiller in German.

3. Thus this is a good opportunity for Mr. Clark to practice his German.

4. Here is the letter which Mr. Clark has written:

New York, May 4, 2005

Dear Mr. Schiller:

I am glad to inform you that I intend to take a trip to Germany. I shall leave New York by plane at 7 p.m. on the 31st of May, and shall arrive at the Munich airport at 10:10 a.m. on June 1st.

I intend to spend two months in Germany. This will be a pleasure trip as well as a business trip. I shall stay two or three weeks in Munich, and from there I will make various excursions to see the most interesting places in the vicinity of Munich.

I shall also visit other parts of Germany, and perhaps Austria and Switzerland.

During my stay in Munich I shall be pleased to get personally acquainted with you. I hope that we will find a suitable date for a meeting. I know that you are very busy and that you travel much. Therefore I am writing you in advance in

Sie viel umherreisen. Deshalb schreibe ich Ihnen schon jetzt in der Hoffnung, dass ein Treffen mit Ihnen möglich sein wird. Ich bitte Sie mich zu benachrichtigen, ob ich das Vergnügen haben werde, Sie in München zu treffen.

Seit sechs Monaten studiere ich Deutsch. Das wird Sie vielleicht überraschen. Ich hoffe, dass es mir möglich sein wird, mich mit Ihnen in Ihrer schönen Sprache zu unterhalten.

In Erwartung Ihrer Antwort verbleibe ich mit besten Grüßen,

Ihr
Robert Clark

the hope that a meeting with you will be possible. Please let me know whether I shall have the pleasure of meeting you in Munich.

I have been studying German for six months. This will perhaps surprise you. I hope that it will be possible for me to converse with you in your beautiful language.

Awaiting your answer, I remain with kind regards.

Yours truly,
Robert Clark

5. Herr Clark wird diesen Brief gleich am nächsten Tag zur Post bringen.
6. Der Brief wird etwa vier Tage bis nach München brauchen. Dann wird Herr Schiller den Brief lesen und sich über den Besuch von Herrn Clark freuen.
7. Herr Schiller wird auch sofort einen Antwortbrief schreiben. Darin wird er schreiben, wann er Herrn Clark in München treffen kann.

5. Mr. Clark will go and bring this letter to the post office on the following day.
6. The letter will take about four days to reach Munich. Then Mr. Schiller will read the letter and be pleased about Mr. Clark's visit.
7. Mr. Schiller will also write a reply letter. In this letter he will write when he can meet Mr. Clark in Munich.

Wortschatz

der Aufenthalt *pl.* -e stay, sojourn
die Begégnung *pl.* -en meeting
die Gelegenheit *pl.* -en opportunity
die Hoffnung *pl.* -en hope
begégnen (+ *dat. object*) to meet
benáchrichtigen to inform

besíchtigen to view, to see
erklären to state, to explain
umher-reisen to travel about
verbinden to combine
beschäftigt busy
einzig single

Strong Verbs

bei-tragen	to contribute	er trägt . . . bei	trug . . . bei	hat beigetragen
halten	to hold	er hält	hielt	hat gehalten
erhalten	to receive	er erhält	erhielt	hat erhalten
gestehen	to confess	er gesteht	gestand	hat gestanden
vor-lesen	to read to, read aloud	er liest . . . vor	las . . . vor	hat vorgelesen

Wichtige Redemittel

einen Ausflug machen to make an excursion.

Ich werde Ausflüge ins Gebirge machen. I'll make excursions (take trips) into the mountains.

Es wird mir lieb sein. I shall enjoy it (*lit.* It will be pleasing to me).

kennen lernen to become acquainted with, to know, to get to know

Es freut mich, Sie kennen zu lernen. I'm pleased to meet you.

sich auf etwas freuen to look forward to something **Ich freue mich auf meine kommende Reise.** I am looking forward to my coming trip.

Formal Letters

Date: The date of all letters (formal and informal) is written in the accusative case.

New York, den 25. Mai 2005   **München, den 11. Juni 2004**

Formal letters usually begin:

Sehr geehrter Herr Schiller!   **Sehr geehrter Herr Professor!**   (**geehrt** = honored)
Sehr geehrte Frau Schiller!   **Sehr geehrte Frau Professor!**

Formal letters end:

Hochachtungsvoll, Karl Engel   Sincerely yours, Karl Engel
Mit besten Grüßen, Maria Engel   Sincerely yours, Maria Engel

Grammar Notes and Practical Exercises

1. THE FUTURE TENSE ("DAS FUTUR")

I shall go, you will go, he, she, it will go, etc.

Ich werde morgen **gehen.**   **Wir werden** morgen **gehen.**
Du wirst morgen **gehen.**   **Ihr werdet** morgen **gehen.**
Er, sie, es wird morgen **gehen.**   **Sie (Sie) werden** morgen **gehen.**

The future tense of a verb is formed by the auxiliary **werden** (shall, will) + the infinitive of the verb. The infinitive must stand at the end of a simple sentence or main clause.

As you have seen (Chapter 22, Grammar Note 1), **werden** may be used as a verb by itself, meaning *to become, to get.*

2. THE PRESENT TENSE WITH FUTURE MEANING

Ich gehe morgen ins Theater.	I am going to the theater tomorrow.
Er kommt übermorgen.	He will come the day after tomorrow.
Nächsten Frühling macht er eine Reise nach Deutschland.	Next spring he will take a trip to Germany.

The present tense is often used in German with future meaning, particularly when the verb is modified by some expression of future time such as: **morgen** tomorrow; **übermorgen** the day after tomorrow; **morgen früh** tomorrow morning; **heute Abend** this evening; **morgen Abend** tomorrow evening; **heute Nachmittag** this afternoon; **bald** soon; **später** later; **nächstes Jahr** next year; **nächste Woche** next week; **nächsten Monat** next month, etc.

Exercise 138

Complete these sentences with the correct form of the auxiliary **werden**.

Beispiel: 1. Herr Clark **wird** einen Brief vorlesen.

1. **Herr Clark _____ einen Brief vorlesen.**
2. **Ich _____ eine Reise nach Deutschland machen.**
3. **Wann _____ Sie New York verlassen?**
4. **Wir _____ am 1. Juni in München ankommen.**
5. **_____ Sie viel Zeit in Deutschland verbringen?**
6. **Wie lange _____ er in München bleiben?**
7. **Ein Freund fragt Herrn Clark „_____ du einige Ausflüge von München machen?"**
8. **Ich _____ meinem Vertreter im Voraus schreiben.**
9. **Wer _____ uns in München begegnen?**
10. **Hoffentlich _____ diese Begegnung möglich sein.**

Exercise 139

Change these sentences to the future.

Beispiel: 1. Die Jungen werden heute einen Ausflug machen.

1. **Die Jungen machen heute einen Ausflug.**
2. **Ich bleibe vier Wochen in München.**
3. **Er besucht andere Teile von Deutschland.**
4. **Du gehst nicht mit.**
5. **Wir sind sehr beschäftigt.**
6. **Ich bin sehr dankbar.**
7. **Schreiben Sie jeden Tag einen Brief?**
8. **Ich komme am 1. Juni in München an.**
9. **Sie ist sehr behilflich.**
10. **Er heiratet eine Amerikanerin.**

3. THE FUTURE TENSE IN SUBORDINATE CLAUSES

Future in Simple Sentences	*Future in Subordinate Clauses*
Er **wird** einen Brief **vorlesen**.	Ich weiß, dass er einen Brief **vorlesen wird**.
Die Kinder **werden** heute Abend nicht ins Kino **gehen**.	Der Vater sagt, dass die Kinder heute Abend nicht ins Kino **gehen werden**.

In a subordinate clause the auxiliary verb of the future tense must stand last, after the infinitive.

Exercise 140

Change each simple sentence in parentheses into a subordinate clause after the given conjunction.

Beispiel: 1. Der Geschäftsmann schreibt, dass er nach München kommen wird.

1. **Der Geschäftsmann schreibt, dass (er wird nach München kommen).**
2. **Der Lehrer fragt mich, ob (ich werde den Brief vorlesen).**
3. **Die Kinder sagen, dass (sie werden ihre Freunde besuchen).**
4. **Ich weiss nicht, ob (das Wetter wird morgen schön sein).**
5. **Ich glaube nicht, dass (unsere Freunde werden heute Abend kommen).**
6. **Ich möchte fragen, wo (Sie werden unterrichten).**
7. **Ich glaube, dass (niemand wird heute kommen).**
8. **Wir wissen, dass (du wirst eine schmackhafte Mahlzeit bereiten).**

Exercise 141

Talking about the weekend: **Es ist Wochenende. Was werden Sie, Ihre Familie und Ihre Freunde machen?**

Beispiel 1. Ich werde ins Kino gehen.

Ich		ins Kino gehen.
Mein Vater		Sport machen.
Meine Schwester		einkaufen gehen.
Mein Onkel		eine Fahrradtour machen.
Peter		in ein Museum gehen.
Herr Müller	werden	nach München fahren.
Herr Schiller		fernsehen.
Du		Baseball spielen.
Angelika		einen Freund besuchen.
Wir		ein Glas Bier trinken.
Sie		das Auto waschen.
. . .		. . .

Weak (Regular) Verbs. No Vowel Changes

Pattern of Principal Parts

Infinitive	*Present*	*Past*	*Present Perfect*
lernen	er lernt	lernte	hat gelernt
arbeiten	er arbeitet	arbeitete	hat gearbeitet

1. frühstücken	1. to breakfast
2. heiraten	2. to marry
3. leben	3. to live
4. plagen	4. to plague
5. bereiten[1]	5. to prepare
6. belästigen	6. to annoy
7. benachrichtigen	7. to inform
8. begegnen[2]	8. to meet
9. langweilen	9. to bore
10. interessieren[3]	10. to interest
11. umher-reisen	11. to travel around
12. ein-wandern	12. to immigrate

NOTES: 1. Verbs with inseparable prefixes **(be-, emp-, ent-, er-, ge-, ver-, zer-)** do not add **ge-** in the past participle: **Sie hat . . . bereitet. 2. begegnen** takes a dative object: **Er begegnete seinem Freund. 3. sich interessieren für** to be interested in: **Ich habe mich für den Sport interessiert.** Verbs in **-ieren** do not add the prefix **ge-** in the past participle.

Strong (Irregular) Verbs. Vowel Changes

	Infinitive	*Present*	*Past*	*Present Perfect*
1. an-fangen	to begin	er fängt an	fing an	hat angefangen
2. an-geben	to give, state	er gibt an	gab an	hat angegeben
3. vor-lesen	to read to	er liest vor	las vor	hat vorgelesen
4. vor-ziehen	to prefer	er zieht vor	zog vor	hat vorgezogen
5. statt-finden	to take place	es findet statt	fand statt	hat stattgefunden
6. gestehen	to confess	er gesteht	gestand	hat gestanden
7. erhalten	to receive	er erhält	erhielt	hat erhalten
8. verstehen	to understand	er versteht	verstand	hat verstanden
9. vergessen	to forget	er vergisst	vergaß	hat vergessen

Redemittel

1. **ohne Zweifel** (*tsvei-fel*) without doubt
2. **im Gegenteil** on the contrary
3. **mit Vergnügen** with pleasure
4. **fertig** finished, done, ready
5. **mit den Fragen fertig werden** to get finished with the questions
6. **Fragen beantworten** or **auf Fragen antworten** to answer questions
7. **einen Ausflug machen** to make an excursion
8. **Deutsch können** to know German. **Ich kann Deutsch (sprechen, lesen, schreiben).** I know German.
9. **jemanden kennen lernen** to get to know (become acquainted with) somebody. **Ich habe ihn kennen gelernt.** I have made his acquaintance.

Exercise 142

Complete the German translation of each English sentence.

1. I want to get to know my business partner.
2. I will ask you questions.
3. You will answer the questions.
4. He has answered all the questions.
5. She knows German and French.

6. Who will make an excursion to the lake?
7. Did your questions annoy him?
8. On the contrary. They pleased him.
9. The examination is over. You have made no mistakes.
10. We have read the letter with pleasure.

1. Ich will meinen Geschäftspartner _____ .
2. Ich werde Ihnen Fragen _____ .
3. Sie werden auf die Fragen _____ .
4. Er hat alle Fragen _____ .
5. Sie _____ Deutsch und Französisch.
6. Wer wird _____ zum See machen?
7. Haben Ihre Fragen ihn _____ ?
8. _____ . Sie haben ihm _____ .
9. Das Examen ist _____ . Sie haben keine Fehler gemacht.
10. Wir haben den Brief _____ gelesen.

Grammar Review and Exercises

1. FIVE TENSES: PRESENT, PAST, PRESENT PERFECT, PAST PERFECT, FUTURE (PRÄSENS, PRÄTERITUM, PERFEKT, PLUSQUAMPERFEKT, FUTUR)

Präsens, *Präterium*	*Perfekt,* *Plusquamperfekt*	*Futur*
Ich lerne	haben-verb: **lernen**	**Ich werde lernen**
Ich lernte	**Ich habe gelernt**	
	Ich hatte gelernt	
Er geht schnell	sein-verb: **gehen**	**er wird gehen**
Er ging schnell	**Er ist gegangen**	
	Er war gegangen	

Intransitive verbs showing a change of place or condition take the auxiliary **sein** instead of **haben** in the compound tenses.

Exercise 143

Change these sentences from the **Präteritum** to the **Perfekt**.

Beispiel: 1. Frau Clark ist zum Markt gegangen.

1. Frau Clark ging zum Markt.
2. Dort machte sie viele Einkäufe.
3. Sie bezahlte für die Einkäufe an der Kasse.
4. Sie brachte alles in ihr Auto.
5. Da vermisste[1] sie ihre Geldtasche.
6. Sie lief zu der Kasse zurück.
7. Gott sei Dank[2] fand sie ihre Geldtasche an der Kasse.
8. Der Kassier reichte ihr die Geldtasche.
9. Frau Clark dankte dem Kassier.
10. Sie stieg ins Auto ein.

NOTES: 1. vermissen to miss. **2.** Thank heavens!

2. SUBORDINATE WORD ORDER OF VERBS IN THE PRESENT PERFECT, PAST PERFECT AND FUTURE

In subordinate word order the auxiliary must stand last, directly after the past participle or the infinitive.

Ich weiß, dass er einen neuen, braunen Anzug **gekauft hat.**

Ich weiß, dass er um drei Uhr nach Hause **gegangen ist.**

Ich weiß, dass er morgen dieses Auto **kaufen wird.**

3. SUMMARY OF SUBORDINATING CONJUNCTIONS

A subordinate clause is introduced by a relative pronoun or by a subordinating conjunction. Here are the most common subordinating conjunctions, most of which you already know:

dass that; **weil** because; **da** since (because); **wenn** when, if; **als** when (with past tenses); **bevor, ehe** before; **bis** until; **während, indem** while; **nachdem** after; **sobald** as soon as; **ob** whether; **obwohl** (*ohp-vohl*) although; and also interrogative words used as subordinate conjunctions in indirect questions: **wer, was, wie, wo, wann, warum.**

Exercise 144

Today everything was different! Form sentences using the **Perfekt**.

Beispiel 1. Jeden Tag gehe ich zu Fuß, aber heute bin ich mit dem Auto gefahren.

1. Jeden Tag gehe ich zu Fuß, aber heute _____ (mit dem Auto fahren)

2. Jeden Tag esse ich Gemüse, aber heute _____ (Fleisch essen)
3. Jeden Tag telefoniere ich mit ihr, aber heute _____ (Brief schreiben)
4. Jeden Tag arbeite ich bis 17 Uhr, aber heute _____ (nur bis 15 Uhr arbeiten)
5. Jeden Tag fährt er mit der U-Bahn, aber heute _____ (mit dem Auto fahren)
6. Jeden Tag lesen Sie die Zeitung, aber heute _____ (ein Buch lesen)
7. Jeden Tag lernt er Deutsch, aber heute _____ (eine Pause machen)
8. Jeden Tag geht ihr zur Arbeit, aber heute _____ (krank sein)

VIER DIALOGE

1. —Wo warst du gestern Abend? —Ich war im Kino. —Was hast du dir angesehen? —Ich sah einen deutschen Film. —Hat der Film dir gefallen? —Sehr. Er war wirklich ausgezeichnet. —War es ein Film mit englischen Untertiteln? —Ja, aber ich habe beinahe alles verstanden, ohne die englischen Untertitel zu lesen.

2. —Herr Braun ist krank. —Das tut mir sehr leid. Wer hat es Ihnen gesagt? —Seine Frau hat mich angerufen. —Wann hat sie angerufen? —Heute früh.

3. Wann sind Sie gestern Abend zu Bett gegangen? —Ich bin erst um 2 Uhr morgens zu Bett gegangen. —Warum denn so spät? —Ich habe heute eine Prüfung in Mathematik und musste mich darauf vorbereiten.

4. —Ich habe heute einen Brief erhalten. —Woher? Von wem? —Von meinem Bruder in Afrika. —Was macht er dort? —Er ist Anthropológe (ăn-troh-poh-lo-ge). Setzen Sie sich zu mir. Ich werde Ihnen den Brief vorlesen.

1. —Where were you last night? —I was at the movies. —What did you see? —I saw a German film. —Did you like the film? —Very much. It was really splendid. —Was it a film with English subtitles? —Yes, but I understood nearly everything without reading the English subtitles.

2. —Mr. Braun is sick. —I am very sorry. Who told you about it? —His wife called me on the phone. —When did she phone? —This morning.

3. —When did you go to bed last night? —I did not go to bed until 2 o'clock in the morning. —But why so late? —I'm taking an examination in mathematics today and had to prepare for it.

4. —I have received a letter today. —From where? From whom? —From my brother in Africa. —What is he doing there? —He is an anthropologist. Sit down beside me. I'll read the letter to you.

FRAU CLARK HAT GEBURTSTAG

Es war der 22. März, der Geburtstag der Frau Clark. An diesem Tag wurde sie fünfunddreißig Jahre alt. Um den Geburtstag zu feiern,[1] ging die Familie Clark zum Essen in ein deutsches Restaurant in New York.

Als sie das Restaurant betraten, sahen sie auf dem Tisch, der für Herrn und Frau Clark gedeckt[2] war, einen schönen Korb[3] voll weißer Rosen. Natürlich war Frau Clark überrascht. Sie dankte ihrem lieben Mann, und dann setzte sich die Familie zum Tisch. Eine junge Kellnerin[4] reichte ihnen die Speisekarte.[5] Alle bestellten[6] ihre Lieblingsgerichte.[7] Am Ende der Mahlzeit holten alle vier Kinder kleine Päckchen[8] für ihre Mutter hervor. In den Päckchen waren Geburtstagsgeschenke.[9] Alle riefen „Alles Gute zum Geburtstag,"[10] und jedes Kind reichte der Mutter sein Geschenk. Marie schenkte ihr ein seidenes Taschentuch, Karl ein Paar Handschuhe, Wilhelm ein wollenes Halstuch und die kleine Anna eine selbst gemalte Zeichnung.

Was für ein schöner Tag, nicht nur für die Mutter sondern auch[11] für Papa und die Kinder.

Zur Übung in Mathematik berechnete Karl die Ausgaben[12] für diesen Tag.

Das Essen für Frau Clark	$19,50
Trinkgeld	3,00
<u>Blumen</u>	<u>12,50</u>
Summe	$35,00

„Der reinste Zufall,"[13] sagte Herr Clark. „Fünfunddreißig Dollar, fünfunddreißig Jahre."

NOTES: 1. to celebrate. **2. Tisch decken** to set a table. **3. der Korb** basket. **4. die Kellnerin** waitress. **5. die Speisekarte** menu. **6.** ordered. **7.** favorite dishes. **8. das Päckchen** package. **9. das Geburtstagsgeschenk** birthday gift. **10.** Happy Birthday. **11. nicht nur . . . sondern auch** not only . . . but also. **12. die Ausgaben** (*pl.*) expenses. **13.** the purest coincidence.

Exercise 145

Lesestück 2

EIN TOLLER[1] FILM IM KINO

Eines Abends gingen Herr und Frau Clark ins Kino. Die Filme aus Hollywood gefielen ihnen nicht, denn an diesem Abend gab es nur Komödien.

Aber an diesem Abend gab es eine außergewöhnliche[2] Vorstellung in einem Kino ganz in der Nähe ihrer Wohnung. Der Film war ein Dokumentarbericht[3] über Deutschland und zwar in deutscher Sprache.

Herr und Frau Clark kamen um 8.30 Uhr (halb neun Uhr) im Kino an. Fast alle Plätze waren schon besetzt. Also mussten sie in der dritten Reihe sitzen. Das gefiel Frau Clark nicht, denn die Bewegungen[4] auf der Leinwand[5] taten ihren Augen weh.[6] Glücklicherweise gelang es ihnen, nach einer Viertelstunde ihre Plätze zu tauschen,[7] und danach saßen sie in der dreizehnten Reihe.

Der Familie Clark gefiel dieser Film außerordentlich.[8] Herr Clark hatte den größten Genuss[9] daran.

Als sie das Kino verließen, sagte Herr Clark zu seiner Frau: „Weißt du, Helene, ich glaube, ich werde mich in Deutschland gut zurecht finden.[10] Ich habe beinahe alles verstanden, was die Schauspieler und Schauspielerinnen auf Deutsch sagten."

NOTES: 1. fantastic. **2.** unusual. **3.** documentary. **4.** movements. **5.** screen. **6. weh-tun** to hurt **7. tauschen** to change. **8.** extremely. **9. der Genuss** enjoyment. **10. zurecht finden** get along.

HERR CLARK ERHÄLT EINE ANTWORT AUF SEINEN BRIEF

Herr Clark hat einige Tage auf eine Antwort auf seinen Brief, den er seinem Geschäftspartner in München geschrieben hat, gewartet. Gestern ist endlich die Antwort auf seinen Brief gekommen.

Herr Clark und Herr Müller sitzen wieder im Arbeitszimmer. Herr Clark sagt aufgeregt: "Dies ist der erste Brief, den ich in deutscher Sprache erhalten habe. Ich hoffe, dass ich alles verstehen werde." Dann liest er die Antwort auf seinen Brief vor. Herr Müller hört aufmerksam zu.

Mr. Clark has been waiting for a few days for an answer to the letter which he had written to his business partner in Munich. Yesterday finally the answer to his letter arrived.

Mr. Clark and Mr. Müller are again sitting in the study. Mr. Clark says excitedly: "This is the first letter I receive in German. I hope to understand everything." Then he reads aloud the answer to his letter. Mr. Müller is listening attentively.

München, den 9. Mai 2005

Sehr geehrter Herr Clark!

Mit großem Vergnügen habe ich Ihren Brief vom 4. Mai gelesen, in dem Sie mich benachrichtigen, dass Sie in der nächsten Zeit eine Reise nach Deutschland unternehmen werden.

Glücklicherweise werde ich während der Monate Juni und Juli in München sein. Daher werde ich Ihnen ganz zur Verfügung stehen. Auch werde ich das Vergnügen haben, Sie um 10.10 Uhr morgens am 1. Juni am Flugplatz zu erwarten. Ich werde mich bemühen, Ihren Aufenthalt in München möglichst angenehm zu gestalten. In Bezug auf ihre Ausflüge rund um München kann ich Ihnen auch gerne mit Rat und Tat zur Seite stehen.

Ich freue mich, dass wir uns in deutscher Sprache unterhalten werden, und ich bin sicher, dass es Ihnen möglich sein wird, unsere Gespräche

Munich, May 9, 2005

Dear Mr. Clark:

I have read with great pleasure your letter of May 4th in which you inform me that you will soon take a trip to Germany.

Luckily I shall be in Munich during the months of June and July. Therefore I shall be entirely at your service. I shall also have the pleasure of awaiting you at the airport at 10:10 a.m. on June 1st. I shall try to make your stay in Munich as pleasant as possible. Concerning your trips around Munich I can help you in many ways.

I am happy that we will converse in the German language, and I am sure that it will be possible for you to carry on the conversation with entire

vollkommen richtig auf Deutsch zu führen. Ihr Brief, den Sie mir ja auf Deutsch geschrieben haben, war in perfektem Deutsch verfasst. Da muss ich Ihnen und Ihrem Lehrer wirklich gratulieren.

In Erwartung, Sie baldigst kennen zu lernen, schließe ich,

Mit freundlichen Grüßen,

Heinrich Schiller

correctness in German. The letter you had written was in perfect German. In this regard I must really congratulate you and your teacher.

I look forward to making your acquaintance soon, and close,

Sincerely yours,

Henry Schiller

Herr Müller sagt: „Das ist wirklich ein sehr netter Brief, Herr Clark. Bisher haben Sie Herrn Schiller nur als einen ernsten und tüchtigen Geschäftspartner gekannt. Sie werden zweifellos erkennen, dass er auch sehr liebenswürdig ist."

Mr. Müller says: "That is really a very nice letter, Mr. Clark. Up to now you have known Mr. Schiller only as an earnest and capable business partner. You will doubtlessly find out that he is also very likable."

„Ich glaube, dass ich mich unter den Deutschen sehr gut zurechtfinden werde, und das Beste ist daran, dass ich die Möglichkeit haben werde, mit ihnen in ihrer eigenen Sprache zu reden."

"I am certain that I shall get along very well among the Germans, and the best thing about it is that I shall have the opportunity of speaking to them in their own language."

„Da haben Sie ganz recht, und ich bin gewiss, Sie werden jede Gelegenheit ergreifen, Deutsch zu sprechen. Nun, Herr Clark, nächsten Donnerstag kann ich leider nicht vor halb neun kommen."

"In this you are quite right, and I am certain that you will take every opportunity to speak German. Well, Mr. Clark, next Thursday unfortunately I cannot come before half past eight."

„Das macht nichts, Herr Müller. Besser spät als nie!"

"That's all right with me, Mr. Müller. Better late than never."

Wortschatz

sich bemühen to try, to endeavor
durch-führen to carry on, accomplish
gratulíeren (+ *dat. object*) to congratulate
aufgeregt excited
aufmerksam attentive, attentively
ernst earnest; **liebenswürdig** likable
eigen own; **in ihrer eigenen Sprache** in their own language.

bisher until now
möglichst as much as is possible
möglichst angenehm as pleasant as possible
tatsächlich as a matter of fact, actually
zugléich at the same time
zweifellos doubtlessly, without doubt
daher therefore

Strong Verbs. Principal Parts

ergreifen	to seize, to take	er ergreift	ergriff	hat ergriffen
schließen	to close	er schließt	schloss	hat geschlossen
unternéhmen	to undertake	er unternímmt	unternáhm	hat unternómmen
sich zurecht- finden	to get along	er findet sich zurecht	fand sich zurecht	hat sich zurecht gefunden

Related Words

begegnen (*w. dat.*) to meet
die Begegnung the meeting
hoffen to hope
die Hoffnung the hope
üben to practice
die Übung the exercise, practice
prüfen to test
die Prüfung the test, examination

unternéhmen to undertake
die Unternéhmung the undertaking
überráschen to surprise
die Überráschung the surprise
leisten to accomplish
die Leistung the accomplishment
sich unterhálten to converse
die Unterháltung the conversation

Note that all nouns ending in **-ung** are feminine.

Wichtige Redemittel

in der nächsten Zeit = bald soon

zur Verfügung stehen to be at the service of. **Ich stehe Ihnen zur Verfügung.** I am at your service.

in Bezug auf in respect to, in the matter of. **Er war uns behilflich in Bezug auf das Geschäft.** He was helpful to us in the matter of business.

mit Rat und Tat zur Seite stehen to help sb in many ways (*lit.* to be at sb's side with advice and actions)

sich zurechtfinden to get along. **Ich werde mich dort zurechtfinden.** I shall get along there.

die Gelegenheit ergreifen to seize (take) the opportunity. **Ich werde jede Gelegenheit ergreifen, Deutsch zu sprechen.** I shall take every opportunity to speak German.

Sprichwort: **Besser spät als nie.** Better late than never.

Grammar Notes and Practical Exercises

1. MIXED VERBS

A small number of verbs form their past tense and past participle by adding -te and -t respectively, like weak (regular) verbs, and also by vowel change, like strong (irregular) verbs. Here are the principal parts of mixed verbs you have already met.

kennen	to know[1]	er kennt	kannte	hat gekannt
erkennen	to find out, recognize	er erkennt	erkannte	hat erkannt
nennen	to name	er nennt	nannte	hat genannt
senden	to send	er sendet	sandte	hat gesandt
denken	to think	er denkt	dachte	hat gedacht
bringen	to bring	er bringt	brachte	hat gebracht
verbringen	to spend	er verbringt	verbrachte	hat verbracht
wissen	to know[1]	er weiß	wusste	hat gewusst

NOTE: 1. kennen to know, be acquainted with (persons or things); **wissen** to know facts.

Exercise 146

Change these sentences to the **Präteritum** and the **Perfekt**.

Beispiel: 1. Ich kannte ihn gut. Ich habe ihn gut gekannt.

1. Ich kenne ihn gut.
2. Wir nennen die Dinge auf Deutsch.
3. Senden Sie ihm einen Brief?
4. Er denkt an seine Freundin.
5. Was bringst du mir?
6. Wie verbringen Sie den Sonntag?
7. Ich weiß nicht wie er heißt.
8. Ihr kennt seinen Bruder.
9. Ich erkenne ihn nicht wieder.
10. Wir denken oft an dich.

2. INFINITIVE WITH *zu*

Ich hoffe, Ihnen dort zu begegnen.	I hope to meet you there.
Es ist schwer, eine Sprache zu lernen.	It is difficult to learn a language.
Er arbeitet, um Geld zu verdienen.	He works in order to earn money.
Es ist schon Zeit wegzugehen.	It is already time to go away.
Er wünschte, mitzugehen.	He wanted to go along.

a. The use of **zu** *with German infinitives usually corresponds to the use of* to *with English infinitives.*

b. If the infinitive is a separable verb, **zu** *stands between the prefix and the verb (wegzugehen, mitzugehen).*

c. Note that the infinitive stands last. Objects and modifiers of an infinitive must precede it.

3. INFINITIVE WITHOUT *ZU*

Ich werde den Arzt rufen.	I will call the doctor.
Ich muss Ihnen gratulieren.	I must congratulate you.
Wir konnten gar nicht schlafen.	We could not sleep at all.
Sie wollten ins Kino gehen.	They wanted to go to the movies.
Darf ich Ihnen einige Fragen stellen?	May I ask you some questions?
Er ließ mich nicht arbeiten.	He didn't let me work.
Sahen Sie das Flugzeug landen?	Did you see the plane land?
Was hörtest du ihn sagen?	What did you hear him say?

a. zu is not used with the infinitive in the future tense.

b. zu is not used with the infinitives after the modal auxiliaries: **dürfen, können, mögen, müssen, sollen, wollen;** *and after* **lassen, sehen** *and* **hören.**

Exercise 147

Complete the sentences on the right with the correct infinitive.

Beispiel: 1. Sie werden die Gelegenheit haben, Deutsch zu sprechen.

1. You will have the chance to speak German.   Sie werden die Gelegenheit haben, Deutsch _____.
2. I hope to get a good job.   **Ich hoffe, eine gute Stellung _____ .**
3. Where will you await me?   **Wo werden Sie mich _____ ?**
4. All had to get up early.   **Alle mussten früh _____ .**
5. It is now time to get up.   **Es ist jetzt Zeit _____ .**
6. May I visit you tomorrow?   **Darf ich Sie morgen _____ ?**
7. We tried to find his home.   **Wir versuchten seine Wohnung _____ .**
8. He let the children play there.   **Er ließ die Kinder dort _____ .**
9. I intend to go to the movies.   **Ich beabsichtige, ins Kino _____ .**
10. What do you wish to say about it?   **Was wünschen Sie dazu _____ ?**
11. One needs money in order to travel.   **Man braucht Geld, um _____ .**
12. I heard him say: "Good-bye."   **Ich hörte ihn _____ : „Auf Wiedersehen!"**

Exercise 148

Complete the following sentences with infinitives.

1. **Ich habe heute keine Zeit, _____ .**
2. **Ich kann heute nicht _____ .**

3. Ich habe keine Lust, _____ .

4. Ich will nicht _____ .

5. Ich habe die Erlaubnis,[1] _____ .

6. Ich darf _____ .

NOTE: 1. I have the permission . . .

Exercise 149

Fragen

Lesen Sie noch einmal den Text: **Herr Clark erhält eine Antwort auf seinen Brief,** und dann beantworten Sie diese Fragen!

1. An wen hatte Herr Clark einen Brief geschrieben?
2. Warum war Herr Clark aufgeregt?
3. Wann hat Herr Clark die Antwort auf seinen Brief bekommen?
4. Was tat der Lehrer, während der Geschäftsmann die Antwort vorlas?
5. Wie fängt Herrn Schillers Antwort an?
6. Wo wird Herr Schiller während der Monate Juni und Juli sein?
7. Wo wird er Herrn Clark erwarten?
8. Wird er sich mit Herrn Clark in deutscher oder englischer Sprache unterhalten?
9. Wem muss Herr Schiller gratulieren?
10. In welcher Beziehung (in what relation) hat Herr Clark seinen Partner bis jetzt gekannt?
11. Was wird er zweifellos erkennen?
12. Wird Herr Clark jede Gelegenheit ergreifen, Englisch zu sprechen?

DIE GEOGRAPHIE VON DEUTSCHLAND, ÖSTERREICH UND DER SCHWEIZ

The Rhine is the most well-known river in Germany.

1. Vor seiner Reise nach Deutschland will sich Herr Clark über die Geographie der deutschsprachigen Länder informieren. Er nimmt ein Lexikon zur Hand und beginnt über Deutschland, Österreich und die Schweiz zu lesen:

Deutschland liegt in Mitteleuropa und grenzt an neun verschiedene Nachbarländer. Berlin ist die Hauptstadt und auch die größte Stadt Deutschlands.

Es gibt auch viele Berge in Deutschland. Im Süden befinden sich die Bayerischen Alpen; im Südwesten der Schwarzwald; in Mitteldeutschland der Harz und der Thüringer Wald. Der höchste Berg Deutschlands ist die Zugspitze. Sie ist 2962 Meter oder 9718 Fuß hoch.

Der Rhein ist der längste und wahrscheinlich auch der wichtigste Fluss Deutschlands.

1. Before his trip to Germany Mr. Clark wants to find out about the geography of the German-speaking countries. He takes an encyclopedia and begins to read about Germany, Austria and Switzerland:

Germany lies in Central Europe and borders on nine different neighboring countries. Berlin is the capital and also the biggest city of Germany.

There are also a lot of mountains in Germany. In the south are the Bavarian Alps; in the southwest the Black Forest; in central Germany the Harz Mountains and the Thuringian Forest. The highest mountain in Germany is the Zugspitze. It is 2962 meters or 9718 feet high.

The Rhine is the longest and probably most important German river. The largest

Der größte See ist der Bodensee, der allerdings auch zu Österreich und der Schweiz gehört. Deutschland grenzt auch an die Nord- und an die Ostsee. Der größte und beste Hafen an der Nordsee ist Hamburg, an der Mündung der Elbe. Ein anderer großer Hafen ist Bremerhaven, an der Mündung der Weser.

Österreich ist kleiner als Deutschland. Die wichtigste Stadt Österreichs ist Wien. Andere bekannte Städte sind Graz, Salzburg und Innsbruck. Österreich ist sehr gebirgig. Der höchste Berg ist der Großglockner mit einer Höhe von 3797 Metern (12 457 Fuß) Die Donau ist der längste Fluss Österreichs. Ebenso wichtig wie der Bodensee ist der Neusiedlersee im Osten von Österreich.

Das kleinste der deutschsprachigen Länder ist die Schweiz. Die größte Stadt der Schweiz ist Zürich, aber die Hauptstadt ist Bern. Die Schweiz ist das gebirgigste Land Europas. Die Alpen im Süden und die Jura im Norden bedecken ca. 70 Prozent der Schweiz. Die Schweiz ist berühmt für ihre Seen. Zu den wichtigsten Seen gehören der Bodensee, der Genfer See und der Lago Maggiore, der auch zu Italien gehört.

2. Zufrieden legt Herr Clark das Lexikon zur Seite. Jetzt weiß er über die Geographie der deutschsprachigen Länder Bescheid. Er denkt sich: "Hoffentlich habe ich die Gelegenheit, viele der wichtigsten und schönsten Orte in Deutschland, Österreich und der Schweiz zu besuchen!"

lake is Lake Constance which also makes part of Austria and Switzerland. Germany borders also on the North and Baltic Seas. Hamburg, at the mouth of the Elbe, is the largest and best German port. Bremerhaven, at the mouth of the Weser, is another big port on the North Sea.

Austria is smaller than Germany. The most important Austrian city is Vienna. Other well known cities are Graz, Salzburg and Innsbruck. Austria is very mountainous. The highest mountain is the Großglockner with a height of 3,797 meters (12,457 feet).

The Danube is the longest Austrian river. As important as Lake Constance is Lake Neusiedel in the east of Austria.

The smallest of the German-speaking countries is Switzerland. The biggest city is Zurich, but Bern is the capital. Switzerland is the most mountainous country in Europe. The Alps in the south and the Jura in the north cover about 70 percent of Switzerland. Switzerland is famous for the many lakes. Lake Constance, Lake Geneva and Lake Maggiore—belonging also to Italy—are the most important Swiss lakes.

2. Satisfied, Mr. Clark put down the encyclopedia. Now he knows all about the geography of the German-speaking countries. He thinks: "I hope that I'll get the chance to visit many of the most important and most beautiful places in Germany, Austria, and Switzerland."

Wortschatz

die Geographíe (*gay-oh-gra-fee*) geography
der Berg *pl.* -e mountain
der Fluss *pl.* ¨-e river
das Gebírge *pl.* - mountain range; **gebirgig** mountainous
der Hafen *pl.* ¨- harbor

die See *pl.* -n sea, ocean
der See *pl.* -n lake
der Norden north; der Süden south
der Osten east; der Westen west
vielmals many times; nie, niemals never

Wichtige Redemittel

Bescheid wissen to know all about

Erlauben Sie! Permit me.

Erlauben Sie, dass ich einige Fragen an Sie stelle! Permit me to ask you a few questions.

meiner Meinung nach according to (in) my opinion

deiner (Ihrer, eurer) Meinung nach according to your opinion

uns(e)rer (ihrer) Meinung nach according to our (her, their) opinion

In the sense of *according to*, **nach** usually follows the noun

1. COMPARISON OF ADJECTIVES

Positive		*Comparative*	*Superlative*
klein	small	kleiner	der, die, das kleinste
breit	wide	breiter	der, die, das breiteste
interessant	interesting	interessanter	der, die, das interessanteste
niedrig	low	niedriger	der, die, das niedrigste
schön	beautiful	schöner	der, die, das schönste
lang	long	länger	der, die, das längste
kurz	short	kürzer	der, die, das kürzeste
wenig	little	weniger	der, die, das wenigste

Die Elbe ist **lang**. Der Rhein ist **länger** als die Elbe, aber nicht so lang wie die Volga. Die Volga ist **der längste** Fluss Europas.

The Elbe is *long*. The Rhine is *longer* than the Elbe, but not as long as the Volga. The Volga is *the longest* river of Europe.

Unser Haus ist **alt**. Euer Haus ist **älter** als unser Haus. Sein Haus ist **das älteste** in dieser Strasse.

Our house is *old*. Your house is *older* than our house. His house is *the oldest* in this street.

a. *The comparative of adjectives is formed by adding -er to the positive.*

b. *The superlative is formed by adding **-st** or **-est** to the positive. **-est** is added for ease in pronunciation when the adjective ends in **-t, -d, -s, -ss, -z, -ch.***

c. *Most one-syllable adjectives add an **Umlaut** to **a, o, u** in the comparative and superlative. You have met the following: **kurz, lang, alt, jung, warm, kalt, schwarz.***

d. *In comparisons **so . . . wie** = as . . . as; **als** = than.*

Er ist **so groß wie** ich. He is *as tall as* I.   Er ist **größer als** ich. He is *taller than* I.

2. SOME ADJECTIVES IRREGULAR IN COMPARISON

groß	big	größer	bigger	der, die, das größte	the biggest
gut	good	besser	better	der, die, das beste	the best
hoch	high	höher	higher	der, die, das höchste	the highest
nah(e)	near	näher	nearer	der, die, das nächste	the nearest
viel	much	mehr	more	der, die, das meiste	the most

Die Zugspitze ist **hoch.** Der Mont Blanc ist **höher** als die Zugspitze. Der Mount Everest ist **der höchste** Berg in der ganzen Welt.

The Zugspitze is *high.* Mont Blanc is *higher* than the Zugspitze. Mount Everest is *the highest* mountain in the whole world.

NOTE: hoch drops the **c** whenever the ending begins with **-e (der hohe Berg).**

Exercise 150

Complete each sentence with the comparative of the adjective in parentheses.

Beispiel: 1. **Der Rhein und die Elbe sind kürzer als die Wolga.**

1. **Der Rhein und die Elbe sind (kurz) als die Wolga.**
2. **Ist Köln (schön) als Nürnberg?**
3. **Der Winter ist (kalt) in Kanada als in den Vereinigten Staaten.**
4. **Karl ist (alt) als Wilhelm.**
5. **Ist Frankfurt (groß) als Hamburg?**
6. **Mein Bruder ist (jung) als ich.**
7. **Was finden Sie (interessant), das Theater oder das Kino?**
8. **Im Sommer sind die Tage (lang) als im Winter.**
9. **Er isst (viel) Fleisch als ich.**
10. **Das Essen ist (gut) zu Hause als im Restaurant.**

3. **CASE ENDINGS IN THE COMPARATIVE AND SUPERLATIVE**

a. **Das kleine Kind** *ist mein Bruder.*
   Das kleinere Kind ist mein Bruder.
   Das kleinste Kind ist mein Bruder.

b. **Mein alter Freund** *kommt heute.*
   Mein älterer Freund kommt heute.
   Mein ältester Freund kommt heute.

c. *Ich trage* **den schweren Koffer.**
   Sie tragen **den schwereren Koffer.**
   Er trägt **den schwersten Koffer.**

d. *Er arbeitete in* **dem großen Zimmer.**
   Sie arbeitete in **dem größeren Zimmer.**
   Wir arbeiteten in **dem größten Zimmer.**

The comparative and superlative of adjectives take the same case endings as the positive.

CHAPTER 32: **DIE GEOGRAPHIE**   201

Exercise 151

In each sentence substitute the comparative of the adjective in place of the positive.

Beispiel: 1. Er kauft sich ein besseres Auto.

1. Er kauft sich ein **gutes** Auto.
2. Der **große** Tisch gehört mir.
3. Ich schreibe mit dem **langen** Bleistift.
4. Ich konnte keine **gute** Wohnung finden.
5. Ich habe einen **jungen** Bruder.
6. Sie hat eine **junge** Schwester.
7. Marie hat eine **alte** Bluse.
8. Die **hohen** Berge befinden sich in Süddeutschland.
9. Ich gab meinem Freund den **guten** Platz.
10. Wie heißt Ihr **junger** Bruder?

Exercise 152

In each sentence, substitute the superlative of the adjective for the positive.

Beispiel: 1. Am Rhein sieht man die ältesten Schlösser.

1. Am Rhein sieht man die **alten** Schlösser.
2. Ich lese jetzt das **interessante** Buch.
3. Ich habe den **guten** Platz gekauft.
4. Die **langen** Tage sind im Sommer.
5. Die **kurzen** Tage sind im Winter.
6. Hier ist das **warme** Zimmer.
7. Sie mag Einkäufe in den **großen** Läden.
8. Er sprach von seinem **alten** Freund.
9. Die **guten** Plätze sind alle besetzt.
10. Die **hohen** Berge sind in der Schweiz.

Exercise 153

Lesen Sie diesen Text! Dann beantworten Sie die Fragen!

Herr Braun ist fünfundvierzig Jahre alt. Herr Engel ist fünfzig Jahre alt. Herr Schumann ist sechzig Jahre alt.

Herr Braun besitzt 500 000 (fünfhunderttausend) Euro. Herr Engel besitzt 400 000 Euro. Herr Schumann besitzt 300 000 Euro.

Herr Braun ist 1,80 m (ein Meter achtzig) groß. Herr Engel ist 1,85 m groß. Herr Schumann ist 1,65 m groß.

1. Wie heißt der älteste Herr?
2. Wie heißt der reichste Herr?
3. Wie heißt der größte (Herr)?
4. Ist Herr Engel älter oder jünger als Herr Braun?
5. Ist Herr Braun größer oder kleiner als Herr Engel?
6. Ist Herr Schumann reicher oder weniger reich als Herr Engel?
7. Wer hat das meiste Geld?
8. Wer hat das wenigste?

Exercise 154

Make comparisons.

Beispiel: 1. Ein Ferrari fährt schneller als ein Subaru.

1. Ferrari—Subaru—schnell fahren
2. Deutschland—Österreich—groß
3. Schweiz—Österreich—klein
4. Großglockner—Zugspitze—hoch
5. Herr Müller—Herr Clark—alt
6. Wein—Wasser—gut
7. Apfel—Orange—gern haben
8. lesen—fernsehen—oft

1. Wie Sie wohl wissen, Herr Clark, bietet die gute deutsche Küche dem Touristen große Abwechslung.

2. Ja, das weiß ich sehr wohl.

3. Sind Sie mit der deutschen Küche ein wenig bekannt?

4. Ja, ich weiß darüber schon ein wenig Bescheid. Wenn mich ein wichtiger Kunde besucht, lade ich ihn ein, mit mir in einem der besten deutschen Restaurants in New York zu essen. Das geschieht oft und bereitet mir viel Vergnügen.

5. Nun in Deutschland findet man die Kost nie eintönig, und da gibt es für den Reisenden immer eine neue Überraschung.

6. Schön. Wenn ich in Deutschland bin, mache ich eine Liste der Gerichte, die mir am besten schmecken. Dann schenke ich meiner Frau ein gutes deutsches Kochbuch, natürlich in englischer Sprache.

7. Eine vorzügliche Idee!

8. Sagen Sie mir bitte, Herr Müller, ist die deutsche Küche sehr kompliziert?

9. Eigentlich nicht. Es gibt nur drei Geheimnisse der guten deutschen Küche. Diese drei sind auch die Geheimnisse jeder guten nationalen Küche, ob der deutschen, der französischen, der italienischen, oder irgendeiner anderen.

10. Was sind diese drei Geheimnisse?

11. Erstens muss alles, was man zum Kochen kauft, von der besten Qualität sein: Fleisch, Fisch, Gemüse, Butter, Eier usw. Zweitens muss man richtig kochen, um den Naturgeschmack der Nahrungsmittel zu behalten. Drittens muss man aber vor allem das Kochen lieben.

1. As you no doubt know, Mr. Clark, good German cooking offers the tourist great variety.

2. Yes, that I know very well.

3. Are you somewhat acquainted with German cooking?

4. Yes, I already know a little about it. When an important customer visits me, I invite him to dine with me in one of the best German restaurants in New York. That happens often and gives me great pleasure.

5. Well, in Germany one never finds the food monotonous, and there is always a new surprise for the traveler.

6. Good. When I am in Germany I shall make a list of the dishes which taste best to me. Then I shall send my wife a good German cookbook, naturally in the English language.

7. An excellent idea!

8. Tell me please, Mr. Müller, is German cooking very complicated?

9. Not really. There are only three secrets of good German cooking. These three are also the secrets of every good national cuisine, whether the German, the French, the Italian or any other.

10. What are these three secrets?

11. First, everything that one buys for cooking must be of the finest quality: meat, fish, vegetables, butter, eggs, etc. Second, one must cook correctly in order to retain the natural flavor of the foods. Third, one must above all love the art of cooking.

12. **Wann nehmen denn die Deutschen ihre Hauptmahlzeit zu sich?**

13. **Die Hauptmahlzeit der Deutschen ist das Mittagessen. Es beginnt gewöhnlich mit einer Suppe. Dann kommt Fleisch, Gemüse und Salat. Statt Fleisch gibt es manchmal (besonders Freitags) Fisch.**

14. **Und wie steht es mit dem Dessert?**

15. **Zum Nachtisch gibt es entweder Obst oder Obstkuchen, zum Beispiel Apfelkuchen oder Pflaumenkuchen.**

16. **Und keinen Strudel? Ich esse Strudel am allerliebsten.**

17. **Ach ja! In Süddeutschland und in Österreich ist der Strudel besonders beliebt.**

18. **Und was trinkt man am Ende der Mahlzeit?**

19. **Während des Essens trinkt man fast immer Bier oder Wein. Viele Deutsche trinken nach dem Essen auch eine Tasse Kaffee.**

20. **Das Wasser läuft mir schon im Mund zusammen.[1] Herr Müller, wollen Sie mit mir vor meiner Abreise in einem deutschen Restaurant speisen?**

21. **Mit Vergnügen. Vielen, vielen Dank!**

12. When do the Germans eat their main meal?

13. The main meal of the Germans is the midday meal. It usually begins with soup. Then comes meat, vegetables and salad. Instead of meat there is sometimes fish (especially on Friday).

14. And what about the dessert?

15. For dessert there is either fruit or fruit cake, for example apple cake or plum cake.

16. And no strudel? I like to eat strudel most of all.

17. Oh yes. In South Germany and Austria strudel is especially popular.

18. And what does one drink at the end of the meal?

19. During the meal one almost always drinks beer or wine. Many Germans also like to drink a cup of coffee at the end of the meal.

20. My mouth is already watering. Mr. Müller, will you dine with me in a German restaurant before my departure?

21. With pleasure. Many thanks.

NOTE: 1. *Lit.* The water is already gathering in my mouth.

Wortschatz

die Abwechslung *pl.* **–en** variety, change
das Dessért = der Nachtisch dessert
das Gehéimnis *pl.* **-se** secret
das Gemüse vegetables
der Geschmáck taste
das Gerícht *pl.* **-e** dish, course
die Küche *pl.* **-n** kitchen, cuisine, cooking
die Nahrungsmittel foods
das Obst fruit; **der Salat** salad
kochen to cook
schicken = senden to send

speisen to dine
bekannt known
kompliziért complicated
nahrhaft nourishing
erstens first, firstly
zweitens second, secondly
drittens third, thirdly
irgendein any
entweder . . . oder either . . . or

Strong Verbs. Principal Parts

behálten	to retain, receive	er behält	behielt	hat behalten
beschréiben	to describe	er beschreibt	beschrieb	hat beschrieben
bieten	to offer	er bietet	bot	hat geboten
ein-laden	to invite	er lädt . . . ein	lud . . . ein	hat eingeladen

Wichtige Redemittel

Bescheid wissen to have knowledge of a thing, to know about, to know one's way. **Über die deutsche Küche wissen wir ein wenig Bescheid.** We know a little about German cuisine. **In dieser Stadt weiß er Bescheid.** He knows his way around this town.

beliebt popular; **beliebt bei** a favorite with. **Der Strudel ist bei uns sehr beliebt.** Strudel is a great favorite with us.

vor allem above all, first of all. **Wir müssen vor allem fleißig arbeiten.** We must above all work diligently. **Ich dachte vor allem an die Geschäftssachen.** I thought first of all of the business matters.

ob . . . oder whether . . . or. **Ob heute oder morgen, wir werden gewiss gehen.** Whether today or tomorrow, we shall surely go.

Sprichwort: Der Mensch ist, was er isst.

Proverb: Man is what he eats.

Grammar Notes and Practical Exercises

1. THE *am -sten* FORM OF THE SUPERLATIVE OF ADJECTIVES

Das Wetter ist **am schönsten.**	The weather is *most beautiful*.
Wir haben **das schönste** Wetter.	We have the most beautiful weather.
In Asien sind die Berge **am höchsten.**	In Asia the mountains are *highest*.
Die höchsten Berge sind in Asien.	The highest mountains are in Asia.

The **am -sten** form is used for the most part in cases where the corresponding English superlative omits *the*. This form is never used before a noun. Some familiar adjectives in the **am -sten** superlative are: **am kleinsten, am größten, am interessantesten, am schönsten, am längsten, am kürzesten, am kältesten, am wärmsten, am heißesten, am jüngsten, am ältesten, am höchsten, am besten.**

Exercise 155

Translate the superlative of the adjective with the **am -sten** form.

1. **Die Berge sind hier** (highest).
2. **Der Herbst ist hier** (most beautiful).

3. **Im Winter sind die Tage** (coldest).
4. **In Afrika ist das Klima** (hottest).
5. **Im Sommer sind die Tage** (shortest).
6. **Diese Zimmer sind** (largest).
7. **In diesem Dorf sind die Häuser** (oldest).
8. **Die Ferientage** (vacation days) **sind** (best).

2. COMPARISON OF ADVERBS

schnell	quickly	**schneller**	more quickly	**am schnellsten**	most quickly
langsam	slowly	**langsamer**	more slowly	**am langsamsten**	most slowly
klar	clearly	**klarer**	more clearly	**am klarsten**	most clearly
spät	late	**später**	later	**am spätesten**	latest
früh	early	**früher**	earlier	**am frühesten**	earliest
gut	good	**besser**	better	**am besten**	best
schlecht	bad	**schlechter**	worse	am schlechtesten	worst
schön	beautiful	**schöner**	more beautiful	**am schönsten**	most beautiful
gern	gladly	**lieber**	more gladly	**am liebsten**	most gladly

Ein Auto fährt **schnell**. Ein Flugzeug fliegt **schneller** als ein Auto. Eine Rakete fliegt **am schnellsten (am allerschnellsten)**.

A car goes *fast*. A plane goes *faster* than a car. A rocket goes *fastest* (*of all*).

a. *Adverbs are compared like adjectives. The superlative of an adverb, however, always has the* **am -sten** *form. Many adjectives can be used also as adverbs.*

Er ist **gut**. Er schreibt **gut**.

He is *good* (*adj.*). He writes *well* (*adv.*).

b. *As you have already learned, a verb* + **gern(e)** *means* to like to; *a verb* + **lieber** *means* to prefer to; *a verb* + **am liebsten** *means* to like most *or* best of all.

Ich esse Apfelkuchen **gern**. Ich esse **lieber** Pflaumenkuchen. Ich esse **am liebsten** Strudel.

I like to eat apple cake. I prefer to eat plum cake. I like to eat strudel most of all.

Exercise 156

Answer according to your own preferences.

1. **Was essen Sie am liebsten?**
2. **Welche Schauspielerin gefällt Ihnen am besten?**
3. **Welchen Song hören Sie am wenigsten gern?**
4. **Wer in Ihrer Familie ist am größten?**
5. **Welches Buch finden Sie am spannendsten?**
6. **Welche Sprache ist am schwierigsten?**

7. Was macht Sie am glücklichsten?
8. Welches Gebäude ist am höchsten?

Exercise 157

Ein Gespräch

DEUTSCHE ODER FRANZÖSISCHE KÜCHE

—Ich habe die deutsche Kost sehr gern. Sie auch?

—Ich habe die deutsche Kost lieber als die italienische. Aber die französische Kost habe ich am liebsten.

—Kennen Sie etwas, was den Appetit besser anregt als ein Bismarckhering?

—Gewiss. Das tun die französischen hors d'oeuvres (Vorspeisen) am allerbesten.

—Wer tüchtig speisen will, isst am besten ein Wiener Schnitzel mit Rotkohl und dazu ein Seidel dunkles Bier.

—Aber nein, man speist nicht weniger gut, wenn man in einem der besseren Pariser Restaurants coq au vin mit haricots verts (Huhn in Wein gekocht mit grünen Bohnen) bestellt.

—Trinken Sie lieber Bier oder Wein zum Mittagessen?

—Ich trinke lieber den französischen Rotwein.

—Wie ist es mit dem Nachtisch? Von allen deutschen Nachspeisen schmeckt mir ein frischer Apfelstrudel am besten.

—Ich esse öfter Obst als Kuchen. Aber unter den Mehlspeisen bestelle ich am häufigsten die wunderbaren französischen crêpes suzettes. Die sind auch viel besser als die deutschen Pfannkuchen.

—Nun, gibt es denn keine deutschen Gerichte, die Sie gern haben?

—Ich habe nichts gegen die deutsche Kost, aber die französische mag ich eben lieber.

—Und ich freue mich am meisten über die deutsche Kost. Es ist doch klar, über den Geschmack lässt sich nicht streiten!

—I like German food very much. Do you?

—I like German food better than the Italian. But I like French food best.

—Do you know of anything that stimulates the appetite better than a Bismarck herring?

—Certainly. The French hors d'oeuvres do that best of all.

—Anyone who wants to dine heartily will find a Vienna veal cutlet with red cabbage and a mug of dark beer on the side most satisfying.

—Oh no, one dines no less well if in one of the better Parisian restaurants one orders coq au vin (capon in wine) with string beans.

—Do you prefer to drink beer or wine with your dinner?

—I prefer to drink French red wine.

—How about dessert? Of all the German desserts I like a fresh apple strudel best.

—I eat fruit more often than cake. But in the line of baked sweets I most often order the wonderful French crêpes suzettes. These are even better than the German pancakes.

—Well, aren't there any German dishes which you like?

—I have nothing against German food, but I just like French food more.

—And I enjoy German cooking most. Well, it's obvious, there's no disputing about taste!

Exercise 158

Ein Rezept: Apfelkuchen

<u>Einkaufsliste</u>: 100g Butter, 100g Staubzucker, 2 Eier, 1 Dotter, geriebene Schale einer halben Zitrone, 1 Pkt. Vanillinzucker, 250g Mehl, Pkt. Backpulver, 1/16 l Milch, 750g Äpfel, 100g Kristallzucker, Saft einer halben Zitrone, Zimt, Gewürznelken

<u>Vorbereitung</u>: Die Äpfel waschen, schälen achteln und vom Kerngehäuse befreien. In einem halben Liter Wasser mit dem Kristallzucker, Zitronensaft und Zitronenschale, einigen Gewürznelken und der Zimtrinde langsam zum Kochen bringen und zugedeckt kochen lassen. Die Apfelspalten vorsichtig aus dem Wasser nehmen und in einem Sieb gut abtropfen lassen.

<u>Zubereitung</u>: Die Butter auf Handwärme bringen und mit dem gesiebten Staubzucker sehr schaumig rühren. Nach und nach Dotter und Eier einrühren, Vanillinzucker und Zitronenschale beifügen und wieder schaumig rühren. Zuletzt löffelweise das mit Backpulver, versiebte Mehl und die warme Milch einrühren. Sodann zwei Drittel der Masse in eine gebutterte und bemehlte Tortenform füllen und mit den Apfelspalten belegen. Die restliche Masse daraufstreichen und den Kuchen im vorgeheizten Backrohr bei 175 Grad etwa 60 Minuten lang backen. In der Form erkalten lassen und nach zwei Stunden Ruhezeit aus der Form lösen.

GUTEN APPETIT!

Exercise 159

Fragen

Lesen Sie noch einmal den Text: **Die deutsche Küche**, und dann beantworten Sie diese Fragen!

1. Wem bietet die deutsche Küche viel Abwechslung?
2. Wo speist Herr Clark oft mit einem wichtigen Kunden?
3. Wo findet man die Kost nie eintönig?
4. Wem wird Herr Clark ein gutes, deutsches Kochbuch senden?
5. Was ist das erste Geheimnis der guten, deutschen Küche?
6. Was ist das dritte?
7. Welches ist die Hauptmahlzeit der Deutschen?
8. Womit beginnt gewöhnlich die Mahlzeit?
9. Was kommt dann?
10. Was gibt es zum Dessert?
11. Welches Dessert hat Herr Clark am liebsten?
12. Wo ist der Strudel besonders beliebt?
13. Was trinkt man am Ende der Mahlzeit?
14. Was trinkt man während der Mahlzeit?

1. Herr Müller und Herr Clark haben heute ihre letzte Deutschstunde, bevor Herr Clark seine Reise nach Deutschland antritt. Natürlich sprechen sie über diese Reise:

   „Nächste Woche werden Sie nach Deutschland abreisen. Wie lange werden Sie in diesem Land bleiben?"

2. „Mir stehen nur sechs Wochen zur Verfügung. Aber ich versichere Ihnen, ich werde versuchen, diese Zeit aufs beste zu nützen."

3. „Wissen Sie schon, welche Städte Sie in Deutschland besuchen werden?"

4. „Ich denke immer daran und informiere mich in meiner Sammlung von Reiseführern. Wie Sie schon wissen, führen mich meine Geschäftsangelegenheiten nach München, wo mein Geschäftspartner, Herr Schiller wohnt."

5. „Und wie lange werden Sie in München bleiben?"

6. „Zwei oder drei Wochen, vielleicht länger."

7. „Und welche Sehenswürdigkeiten wollen Sie dort besuchen?"

8. „Sie wissen, man nennt München das moderne Athen, mit berühmten Kunstmuseen, die ich besuchen will. Das Deutsche Museum soll das größte technische Museum Europas sein.

   Natürlich muss ich auch die weltberühmte Liebfrauenkirche und das Rathaus mit dem Glockenspiel[1] besuchen. Außerdem gibt es Theater und Oper, auch Wein stuben und Bierzelte. Ich muss auch einen langen Spaziergang im berühmten Englischen Garten[2] machen."

1. Today Mr. Müller and Mr. Clark have their last German lesson before Mr. Clark travels to Germany. Naturally they are talking about this journey.

   "Next week you will be setting out for Germany. How long will you stay in that country?"

2. There are only six weeks at my disposal. But I assure you, I shall try to make use of this time to the best advantage.

3. Do you already know which cities of Germany you will visit?

4. I'm thinking about this matter all the time, and reading diligently in my collection of guidebooks. As you know, business matters are taking me to Munich, where my business partner, Mr. Schiller, lives.

5. And how long will you stay in Munich?

6. Two or three weeks, perhaps longer.

7. And what places of interest do you expect to visit there?

8. You know they call Munich the modern Athens, with famous art museums which I want to visit. The German Museum is said to be the largest technical museum in Europe.

   Of course I must visit the world-famous Church of Our Lady and the City Hall with the "Chimes." Besides these two things there is theater and opera, also taverns and beer tents among other things. I must also take a long walk in the famous English Garden.

9. „Denken Sie auch, Ausflüge in die Umgebung zu machen?"

10. „Ja, gewiss. München ist das Tor zu den Bayerischen Alpen und zur Seegegend. Ich werde den Tegernsee und die anderen malerischen Seen besuchen. Ich möchte auch einen Ausflug zum interessanten Dorf Oberammergau und zum nahe gelegenen Garmisch-Partenkirchen machen. Das soll eine der schönsten Berggegenden der Welt sein."

11. „Werden Sie noch andere Städte in der Nähe von München besuchen?"

12. „Jawohl. Ich denke vor allem an Nürnberg, die Stadt der Meistersinger, und an Bayreuth, die Stadt, in der Richard Wagner lebte und komponierte.

Ich glaube Herr Schiller wird mir bei meinen Ausflügen behilflich sein, soweit es seine Zeit erlauben wird."

13. „Wird Sie Ihre Reise auch in andere Teile Deutschlands führen?"

14. „Ach, ja. Ich werde in Frankfurt einige Geschäfte erledigen. Dann will ich eine Rheinreise machen, und dabei werde ich Bonn, die alte Hauptstadt Deutschlands, und die Rheinstädte, Köln und Düsseldorf, den Geburtsort von Heinrich Heine,[3] besuchen können. Von dort wird's nach Hamburg gehen, von wo aus ich per Flugzeug die Heimreise unternehmen werde. Was denken Sie darüber, Herr Müller?"

15. „Was ich darüber denke? Ich beneide Sie, Herr Clark, und ich würde Sie am liebsten begleiten. Das ist aber leider unmöglich. Ich werde zu Hause bleiben müssen."

16. „Wie schade, Herr Müller. Es tut mir aufrichtig leid."

9. Are you thinking also of taking excursions out into the surroundings?

10. Yes, surely. Munich is the gateway to the Bavarian Alps and the lake region. I shall visit the Tegernsee and the other picturesque lakes. I should also like to take a trip to the interesting village of Oberammergau and to Garmisch-Partenkirchen nearby. That is said to be one of the most beautiful mountain regions in the world.

11. Will you visit other cities near Munich?

12. Yes, indeed. I think first of all of Nuremberg, city of the mastersingers, and of Bayreuth, the city in which Richard Wagner lived and composed.

I believe Mr. Schiller will be helpful to me in my travels, as far as his time will permit.

13. Will your trip include other parts of Germany too?

14. Oh yes. I shall take care of some business matters in Frankfurt. Then I will take a Rhine trip and at the same time I shall be able to visit Bonn, the old capital of Germany, and the Rhine cities of Cologne and Düsseldorf, the birthplace of Heinrich Heine. From there the next stop will be Hamburg, from which place I shall make the home journey by airplane. What do you think of this, Mr. Müller?

15. What do I think of it? I envy you, Mr. Clark, and I would like to accompany you. However, that is unfortunately impossible. I shall have to stay at home.

16. That's too bad, Mr. Müller. I'm really very sorry.

NOTES: 1. **Das Glockenspiel** a remarkable clock with chimes on the **Rathaus** (City Hall) in Munich. Every day at 11 A.M. wooden figures come out and dance to the music of the bells. 2. **Der Englische Garten** a large, beautiful park in Munich. 3. **Heinrich Heine, 1797–1856.** Great German lyric poet. Among his most famous poems are **Die Lorelei, Du bist wie eine Blume** and **Die Zwei Grenadiere.**

Wortschatz

das Dorf *pl.* ¨-er village
der Gebúrtsort *pl.* -e birthplace
die Gegend *pl.* -en region
die Kirche *pl.* -n church
das Tor *pl.* -e gate
die Sammlung *pl.* -en collection
die Sehenswürdigkeit *pl.* -en place of interest
ab-reisen to set out
nützen to make full use of
beneíden to envy
besórgen to take care of, attend to
komponiéren to compose
versíchern to assure
bekánnt known; **altbekannt** long known
nahe gelegen nearby
technisch technical
soweít as far as
dabeí at the same time; in connection with that

Munich is well-known for its gardens.

Strong Verbs. Principal Parts

ein-schließen	to include	er schließt . . . ein	schloss . . . ein	hat eingeschlossen
bleiben	to remain	er bleibt	blieb	ist geblieben
tun	to do	er tut	tat	hat getan

Wichtige Redemittel

schade! wie schade! what a pity
Es ist sehr schade. It's a great pity.
ja, gewiss yes, surely

einen Spaziergang machen to take a walk
Jeden Tag hat er einen Spaziergang im Park gemacht. Every day he took a walk in the park.

Grammar Notes and Practical Exercises

1. THE FUTURE TENSE OF MODAL AUXILIARIES

I will have to go, you will have to go, etc.

Ich werde heute gehen **müssen.**
Du wirst heute gehen **müssen.**
Er (sie, es) wird heute gehen **müssen.**

Wir werden heute gehen **müssen.**
Ihr werdet heute gehen **müssen.**
Sie (Sie) werden heute gehen **müssen.**

a. In the future tense the infinitive of the modal auxiliary stands last.
b. The present tense of modal auxiliaries is often used to express future time.

Ich muss morgen gehen = Ich werde morgen gehen müssen.

Er kann mich morgen nicht begleiten = Er wird mich morgen nicht begleiten können.

Exercise 160

Above is the future of **müssen**. Practice the future of the other modals by substituting **dürfen, können, mögen, sollen, wollen** for **müssen**.

Exercise 161

Ein Gespräch. Practice aloud.

—**Wohin werden Sie im nächsten Sommer fahren?**

—**Ich werde nach Deutschland reisen.**

—**Wann werden Sie New York verlassen?**

—**Ich werde am 31. Mai abfahren.**

—**Wie viel Zeit werden Sie in Deutschland verbringen?**

—**Ich werde dort drei Monate verbringen.**

—**Werden Sie Ihren Geschäftspartner in München sehen?**

—**Jawohl, er wird mich am Flugplatz erwarten.**

—**Wie lange werden Sie in München bleiben?**

—**Ich werde dort drei oder vier Wochen lang bleiben.**

—**Wollen Sie eine Reise nach Berlin machen?**

—**Ja, ich will nach Berlin reisen, wenn ich Zeit habe.**

—**Kann Herr Müller Sie begleiten?**

—**Es wird ihm leider nicht möglich sein, mich zu begleiten;** *or* **Er kann mich nicht begleiten;** *or*

Er wird mich nicht begleiten können.

Exercise 162

Complete the translation of each English sentence.

Beispiel: 1. Er wird drei Wochen in Berlin bleiben müssen.

1. He will have to stay in Berlin three weeks.
2. Which cities will he visit?
3. I do not know which cities he will visit.
4. This lake is said to be beautiful.
5. We shall visit all places of interest.
6. In Cologne we shall be able to visit the Cathedral.
7. The tourists will want to see the German Museum.
8. We shall make many excursions to the country.
9. Will you be able to accompany me?
10. Will Mr. Schiller await you at the airport?

1. **Er wird drei Wochen in Berlin bleiben _____ .**
2. **_____ wird er besuchen?**
3. **Ich weiß nicht, welche Städte er _____ .**
4. **Dieser See _____ schön sein.**
5. **Wir werden _____ besuchen.**
6. **In Köln werden wir den Dom besuchen _____ .**
7. **Die Touristen werden das Deutsche Museum sehen _____ .**
8. **Wir werden _____ aufs Land machen.**
9. **Werden Sie mich begleiten _____ ?**
10. **Wird Herr Schiller Sie am Flugplatz _____ .**

2. THE FUTURE PERFECT TENSE

I will have learned German, etc.

Ich werde Deutsch gelernt haben.
Du wirst Deutsch gelernt haben.
Er wird Deutsch gelernt haben.
Wir werden Deutsch gelernt haben.
Ihr werdet Deutsch gelernt haben.
Sie werden Deutsch gelernt haben.

I will have gone home, etc.

Ich werde nach Hause gegangen sein.
Du wirst nach Hause gegangen sein.
Er wird nach Hause gegangen sein.
Wir werden nach Hause gegangen sein.
Ihr werdet nach Hause gegangen sein.
Sie werden nach Hause gegangen sein.

The future perfect tense in German, like this tense in English, is rarely used.

Exercise 163

Write about what you will have done in the future.

Beispiel: In drei Jahren werde ich mein Elternhaus verlassen haben.

1. In drei Jahren . . .
2. In fünf Jahren . . .
3. In zehn Jahren . . .
4. In zwanzig Jahren . . .
5. In dreißig Jahren . . .
6. In fünfzig Jahren . . .

Exercise 164

Fragen

Lesen Sie noch enmal den Text: **Welche Städte werden Sie besuchen, Herr Clark?** und dann beant-worten Sie diese Fragen!

1. Wie lange wird Herr Clark in Deutschland bleiben?
2. In welchen Büchern liest er oft?
3. Wie lange wird er in München bleiben?
4. Wie nennt man München?
5. Welches Museum soll das größte technische Museum Europas sein?
6. In welchem berühmten Park will Herr Clark einen Spaziergang machen?
7. Zu welchem interessanten Dorf möchte er einen Ausflug machen?
8. Welche Stadt ist die Stadt der Meistersinger?
9. In welcher Stadt lebte und komponierte Richard Wagner?
10. Welche Städte am Rhein wird Herr Clark besuchen?
11. Wo wurde Heinrich Heine geboren?
12. Von wo aus wird Herr Clark die Heimreise unternehmen?
13. Wer möchte Herrn Clark auf seiner Reise begleiten?
14. Wird er ihn begleiten können?

HERR CLARK REIST NACH DEUTSCHLAND AB

1. Herr Clark hat nun sechs Monate Deutsch gelernt. Er hat viel Zeit mit Gesprächen mit seinem Lehrer, Herrn Müller verbracht. Er hat auch die wichtigsten Regeln der Grammatik gelernt und einige Bücher über Deutschland gelesen. Er hat ernst und fleißig gearbeitet. Jetzt kann er Deutsch sprechen, und freut sich darauf, seine Kenntnisse in Deutschland auszunutzen.

2. Herr Clark hat seinen Reisepass besorgt und sein Flugticket gekauft. Er hat nun alles, was er braucht.

3. Natürlich hat Herr Clark seinem Geschäftspartner in München einen Brief geschrieben, um ihm die Zeit seiner Ankunft mitzuteilen. Herr Schiller, der Vertreter, hat versprochen, ihn am Münchener Flughafen abzuholen.

4. Endlich kommt der 31. Mai, der Tag der Abreise. Das Flugzeug, in dem Herr Clark reisen wird, verlässt den JFK-Flughafen punkt 19.00 Uhr (sieben Uhr abends). Er muss zwei Stunden früher am Flugplatz sein, um sein Ticket vorzuzeigen und sein Gepäck aufzugeben.

5. Die Familie begleitet ihn nicht nach Deutschland, denn die Kinder müssen ja in die Schule gehen, und seine Frau muss zu Hause bleiben, um für die Kinder zu sorgen. Außerdem ist das Reisen mit vier Kindern kostspielig.

6. Natürlich ist die Familie sehr aufgeregt. Die Kinder haben nicht viel geschlafen, und um sieben Uhr dreißig früh sind alle wach, gewaschen und angezogen.

1. Mr. Clark has now studied German for six months. He has spent much time in conversation with his teacher, Mr. Müller. He has also learned the most important rules of German grammar and has read some books about Germany. He has worked earnestly and industriously. Now he can speak German and is looking forward to make use of his knowledge in Germany.

2. Mr. Clark has obtained his passport and has bought his plane ticket. He now has everything that he needs.

3. Naturally, Mr. Clark has written a letter to his business partner in Munich to inform him of the time of his arrival. Mr. Schiller, the partner, has promised to pick him up at the Munich airport.

4. Finally the 31st of May arrives, the day of departure. The plane on which Mr. Clark will travel leaves the JFK-Airport at exactly seven o'clock in the evening. He must be at the airport two hours earlier in order to present his ticket and have his baggage checked in.

5. His family is not accompanying him to Germany, for the children must go to school, and his wife must remain at home in order to look after the children. Besides, traveling with four children is costly.

6. Naturally the family is very excited. The children have not slept much and at seven-thirty in the morning they are all awake, washed and dressed.

7. Um 5 Uhr nachmittags ist die ganze Familie bereit, zum Flughafen zu fahren. Herr Clark ist reisefertig. Er hat zwei Koffer gepackt und bereits in das Auto gestellt. Sie steigen alle ein. Herr Clark fährt selbst und sie kommen um Viertel nach sechs am Flughafen an.

8. Herr Clark muss seine Karte und seinen Reisepass vorzeigen und sein Gepäck abwiegen lassen. Und nun ist es Zeit, das Flugzeug zu besteigen.

9. Jetzt umarmt und küsst Herr Clark seine Frau und Kinder, die ihm „Gute Reise" wünschen. Bevor er das Flugzeug besteigt, winkt er seiner Familie, die ihm traurig nachschaut. Um punkt 19.00 Uhr (sieben Uhr abends) steigt das Flugzeug auf.

10. Herr Clark ist auf dem Weg nach Deutschland!

7. At 5 o'clock in the afternoon the whole family is ready to ride to the airport. Mr. Clark is ready to start. He has packed two suitcases and has already put them in the car. They all get in. Mr. Clark drives himself and they arrive at the airport at a quarter past six.

8. Mr. Clark must show his ticket and passport and have his baggage weighed. And now it is time to get on the plane.

9. Now Mr. Clark embraces and kisses his wife and children, who wish him "Happy Voyage." Before getting on the plane, he waves to his family, who are watching him sadly. At 7:00 o'clock sharp (seven o'clock in the evening) the plane takes off.

10. Mr. Clark is on his way to Germany.

Wortschatz

die Abreise *pl.* **-n** departure
die Kenntnis *pl.* **-se** knowledge
das Reisen traveling
die Regel *pl.* **-n** rule
wiegen to weigh
ab-holen to call for; pick up, meet
küssen to kiss
mit-teilen to inform
nach-prüfen to check
nach-schauen to watch, look after
packen to pack
sorgen für to take care of, look after
umármen to embrace
vor-zeigen to present
winken to beckon, wave
aufgeregt excited
traurig sad
kostspielig = **teuer** costly
reisefertig ready to start
schwierig difficult; **wach** awake
nicht nur . . . sondern auch not only . . . but also

Strong Verbs. Principal Parts

auf-steigen	to arise, get on	er steigt . . . auf	stieg . . . auf	ist aufgestiegen
besteigen	to get on, mount	er besteigt	bestieg	hat bestiegen
schlafen	to sleep	er schläft	schlief	hat geschlafen
versprechen	to promise	er verspricht	versprach	hat versprochen
bringen	to bring	er bringt	brachte	hat gebracht
verbringen	to spend (time)	er verbringt	verbrachte	hat verbracht
wiegen	to weigh	er wiegt	wog	hat gewogen

Two Word Families

reisen to travel
das Reisen[1] traveling
die Reise trip
ab-reisen to depart
die Abreise departure
der Reisende traveler
reisefertig ready to depart, ready for travel
Reiseführer guide
Reisetasche traveling bag

sprechen to speak
das Sprechen[1] speaking
versprechen to promise
aus-sprechen to pronounce
die Sprache speech, language
die Aussprache pronunciation
das Gespräch conversation
sprachlos speechless
der Sprecher speaker, orator, announcer

NOTE: 1. Infinitives may be used as neuter nouns. The translation is usually a noun ending in **-ing: das Schreiben** writing, **das Lesen** reading.

Wichtige Redemittel

punkt 18.00 six o'clock sharp
Das Flugzeug steigt auf. The plane takes off.
etwas tun lassen to have something done.

Er lässt sein Gepäck wiegen. He has his baggage weighed.
Ich ließ meinen Reisepass überprüfen. I had my passport checked.

Grammar Notes and Practical Exercises

1. ABOUT THE VERBS *lassen* (*er lässt, ließ, hat gelassen*) and *verlassen*

a. lassen + *an infinitive without* zu = *to let, to allow, to have something done.*

Sie lässt uns hier spielen.
Lasst uns fertig werden!
Er lässt das Gepäck wiegen.
Ich lasse mir einen Anzug machen.

She lets us play here.
Let's get finished!
He has the baggage weighed.
I'm having a suit made (for myself).

b. lassen + *a direct object* = *to leave, to let.*

Er ließ seinen Hut auf dem Tisch.
Ich ließ ihn gestern fortgehen.

He left his hat on the table.
I let him go yesterday.

c. verlassen *to leave (go away from, abandon)*

Am Mittwoch hat er die Stadt verlassen.   On Wednesday he left the city.

Exercise 165

Change these sentences to the present.

Beispiel: 1. Herr Clark lernt die Regeln der Grammatik.

1. Herr Clark hat die Regeln der Grammatik gelernt.
2. Er hat einige Bücher über Deutschland gelesen.
3. Er hat seinen Reisepass besorgt.
4. Er hat seine Fahrkarte gekauft.
5. Er hat seinem Geschäftspartner einen Brief geschrieben.
6. Er hat eine Antwort bekommen.
7. Herr Schiller hat versprochen, ihn abzuholen.
8. Die Kinder haben viel geschlafen.
9. Sie haben sich gewaschen.
10. Sie haben sich angezogen.
11. Die Familie ist zum Flughafen gefahren.
12. Das Flugzeug ist aufgestiegen.
13. Herr Clark hat das Flugzeug bestiegen.
14. Er ist abgereist.
15. Er hat seine Frau und Kinder zu Hause gelassen.
16. Die Familie hat um sieben Uhr den Flughafen verlassen.

Exercise 166

Complete these sentences by choosing the infinitive with or without **zu** as each sentence requires.

Beispiel: 1. Herr Schiller hat versprochen, ihn **abzuholen.**

1. Herr Schiller hat versprochen, ihn (abholen, abzuholen).
2. Ich hoffe, Ihnen in München (begegnen, zu begegnen).
3. Wir müssen alle unsere Kenntnisse (ausnützen, auszunützen).
4. Die Passagiere kommen früh, um ihre Reisepässe (vorzeigen, vorzuzeigen).
5. Der Beamte will unsere Koffer (wiegen, zu wiegen).
6. Wir ließen unsere Reisepässe (nachprüfen, nachzuprüfen).
7. Ich werde Ihnen schreiben, um die Zeit meiner Ankunft (mitteilen, mitzuteilen).
8. Ich beabsichtige, Sie am Flugplatz (abholen, abzuholen).
9. Ich werde die Gelegenheit haben, meine Kenntnisse (ausnützen, auszunützen).
10. Herrn Clarks Frau und Kinder können nicht (mitgehen, mitzugehen).
11. Alle sind bereit, zum Flughafen (fahren, zu fahren).
12. Es ist jetzt Zeit, das Flugzeug (besteigen, zu besteigen).

Exercise 167

Find the following cities!

1. **Wo ist Berlin?**
2. **Zeigen Sie mir, wo Köln ist?**
3. **Können Sie mir sagen, wo Frankfurt ist?**
4. **Ist Hamburg im Süden von Deutschland?**
5. **Welche große Stadt liegt am Rhein?**
6. **Zeigen Sie mir bitte die Stadt, in der Herr Clark mit dem Flugzeug landet.**
7. **Wo ist Bremen?**
8. **Welche große Stadt liegt an der Nordsee?**

Exercise 168

Fragen

Lesen Sie noch einmal den Text: **Herr Clark reist nach Deutschland ab,** und dann beantworten Sie diese Fragen!

1. **Wie lange hat Herr Clark Deutsch gelernt?**
2. **Mit wem hat er viel Zeit im Gespräch verbracht?**
3. **Was hat er gelesen?**
4. **Kann er jetzt Deutsch sprechen?**
5. **An wen hat er einen Brief geschrieben?**
6. **Was hat sein Geschäftspartner ihm versprochen?**
7. **Welcher Tag kommt endlich?**
8. **Um wie viel Uhr verlässt das Flugzeug den JFK-Flughafen?**
9. **Begleiten ihn Frau und Kinder auf der Reise?**
10. **Warum müssen die Kinder zu Hause bleiben?**
11. **Warum muss Frau Clark zu Hause bleiben?**
12. **Um wie viel Uhr ist die ganze Familie bereit, zum Flughafen zu fahren?**
13. **Wann kommen sie am Flughafen an?**
14. **Was tut Herr Clark, bevor er das Flugzeug besteigt?**
15. **Wie sehen ihm Frau und Kinder nach, während er das Flugzeug besteigt?**

REVIEW OF CHAPTERS 31–35

Weak (Regular) Verbs. No Vowel Changes

1.	führen	1.	to lead, carry on
2.	schicken	2.	to send
3.	schmecken	3.	to taste (*no obj.*)
4.	speisen	4.	to dine
5.	sorgen für	5.	to look after
6.	packen	6.	to pack
7.	küssen	7.	to kiss
8.	schauen	8.	to look
9.	leben	9.	to live
10.	versuchen	10.	to try, taste + *obj.*
11.	begegnen	11.	to meet + *dat.*
12.	gratulieren	12.	to congratulate + *dat.*
13.	ab-reisen	13.	to set out
14.	aus-nützen	14.	to make full use of
15.	mit-teilen	15.	to inform
16.	ab-holen	16.	to go to meet, pick up
17.	zu-hören	17.	to listen
18.	sich bemühen	18.	to try

Strong (Irregular) Verbs. Vowel Changes

bieten	to offer	er bietet	bot	hat geboten
essen	to eat	er isst	aß	hat gegessen
trinken	to drink	er trinkt	trank	hat getrunken
bitten (um)	to ask (for)	er bittet	bat	hat gebeten
schließen	to close	er schließt	schloss	hat geschlossen
schlafen	to sleep	er schläft	schlief	hat geschlafen
beschreiben	to describe	er beschreibt	beschrieb	hat beschrieben
besteigen	to mount	er besteigt	bestieg	hat bestiegen
ein-steigen	to get in	er steigt ein	stieg ein	ist eingestiegen
ein-laden	to invite	er lädt ein	lud ein	hat eingeladen
ergreifen	to seize	er ergreift	ergriff	hat ergriffen
unternehmen	to undertake	er unternimmt	unternahm	hat unternommen

Deutsche Ausdrücke

1. **mit Recht** rightly; **vor allem** above all
2. **reisefertig** ready to start
3. **ja, gewiss** yes, indeed; yes, surely
4. **auf dem Land** in the country (opposite of city); **aufs Land** to the country; **Wir machen einen Ausflug aufs Land.** We are taking a trip to the country. **Er wohnt auf dem Lande.** He lives in the country.
5. **zum Essen ein-laden,** to invite to dinner. **Ich habe sie zum Essen eingeladen.** I have invited her (them) to dinner.
6. **meiner (seiner, ihrer, Ihrer, usw.) Meinung nach.** according to my (his, her, your, etc.) opinion. **nach,** in the sense of according to, follows its noun.
7. **einen Spaziergang machen** to take a walk
8. **die Gelegenheit ergreifen** to take the opportunity
9. **Das ist mir angenehm.** That's agreeable to me.
10. **Der Mensch ist, was er isst. (Sprichwort)** Man is what he eats.
11. **Besser spät als nie. (Sprichwort)** Better late than never.

Exercise 169

Ergänzen Sie diese Sätze auf Deutsch! Complete these sentences in German.

1. **Wann fahren Sie** (to the country)?
2. **Sie nennen** (rightly) **München das moderne Athen.**
3. **Sie lebten das ganze Jahr** (in the country).
4. **Warum** (don't take the opportunity) **auf die Universität zu gehen?**
5. (Do you like) **die deutsche Küche?**
6. **Jeden Tag** (he took a walk) **im Englischen Garten.**
7. **Wir waren schon** (ready for travel), **als das Auto ankam.**
8. (Take every opportunity), **Deutsch zu reden!**
9. (According to his opinion) **ist München die schönste Stadt Deutschlands.**
10. (According to her opinion) **ist Köln schöner als München.**
11. (We have invited him), **uns zu besuchen.**

Exercise 170

Review the principal parts of the strong and weak verbs at the beginning of this chapter. Then complete these sentences with the given tense of the verbs in parentheses.

Beispiel: 1. Der Lehrer hörte aufmerksam zu, als er den Brief las.

1. (zu-hören *Prät.*) Der Lehrer _____ aufmerksam _____ , als er den Brief vorlas.
2. (essen *Perf.*) Zum Mittagessen _____ wir Fleisch mit Gemüse _____ .
3. (schmecken *Prät.*) Alles _____ sehr gut.
4. (ein-laden *Perf.*) Ich _____ meinen besten Kunden zum Mittagessen _____ .
5. (trinken *Prät.*) Beim Abendessen _____ jeder von uns zwei Glas Bier.
6. (sich zurecht-finden *Fut.*) Ich _____ mich gewiss in Deutschland _____ .
7. (ergreifen *Imp.*) _____ Sie jede Gelegenheit Deutsch zu sprechen!
8. (beschreiben *Fut.*) Wir _____ alle Sehenswürdigkeiten _____ .
9. (speisen *Perf.*) Wo _____ Sie gestern abend _____ ?
10. (sich bemühen *Plu.perf.*) Er _____ sich _____ , behilflich zu sein.
11. (auf-stehen *Perf.*) Die Kinder _____ um sieben Uhr dreißig _____ .
12. (bieten *Präs.*) _____ man etwas Gutes heute?
13. (müssen *Prät.*) Die Mütter _____ für die Kinder sorgen.
14. (besteigen *Plu.perf.*) Nachdem er das Flugzeug _____ , winkte er mit der Hand.
15. (ein-steigen *Perf.*) Um drei Uhr nachmittags _____ alle in den Zug _____ .
16. (bitten um *Präs.*) Dort ist ein Reisender, der um Auskunft _____ .

Exercise 171

Positive, Comparative, Superlative: Fill in the grid!

Positive	Comparative	Superlative
		am größten
	dicker	
schnell		
gut		
		am klügsten
	höher	
nahe		
gern		
		am wenigsten

DIALOG 1
DEUTSCHE ODER AMERIKANISCHE FILME?

—Sind die deutschen Filme Ihrer Meinung nach besser als die amerikanischen?

—Nun, manche[1] sind besser und manche sind schlechter. In beiden Ländern gibt es gute, ernsthafte Filme und auch viele schlechte. In beiden Ländern findet man sehr gute und auch sehr schlechte Filme.

—Wie gefallen Ihnen die Hollywood-Filme?

—Die gefallen mir meistens nicht. Sie bieten viel Kitsch, aber ich muss gestehen, dann und wann kommen auch hervorragende Filme aus Hollywood. Am besten gefallen mir Kultur- und Dokumentarfilme.

—Ich nehme an, dass Sie Kriminalfilme nicht mögen.

—Da haben Sie Recht! Die Darstellung von Gewalt und Verbrechen ist nicht nach meinem Geschmack.

—Solche Bilder scheinen einem großen Teil des amerikanischen Publikums zu gefallen.

—Nun, über, den Geschmack lässt sich nicht streiten.

—In your opinion, are the German films better than the American ones?

—Well, some are better and some are worse. In both countries there are good, serious films and also many bad, inferior ones. In both countries one finds very good as well as very bad films.

—How do you like the Hollywood films?

—Generally I do not like these. They offer a great deal of trash and junk, but I must admit that now and then some outstanding films do come out of Hollywood. I like cultural and documentary films best.

—I assume that you don't care for thrillers.

—That's right! The acting out of violence and crime is not to my taste.

—Such pictures seem to please a large part of the American public.

—Well, there's no disputing about taste.

NOTE: 1. **mancher** many a, *plural* many, some. **Mancher** is a **der**-word: **mancher Mann, manche Frau, manches Kind; manche Männer.**

DIALOG 2
IM RESTAURANT

—Guten Tag, mein Herr. Hier ist die Speisekarte.

—Danke. Was empfehlen Sie heute?

—Es gibt Beefsteak mit Kartoffeln, Wiener Schnitzel, Rührei mit Schinken, oder Spiegeleier, auch kalten Aufschnitt, Bismarckhering oder eine Gemüseplatte.

—Sehr gut. Ich möchte Wiener Schnitzel. Aber bringen Sie mir zuerst einen Bismarckhering.

—Bitte. Wünschen Sie zu dem Wiener Schnitzel Gemüse? Die übliche Beilage ist Rotkohl.

—Nein, danke. Ich nehme nur grünen Salat dazu. Nichts mehr.

—Good morning, sir. Here's the menu.

—Thanks. What do you recommend today?

—There's beefsteak with potatoes, veal cutlet, scrambled egg with ham, or fried eggs, besides cold cuts, Bismarck herring, or a vegetable plate.

—Fine. I should like veal cutlet. But bring me a Bismarck herring to start with.

—Certainly. Do you wish some vegetable with the veal cutlet? The usual side dish is red cabbage.

—No, thanks. I'll just take lettuce with it. That will be all.

—Schön. Wünschen Sie etwas Obst?

—Very well. Do you care for some fruit?

—Ach ja. Wie sind die Birnen?

—Yes indeed. How are the pears?

—Sehr gut.

—Very good.

—Schön. Und dazu bringen Sie mir eine Tasse Kaffee.

—All right. And with it bring me a cup of coffee.

—Und was trinken Sie zum Essen? Vielleicht eine Flasche Wein?

—And what will you have to drink with your meal? How about a bottle of wine?

—Nein, lieber ein Seidel Bier.

—No, I'd prefer a mug of beer.

—Schön. Ich komme gleich zurück.

—Okay, I'll be right back.

Am Ende der Mahlzeit sagt Herr Clark: „Bitte, zahlen, Herr Ober!"

At the end of the meal Mr. Clark says, "The check please, waiter."

—Hier ist die Rechnung.

—Here is your bill.

—Ist der Bedienungszuschlag schon darin enthalten?

—Is the service charge included?

—Jawohl, zehn Prozent Bedienung.

—Yes, sir, ten percent for service.

Herr Clark bezahlt die Rechnung und verlässt das Restaurant.

Mr. Clark pays the bill and leaves the restaurant.

Exercise 172

Lesestück. The following text shows that the English influence on German is undeniable.

FRAU CLARK SHOPPT IM INTERNET

Heute hat Frau Clark keine Lust[1] nach New York zum Shopping zu fahren. Also setzt sie sich an ihren Laptop und surft ein wenig im Internet. Zuerst sucht sie nach der neuesten Mode. Sie will keine Designerkleidung, denn die ist ihr zu teuer. Nach einer Weile findet sie ein Paar Jeans, die ihr sehr gut gefallen. Mit einem Mausklick landen die Jeans in ihrem virtuellen Warenkorb.[2] Nun braucht sie noch ein trendiges Top. Sie muss nicht lange suchen, bis sie etwas Passendes gefunden hat. Wieder ein Mausklick. Danach beginnt Frau Clark nach einer Musik-CD mit dem neuesten Hit aus der Hitparade zu suchen. Klick. Vielleicht noch eine DVD für den heutigen Abend vor dem Videorecorder? Klick. Zuletzt will sich Frau Clark noch etwas zum Lesen kaufen. Sie möchte unbedingt den Bestseller lesen, von dem sie im Fernsehen gehört hat. Klick. Klick. Zum Bezahlen kann Frau Clark ihre Kreditkarte benutzen. Sie hat zwar viel mehr gekauft als sie eigentlich wollte, aber sie konnte alles zu Hause von ihrem Computer aus erledigen.

NOTES: 1. keine Lust haben not to feel like it; **Sie hat keine Lust** she doesn't feel like it. **2.** virtual shopping basket.

ANKUNFT IN MÜNCHEN

DER ERSTE BRIEF AUS MÜNCHEN AN HERRN MÜLLER

München, den 4. Juni 2005

Lieber Freund!

1. *Als das Flugzeug in München landete, kam ich ohne Probleme durch den Zoll und ging in die Ankunftshalle.*
2. *Sofort kam mir ein gut gekleideter Herr entgegen und fragte: „Entschuldigung, sind Sie Herr Clark?"*
3. *Ich antwortete: „Ja, ich bin's. Und Sie sind Herr Schiller, nicht wahr? Es freut mich sehr, Sie kennen zu lernen." Wir gaben uns die Hand.*
4. *„Das Vergnügen ist ganz meinerseits," erwiderte Herr Schiller.*
5. *Dann gingen wir zusammen hinaus und fuhren mit einem Taxi zu dem Hotel Königshof.*
6. *Das Taxi fuhr sehr schnell durch die Stadt. Ich dachte mir: Die Taxifahrer sind überall gleich.*
7. *Endlich kamen wir beim Hotel an und stiegen aus. Herr Schiller ging mit mir ins Hotel hinein.*
8. *Ich ging zum Empfangschef und sagte zu ihm: „Guten Tag. Haben Sie ein Zimmer für Clark reserviert?"*
9. *„Willkommen in München, Herr Clark. Gewiss haben wir für Sie ein schönes Zimmer reserviert. Es ist im fünften Stock, Nummer 55."*
10. *„Sehr nett, schönen Dank. Was ist der Zimmerpreis, bitte?"*
11. *„Fünfundsiebzig Euro pro Tag, mit Frühstück."*

Munich, June 4, 2005

Dear Friend:

1. *When the plane landed in Munich I went through customs without any problems and went into the hall for arrivals.*
2. *Immediately a well-dressed man came toward me and asked: "Excuse me, are you Mr. Clark?"*
3. *I answered: "Yes I am. And you are Mr. Schiller, aren't you? I am very glad to make your acquaintance." We shook hands.*
4. *"The pleasure is all mine," answered Mr. Schiller.*
5. *Then we went out together and went by taxi to the Königshof Hotel.*
6. *The taxi drove rapidly through the city. I thought to myself: Taxi drivers are the same everywhere.*
7. *Finally we arrived at the hotel and got out. Mr. Schiller went in with me.*
8. *I went to the manager and said to him: "Good day. Have you reserved a room for Clark?"*
9. *"Welcome to Munich, Mr. Clark. Of course we have reserved a beautiful room for you. It is on the fifth floor, No. 55."*
10. *"Very nice, thank you. And what is the cost of the room please?"*
11. *"Seventy-five euros per day, including breakfast."*

12. „*Schön. Wollen Sie bitte mein Gepäck hinauftragen lassen?*"

13. „*Sofort, Herr Clark. —Aber Sie sprechen sehr gut Deutsch. Wie lange sind Sie schon in Deutschland?*"

14. „*Ich bin soeben angekommen,*" *sagte ich, und war auf mich selbst recht stolz.*

15. „*Sind Sie zum Vergnügen hergereist?*"

16. „*Es ist eine Vergnügungsreise und auch eine Geschäftsreise.*"

17. *Ich plauderte noch ein wenig mit Herrn Schiller, und dann verabschiedeten wir uns. Als er mich verließ, versprach Herr Schiller, mich anzurufen, um einen Termin für den nächsten Tag auszumachen.*

18. *Ich fuhr mit dem Fahrstuhl zu meinem Zimmer hinauf. Es ist ein sehr bequemes Zimmer. Mir fehlt nichts. Ich glaube, Herr Müller, dass es mir in Deutschland sehr gut gefallen wird.*

Mit herzlichem Gruß,

Ihr Freund R. Clark

12. "Good. Will you please have my baggage taken up?"

13. "Immediately, Mr. Clark. —But you speak German very well. How long have you been in Germany?"

14. "I have just arrived," said I, and was very proud of myself.

15. "Have you come here for a pleasure trip?"

16. "It is a pleasure trip and also a business trip."

17. I chatted with Mr. Schiller a little longer and then we said good-bye. When he left me, Mr. Schiller promised to telephone me in order to arrange a definite appointment for the next day.

18. I went up in the elevator to my room. It is a very comfortable room. I lack nothing. I believe, Mr. Müller, that I shall like Germany very well.

With hearty greetings,

Your friend R. Clark

Wortschatz

der Fahrstuhl = der Lift elevator
der Empfángschef hotel manager
die Geschwíndigkeit speed
der Termin, die Verábredung appointment
der Zoll customs
sich erínnern to remember

fest-setzen to set, fix, arrange
um-schauen to look around
stolz (auf + *acc.*) proud (of)
schließlich finally
soében just now
meinerseits on my part

Strong Verbs

an-rufen to call up	er ruft an	rief an	hat angerufen
an-schreien to cry out	er schreit an	schrie an	hat angeschrien
hinauf-tragen to carry up	er trägt hinauf	trug hinauf	hat hinaufgetragen
gefallen + *dat.* to please	er gefällt	gefiel	hat gefallen

Wichtige Redemittel

kennen lernen to become (get) acquainted, to get to know.

Es freut mich, Sie kennen zu lernen. I'm pleased to meet you.

Wann hast du sie kennen gelernt? When did you make her acquaintance?

Ich habe sie nie kennen gelernt. I have never met her.

Ich möchte sie kennen lernen. I should like to meet her.

Nun, morgen wirst du sie kennen lernen. Well, tomorrow, you will meet her.

Nichts fehlt mir. I lack nothing (*lit.* nothing is lacking to me).

Ihm (ihr, Ihnen, etc.) **fehlt nichts.** He (she, you, etc.) lacks nothing.

Exercise 173

DER ERSTE DIALOG
AM FLUGHAFEN

1. **Guten Tag, Herr Schiller. Erwarten Sie jemand?**
2. **Jawohl, ich warte auf Herrn Clark, den Chef der Firma, die ich in München vertrete.**
3. **Kennen Sie ihn?**
4. **Ich kenne ihn nicht persönlich. Aber ich habe ein Foto von ihm, und ich glaube, ich werde ihn erkennen. Er ist ein Mann von ungefähr vierzig.**
5. **Um wie viel Uhr kommt er an?**
6. **Das Flugzeug soll um 10.10 Uhr ankommen.**
7. **Hat es Verspätung?**
8. **Nein, es kommt pünktlich. Aha, es ist eben gelandet.**
9. **Entschuldigen Sie mich, bitte, ich gehe hinüber, um Herrn Clark zu begrüßen.**

1. Good morning, Mr. Schiller. Are you expecting someone?
2. Yes, sir, I am waiting for Mr. Clark, the head of the firm I represent in Munich.
3. Do you know him?
4. I don't know him personally. But I have his photo and I think I'll be able to recognize him. He is a man of about forty.
5. At what time is he due?
6. The plane is scheduled to arrive at 10:10.
7. Is it late?
8. No, it's on time. Ah, it has just landed!
9. Excuse me, sir, I'm going over to greet Mr. Clark.

Exercise 174

DER ZWEITE DIALOG
WILLKOMMEN IN DEUTSCHLAND

1. Sind Sie Herr Clark?	1. Are you Mr. Clark?
2. Ja, ich bin's. Und Sie sind Herr Schiller, nicht wahr?	2. Yes, I'm he. And you are Mr. Schiller, aren't you?
3. Jawohl. Willkommen in Deutschland, Herr Clark. Wie ist es Ihnen auf der Reise gegangen?	3. Right. Welcome to Germany, Mr. Clark. How did the trip go?
4. Außerordentlich gut! Ich freue mich, in Deutschland zu sein.	4. Marvelously! I am very happy to be in Germany.
5. Ich bin sicher, dass es Ihnen hier sehr gut gefallen wird.	5. I am sure that you will like it here very much.

Grammar Notes and Practical Exercises

1. THE PRESENT PARTICIPLE USED AS AN ADJECTIVE

The present participle is formed by adding **-d** to the infinitive. Thus:

redend speaking	**folgend** following	**aussehend** looking
lachend laughing	**plaudernd** chatting	**kommend** coming

Used as an adjective, the present participle takes adjective case endings:

Ein fein aussehender Mann kam mir entgegen.	A good-looking man came toward me.
Ich freue mich auf die kommenden Ferien.	I am looking forward to the coming vacation.

Exercise 175

Add the correct case endings (for present participles and adjectives).

Ein amerikanisch _____ Lehrer musste nach einer verloren _____ Wette vor seinen lachend _____ Schülern vier Würmer verspeisen. Chuck Matlock aus Michigan hatte gewettet, dass seine zwölfjährig _____ Schüler es nicht schaffen würden, in einem Monat über tausend Bücher zu lesen. Die fleißig _____ Schüler aber wurden zu Bücherwürmern und gewannen die skurril _____ Wette. Matlock warf dann vor den staunend _____ Schülern vier Würmer in kochend _____ Wasser, salzte und verspeiste sie. Der kauend _____ Lehrer erklärte sich bereit, im kommend _____ Jahr eine ähnliche Wette abzuschließen.

2. MORE *sein*-VERBS (INTRANSITIVE VERBS DENOTING A CHANGE OF PLACE OR CONDITION)

Note the **sein**-verbs in the text, some familiar, some new.

landen	to land	er landet	landete	ist gelandet
eilen	to hurry	er eilt	eilte	ist geeilt
rasen	to rush (madly)	er rast	raste	ist gerast
her-reisen	to travel here	er reist her	reiste her	ist hergereist
werden	to become, to get	er wird	wurde	ist geworden
fahren	to ride	er fährt	fuhr	ist gefahren
hinauf-gehen	to go up	er geht hinauf	ging hinauf	ist hinaufgegangen
hinein-gehen	to go in	er geht hinein	ging hinein	ist hineingegangen
aus-steigen	to get out	er steigt aus	stieg aus	ist ausgestiegen
an-kommen	to arrive	er kommt an	kam an	ist angekommen

Exercise 176

Change these sentences to the **Perfekt**. All the verbs are **haben**-verbs.

Beispiel: 1. Der Kaufmann hat Deutsch studiert.

1. Der Kaufmann studierte Deutsch.
2. Das Taxi nahm den kürzesten Weg in die Stadt.
3. Ich hatte gar keine Eile.
4. Sie plauderten noch ein wenig.
5. Mir fehlte nichts.
6. Es gefiel ihm in Deutschland sehr gut.
7. Er verbrachte viel Zeit in München.
8. Sein Freund versprach, ihm zu begegnen.
9. Er kaufte sich eine Fahrkarte.
10. Wann verließen Sie die Stadt?

Exercise 177

Change these sentences to the **Perfekt**. All the verbs are **sein**-verbs.

Beispiel: 1. Das Flugzeug ist in München gelandet.

1. Das Flugzeug landete in München.
2. Er wurde beim Zoll bald fertig.
3. Dann gingen sie zusammen hinaus.
4. Ein gut gekleideter Herr kam ihm entgegen.
5. Sie fuhren mit dem Taxi zum Hotel.

6. Das Taxi raste um die Ecke.
7. Es fuhr mit hoher Geschwindigkeit.
8. Endlich kam der Geschäftsmann im Hotel an.
9. Die zwei Herren gingen hinein.
10. Um wie viel Uhr stiegst du aus dem Taxi?

Exercise 178

Fragen

Lesen Sie noch einmal den Text: Ankunft in München, und dann beantworten Sie diese Fragen!

1. Wohin ging Herr Clark, als er beim Zoll fertig wurde?
2. Wer kam ihm in der Ankunftshalle entgegen?
3. Was fragte dieser Herr?
4. Was erwiderte Herr Clark?
5. Wohin fuhren die zwei Herren in einem Taxi?
6. Fuhr das Taxi langsam oder mit hoher Geschwindigkeit?
7. Wo sind sie endlich angekommen?
8. Wer ging mit Herrn Clark hinein?
9. Was für ein Zimmer hatte man für Herrn Clark reserviert?
10. In welchem Stock befand sich dieses Zimmer?
11. Wie hoch war der Zimmerpreis?
12. Was versprach Herr Schiller, als er Herrn Clark verließ?

HERR CLARK BESUCHT DIE FAMILIE SCHILLER

1. Einen Tag nach Herrn Clarks Ankunft in München hat Herr Schiller Herrn Clark angerufen, um ihn für den folgenden Tag zum Essen einzuladen. Natürlich hat Herr Clark die Einladung sofort angenommen, denn er freute sich darauf, eine deutsche Familie zu besuchen.

2. Er rief sich ein Taxi, und um sieben Uhr kam er vor einem modernen Miethaus in der Thomasstraße an.

3. Herr Clark fuhr mit dem Lift in den vierten Stock und klingelte. Frau Schiller öffnete die Tür und lud ihn ein, hereinzukommen.

4. Herr Schiller kam ihm sogleich entgegen und begrüßte Herrn Clark herzlich. „Guten Abend, Herr Clark," sagte er, „es macht mir große Freude, Sie bei mir im Hause begrüßen zu dürfen."

5. Dann betraten sie das Wohnzimmer, das modern und geschmackvoll möbliert war. Herr Clark sagte zu Herr und Frau Schiller: „Diese Wohnung ist sehr hübsch." Herr Schiller stellte auch noch seine zwei Kinder vor.

6. Die Jungen gehen in das Gymnasium. Der ältere möchte Arzt werden, und der jüngere will Anwalt werden.

7. Dann setzten sich alle zu Tisch, und Frau Schiller wartete mit einem ausgezeichneten deutschen Essen auf. Dieses begann mit einer Vorspeise, danach gab es Suppe, Fleisch mit zwei Sorten Gemüse, Salat, Obst, mehrere Weinsorten, einen Apfelstrudel und Kaffee.

1. One day after Mr. Clark's arrival in Munich Mr. Schiller telephoned Mr. Clark to invite him for dinner on the following day. Naturally Mr. Clark accepted the invitation at once, because he was looking forward to visiting a German family.

2. He called a taxi, and at seven o'clock he arrived in front of a modern apartment house on Thomas Street.

3. Mr. Clark rode up to the fourth floor in the elevator, and rang. Mrs. Schiller opened the door and invited him to come in.

4. Mr. Schiller came immediately toward him and greeted Mr. Clark cordially. "Good evening, Mr. Clark," he said. "It gives me great pleasure to see you here in my house."

5. Then they entered the living room, which was furnished tastefully in modern style. Mr. Clark said to Mr. and Mrs. Schiller: "This apartment is very nice." Mr. Schiller introduced also his children.

6. The boys are studying at a German high school. The older would like to become a doctor and the younger wants to become a lawyer.

7. Then they sat down at the table and Mrs. Schiller served an excellent German meal. This began with an appetizer, then there was soup, meat with two kinds of vegetables, a salad, fruit, several kinds of wine, apple strudel and coffee.

8. **Bei Tisch unterhielten sich die zwei Geschäftspartner über das Leben in Deutschland, über Kunst und Musik.**

9. **Nach dem Essen zogen sich die Jungen auf ihre eigenen Zimmer zurück, um ihre Hausaufgaben zu machen.**

10. **Nun hatten Herr Clark und Herr Schiller die Gelegenheit, ein wenig über das Geschäft zu sprechen.**

11. **Nach dem gemütlichen Abend bei seinen neuen deutschen Freunden stand Herr Clark auf, bedankte sich bei der Hausfrau für das wunderbare Essen, verabschiedete sich bei allen und verließ die Wohnung.**

12. **Dann fuhr Herr Clark zurück nach Hause, das heißt zu seinem Hotel.**

8. At table the two business partners talked about life in Germany, about art and music.

9. After the meal the boys retired to their own rooms in order to do their homework.

10. Now Mr. Clark and Mr. Schiller had the chance to talk a little bit about business.

11. After spending such a pleasant evening with his new German friends Mr. Clark got up, thanked the housewife for the wonderful meal, said good-bye to everyone and left the house.

12. Then Mr. Clark went home, that is to say, to his hotel.

Wortschatz

der Anwalt *pl.* ¨-e lawyer
die Etáge = der Stock story (of house)
die Hausaufgabe *pl.* -n homework
das Miethaus *pl.* ¨-er apartment house
die Vorspeise *pl.* -n appetizer
die Sorte *pl.* -n kind

klingeln to ring (bell)
auf-warten to serve, wait on
begrüßen to greet
halt-machen to stop
mieten to rent
hübsch pretty

Strong Verbs. Principal Parts

an-nehmen	to accept	er nimmt an	nahm an	hat angenommen
an-halten	to stop	er hält an	hielt an	hat angehalten
an-rufen	to call to, phone	er ruft an	rief an	hat angerufen
betreten	to step into	er betritt	betrat	hat betreten
sich zurück ziehen	to withdraw	er zieht sich zurück	zog sich zurück	hat sich zurückgezogen

Wichtige Redemittel

entzückt von delighted with

Er war von seinen Freunden entzückt. He was delighted with his friends.

anrufen to call on the phone

Sie haben mich angerufen. They called me on the telephone.

jemanden einladen to invite someone

Wir haben ihn zum Essen eingeladen. We invited him to dinner.

eine Einladung annehmen to accept an invitation

Er hat unsere Einladung angenommen. He accepted our invitation.

jemanden vorstellen to introduce somebody

Er stellte mich seiner Frau vor. He introduced me to his wife.

das heißt that is to say

Er will Arzt (Anwalt) werden. He wants to become a doctor (a lawyer).

Exercise 179

Ein Telefongespräch

Herr Schiller ruft Herrn Clark an.

Schiller: Bitte, ich möchte mit Herrn Clark sprechen.

Clark: Hier Clark. Wer spricht?

Schiller: Hier Schiller. Nun, Herr Clark, wie geht es Ihnen?

Clark: Danke, recht gut.

Schiller: Herr Clark, können Sie morgen Abend zu uns zum Essen kommen? Meine Frau und ich würden uns sehr freuen, wenn wir den Abend mit Ihnen verbringen könnten.

Clark: Danke vielmals, Herr Schiller. Ich nehme Ihre freundliche Einladung mit Vergnügen an.

Schiller: Schön. Wir erwarten Sie also um sieben Uhr. Auf Wiedersehen, bis morgen Abend.

A Telephone Conversation

Mr. Schiller calls up Mr. Clark on the telephone.

Schiller: I'd like to speak to Mr. Clark, please.

Clark: This is Clark. Who is speaking?

Schiller: Schiller speaking. Well, Mr. Clark, how are you?

Clark: Quite well, thank you.

Schiller: Mr. Clark, can you come to dinner at our house tomorrow evening? My wife and I would be very happy if we could spend the evening with you.

Clark: Thanks a lot, Mr. Schiller. I accept your kind invitation with pleasure.

Schiller: Good. Then we'll expect you at seven o'clock. Good-bye, until tomorrow evening.

Exercise 180

Sich Vorstellen

Herr Clark, Herr Schiller, Frau Schiller und die Kinder.

Clark: Guten Abend, Herr Schiller.

Schiller: Guten Abend, Herr Clark. Darf ich Ihnen meine Frau Marie vorstellen?

Clark: Es freut mich, Sie kennen zu lernen, Frau Schiller.

Frau Schiller (lächelnd): Das Vergnügen ist ganz meinerseits. (Sie geben sich die Hand.)

Schiller: Und hier sind meine Jungen, Hans und Paul.

Clark: Es freut mich, euch kennen zu lernen.

Hans, Paul: Gleichfalls, Herr Clark.

(Sie geben sich die Hand.)

An Introduction

Mr. Clark, Mr. Schiller, Mrs. Schiller and the children.

Clark: Good evening, Mr. Schiller.

Schiller: Good evening, Mr. Clark. May I introduce my wife Mary to you?

Clark: I'm happy to make your acquaintance, Mrs. Schiller.

Mrs. Schiller (smiling): The pleasure is all mine. (They shake hands.)

Schiller: And here are my boys, John and Paul.

Clark: Glad to make your acquaintance.

John, Paul: Same here, Mr. Clark.

(They shake hands.)

Grammar Notes and Practical Exercises

1. PREPOSITIONS WITH SPECIAL MEANINGS AFTER CERTAIN VERBS

You know the usual meanings of nearly all prepositions. After certain verbs some prepositions have special meanings. You are familiar with the following:

denken an + *acc.* to think of (to have in mind). **Der Geschäftsmann denkt immer an das Geschäft.** The business man always thinks of business.

denken über + *acc.* to think about (have an opinion about). **Was denken Sie über meine kommende Reise?** What do you think about my coming trip?

warten auf + *acc.* to wait for. **Er wartete auf seinen Freund im Arbeitszimmer.** He was waiting for his friend in the study.

sich interessieren für + *acc.* to be interested in. **Er hat sich gar nicht für den Sport interessiert.** He was not at all interested in sports.

sich unterhalten über + *acc.* to converse about. **Sie unterhielten sich über das Klima in Deutschland.** They were discussing the climate of Germany.

sich freuen über + *acc.* to be happy about. **Sie freut sich über ihr neues Kostüm.** She is happy about her new suit.

sich freuen auf + *acc.* to look forward to. **Wir freuen uns auf die kommenden Ferien.** We are looking forward to the coming vacation.

sich vorbereiten auf + *acc.* to prepare for. **Er musste sich auf die Prüfung vorbereiten.** He had to prepare for the examination.

bitten um + *acc.* to ask for. **Er bat um die Speisekarte.** He asked for the menu.

Note carefully the case which follows prepositions with special meanings. The *place where, place to which* rule does not apply to doubtful prepositions with special meanings. The prepositions **auf** and **über** are <u>always</u> followed by the accusative; **an, unter, vor** and **in** are <u>almost always</u> followed by the accusative.

Exercise 181

Complete these sentences in German.

Beispiel: 1. Bei Tisch haben wir uns über Kunst und Musik unterhalten.

1. **Bei Tisch haben wir uns** (about art and music) **unterhalten.**
2. **Ich freute mich** (about the invitation) **zum Abendessen und nahm sie sofort an.**
3. (I am looking forward to) **einen gemütlichen Abend.**
4. **Die Jungen des Kaufmanns** (are interested in) **Sport.**
5. (What do you think) **darüber?**
6. **Der Reisende** (is asking for) **eine Fahrkarte.**
7. **Herr Clark wartete gewöhnlich** (for his teacher) **im Arbeitszimmer.**
8. **Haben Sie sich** (for the trip) **vorbereitet?**

9. **Wir denken immer** (of the coming examinations).
10. (I am not thinking) **daran**.

Exercise 182

Which sentences belong together?

1. **Frau Clark bittet**
2. **Herr Müller denkt immer**
3. **Karl ist vorbereitet**
4. **Was denkst du**
5. **Die Kinder freuen sich**
6. **Die Herren unterhalten sich**
7. **Marie interessiert sich**
8. **Herr Schiller hat**

a. auf Herrn Clark gewartet.
b. über Fußball.
c. um ein Glas Wasser.
d. an seinen Schüler.
e. nur für ihre Puppen.
f. auf seine Mathematikprüfung.
g. über Deutschland?
h. auf ihren Vater.

Exercise 183

Fragen

Lesen Sie noch einmal den Text: **Herr Clark besucht die Familie Schiller,** und dann beantworten Sie diese Fragen!

1. **Wer hat Herrn Clark zum Abendessen eingeladen?**
2. **Wie kam Herr Clark zu der Wohnung des Herrn Schiller?**
3. **Wo machte das Taxi halt?**
4. **In welchem Stock befand sich die Wohnung der Familie Schiller?**
5. **Wer lud den Kaufmann ein, hereinzukommen?**
6. **Wie begrüßte ihn Herr Schiller?**
7. **Wie war das Wohnzimmer möbliert?**
8. **Wem stellte ihn Herr Schiller vor?**
9. **Wo studieren die zwei Jungen?**
10. **Mit was für einem Essen wartete Frau Schiller auf?**
11. **Was gab es zum Dessert?**
12. **Worüber unterhielten sie sich bei Tisch?**
13. **Was taten die zwei Jungen nach dem Essen?**
14. **Was für einen Abend hatte Herr Clark verbracht?**

EIN AUSFLUG AN DEN AMMERSEE

ZWEITER BRIEF AUS MÜNCHEN AN HERRN MÜLLER

Lieber Freund!

1. *Gestern rief ich die zwei Söhne des Herrn Schiller an und fragte sie: „Wollt ihr mit mir einen Ausflug im Auto zum Ammersee machen?" Sie nahmen mit Vergnügen an.*

2. *Heute früh warteten meine jungen Freunde um 8.30 vor meinem Hotel.*

3. *Die Jungen trugen einen Korb, in dem sich ein guter Imbiss befand, den Frau Schiller für uns zubereitet hatte.*

4. *Wir stiegen redend und lachend in das Auto, das ich gemietet hatte, ein und fuhren los.*

5. *Ich saß am Lenkrad und fuhr gemütlich an den Vororten der Stadt entlang, als ich plötzlich einen Lärm hörte, den ich sofort erkannte.*

6. *„Was ist das? Was ist geschehen?" fragten die Jungen.*

7. *Ich hielt das Auto an, und wir stiegen aus. „Wir haben eine Reifenpanne," antwortete ich.*

8. *Ich wollte den Reifen wechseln, und die Jungen wollten mir helfen. Doch leider befand sich kein Wagenheber in dem Kofferraum. Was tun?*

9. *Autos fuhren mit großer Geschwindigkeit an uns vorbei. Trotz unsrer offensichtlichen Panne und unsrer Signale hielt niemand an.*

10. *Es war sehr heiß, und die Sonne brannte auf unsere Köpfe nieder.*

11. *Endlich kam ein Lastwagen, der plötzlich vor uns anhielt. Der Fahrer stieg aus.*

Dear Friend,

1. *Yesterday I telephoned the two sons of Mr. Schiller and asked them: "Do you wish to take a trip with me by car to the Ammersee?" They accepted with pleasure.*

2. *This morning my young friends waited for me at 8:30 at my hotel.*

3. *The young men were carrying a basket in which there was a good lunch that Mrs. Schiller had prepared for us.*

4. *Talking and laughing we got into the car I had rented and drove away.*

5. *I was at the wheel driving calmly along the suburbs of the city when all of a sudden I heard a noise that I recognized at once.*

6. *"What is it? What has happened?" the boys asked.*

7. *I stopped the automobile and we got out. "We have a punctured tire," I answered.*

8. *I wanted to change the tire and the boys wanted to help me. But unfortunately there was no jack in the trunk of the car. What to do?*

9. *Cars passed us at great speed. In spite of our obvious breakdown and our signals nobody stopped.*

10. *It was very hot and the sun was burning down upon our heads.*

11. *Finally a truck approached and then stopped suddenly in front of us. The truck driver got out.*

12. „Habt ihr eine Panne? Braucht ihr Hilfe?"

13. „Ja, wir haben leider einen Platten, aber wir haben keinen Wagenheber," sagte ich zu ihm. „Glücklicherweise haben wir ein Ersatzrad."

14. Der Lastwagenfahrer lieh uns seinen Wagenheber, und wir gingen alle an die Arbeit. In fünf Minuten war alles fertig.

15. Wir dankten ihm tausendmal, und ich versuchte, ihn für seine Hilfe zu bezahlen, aber er wollte nichts annehmen.

16. Dann gaben wir einander die Hand und verabschiedeten uns. Der Lastwagenfahrer machte sich wieder auf den Weg nach München, und wir fuhren weiter auf der Landstraße in Richtung Ammersee.

17. Ohne weitere Zwischenfälle erreichten wir unser Ziel. Wir ließen das Auto am Parkplatz und vertraten uns die Beine, indem wir eine kurze Strecke am See spazierten.

18. Dann mieteten wir ein Segelboot, und bald schaukelten wir über die Wellen. Wir öffneten unseren Picknickkorb und aßen mit großem Appetit. Bei Singen, Scherzen und Lachen verging die Zeit angenehm und schnell.

19. Es war schon spät am Nachmittag, als wir glücklich wieder bei meinem Hotel ankamen. Die beiden Jungen dankten mir herzlich für den lustigen und abenteuerlichen Ausflug.

20. Nun muss ich aber schließen, denn heute Abend gehe ich ins Konzert, und jetzt muss ich mich umziehen. So verbleibe ich mit den herzlichsten Grüßen Ihr Freund,

Robert Clark

12. "Have you a flat? Do you want help?"

13. "Yes, unfortunately we've got a flat, but we don't have a jack," I said to him. "But fortunately we have a spare wheel."

14. The truck driver loaned us his jack and we all set to work. In five minutes everything was ready.

15. We thanked him a thousand times, and I offered to pay him for his help, but he would not accept anything.

16. Then we shook hands and said good-bye. The truck driver again took the road toward Munich and we continued on the road toward the Ammersee.

17. Without further mishaps we reached our goal. We left the car in the parking area and stretched our legs by walking a short distance along the lake.

18. Then we hired a sailboat, and soon we were rocking gently on the waves. We opened our lunch basket and ate with hearty appetites. With singing, jesting, and laughing the time passed pleasantly and quickly.

19. It was already late in the afternoon when we arrived safely again at my hotel. The two boys thanked me heartily for the entertaining and adventurous excursion.

20. But now I must close, for I am going to a concert tonight and now I must change clothes. And so I remain with the most cordial greetings your friend,

Robert Clark

Wortschatz

das Bein *pl.* **-e** leg
die Hilfe help
der Imbiss snack, lunch
der Kopf *pl.* **¨-e** head
die Landstraße *pl.* **-n** road, highway
das Segelboot *pl.* **-e** sailboat
das Signál *pl.* **-e** signal
der Zwischenfall *pl.* **¨-e** mishap
die Welle *pl.* **-n** wave; **das Ziel** *pl.* **-e** goal
lachen to laugh

scherzen to joke, jest
strecken to stretch
spaziéren to walk
zu-bereiten to prepare
sich um-kleiden to change clothes
unterwegs on the way
trotz (*prep.* + *gen.*) in spite of
einánder each other
nieder down; **nieder-brennen** to burn down

Some Automobile Terms

das Auto, das Automobil, der Wagen, der PKW car, automobile
VW (*fow-vay*) short for **Volkswagen**
der Fahrer driver
der Lastwagen, der LKW truck
der Kofferraum trunk
der Tank (Benzintank) tank, gas tank

der Reifen tire
die Panne breakdown
der Platten puncture, flat
das Lenkrad steering wheel
der Wagenheber jack
die Werkstatt garage
der Parkplatz parking place
das Ersatzrad spare wheel
lenken to steer

Wichtige Redemittel

an die Arbeit gehen to set to work
Sie gingen alle an die Arbeit. They all set to work.
Wir gaben einander die Hand. We shook hands (*lit.* We gave to each other the hand).

sich auf den Weg machen to set out
Sie machten sich wieder auf den Weg. They set out (took to the road) again.
Das Auto hält an. The car stops.
Er hielt das Auto an. He stopped the car.
sich die Beine vertreten to stretch one's legs

Informal Letters

Salutations: **Lieber Freund! Liebe Freundin! Lieber Karl! Liebe Anna! Liebes Fräulein Helene!** etc.

Dear Friend: Dear Charles: Dear Anna: Dear Miss Helen: etc.

Endings: **Mit herzlichem Gruß**
Mit den herzlichsten Grüßen
Deine Freundin
Ihr Freund, Ihre Freundin, Dein Freund, Ihr Hans, Ihre Marie, Dein Hans, Deine Marie

With a hearty greeting
With the heartiest greetings
Your friend
Your Hans, Your Marie

Forms of **sie** and **ihr (P.F.)** are capitalized when used in a letter. Thus:

Sehr geehrte Frau Müller! Ich habe heute Ihren Brief erhalten. Es freut mich zu hören, dass Sie Ihre Prüfungen gut bestanden haben. Ich gratuliere Ihnen.

Dear Mrs. Müller: Today I received your letter. I am glad to hear that you passed the examinations well. I congratulate you.

Grammar Notes and Practical Exercises

1. MORE STRONG (IRREGULAR) VERBS. PRINCIPAL PARTS

helfen + *dat. obj.*	to help	**er hilft**	**half**	**hat geholfen**
heran-fahren	to ride up	**er fährt heran**	**fuhr heran**	**ist herangefahren**
entlang-fahren	to ride along	**er fährt entlang**	**fuhr entlang**	**ist entlanggefahren**
vorbei-fahren	to ride past	**er fährt vorbei**	**fuhr vorbei**	**ist vorbeigefahren**
leihen	to lend	**er leiht**	**lieh**	**hat geliehen**
vergehen	to pass, to elapse	**es vergeht**	**verging**	**ist vergangen**
sich befinden	to be (located)	**er befindet sich**	**befand sich**	**hat sich befunden**

Exercise 184

Change these sentences to the **Plusquamperfekt**. Remember! **Haben**-verbs have in the **Plusquamperfekt** the auxiliary verb **ich hatte, du hattest,** etc.; **sein**-verbs have the auxiliary **ich war, du warst,** etc.

Beispiel: 1. **Er hatte die zwei Söhne seines Kollegen angerufen.**

1. **Er rief die zwei Söhne seines Kollegen an.**
2. **Die Jungen holten ihn im Hotel ab.**
3. **Was trugen Sie im Korb?**
4. **Im Korb befand sich ein guter Imbiss.**
5. **Wer bereitete diesen guten Imbiss zu?**
6. **Wartete er lange auf sie?**
7. **Sie fuhren an den Vororten entlang.**
8. **Erkanntest du bald den Lärm?**
9. **Plötzlich hielt der Lastwagen vor ihnen an.**
10. **Was ist geschehen?**
11. **Der Fahrer half ihnen, den Reifen zu wechseln.**
12. **Er lieh ihnen seinen Wagenheber.**

2. THE PRINCIPAL PARTS OF THE MODAL AUXILIARIES

Infinitive	Present (Präsens)	Past (Präteritum)	Present Perfect (Perfekt)
dürfen	er darf	durfte	hat gedurft (dürfen)
können	er kann	konnte	hat gekonnt (können)
mögen	er mag	mochte	hat gemocht (mögen)
müssen	er muss	musste	hat gemusst (müssen)
sollen	er soll	sollte	hat gesollt (sollen)
wollen	er will	wollte	hat gewollt (wollen)

The principal parts of modals follow the pattern of weak verbs, except that the present tense is irregular and the **Umlaut** is dropped in the participle. Note, however, that each modal has a substitute for the past participle, which is identical in form with the infinitive. The past participle is used when the modal has no complementary infinitive. The infinitive substitute is used when the modal has a complementary infinitive. Thus:

Der Mann hat kein Geld **gewollt.**	The man did not want any money.
Der Mann hat kein Geld **annehmen wollen.**	The man did not want to accept any money.

Compare a modal in five tenses with and without a complementary infinitive.

	without a complementary infinitive	with a complementary infinitive
Präsens	**Wir mögen** ihn nicht.	**Wir mögen** ihn nicht **sehen.**
Präteritum	**Wir mochten** ihn nicht.	**Wir mochten** ihn nicht **sehen.**
Perfekt	**Wir haben** ihn nicht **gemocht.**	Wir haben ihn nicht **sehen mögen.**
Plusquamperfekt	**Wir hatten** ihn nicht **gemocht.**	Wir hatten ihn nicht **sehen mögen.**
Futur	**Wir werden** ihn nicht **mögen.**	**Wir werden** ihn nicht **sehen mögen.**

In general, use the **Präteritum** of the modal rather than the **Perfekt** to express past time.

3. THE DOUBLE INFINITIVE WITH *lassen, sehen* and *hören*

The double infinitive construction (see above with the modals) is also generally used with **lassen, sehen** and **hören** when these verbs have a complementary infinitive.

Ich habe es dort gelassen.	I have left it there.
Ich habe es dort liegen lassen.	I have left it lying there.
Wir haben ihn gesehen.	We have seen him.
Wir haben ihn tanzen sehen.	We have seen him dance.

Exercise 185

Change these sentences to the **Perfekt** and the **Plusquamperfekt**.

Beispiel: 1. Herr Clark hat (hatte) eine Reise machen müssen.

1. Herr Clark musste eine Reise machen.
2. Die Jungen wollten helfen.
3. Du durftest das Zimmer verlassen.
4. Ich konnte leider nicht mitgehen.
5. Wir mochten nicht spielen.
6. Ich musste einen Brief schreiben.
7. Der Mann wollte nichts annehmen.
8. Während des Sommers konnten wir nicht aufs Land geben.
9. Trotz der Hitze mussten sie in der Stadt bleiben.
10. Trotz des Regens wollten sie Fußball spielen.

Exercise 186

Form correct sentences.

Beispiel 1. Ich habe ihn treffen wollen.

1. treffen—habe—wollen—ihn—Ich.
2. Kinder—liegen—haben—Die—Garten—Ball—im—den—lassen.
3. sie—Wir—kommen—hören—haben.
4. wollten—Segelboot—mieten—Wir—ein.
5. haben—wir—Segelboot—wollen—ein—mieten.
6. Wir—kommen—LKW—sehen—haben—den.
7. Wir—LKW—gesehen—den—haben.
8. Jungen—müssen—wechseln—Reifen—haben—den—Die.

Exercise 187

Fragen

Lesen Sie noch einmal den Text: **Ein Ausflug an den Ammersee**, und dann beantworten Sie diese Fragen!

1. Wen rief Herr Clark an?
2. Wohin wollte Herr Clark einen Ausflug im Auto machen?
3. Wen lud er ein, mit ihm zu fahren?
4. Wo warteten die Jungen auf Herrn Clark?
5. Was war in dem Korb, den die Jungen trugen?
6. Wer hatte den guten Imbiss für sie zubereitet?
7. Was hörte Herr Clark plötzlich, als er am Steuer saß?
8. Was war geschehen?
9. Warum konnten sie den Reifen nicht wechseln?
10. Was für ein Wagen hielt plötzlich vor ihnen an?
11. Was lieh ihnen der LKW-fahrer?
12. In wie vielen Minuten war alles fertig?

CHAPTER 40

HERR CLARK VERLÄSST DEUTSCHLAND

Vienna, Austria, is a capital of German culture. The Opera House there is world renowned for its architecture.

BRIEF AUS HAMBURG

Lieber Freund!

1. *Als ich New York verließ, hatte ich bereits vieles über Deutschland gelernt. Ich hatte einige interessante Bücher über die Geschichte und die Bräuche dieses Landes gelesen. Ich konnte schon ziemlich gut Deutsch sprechen. Nun, da ich im Begriff bin, Deutschland zu verlassen, scheint es mir, dass ich viel fließender Deutsch spreche.*

2. *Ich habe viele Plätze besucht, von denen wir geredet hatten. Wie Sie sich wohl vorstellen können, gefielen mir die Sehenswürdigkeiten Deutschlands sehr, seine schöne Landschaft, seine alten Städte, seine Musik, seine gute Küche. Es machte mir viel Freude, mit den Deutschen in ihrer eigenen Sprache zu reden, wodurch ich vieles über sie lernte, was ich nicht aus den Büchern erlernen konnte.*

3. *Das Leben in den Städten Deutschlands scheint mir nicht ruhiger zu sein als in unseren Städten, allerdings kann man die Stadt meist schnell verlassen und ist in wenigen Minuten im Grünen.*

Dear Friend:

1. *When I left New York I had already learned a great deal about Germany. I had read some interesting books on the history and customs of that country. I already knew how to speak German fairly well. Now that I am about to leave Germany, it seems to me that I am speaking German much more fluently.*

2. *I have visited many places of which we have spoken in our conversations. As you may well imagine, I liked immensely the places of interest in Germany, its beautiful landscape, its old cities, its music, its good cuisine. I enjoyed talking to Germans in their own language, thus learning many things about them which I could not acquire from books.*

3. *Life in the cities of Germany does not seem more tranquil to me than in our cities, but one can leave the city quickly and in a few minutes one is in the country.*

4. Wie Sie wissen, war meine Reise nach Deutschland nicht nur eine Geschäftreise, sondern auch eine Vergnügungsreise. Glücklicherweise konnte ich die Geschäftsangelegenheiten rasch erledigen und danach konnte ich mich ganz dem Vergnügen widmen. Ich habe kaum Zeit gefunden, Ihnen auch nur ein paar Briefe aus Deutschland zu schreiben. Ich werde Ihnen aber viel über die Leute erzählen, die ich kennen gelernt habe, die Plätze, die ich besucht habe, und über alles, was ich von dem Leben, den Bräuchen, und der Kultur Deutschlands gelernt habe.

5. Ich werde sicherlich Deutschland bald wieder besuchen. Ich möchte sogar schon im kommenden Jahr wieder dahin. Aber nächstes Mal nehme ich meine Familie mit. Ich muss Ihnen gestehen, ich habe meine Frau und Kinder auf meiner Reise sehr vermisst und hatte oft Heimweh.

   Dies ist der letzte Brief, den ich Ihnen schreibe, ehe ich nach New York abreise. Es wird mir ein Vergnügen sein, Sie bei meiner Ankunft anzurufen, um Sie einzuladen, möglichst bald bei uns zu Abend zu essen.

6. Zweifellos werden wir viele Stunden im Gespräch über Deutschland verbringen, besonders über München und Umgebung, denn diese Stadt lernte ich wirklich lieben.

Mit herzlichen Grüßen

Ihr Freund

R. Clark

4. As you know, my trip to Germany was not only a business trip but also a pleasure trip. Luckily I was able to settle my business matters quickly, and after that I was able to devote myself entirely to recreation. I have hardly found time to send you even a few letters from Germany. I shall, however, have much to tell you about the persons I have met, the places I have visited, and all I have learned about the life, customs and culture of Germany.

5. I am sure I shall visit Germany again soon. I should even like to go next year. But the next time I go I shall take my family with me. I must confess to you I missed them very much on my trip and was often homesick.

   This is the last letter which I am writing you before I leave for New York. I shall take pleasure in telephoning you on my arrival and inviting you to have dinner with us as soon as possible.

6. Without doubt we shall spend many hours speaking of Germany and of Munich and its surroundings, for I have really learned to love this city.

With heartiest greetings

Your friend

R. Clark

Wortschatz

das Heimweh homesickness
die Sitte *pl.* **-n** custom
einhér-rasen to rush madly about
erlérnen to learn, acquire
erlédigen to settle, finish
handeln von to deal with

sich hin-geben to devote oneself
scheinen to seem, shine (*past* **schien**)
speisen to dine
vermíssen to miss
kaum scarcely, hardly
sogar even

Deutsche Ausdrücke

Heimweh haben to be homesick
Er hatte Heimweh, als er in Deutschland war.
He was homesick when he was in Germany

sich erinnern an + *acc.* to remember, to recall
(*lit.* to remind oneself of)

Erinnern Sie sich an Ihre Ankunft in Deutschland? Do you remember your arrival in Germany?

Ja, ich erinnere mich daran. Yes, I remember it (*lit.* I remind myself of it).

Wir erinnern uns alle daran. We all remember it.

Grammar Notes and Practical Exercises

1. SUMMARY OF GERMAN WORD ORDER IN SIMPLE SENTENCES AND MAIN CLAUSES

a. *Normal word order*
Der Geschäftsmann schrieb gestern an seinen Geschäftspartner.
In normal word order the verb follows the subject.

b. *Inverted word order*
Gestern schrieb der Geschäftsmann einen Brief an seinen Geschäftspartner.
Schrieb der Geschäftsmann gestern einen Brief an seinen Partner?

In inverted word order the verb precedes the subject. Inverted word order is used in questions and when the sentence or noun clause begins with words other than the subject (adverbs, phrases, objects).

c. *Position of the separable prefix*
Die Kinder stehen gewöhnlich früh **auf.**
Am Tage der Abfahrt **standen die Kinder** früh **auf.**
In the present and past tenses the separable prefix stands at the end of the simple sentence or main clause.

d. *Position of the past participle*
Er hat vieles über Deutschland **gelernt.**
Ich hatte einige interessante Bücher **gelesen.**
Die ganze Familie ist heute früh **aufgestanden.**

In the present perfect and past perfect tenses the past participle stands at the end of a simple sentence or main clause. The **ge-** of the past participle of a separable verb stands between the prefix and the verb.

e. *Position of the infinitive*
1. Ich werde Deutschland bald wieder **besuchen.**
2. **Ich konnte** die Geschäftsangelegenheiten rasch **erledigen.**
3. Ich bin jetzt im Begriff, **Deutschland zu verlassen.**
4. Die Passagiere begannen, **in den Zug einzusteigen.**

In the future the infinitive stands last in the sentence or main clause (Sentence 1).

Complementary infinitives stand last (Sentences 2, 3, 4). If the infinitive has **zu**, it is set off by commas, after the rest of the sentence or clause (Sentences 3, 4).

2. SUMMARY OF WORD ORDER IN SUBORDINATE CLAUSES

a. *Es scheint mir*, **dass ich** *schon fliessender Deutsch* **spreche**.
Er las einige Bücher, **die** von der Geschichte Deutschlands **handelten**.

In subordinate clauses, whether introduced by a subordinate conjunction or by a relative pronoun, the verb stands last.

b. *Ich bin sicher*, **dass ich** *Deutschland wieder* **besuchen werde**.
Ich habe die Städte besucht, **von denen** wir heute **geredet haben**.
If the verb in the subordinate clause has an auxiliary, the auxiliary part of the verb stands last.

c. **Als Herr Clark** *nach Deutschland* **abreiste**, sprach er *schon ziemlich gut Deutsch*.
The separable prefix does not separate from the verb in subordinate word order.
If the subordinate clause comes first, the main clause has inverted word order.

Exercise 188

Ergänzen Sie diese Sätze auf Deutsch! (Complete these sentences in German.)

Beispiel: 1. Ehe er New York verließ, hatte er vieles über Deutschland gelernt.

1. (Before he left New York), **hatte er vieles über Deutschland gelernt.**
2. **Hatte er** (some interesting books) **gelesen?**
3. **Kannst du** (speak German quite well)?
4. **Es scheint mir,** (that he is speaking German much more fluently).
5. **Er besuchte alle Plätze,** (about which we have spoken).
6. (Did you like) **die Sehenswürdigkeiten Deutschlands?**
7. **Mir gefielen** (its music and cuisine).
8. **Er lernte vieles, was** (he could not acquire out of books).
9. **Das Leben in den deutschen Städten** (is not more tranquil than in our cities).
10. **Meine Reise war** (not only) **eine Geschäftsreise,** (but also) **eine Vergnügungsreise.**
11. **Konnten Sie die Geschäftsangelegenheiten** (to finish quickly)?
12. (Yes, and after that I was able) **mich ganz dem Vergnügen hingeben.**
13. **Er hat vieles** (about the life and customs) **Deutschlands gelernt.**
14. **Sobald ich zu Hause bin,** (I shall telephone you).
15. (He was homesick), **weil er seine Frau und Kinder vermisste.**
16. **Nächstes Mal** (he will take the family along).
17. **Werden Sie** (have supper with us)?
18. **Dies ist der letzte Brief,** (which I shall write).
19. **Später** (I shall tell you everything).

Exercise 189

Start the sentences with the underlined word.

Beispiel 1. Gestern habe ich ihn am Bahnhof getroffen.

1. Ich habe ihn gestern am Bahnhof getroffen.
2. Der LKW ist plötzlich stehen geblieben.
3. Herr Clark konnte leider keinen Wagenheber im Auto finden.
4. Er hat in Deutschland viele Sehenswürdigkeiten gesehen.
5. Er muss nun nach New York zurückkehren.

Exercise 190

Form correct sentences starting with **Ich glaube, dass** . . .

Beispiel 1. Ich glaube, dass Herr Clark gern in Deutschland war.

1. Herr Clark war gern in Deutschland.
2. Er hatte jedoch Heimweh.
3. Herr Clark hat einige Briefe in die USA geschrieben.
4. Das nächste Mal wird er seine Familie nach Deutschland mitnehmen.
5. Er kann nun fließend Deutsch sprechen.
6. In New York wird er Herrn Müller anrufen.

Exercise 191

Lesen Sie noch einmal den Text: **Herr Clark verlässt Deutschland,** und dann beantworten Sie diese Fragen!

1. Wer ist im Begriff, Deutschland zu verlassen?
2. Was hat ihm in Deutschland sehr gefallen?
3. War Herrn Clarks Reise nur eine Geschäftsreise?
4. Was konnte er rasch erledigen?
5. Hat er Zeit gefunden, viele Briefe zu schreiben?
6. Wann möchte Herr Clark wieder nach Deutschland reisen?
7. Beabsichtigt er, allein zu gehen?
8. Wen hatte er vermisst?
9. Wen wird er bei seiner Ankunft in New York anrufen?
10. Wie wird er viele Stunden mit Herrn Müller verbringen?

Weak (Regular) Verbs. No Vowel Changes

1.	eilen	1.	to hurry
2.	handeln (von)	2.	to deal (with)
3.	lachen	3.	to laugh
4.	landen	4.	to land
5.	scherzen	5.	to joke
6.	spazieren	6.	to walk
7.	begrüßen	7.	to greet
8.	erwidern	8.	to answer
9.	erledigen	9.	to settle, finish
10.	erlernen	10.	to acquire (learn)
11.	auf-warten	11.	to serve, to wait on
12.	ab-holen	12.	to call for
13.	halt-machen	13.	to stop
14.	her-reisen	14.	to travel here
15.	vor-stellen	15.	to introduce
16.	zu-bereiten	16.	to prepare
17.	sich um-kleiden	17.	to change clothes
18.	sich um-schauen	18.	to look around

Strong (Irregular) Verbs. Vowel Changes

helfen	to help	er hilft	half	hat geholfen
leihen	to lend	er leiht	lieh	hat geliehen
scheinen	to shine; to seem	er scheint	schien	hat geschienen
betreten	to enter, step into	er betritt	betrat	hat betreten
vergehen	to pass, elapse	er vergeht	verging	ist vergangen
an-nehmen	to accept	er nimmt an	nahm an	hat angenommen
an-rufen	to call to	er ruft an	rief an	hat angerufen
an-schreien	to cry out to	er schreit an	schrie an	hat angeschrien
an-halten	to stop	er hält an	hielt an	hat angehalten
fliegen	to fly	er fliegt	flog	ist geflogen

Wichtige Redemittel

1. **kennen lernen** to become acquainted with
   Ich habe ihn eben kennen gelernt.
2. **anrufen** to telephone
   Ich habe ihn angerufen.
3. **jemanden vorstellen** to introduce somebody
   Herr Schiller hat ihn seiner Frau vorgestellt.
4. **an die Arbeit gehen** to set to work
   Sie gingen sofort an die Arbeit.
5. **Heimweh haben** to be homesick
   Herr Clark hatte Heimweh.
6. **sich erinnern an** to remember
   Ich konnte mich nicht an ihn erinnern.
   I could not remember him.

Exercise 192

Complete the translation of each English sentence.

1. I have helped him with the letter.
2. The truck driver loaned them a jack.

3. On the way they were joking and laughing.
4. The time passed quickly and merrily.
5. He has invited us to dinner.
6. We have accepted the invitation.
7. "Stop!" he cried out to the driver.
8. The taxi driver did not stop.
9. We entered a nicely furnished living room.

10. Mr. Schiller greeted us most warmly.

11. May I introduce my wife Mary to you?
12. After dinner we shall take a walk to the English Garden.

1. Ich _____ ihm mit dem Brief _____.
2. Der Lastwagenfahrer _____ ihnen einen Wagenheber.
3. Am Wege _____ und _____ sie.
4. Die Zeit _____ schnell und fröhlich.
5. Er _____ uns zum Essen _____.
6. Wir _____ die Einladung _____.
7. „Halt!" _____ er dem Fahrer zu.
8. Der Taxifahrer _____ nicht an.
9. Wir _____ ein schön möbliertes Wohnzimmer.
10. Herr Schiller _____ uns aufs herzlich-ste.
11. Darf ich Ihnen meine Frau Marie _____?
12. Nach dem Essen _____ wir einen Spaziergang im Englischen Garten _____.

Exercise 193

Ergänzen (Complete) **Sie die Sätze auf deutsch!**

1. **Herr Clark** (is a businessman in New York).
2. **Er machte eine Reise nach München,** (in order to visit the business partner of his firm).

3. (He wanted) **ihn persönlich kennen lernen.**
4. **Bevor er New York verließ,** (he had learned German).
5. (He had) **einen sehr guten Lehrer.**
6. **Er konnte** (speak, read and write German).
7. **Er las einige Bücher** (about Germany).
8. (He wrote) **einen Brief an seinen Geschäftspartner.**
9. **Nach einigen Tagen** (he received an answer).
10. ("I shall call for you at the airport,") **schrieb ihm Herr Schiller.**
11. **Herr Schiller** (called for him there).
12. **Sie nahmen ein Taxi,** (and rode to the hotel).
13. (Luckily) **erledigte er bald seine Geschäftsangelegenheiten.**
14. **Während seines Aufenthalts in München** (he took a trip to the Ammersee).
15. **Die Söhne des Herrn Schiller** (went with him).
16. (He visited the places) **in der Nähe von München.**
17. **Nach zwei Wochen,** (he left Munich and took a Rhine trip).
18. **Der Rhein ist** (the longest, the broadest and the most beautiful) **Fluß Deutschlands.**
19. (Finally he rode) **mit dem Zug nach Hamburg.**
20. **Von Hamburg** (he flew back to New York).
21. **Nächstes Jahr** (Mr. Clark will again take a trip to Germany).
22. **Aber diesmal** (he will take his family along).

DIALOG

An der Tankstelle

Herr Clark fährt zur Tankstelle, um zu tanken, denn das Benzin ist beinahe alle. Sofort nähert sich ein junger Tankwart, um ihn zu bedienen.

T.: **Guten Tag, mein Herr, kann ich Ihnen helfen?**

C: **Guten Tag. Volltanken, bitte.**

T.: **Diesel, Normalbenzin, oder Super?**

C.: **Was kostet das Normalbenzin?**

T.: **Normal kostet 99 Cent, Super 1 Euro, 12 Cent.***

C.: **Für diesen Wagen genügt Normalbenzin. Können Sie bitte auch Öl, Luft und Kühlwasser nachsehen?**

T.: **Gerne.**

Der junge Mann füllt den Tank, prüft das Öl, Kühlwasser und die Reifen.

T.: **Alles in Ordnung.**

C.: **Schönen Dank. Wie viel bin ich schuldig?**

At the Gas Station

Mr. Clark drives to the gas station to have the car filled up, for the gasoline is almost all used up. At once a young attendant approaches to serve him.

A.: How do you do, sir, what can I do for you?

C.: How do you do. Fill up the tank, please.

A.: Diesel, regular or super?

C.: What is the price of the gasoline?

A.: Regular costs 99 cents, super costs 1 euro 12 cents.*

C.: For this car the plain gasoline is good enough. And will you please check the oil, air and water?

A.: With pleasure.

The young man fills up the tank, checks the oil, water and the tires.

A.: Everything is okay.

C.: Thank you very much. How much do I owe you?

T.: Im Ganzen 34 Euro vierzig.

A.: All together 34 euros and forty cents.

Herr Clark gibt ihm zwei Zwanzigeuroscheine, und der junge Mann gibt ihm fünf Euro und sechzig Cent zurück.

Mr. Clark gives him two twenty-euro notes and the young man gives him five euros and sixty cents in change.

*NOTE: gasoline prices may differ from those given here.

Exercise 194

Lesestück l

DAS DEUTSCHE FERNSEHEN[1]

Ebenso wie in den Vereinigten Staaten besitzen fast alle Einwohner Deutschlands einen Fernsehapparat. Viele Familien haben zwei oder mehrere Fernseher. Dazu kommen noch Video- bzw. DVD-Rekorder. Auch viele Kinder haben ihren eigenen Fernsehapparat im Zimmer.

In Deutschland gibt es private und staatliche Fernsehsender.[2] Es gibt einen wichtigen Unterschied zwischen den privaten und den staatlichen Fernsehsendern. Jeder hat sich schon einmal über die Werbung[3] geärgert, die in den Vereinigten Staaten fast jede Fernsehsendung unterbricht, sei es ein Film, eine Reportage,[4] die Nachrichten[5] oder eine Sportübertragung.[6]

Im deutschen öffentlichen Fernsehen gibt es keine Werbung während der Filme, also kann der deutsche Fernsehteilnehmer die interessantesten Fernsehprogramme ohne störende Unterbrechungen[7] genießen. Allerdings muss jeder Besitzer eines Fernsehapparats eine monatliche Fernsehgebühr[8] zahlen. Dieses Geld erhält das staatliche Fernsehen. Da private Fernsehsender nichts von den Fernsehgebühren bekommen, finanzieren sie sich wie in den USA über häufige Werbeeinschaltungen.

NOTES: 1. television. **2.** state-owned TV company. **3.** advertisement, advertising. **4.** on-the-spot reporting. **5.** news. **6.** sports transmission. **7.** disturbing interruptions. **8.** television fee.

Exercise 195

Lesestück 2

Herrn Clarks Rheinreise

Nachdem er seine Geschäfte in München erledigt hatte, machte Herr Clark eine Vergnügungsreise durch das Rheinland, zum Teil per Schiff und zum Teil mit der Eisenbahn.

Man behauptet[1] mit Recht, dass der Rhein einer der schönsten Flüsse Europas ist. Auf der Strecke von Mainz bis Köln bewunderte Herr Clark die dunklen Wälder, die terrassenförmigen Weinberge,[2] die kleinen Dörfer mit ihren altertümlichen[3] Kirchen und Häusern, und die Ruinen alter Schlösser.

Jetzt fuhr das Rheinschiff an dem Loreleifelsen vorbei. Jedermann kennt die Legende von der Zauberin,[4] die mit ihrem Singen die armen Schiffer in den Tod lockte.[5] Diese Legende hat Heinrich Heine verewigt[6] in dem berühmten Liede: „Ich weiß nicht, was soll es bedeuten, dass ich so traurig bin."

Bald danach erschien[7] der Drachenfels,[8] wo (der Legende nach) der Held Siegfried einen Drachen erschlug.[9] Die Legende erzählt, dass er sich im Blut des Drachen badete, um unverwundbar[10] zu werden. In solchen Legenden aus dieser Gegend fand Richard Wagner den Stoff für manche seiner bekannten Opern, wie z.B. *Das Rheingold, Siegfried* usw.

In einigen der berühmten Rheinstädte hielt das Schiff an. Also konnte Herr Clark die Stadt Mainz besuchen, den Geburtsort von Johann Gutenberg, der die Buchdruckerkunst[11] erfunden hat.[12]

Dann kam Bonn, die Stätte einer alten Universität und nach dem Zweiten Weltkrieg die Hauptstadt Westdeutschlands. In dieser Stadt wurde Ludwig van Beethoven geboren.

Der nächste Haltepunkt war Köln. Bewundernswert[13] vor allem ist hier der weltberühmte Kölner Dom, dessen Türme mehr als 165 Meter in die Höhe ragen.[14]

Die letzte Rheinstadt, die Herr Clark besuchte, war Düsseldorf, die Geburtsstadt des großen deutschen Lyrikers[15] Heinrich Heine.

Von Düsseldorf ging's nach Hamburg, wo Herr Clark einige Geschäfte zu erledigen hatte, und von wo aus er die Heimreise per Flugzeug antrat.

Als Herr Clark wieder zu Hause war, sprach er oft von seiner interessanten und angenehmen Rheinreise.

NOTES: 1. asserts. **2.** terraced vineyards. **3.** ancient. **4.** sorceress. **5.** enticed. **6.** immortalized. **7. erscheinen (erschien, ist erschienen)** to appear. **8.** Dragon Rock. **9. erschlagen (erschlug, hat erschlagen)** to kill. **10.** invulnerable. **11.** art of printing. **12. erfinden (erfand, hat erfunden)** to invent. **13.** worthy of admiration, remarkable. **14. in die Höhe ragen** tower above. **15.** lyric poet.

Lieber Freund!

Ich bekam deinen lieben Brief gerade, als ich im Begriff war, meine Rückreise in die Heimat anzutreten. Du batest mich, deine Verwandten in Hamburg aufzusuchen. Das hätte ich gern getan, wenn ich Zeit gehabt hätte. Wenn dein Brief nur ein paar Tage früher angekommen wäre, so hätte ich sicher deinen Onkel besucht.

Ich dachte, dass es sehr nett sein würde, wenn ich den Onkel wenigstens telefonisch sprechen könnte. Als ich anrief, bekam ich aber leider keine Antwort.

Ich freue mich Dir mitzuteilen, dass meine Reise sehr erfolgreich gewesen ist. Wenn ich aber nicht einen tüchtigen Geschäftspartner in München hätte, der sehr fleißig und zuvorkommend ist, so wäre es mir nicht möglich gewesen, meine Geschäfte so schnell und leicht zu erledigen. Dank seiner Hilfe habe ich auch die Gelegenheit gehabt, so viele Sehenswürdigkeiten und so viele nette Leute kennen zu lernen.

Wenn Du in der nächsten Zeit nach New York kommen solltest, so würde es mich sehr freuen, einige Zeit mit Dir zu verbringen.

Mit herzlichsten Grüßen

Dein Freund Robert

Dear Friend:

I received your letter just as I was about to start my journey home.

You asked me to look up your relatives in Hamburg. This I would have done gladly if I had had time. If only your letter had come a few days sooner I would surely have visited your uncle.

I thought it would be very nice if I could at least talk to your uncle on the telephone. But when I called, unfortunately I received no answer.

I am glad to inform you that my trip has been very successful. But if I did not have a capable business partner in Munich who is very industrious and very obliging it would not have been possible for me to dispose of my business so quickly and easily. And thanks to his help I had the opportunity to get to know so many places of interest and so many nice people.

If you should come to New York in the near future, I would be very happy to spend some time with you.

With kindest greetings,

Your friend Robert

Wortschatz

die **Heimat** home, home country
der **Verwándte** *pl.*-n relative
mit-teilen to inform

erfólgreich successful
zuvórkommend obliging, gracious

Grammar Notes and Practical Exercises

1. ABOUT THE SUBJUNCTIVE

Subjunctive verb forms have almost disappeared in modern English. About the only survivor is "were" instead of "was" in such expressions as: If he were here, he would be happy. She acts as if she were sick. If this were only true!

In the foregoing chapters of this book all the verb forms you have learned have been in what is called the "indicative" mood. But modern German also has verb forms in what is called the "subjunctive" mood. In this chapter you will learn verb forms of the subjunctive and their use in certain types of conditional sentences.

2. THE PRESENT SUBJUNCTIVE

lernen	gehen	sehen	fahren	haben	sein	werden	können
ich lerne	gehe	sehe	fahre	habe	sei	werde	könne
du lernest	gehest	sehest	fahrest	habest	seiest	werdest	könnest
er lerne	gehe	sehe	fahre	habe	sei	werde	könne
wir lernen	gehen	sehen	fahren	haben	seien	werden	können
ihr lernet	gehet	sehet	fahret	habet	seiet	werdet	könnet
sie lernen	gehen	sehen	fahren	haben	seien	werden	können

To form the present subjunctive of any verb, drop the infinitive ending (**-en** or **-n**) and add the personal endings **-e, -est, -e; -en, -et, -en.** The verb **sein** is the only exception to this rule. It lacks the ending **-e** in the first and third person singular (**ich sei, er sei**).

There are no contractions or vowel changes in the present subjunctive. Thus:

Indicative	du **hast**	du **siehst**	du **fährst**	du **wirst**	du **kannst**
Subjunctive	du **habest**	du **sehest**	du **fahrest**	du **werdest**	du **könnest**

3. THE PAST SUBJUNCTIVE

Past Indicative

ich **lernte**	**ging**	**sah**	**fuhr**	**hatte**	**war**	**wurde**	**konnte**

Past Subjunctive

ich lernte	ginge	sähe	führe	hätte	wäre	würde	könnte
du lerntest	gingest	sähest	führest	hättest	wärest	würdest	könntest
er lernte	ginge	sähe	führe	hätte	wäre	würde	könnte
wir lernten	gingen	sähen	führen	hätten	wären	würden	könnten
ihr lerntet	ginget	sähet	führet	hättet	wäret	würdet	könntet
sie lernten	gingen	sähen	führen	hätten	wären	würden	könnten

a. The endings of the past subjunctive are the same as those for the present: -e, -est, -e; -en, -et, -en.

b. The verbs haben, sein *and* werden *have an* umlaut *in the past subjunctive* (hätte, wäre, würde).

c. All strong verbs add an umlaut *to the stem vowel* a, o *or* u *in the past subjunctive (*sah > sähe, bot > böte, fuhr > führe*).*

d. The modals dürfen, können, mögen, müssen *and the mixed verbs* bringen, denken, wissen *have an* umlaut *in the past subjunctive.* Sollen *and* wollen *do not add an* Umlaut *(*sollte, wollte*).*

Indicative	**durfte**	**konnte**	**musste**	**mochte**	**brachte**	**dachte**	**wusste**
Subjunctive	**dürfte**	**könnte**	**müsste**	**möchte**	**brächte**	**dächte**	**wüsste**

4. THE COMPOUND TENSES OF THE SUBJUNCTIVE

Present Perfect		*Past Perfect*	
ich **habe** gelernt	ich **sei** gegangen	ich **hätte** gelernt	ich **wäre** gegangen
du **habest** gelernt	du **seiest** gegangen	du **hättest** gelernt	du **wärest** gegangen
er **habe** gelernt	er **sei** gegangen	er **hätte** gelernt	er **wäre** gegangen
wir **haben** gelernt	wir **seien** gegangen	wir **hätten** gelernt	wir **wären** gegangen
ihr **habet** gelernt	ihr **seiet** gegangen	ihr **hättet** gelernt	ihr **wäret** gegangen
sie **haben** gelernt	sie **seien** gegangen	sie **hätten** gelernt	sie **wären** gegangen

Future		*Future Perfect*	
ich **werde** lernen	(gehen)	ich **werde** gelernt haben	(gegangen sein)
du **werdest** lernen	(gehen)	du **werdest** gelernt haben	(gegangen sein)
er **werde** lernen	(gehen)	er **werde** gelernt haben	(gegangen sein)
wir **werden** lernen	(gehen)	wir **werden** gelernt haben	(gegangen sein)
ihr **werdet** lernen	(gehen)	ihr **werdet** gelernt haben	(gegangen sein)
sie **werden** lernen	(gehen)	sie **werden** gelernt haben	(gegangen sein)

The compound tenses in the subjunctive are formed in the same way as in the indicative, except that the subjunctive forms of the auxiliary verbs **haben, sein, werden** are used.

Exercise 196

Change the following indicative verb forms to the subjunctive.
Beispiel: 1. ich **wäre.** 2. sie **wären.**

1. ich war
2. sie waren
3. er hatte
4. wir hatten
5. er schreibt
6. er schrieb
7. ich las
8. sie lasen
9. er lernt
10. du lerntest
11. du siehst
12. du sahst
13. er kommt
14. wir kamen
15. sie geht
16. sie ging
17. er fährt
18. er fuhr
19. ich kann
20. er konnte
21. wir müssen
22. wir mussten
23. ich weiß
24. er wusste
25. er hat gehabt
26. sie hat studiert
27. ich bin gewesen
28. ich war gewesen
29. wir sind gekommen
30. wir waren gekommen
31. du hast gelebt
32. du hattest gelebt

5. THE "WÜRDE"-FORM

In spoken German it is possible to substitute the more difficult forms of the subjunctive with "**würde + inf.**" Thus **Ich würde gehen** instead of **Ich ginge** or **Ich würde lernen** instead of **Ich lernte.** The **würde + inf.** reminds us of the English conditional. Thus:

I should learn (go), you would learn (go), would learn (go), etc.		*I should have learned (gone), you would have he learned (gone), etc.*	
ich **würde** lernen	(gehen)	ich **würde** gelernt haben	(gegangen sein)
du **würdest** lernen	(gehen)	du **würdest** gelernt haben	(gegangen sein)
er **würde** lernen	(gehen)	er **würde** gelernt haben	(gegangen sein)
wir **würden** lernen	(gehen)	wir **würden** gelernt haben	(gegangen sein)
ihr **würdet** lernen	(gehen)	ihr **würdet** gelernt haben	(gegangen sein)
sie **würden** lernen	(gehen)	sie **würden** gelernt haben	(gegangen sein)

The **würde**-from in present and past is formed like the future and future perfect, except that the auxiliary verb is **würden** (should, would) instead of **werden** (shall, will).

6. USE OF THE SUBJUNCTIVE IN CONDITIONAL SENTENCES

A conditional sentence consists of a subordinate clause with the conjunction **wenn** (if), called the conditional clause, and of a main clause, called the conclusion. There are two types of conditions, *simple* and *contrary-to-fact.*

Simple Conditions

Wenn **er** das Geld **bekommt, wird er** das Auto **kaufen.**

If *he receives* the money, *he will buy* the car.

Wenn **er** seine Fahrkarte **verloren hat, muss** er zu Fuß **gehen.**

If *he has lost* his ticket, *he must walk.*

The **wenn** (if) clause of a simple condition assumes something which may or may not be true. In both clauses German and English use the same tenses of the verbs. The verbs in both clauses of simple conditions are in the indicative mood.

Contrary-to-Fact Conditions

a. Denoting present or future time

Wenn **ich** Zeit **hätte,** (so) **würde ich gehen,** *or* (so) **ginge ich.** If *I had* time *I would go.*

b. Denoting past time

Wenn **ich** Zeit **gehabt hätte,** (so) **würde ich gegangen sein** *or* (so) **wäre ich gegangen.** If *I had had* time *I would have gone.*

In contrary-to-fact conditions the **wenn** (if) clause assumes something which is not true (present contrary-to-fact) or was not true (past contrary-to-fact).

Pattern of Contrary-to-Fact Conditions

Denoting Present or Future Time   *Denoting Past Time*   **würde** (present)

Wenn-clause: past subjunctive   *Conclusion or*
                                                                                                          past subjunctive **würde** (past)

Wenn-clause: past perfect subjunctive   *Conclusion or*
                                                                                                          past perfect subjunctive

In the conclusion of contrary-to-fact conditions denoting present or future time, German prefers the **würde**-form (present). In the conclusion of contrary-to-fact conditions denoting past time, German prefers the past perfect subjunctive.

7. WORD ORDER IN CONDITIONAL SENTENCES

Wenn er nicht krank wäre, (so) würde er spielen.   If he were not sick, (then) he would play.
Er würde spielen, wenn er nicht krank wäre.   He would play, if he were not sick.

A conditional sentence may begin with the **wenn**-clause or with the main clause. If the sentence begins with the **wenn**-clause, the main clause has inverted word order and may be preceded by **so** (then).

8. OMISSION OF *wenn*

Hätte ich Hunger, (so) würde ich essen.   Were I hungry, I would eat.
Hätte es nicht geregnet, (so) wären wir   Had it not rained, we would have gone.
gegangen.

The conjunction **wenn** may be omitted. The conditional clause must then have inverted word order.

Exercise 197

Read each sentence aloud three times. This will help you to get the "feel" of conditional contrary-to-fact sentences.

1. **Wenn ich genug Geld hätte, so würde ich eine Reise machen.**
2. **Wenn das Haus größer wäre, so würde ich es kaufen.**
3. **Wenn ich jetzt Ferien hätte, so würde ich nach Europa reisen.**
4. **Wenn das Wetter schön wäre, so würde ich einen Spaziergang machen.**
5. **Wenn sie Zeit hätte, so würde sie uns öfter schreiben.**
6. **Wenn er heute käme, so würden wir uns freuen.**
7. **Wenn wir Tennis spielen könnten, so würden wir euch begleiten.**
8. **Wir würden uns auf den Weg machen, wenn unsere Freunde schon dort wären.**
9. **Das Kind würde nicht fallen, wenn es nicht so schnell liefe.**
10. **Sie könnten es tun, wenn sie es tun wollten.**

11. Wenn er Zeit gehabt hätte, so hätte er das Deutsche Museum besucht.
12. Wenn wir einen Wagenheber gehabt hätten, so wären wir gleich an die Arbeit gegangen.
13. Ich hätte es nicht geglaubt, wenn ich es nicht selber gesehen hätte.
14. Wir wären zu Hause geblieben, wenn wir das gewusst hätten.
15. Hätte Herr Clark keinen Partner in München gehabt, so hätte er seine Geschäfte nicht so schnell erledigt.

Exercise 198

Which sentences belong together?

1. Wenn ich viel Geld hätte,
2. Wenn er Zeit gehabt hätte,
3. Wenn er schneller gefahren wäre,
4. Wenn er besser Deutsch könnte,
5. Wenn sie in Europa geblieben wäre,
6. Wenn wir keinen Hunger hätten,

a. würde er alles genau verstehen.
b. wäre er nach Österreich gefahren.
c. würde ich viele Souvenirs kaufen.
d. wären wir nicht essen gegangen.
e. wäre er nicht zu spät gekommen.
f. hätte sie ihre Freunde besuchen können.

Exercise 199

Complete the sentences.

1. Wenn ich im Lotto gewänne, _____ .
2. Wenn ich ein Schauspieler wäre, _____ .
3. Wenn ich viele Sprachen könnte, _____ .
4. Wenn Tiere reden könnten, _____ .
5. Wenn ich in Deutschland lebte, _____ .
6. Wenn ich sehr krank wäre, _____ .
7. Wenn ich meiner Traumfrau / meinem Traummann begegnen könnte, _____ .
8. Wenn ich kein Auto hätte, _____ .

BERICHT EINES GESPRÄCHS ZWISCHEN HERRN CLARK UND HERRN MÜLLER

Report of a Conversation between Mr. Clark and Mr. Müller

Reread the conversation between Mr. Clark and Mr. Müller in Chapter 28. Here is a report of that conversation. It tells what Mr. Müller said, related or answered and what Mr. Clark said or asked, but not in the exact words of the two speakers. You will note that subjunctive forms appear in this reported conversation. The use of the subjunctive in reported statements and reported questions will be treated in the "Grammar Notes and Practical Exercises" of this chapter.

Herr Müller begann das Gespräch.

1. Er sagte, dass er etwas von sich selbst erzählen werde; dass er selber das Gesprächsthema sein werde.

2. Herr Clark bemerkte, dass das sicherlich interessant wäre, und fragte, ob er Fragen an ihn stellen dürfe.

3. Herr Müller erwiderte, dass es ihn immer freue, Fragen zu beantworten. Dann fügte er hinzu, dass er in Deutschland geboren sei. Er sei jetzt Bürger der Vereinigten Staaten. Er sei verheiratet und habe zwei Kinder.

4. Herr Clark fragte, was sein Beruf sei.

5. Herr Müller antwortete ausführlich. Er sagte, er sei Lehrer. Er unterrichte an einer Sekundarschule. Er lehre Deutsch und Französisch.

   Dann fügte er hinzu, dass er Französisch und Englisch lese, spreche und schreibe. Er habe auf dem Gymnasium und auf der Universität Französisch und Englisch studiert. Er habe vier Jahre lang in Paris gelebt.

6. Herr Clark fragte, wann er in Paris gewesen sei.

Mr. Müller began the conversation.

1. He said that he would relate something about himself, that he himself would be the topic of conversation.

2. Mr. Clark remarked that this would surely be interesting and asked whether he might ask him questions.

3. Mr. Müller answered that he was always glad to answer questions. Then he added he had been born in Germany. He was now a citizen of the United States. He was married and had two children.

4. Mr. Clark asked what his profession was.

5. Mr. Müller answered in detail. He said he was a teacher. He was teaching in a secondary school. He was teaching German and French.

   Then he added that he spoke, read and wrote French and English. He had studied French and English at the gymnasium and the university. He had lived four years in Paris.

6. Mr. Clark asked when he had been in Paris.

7. Herr Müller antwortete, er sei vom Jahre 1978 bis zum Jahre 1983 dort gewesen. Er habe dort als Zeitungskorrespondent gearbeitet.

7. Mr. Müller answered he had been there from the year 1978 until the year 1983. He had worked there as a newspaper correspondent.

8. Herr Clark fragte, wann er nach Amerika gekommen sei.

8. Mr. Clark asked when he had come to America.

9. Herr Müller antwortete, das er im Jahre 1983 hergekommen sei.

9. Mr. Müller answered that he had come here in the year 1983.

10. Herr Clark fragte, ob er hier geheiratet habe.

10. Mr. Clark asked whether he had married here.

11. Herr Müller antwortete, dass er hier eine Amerikanerin geheiratet habe.

11. Mr. Müller answered that he had married an American here.

12. Zuletzt dankte Herr Clark Herrn Müller, und fragte, ob die Fragen ihn belästigt hätten.

12. Finally Mr. Clark thanked Mr. Müller and asked whether the questions had annoyed him.

13. Herr Müller antwortete, dass es ihm ein Vergnügen gewesen sei.

13. Mr. Müller answered that it had been a pleasure.

1. THE SUBJUNCTIVE IN INDIRECT DISCOURSE

A statement or question is said to be in *direct discourse* when the exact words or thoughts of a person are reported directly, that is, quoted after verbs of saying, telling, relating, thinking, asking and the like. A statement or question is said to be in *indirect discourse* when the statement or question is reported but not in the exact words of the speaker or thinker.

Direct statements are put in quotation marks.

Compare the direct statements with the indirect statements in the following English sentences.

	Direct Discourse	*Indirect Discourse*
	He said,	He said,
Present	"I speak well."	that he spoke well.
Past	"I spoke well."	that he had spoken well.
Present Perfect	"I have spoken well."	
Past Perfect	"I had spoken well."	
Future	"I shall speak well."	that he would speak well.

Now compare the direct discourse with the indirect discourse in the corresponding German sentences.

	Direct Discourse	*Indirect Discourse*
	Er sagte:	**Er sagte,**
Present	„Ich spreche gut."	dass er gut spreche *or* spräche.
Past	„Ich sprach gut."	dass er gut gesprochen habe *or*
Present prefect	„Ich habe gut gesprochen."	gesprochen hätte
Past perfect	„Ich hatte gut gesprochen."	
Future	„Ich werde gut sprechen."	dass er gut sprechen werde *or* würde

Pattern of Tenses in Direct and Indirect Discourse in German

Direct Discourse	*Indirect Discourse*
Present	I. Present Subjunctive *or* II. Past Subjunctive
Past	I. Present Perfect Subjunctive *or* II. Past Perfect
Present Perfect	Subjunctive
Past Perfect	I. Future Subjunctive *or* II. **würde** (present)
Future	I. Future Perfect Subjunctive *or* II. **würde** (past)
Future Perfect	

a. *Note that the tenses in Type II correspond exactly to those used in English indirect discourse. In German either Type I or Type II may be used. If, however, the verb form in Type I is identical in the indicative and subjunctive, Type II is used more often.*

Sie sagte: „**Wir haben Geld.**"   Sie sagte, dass sie Geld **hätten** (*not* **haben**).

b. *The same tense pattern is used for indirect questions as for indirect statements.*

Wir fragten ihn: „**Haben Sie Geld?**"   Wir fragten ihn, **ob er Geld habe** (*or* **hätte**).

c. **dass** *like* **that** *in English may be omitted in indirect discourse.*

If **dass** is used, subordinate word order is required.

Er sagte, **dass er in München geboren sei.**   Er sagte, **er sei in München geboren.**

d. *An indirect command is expressed by the present or past subjunctive of* **sollen** *plus an infinitive.*

Er sagte zu mir: „**Tue es sofort!**"   **Er sagte mir, ich soll (sollte) es sofort tun.**
He said to me, "Do it at once!"   He said to me I should do it at once.

e. The indicative might be used in indirect discourse if the introductory verb is in the present tense.

Er sagt: „Sie **ist** hier." Sie fragt: „**War** er gestern **hier**?"   Er sagt, dass sie hier **ist**.

Sie fragt, ob er gestern hier **war**.

Exercise 200

Read each sentence aloud in the direct and indirect discourse. Note how the German tenses in Type II correspond exactly to the English tenses.

1. Er sagte: „Ich habe einen Geschäftspartner in München." Er sagte, dass er einen Geschäftspartner in München habe (hätte).
2. Jemand fragte ihn: „Spricht Herr Schiller kein Englisch?" Jemand fragte ihn, ob Herr Schiller kein Englisch spreche (spräche).
3. Er sagte: „Ich will mit ihm Deutsch reden." Er sagte, dass er mit ihm Deutsch reden wolle (wollte).
4. Jemand fragte ihn: „Haben Sie die Stadt nicht gern?" Jemand fragte ihn, ob er die Stadt nicht gern habe (hätte).
5. Er antwortete: „Ich habe die Stadt nicht gern. Es gibt dort zu viel Lärm." Er antwortete, er habe (hätte) die Stadt nicht gern. Es gebe (gäbe) dort zu viel Lärm.
6. Der Reisende fragte: „Wann fährt der Zug nach Bonn ab?" Er fragte, wann der Zug nach Bonn abfahre (abführe).
7. Er sagte: „Man kann auf einer Reise nicht ohne viel Geld auskommen." Er sagte, man könne (könnte) auf einer Reise nicht ohne viel Geld auskommen.
8. Die Mutter sagte: „Die kleine Anna war gestern krank." Sie sagte, die kleine Anna sei (wäre) gestern krank gewesen.
9. Sie sagte: „Der Doktor ist gestern Abend hier gewesen." Sie sagte, der Doktor sei (wäre) gestern Abend hier gewesen.
10. Die Kinder sagten: „Wir sind heute früh aufgestanden. Wir haben uns schnell angezogen." Sie sagten, sie seien (wären) früh aufgestanden. Sie hätten sich schnell angezogen.
11. Die Eltern fragten: „Sind die Kinder noch nicht zu Bett gegangen?" Sie fragten, ob die Kinder noch nicht zu Bett gegangen seien (wären).
12. Er sagte: „Wir haben nach dem Essen einen Spaziergang gemacht." Er sagte, dass sie nach dem Essen einen Spaziergang gemacht hätten.
13. Sie sagte: „Ich werde am 1. Mai abreisen." Sie sagte, dass sie am 1. Mai abreisen werde (würde).
14. Ich fragte die Kinder: „Werdet ihr heute Abend ins Kino gehen?" Ich fragte sie, ob sie heute Abend ins Kino gehen würden.
15. Der Junge sagte zu mir: „Kommen Sie herein!" Er sagte mir, dass ich hereinkommen solle.
16. Sie sagte zu uns: „Setzen Sie sich!" Sie sagte uns, dass wir uns setzen sollten.

Exercise 201

Put the following sentences into indirect speech. Start with **Er sagte, dass . . .**

1. "Ich habe leider keine Zeit."
2. "Ich bin viel herumgereist."
3. "Wir hatten zuvor intensiv Deutsch gelernt."
4. "Ich werde wieder nach Deutschland reisen."
5. "Ich will meine Familie mitnehmen."
6. "Ich hatte nämlich großes Heimweh."
7. "Deutschland ist ein sehr interessantes Land."
8. Ich will auch Österreich und die Schweiz besuchen."

Was Geschieht im Hotel?

Das Handgepäck wird von dem Gepäckträger hineingetragen. Der Gast, Herr Clark, wird von dem Geschäftsführer des Hotels begrüßt. Der Zimmerschlüssel wird ihm ausgehändigt. Indessen wird sein Zimmer vorbereitet. Die Fenster werden von dem Zimmermädchen geöffnet. Die Vase mit frischen Blumen wird auf den Tisch gestellt. Eine Flasche Mineralwasser und Wassergläser werden von dem Zimmerkellner auf die Kommode gestellt. Herr Clark wird von dem Hotelboy im Fahrstuhl auf sein Zimmer gebracht. Er ist mit allem zufrieden.

What Happens in the Hotel?

The hand baggage is carried in by the porter. The guest, Mr. Clark, is greeted by the manager of the hotel. The key is given to him. In the meantime his room is being prepared. The windows are opened by the maid. The vase with fresh flowers is put on his table. A bottle of mineral water and water tumblers are placed on the bureau by the room waiter. Mr. Clark is taken in the elevator to his room by the bellboy. He is pleased with everything.

Wortschatz

die Blume *pl.* -n flower
das Mineralwasser *pl.* - mineral water
der Gepäckträger *pl.* - porter
der Gast *pl.* ¨-e guest
die Gastfreundlichkeit hospitality

die Kommode *pl.* -n chest of drawers
der Zimmerkellner *pl.* - room waiter
das Zimmermädchen *pl.* - chambermaid
indéssen in the meantime
aushändigen to give, to hand over

Was Geschah auf dem Ausflug?

Als Herr Clark mit den Söhnen des Herrn Schiller nach Hause kam, fragte dieser: „Nun, was geschah auf dem Ausflug?" Herr Clark antwortete:

„Anfangs ging alles glatt. Die Strecke durch Stadt und Vorstadt wurde schnell zurückgelegt. Unterwegs wurden von mir und den Jungen allerlei Anekdoten erzählt. Es wurde viel gelacht und gesungen. Plötzlich wurden wir durch einen lauten Knall erschreckt. Es war eine Reifenpanne. Während wir auf Hilfe warteten, brannte die Sonne auf uns nieder. Endlich wurde unsere Lage von einem vorbeifahrenden Lastwagenfahrer erkannt. Mit seiner Hilfe wurde der Reifen gewechselt."

What Happened on the Excursion?

When Mr. Clark got home with the sons of Mr. Schiller, the latter asked him, "Well, what happened on the excrusion?" Mr. Clark answered:

"At first everything went smoothly. The stretch through town and suburbs was covered rapidly. On the way, all sorts of stories were related by me and the boys. There was a great deal of laughter and singing. Suddenly we were frightened by a loud bang. It was a blowout. While we waited for help the sun burned down upon us. Finally our situation was recognized by a passing truck driver. With his help the tire was changed."

Wortschatz

die **Anekdóte** *pl.* **-n** anecdote
die **Lage** *pl.* **-n** situation, place
die **Rückfahrt** *pl.* **-en** return journey
erschrécken to frighten

zurück-legen to put behind, to cover
anfangs at first
glatt smoothly
sogléich = **sofort** at once

1. USES OF THE VERB *werden* already learned

a. As a main verb meaning to get, to become, werden *is, as you know, used in all tenses.*

Principal parts: **werden, er wird, wurde, ist geworden.**

Das Wetter ist schön geworden.　　　　　　The weather has become nice.

b. As an auxiliary meaning shall *or* will, werden *plus the infinitive of a verb is used to form the future.*

Er *wird* uns morgen *besuchen.*　　　　　　He will visit *us* tomorrow.

You will now learn how **werden** is used as an auxiliary verb to form all tenses of the passive voice.

2. THE PASSIVE VOICE

In the active voice the subject performs some act. In the passive voice the subject is acted upon.

Active: The teacher tests the pupil.　　　　　*Passive:* The pupil is tested by the teacher.

The person *by whom* or the thing *by which* an act is performed is called the *agent.* Now study the formation of the passive in German.

Present

Ich werde von dem Lehrer **geprüft.**
Du wirst von dem Lehrer **geprüft.**
Er wird von dem Lehrer **geprüft.**
Wir werden von dem Lehrer **geprüft.**
Ihr werdet von dem Lehrer **geprüft.**
Sie werden von dem Lehrer **geprüft.**
Der Schüler wird von ihm **geprüft.**
Die Schüler werden von ihm **geprüft.**

I am (being) tested by the teacher.
You are (being) tested by the teacher.
He is (being) tested by the teacher.
We are (being) tested by the teacher.
You are (being) tested by the teacher.
They are (being) tested by the teacher.
The pupil is (being) tested by him.
The pupils are (being) tested by him.

Past

Ich wurde von ihm **geprüft,** usw.
Die Schüler wurden von ihm **geprüft.**

I was tested by him, etc.
The pupils were tested by him.

Present Perfect

Ich bin von ihm **geprüft worden,** usw.	*I have been tested* by him, etc.
Die Schüler sind von ihm **geprüft worden.**	*The pupils have been tested* by him.

Past Perfect

Ich war von ihm **geprüft worden,** usw.	*I had been tested* by him, etc.
Die Schüler waren von ihm **geprüft worden.**	*The pupils had been tested* by him.

Future

Ich werde von ihm **geprüft werden,** usw.	*I shall be tested* by him, etc.
Die Schüler werden von ihm **geprüft werden.**	*The pupils will be tested* by him.

Future Perfect (Very Rarely Used)

Ich werde von ihm **geprüft worden sein,** usw.	*I shall have been tested* by him, etc.
Die Schüler werden von ihm **geprüft worden sein.**	*The pupils will have been tested* by him.

The passive in English is formed by tenses of the auxiliary verb *to be* plus the past participle of the main verb; the passive in German is formed by tenses of the auxiliary verb **werden** plus the past participle of the main verb. Note, however, that the past participle of **werden** used in the passive construction is **worden,** not **geworden.**

The agent in the passive is preceded by **von** if the agent acted directly, by **durch** if the agent acted indirectly.

Die Patientin wurde *von dem Arzt* **gerettet.**	The patient was saved *by the doctor.*
Die Patientin wurde *durch die Operation* **gerettet.**	The patient was saved *by the surgery.*

3. THE PASSIVE INTRODUCED BY *ES*

The passive is often introduced by **es** when no particular subject is stated; or when some indefinite word like **etwas, nichts, alles** is the subject.

Es wird viel gelacht und gesungen.	There is much laughter and singing.
Es wurde nichts gesagt.	Nothing was said.

4. SUBSTITUTES FOR THE PASSIVE

a. In general it is preferable and easier to use the active.

(active) **Wagner hat viele Opern geschrieben.**	*(active)* Wagner has written many operas.
(passive) **Viele Opern sind von Wagner geschrieben worden.**	*(passive)* Many operas have been written by Wagner.

b. An active sentence with the subject man *is often used instead of a corresponding passive. Such sentences are often rendered in English by the passive.*

man sagt (*passive:* **es wird gesagt**)

one says; they, people, etc. say (*passive:* it is said)

Hier spricht man Deutsch (*passive:* **Hier wird Deutsch gesprochen**).

Here one speaks German (*passive:* Here German is spoken).

Man sah viele Schüler dort (*passive:* **Viele Schüler wurden dort gesehen**).

One saw many pupils there (*passive:* Many pupils were seen there).

Exercise 202

Fill in the appropriate forms of **werden.**

1. Der Baum _____ gestern gefällt. (Präteritum)
2. Der Mann _____ gerade operiert. (Präsens)
3. Ich weiß, dass das Buch von vielen Menschen gelesen _____ . (Futur)
4. Ich _____ im Hotel sehr freundlich gegrüßt _____ . (Perfekt)
5. Wir _____ immer gut bedient _____ . (Perfekt)
6. Herr Clark _____ von seiner Frau und seinen Kindern am Flughafen erwartet. (Präsens)
7. Der Mann _____ von einem Hunde gebissen. (Präteritum)
8. Der Dieb _____ noch immer von der Polizei verfolgt. (Präsens)

Exercise 203

von or **durch**? Fill in the gaps.

1. **Das Buch wird dem Schüler _____ Lehrer überreicht.**
2. **Die Stadt wurde _____ ein Erdbeben zerstört.**
3. **Herr Müller wurde _____ einen Unfall verletzt.**
4. **Er wurde _____ einem Auto angefahren.**
5. **Dann wurde er _____ einem Arzt ins Spital gebracht.**

Exercise 204

Fragen

Lesen Sie noch einmal die Texte: **Was geschieht im Hotel** und **Was geschah auf dem Ausflug,** und dann beantworten Sie diese Fragen!

1. **Was wird von dem Gepäckträger hineingetragen?**
2. **Von wem wird der Gast begrüßt?**

3. Was wird ihm ausgehändigt?
4. Was wird indessen vorbereitet?
5. Von wem werden die Fenster geöffnet?
6. Wo werden die Blumen hingestellt?
7. Von wem werden die Wassergläser auf die Kommode gestellt?
8. Von wem wird der Gast auf sein Zimmer gebracht?
9. Wodurch wurden Herr Clark und die Jungen plötzlich erschreckt?
10. Was wurde von dem LKW-Fahrer erkannt?
11. Was wurde mit Hilfe des Lastwagenfahrers gewechselt?

CHAPTER 45

ANSWER SECTION

Exercise 1

1. Here is the glass. It is full of water. The water is fresh and clear. Here is the child. The child drinks water.
2. The child plays ball. The ball is red. The ball rolls under the bed.
3. Here is the tea. There is the coffee. The tea is warm. The coffee is cold. The father drinks coffee. The mother drinks tea.
4. The month of June is warm. The winter is cold in Canada. The summer is warm here.
5. Is the coffee cold? Is the tea warm? Is the beer cold? Is the soup warm? Who drinks tea? Who drinks coffee?
6. Karl is four years old. Mary is seven years old. How old is Jack? How old is the father? How old is the mother? How old is the child?

Exercise 3

1. sie
2. er
3. sie
4. er
5. es
6. es
7. sie
8. sie
9. er
10. er

Exercise 4

1. der Vater; die Schwester; der Lehrer, der Doktor; der Onkel; die Mutter; der Bruder; der Mann; das Kind; die Tante.
2. die Schule; der Ball; der Hut; die Butter; das Glas; das Wasser; der Tee; der Kaffee; die Klasse; das Brot; der Schuh; der Hut.

Exercise 5

Guten Tag!
Guten Tag!
Wie heißen Sie?
Ich heiße Angelika Müller.
Wie heißen Sie?
Ich heiße Robert Clark.
Auf Wiedersehen.
Auf Wiedersehen.

Exercise 6

1. Ein (kein) Plan
2. Ein (kein) Bett
3. Ein (kein) Auto
4. Eine (keine) Tochter
5. Eine (keine) Frau
6. Ein (kein) Bruder
7. Eine (keine) Schwester
8. Eine (keine) Tür
9. Ein (kein) Glas
10. Eine (keine) Schule
11. Ein (kein) Haus
12. Eine (keine) Tochter

Exercise 7

2. Wir lernen
3. Sie kauft
4. Der Stuhl steht
5. Ich spiele
6. Das Kind hat
7. Der Doktor kommt
8. Wer trinkt
9. Er trinkt
10. Der Schüler lernt
11. Wir spielen
12. Es steht
13. Marie singt
14. Sie singt
15. Wir haben
16. Er zählt
17. Wer spielt
18. Was steht

Exercise 8

2. Ist Herr Clark hungrig?
3. Ist das Brot da?
4. Heißt sie Angelika?
5. Kommt sie in die Küche?

Exercise 9

2. Nein, der Schüler geht nicht nach Hause.
3. Der Bruder ist nicht zwölf Jahre alt.
4. Das Wetter ist nicht kühl.
5. Der Mann kauft das Auto nicht.
6. Er ist nicht älter als die Schwester.
7. Das Haus ist nicht sehr alt.
8. Marie singt nicht schön.
9. Der Doktor kommt heute nicht.
10. Sie kommt nicht spät nach Hause.

Exercise 10

2. die Jungen
3. die Bücher
4. die Mädchen
5. die Lehrer
6. die Lampen
7. die Fräulein
8. die Herren
9. die Hüte
10. die Söhne
11. die Brüder
12. die Männer

Exercise 11

wohnen: ich wohne, du wohnst, er wohnt
singen: singe, singst, singt
zählen: zähle, zählst, zählt
spielen: spiele, spielst, spielt
stehen: stehe, stehst, steht
hören: höre, hörst, hört
trinken: trinken, trinkt, trinken
lernen: lernen, lernt, lernen
wünschen: wünschen, wünscht, wünschen
kommen: kommen, kommt, kommen
kaufen: kaufen, kauft, kaufen
gehen: gehen, geht, gehen

Exercise 12

1. kaufen Sie; ich kaufe
2. kauft Herr; er kauft
3. kommen die Mädchen; sie kommen
4. singen die Mädchen; sie singen
5. Spielt ihr; wir spielen
6. lernst du; ich lerne
7. wohnt der Kaufmann; er wohnt
8. ich höre; wer spielt
9. stehen die Stühle; sie stehen
10. trinkst du; ich trinke

Exercise 13

1. Herr Clark ist Geschäftsmann.
2. Nein, er ist kein Deutscher.
3. Sein Büro ist in New York.
4. Er wohnt nicht in New York.
5. Er ist vierzig Jahre alt.
6. Sie heißt Helene.
7. Sie ist vierunddreißig Jahre alt.
8. Sie haben vier Kinder.
9. Die Knaben heißen Karl und Wilhelm.
10. Sie sind zwölf und zehn Jahre alt.
11. Die Mädchen heißen Marie und Anna.

Exercise 14

1. Wie heißt das Mädchen?
2. Was ist er von Beruf?
3. Wie alt sind Sie?
4. Wohnen sie in New York?

5. Wo geht Karl hin?
6. Ist Herr Clark Deutscher?

Exercise 15

2. geht
3. spielt
4. trink
5. singen Sie
6. kommen Sie
7. antwortet
8. kauf
9. zähle
10. kaufen Sie

Exercise   16

Ich sehe die Mädchen, den Lehrer, die Verkäuferin, den Vater, den Geschäftsmann, die Frau, das Kind.

Er sieht ein Brot, ein Geschäft, ein Büro, eine Schule, keine Flasche, kein Haus, keinen Hut.

Exercise 17

Guten Tag.

Guten Tag.

Wie viel kosten die Eier? Wie viel kostet das Brot? Wie viel kostet der Aufschnitt?

Ein Dutzend Eier kostet 2 Euro.

Geben Sie mir bitte Eier und einen Laib Brot.

Bitte schön.

Vielen Dank. Auf Wiedersehen.

Exercise 18

1. Die Tische sind rund.
2. Die Fenster sind offen.
3. Die Türen sind nicht offen.
4. Die Bilder sind schön.
5. Die Fräulein spielen nicht Tennis.
6. Die Herren lernen Englisch.
7. Die Frauen singen schön.
8. Die Schüler spielen Ball.
9. Die Stühle stehen dort.
10. Die Schulen sind nicht weit von hier.

Exercise 19

ihn, sie, sie, es

Exercise 20

2. es
3. ihn
4. sie
5. sie
6. sie
7. es
8. ihn
9. sie
10. sie

Exercise 21

a. Hausflur
b. Lehrer
c. Koch
d. Wein
e. keine
f. ein
g. bitte

Exercise 26

2. Deswegen lernt er Deutsch.
3. Jeden Dienstag hat Herr Clark eine Deutschstunde.
4. Nicht weit von hier wohnt der Lehrer.
5. Hier spricht man Deutsch.
6. Durch die Fenster sehen wir einen Garten.
7. Um den Tisch stehen sechs Stühle.
8. Heute gehen die Kinder nicht zur Schule.

Exercise 27

Ich will den Lehrer fragen.
Du willst die Mutter besuchen.
Er will Deutsch lernen.
Wir wollen fleißig sein.
Ihr wollt Brot kaufen.
Sie wollen Deutschland besuchen.

Exercise 28

1. Wer spricht Deutsch? Herr M. spricht Deutsch.
2. Sprechen Sie Deutsch? Nein, ich spreche nicht Deutsch.
3. Wer fragt: Was ist dies? und Was ist das?
4. Antwortet Herr C. gut? Ist er intelligent und fleißig?
5. Wen will Herr C. besuchen? Er will seinen Geschäftspartner in München besuchen.
6. Ich will eine Reise nach Deutschland machen. Deshalb lerne ich Deutsch.
7. Herr C. ist weder Lehrer noch Arzt. Er ist Geschäftsmann.
8. Die Knaben sind nicht faul sondern fleißig.

Exercise 29

2. dem Kind
3. dem Freund
4. der Tochter
5. der Mutter
6. den Kindern
7. den Schülern
8. den Mädchen

Exercise 30

2. ihnen
3. ihr
4. ihm
5. ihnen
6. ihm
7. ihr
8. ihr

Exercise 31

ihm, ihr, wem, den, der, ihr, den, ihnen

Exercise 32

1. aus dem Haus
2. bei dem Lehrer
3. mit einem Buch
4. von der Schule
5. nach einer Stunde
6. mit einem Füller
7. zu dem Geschäftsmann
8. von der Mutter
9. bei dem Arzt
10. mit den Schülern
11. von den Bildern
12. zu den Kindern
13. von den Herren
14. seit zwei Jahren
15. seit zwei Monaten

Exercise 34

2. in dem Arbeitszimmer
3. an die Wand
4. in der Stadt
5. in die Stadt
6. neben den Lehrer
7. auf der Straße
8. unter den Büchern
9. auf den Tisch
10. hinter der Tür
11. hinter die Tür
12. zwischen den Fenstern

Exercise 36

1. Sie gehen in das Arbeitszimmer.
2. Er setzt sich auf das Sofa.
3. Er setzt sich in den Lehnstuhl.
4. Eine Flasche Rotwein steht auf dem Tisch.
5. Daneben stehen zwei Gläser.
6. Er wohnt in der Vorstadt.
7. Er fährt in die Stadt.
8. Sein Büro ist in der Stadt.
9. Er wohnt lieber in der Vorstadt.
10. Frau Clark fährt manchmal in die Stadt.
11. Es ist still und gemütlich.
12. Sie sind in der Vorstadt besser.
13. Herr Clark macht große Fortschritte im Deutschen.

Exercise 39

1. des Geschäftsmanns
2. des Klaviers
3. des Autos
4. der Kleider
5. der Tinte
6. der Sofas
7. einer Frau
8. eines Mannes
9. der Landkarte

10. des Arztes
11. des Tages, der Nacht
12. des Lärms

Exercise 40

2. Die Bücher des Kindes.
3. Das Auto der Frau.
4. Die Bilder des Mädchens.
5. Das Wohnzimmer der Familie Clark.
6. Das Glas des Lehrers.
7. Die Päckchen der Jungen.
8. Das Büro des Geschäftsmanns.
9. Die Wohnung des Arztes.
10. Der Garten des Onkels.

Exercise 41

1d 2g 3f 4b 5j 6c 7a 8e 9h 10i

Exercise 42

1. **die Haustür** house door
2. **die Wanduhr** wall clock
3. **das Schlafzimmer** bedroom
4. **das Bilderbuch** picture book
5. **das Gartenhaus** garden house
6. **der Deutschlehrer** teacher of German
7. **das Wörterbuch** dictionary
8. **die Geschäftsreise** business trip
9. **das Musikinstrument** musical instrument
10. **das Vaterland** fatherland

Exercise 44

2. eine Wohnung in der Vorstadt
3. die Zimmer der Wohnung
4. die Freunde der Kinder
5. die Wände des Zimmers
6. Bilder . . . den Wänden
7. dem Esszimmer . . . einen Tisch.
8. der Tisch
9. den Tisch
10. der Lehrer . . . einem Stuhl
11. der Geschäftsmann . . . das Sofa
12. dem Klavier . . . einer Frau
13. einen Geschäftspartner
14. den Partner
15. eine Stadt

Exercise 45

2. Die Kinder des Geschäftsmanns spielen im Garten.
3. Ich bringe der Schwester den Hut.
4. Die Kinder lieben die Lehrerinnen.
5. Die Jungen suchen den Ball.
6. Der Lehrer spricht zu den Schülern.
7. Das Porträt der Frau hängt im Wohnzimmer.
8. Der Junge schreibt mit dem Bleistift.
9. Das Mädchen schreibt mit der Füllfeder.
10. Der Vater fragt die Kinder.
11. Ich gebe der Mutter die Briefe.

Exercise 46

Mr. Clark Is Learning German

Mr. Clark is a business man. His office is in a skyscraper in the city of New York. His dwelling, however, is not in the city but in a suburb not far from it. Every weekday Mr. Clark drives into the city and carries on his business there.

The firm of Mr. Clark has a business partner in Germany. His name is Heinrich Schiller and he lives in the city of Munich. In the spring of this year Mr. Clark is taking a trip to Germany in order to visit Mr. Schiller. He wants to talk with his partner about important business matters. Mr. Clark also wants to understand the people in Germany. Therefore Mr. Clark is beginning to learn German.

Mr. Clark has a good teacher, Karl Müller. Every Tuesday and Thursday the teacher comes to the home of his pupil in order to give him a German lesson. Mr. Clark is industrious and smart and learns quickly. During the first hour he learns these German expressions by heart: Good day; How are you?; Many thanks; Please; Good-bye, etc. (and so forth). He already knows the German names for many things in his living room and can answer these questions correctly: What is this? What is that? Where is that? Why is that? etc.

Mr. Müller is very satisfied with the progress of his student and says: "Very good. That is enough for today. I'll come again Thursday. Good-bye."

Exercise 47

The German-speaking Countries

In Germany one obviously speaks German. But also in Austria and Switzerland one speaks German. All three countries lie in Central Europe. After the end of the Second World War Germany was divided into two parts, West Germany and East Germany. The Elbe separated the two parts of Germany. Now West and East Germany are unified again.

The capital of Germany is Berlin. Among the large cities in the west are Cologne, Munich, Stuttgart, Frankfurt, Düsseldorf and the large port cities Hamburg and Bremen. Among the large cities in the east are Leipzig, Dresden, and Chemnitz.

The capital of Austria is Vienna. Many tourists also come to Salzburg in order to visit the birthplace of Wolfgang Amadeus Mozart or to ski in the mountains.

There are high mountains also in Switzerland. In Switzerland one doesn't speak only German, but also French and Italian.

Exercise 49

1. deines
2. eu(e)re Eltern
3. Ihr
4. ihrer
5. seines
6. ihres
7. uns(e)ren
8. Ihrer

9. mein
10. ihre
11. uns(e)rem
12. Ihren

Exercise 51

eure Bücher—unsere Bücher
euren Ball—unseren Ball
euer Flugticket—unser Flugticket
euer Geld—unser Geld
eure Füller—unsere Füller
euer Deutschbuch—unser Deutschbuch
eure Fotos—unsere Fotos
eure Hüte—unsere Hüte
eure Landkarte—unsere Landkarte

Exercise 52

1. Er ist ein Freund von Herrn Clark.
2. Es ist im selben Gebäude wie das Büro des Herrn Clark.
3. Er spricht Deutsch.
4. Er will erfahren, was für Fortschritte Herr Clark macht.
5. Er sitzt an seinem Schreibtisch.
6. Er liest Briefe.
7. Plötzlich tritt sein Freund, Herr Engel, ins Büro.
8. Er beginnt sofort, auf Deutsch zu sprechen.
9. Herr Clark antwortet seinem Freund auf Deutsch.
10. Er lernt schon seit einigen Monaten Deutsch.
11. Er beabsichtigt, im Sommer eine Reise nach Deutschland zu machen.
12. Morgen geht er zum Reisebüro.
13. Die Herren geben sich die Hand.

Exercise 53

a. dreißig
b. zehn
c. fünfzig
d. zwölf
e. sieben
f. sechzig
g. siebzig
h. neunzehn
i. vierzehn
j. einunddreißig
k. fünfundzwanzig
l. dreiundvierzig
m. neunundachtzig
n. neunzig
o. hundert
p. neununddreißig
q. achtundzwanzig
r. sechsunddreißig
s. fünfzehn
t. zwölf

Exercise 54

2. Ein Jahr hat zwölf Monate.
3. Ein Tag hat vierundzwanzig Stunden.
4. Ein Stunde hat sechzig Minuten.
5. Ein Minute hat sechzig Sekunden.

6. Der Monat September hat dreißig Tage.
7. Der Monat Juli hat einunddreißig Tage.
8. In den Vereinigten Staaten sind fünfzig Staaten.
9. Der Vater ist vierzig Jahre alt.
10. Die Mutter ist sechsunddreißig Jahre alt.
11. Ein Dutzend ist zwölf.
12. Die Hand hat fünf Finger.

Exercise 55

kann
Können
kann
kann
könnt
Können
können
kannst

Exercise 57

2. dieses (jenes) Geschäftsmanns
3. in diesem (jenem) Wolkenkratzer
4. diese (jene) Landkarte
5. diesem (jenem) Haus
6. diese (jene) Wörter
7. diesen (jenen) Mädchen
8. dieses (jenes) Wort
9. dieser (jener) Kinder
10. dieser (jener) Frau

Exercise 58

2. Welcher Mann
3. Welcher Lehrer
4. Welches Schlafzimmer
5. Welche Bücher
6. Welche Wörter weiß der Schüler?
7. Welche Herren kennen wir nicht?
8. Welche Wörter muss sie schreiben?

Exercise 59

welchen Pullover—diesen—jenen
welches Hemd—dieses—jenes
welchen Hut—diesen—jenen
welchen Mantel—diesen—jenen
welche Schuhe—diese—jene
welches T-Shirt—dieses—jenes

Exercise 61

a. fünfhundert
b. sechshundertfünfundzwanzig.
c. siebenhundertsechsundvierzig
d. zweihundertsiebenundvierzig
e. hundertsechsunddreißig
f. neunhundertneunundneunzig
g. tausendsechshundertvierzig
h. fünftausenddreihundertzwanzig
i. im Jahre sechzehnhundertzwanzig
j. im Jahre neunzehnhundertsiebzig

Exercise 63

2. . . . zur Schule, wenn das Wetter schön ist.
3. Wir wissen, dass dieser Geschäftsmann einen Partner in München hat.
4. . . . schnell, denn er ist . . .
5. Wenn ich in München bin, will ich mit diesem Mann reden.
6. Ich weiß, dass Sie im Sommer eine Reise nach Deutschland machen.
7. . . . kaufen, aber es ist viel zu teuer.
8. . . . nennen, wenn man in Deutschland ist.
9. . . . kommen, denn ich habe viel zu tun.
10. . . . Kino, und wir müssen zu Hause bleiben.

Exercise 64

1. Ein Euro hat hundert Cent.
2. Der Dollar ist ungefähr fünfundsiebzig Cent wert.
3. Ich bekomme 350 (dreihundertfünfzig) Euro zurück.
4. Ich bekomme 210 (zweihundertzehn) Euro zurück.
5. Ich habe im ganzen 1253,50 Euros (tausendzweihundertdreiundfünfzig Euro und fünfzig Cent).
6. Ich bekomme 90 (neunzig) Euro zurück.
7. Eine Million geteilt durch zehn ist hunderttausend.

Exercise 65

Ich glaube, dass der Hut 9,99 € kostet.
. . . dass der Bleistift 0,65 € kostet.
. . . dass die Fahrkarte 2,20 € kostet.
. . . dass das Kleid 27,50 € kostet.
. . . dass die Wohnung 178 000 € kostet.

Exercise 66

2. des schweren Koffers
3. diesem schweren Koffer
4. die schweren Koffer . . . im großen Wartesaal
5. der runde Tisch
6. diesen runden Tisch
7. dem roten Bleistift
8. die neuen Hefte
9. jene deutschen Bücher
10. dieser deutschen Landkarte
11. welche englischen Bücher

Exercise 67

1. ein amerikanischer Geschäftsmann
2. in einem kleinen Vorort
3. in einem schönen Einfamilienhaus
4. ein kleiner Garten
5. in ihrem kleinen Garten
6. in der großen Stadt . . . einen tüchtigen Geschäftspartner
7. eine kurze Reise
8. seinen deutschen Geschäftspartner
9. eine große Bestellung
10. ein schwerer Koffer

Exercise 68

Ich ziehe ein grünes Hemd an, einen hellroten Pullover, eine schwarze Hose, einen hellgrünen Rock, ein rosa Kleid, ein violettes Sakko, ein weißes T-Shirt, etc.

Exercise 69

a. Viertel nach eins
b. zehn Minuten nach fünf
c. Viertel nach acht
d. Viertel vor drei
e. zwanzig Minuten nach drei
f. fünf Minuten vor vier
g. elf Uhr
h. zwanzig Minuten nach vier
i. halb eins
j. halb acht
k. Viertel vor zehn
l. dreiundzwanzig Minuten nach zehn

Exercise 70

2. siebzehn Uhr fünfundzwanzig
3. fünfzehn Uhr vierzehn
4. acht Uhr fünfundzwanzig
5. sechs Uhr fünfundzwanzig—achtzehn Uhr fünfzig
6. neunzehn Uhr—zehn Uhr zehn
7. neunzehn Uhr dreißig
8. vierzehn Uhr dreißig
9. zweiundzwanzig Uhr dreißig

Exercise 71

2. gibt . . . zurück
3. fährt . . . ab
4. stehen . . . auf
5. kommst . . . zurück
6. fangen . . . an
7. kommt. . . an
8. fangen . . . an
9. steht . . . auf
10. komme . . . zurück

Exercise 72

auf, aus, ein, mit, zu, ab, an, weg

Exercise 73

1. mich
2. mir
3. Sie
4. uns
5. Ihnen
6. euch
7. dir
8. dich
9. mich
10. Sie
11. mir

Exercise 74

1. Euro in Dollar wechseln.
2. gute Reise
3. macht große Fortschritte.
4. Auskunft
5. zu Fuß
6. ich denke an

7. Eines Abends
8. Seit wann
9. Ich lerne
10. Ich gebe ihm die Hand
11. Ich freue mich
12. Fangen wir an

Exercise 75

1. —What are you reading? —I am reading the German newspaper. —What is he reading? —He is reading an English newspaper.
2. —What are you giving Mother for her birthday? —I am giving her a silk handkerchief. —What is Karl giving her? —He is giving her a pretty scarf.
3. —Does Herr Kurz speak English and French? —He speaks neither English nor French. He speaks only German.
4. —Which suit is he wearing today? —He is wearing his new brown suit.
5. —At what time does he leave the house every day? —He leaves the house at seven o'clock sharp.
6. —How long are you remaining here in this city? —I am remaining here a whole year.
7. —Have you a large valise? —I have a large one and a small one. —Please lend me the large one. —Gladly.
8. —What a pretty dress! —What a lovely garden! —What a beautiful lady!

Exercise 76

1e 2f 3a 4h 5b 6j 7i 8c 9g 10d

Exercise 77

2. dem roten Bleistift
3. einen schweren Koffer
4. den schweren Koffer
5. einer schönen Frau
6. dieses amerikanischen Geschäftsmanns
7. jenem kleinen Tisch
8. den runden Tisch
9. ein schönes Mädchen!
10. dem europäischen Kontinent
11. dieser großen Firma
12. dem gemütlichen Zimmer
13. kein altes Auto
14. uns(e)res schweren Koffers
15. seinen deutschen Geschäftspartner

Exercise 78

2. diese schönen Bilder kosten
3. unseren deutschen Lehrern
4. diese kleinen Mädchen
5. Wo sind die Wohnungen deiner neuen Freundinnen?
6. Die deutschen Übungen sind . . .
7. Wo sind die neuen Hefte?
8. keine deutschen Bücher.
9. jener hübschen Kinder
10. den deutschen Zeitungen
11. Liebe Freunde!
12. Liebe Freundinnen!

Exercise 79

1. uns
2. ihn
3. Sie
4. uns
5. ihm
6. ihr
7. Sie
8. dir
9. sie
10. er
11. sie
12. es

Exercise 80

Charles Does Not like to Study Mathematics

One day Charles comes from school and says to his mother, "I don't like to learn mathematics. It is too difficult. Why must we do so many exercises and assignments? We have calculators and computers, haven't we?"

The mother looks at her son and says: "You are wrong, my child. One can do nothing without mathematics. We use mathematics not only in all fields of science but also in daily life." The mother stops talking, for she sees her son is not paying attention to what she is saying.

"Just tell me, my dear boy, doesn't baseball interest you?"

"Of course it interests me."

"Well then, if the Dodgers win eighty games and lose thirty, do you know what percentage of games they win?"

Charles answers: "For the percentage of games I don't need any mathematics. I find all math figured out in the newspaper. But you're right, Mother. I must study better. I hope to go to a university some day and therefore I must pass the school examinations, not only in mathematics but also in the other subjects."

Exercise 84

2. sich
3. mich
4. sich
5. sich
6. uns
7. uns
8. sich
9. dich—dich
10. sich
11. uns

Exercise 85

1. mir
2. euch
3. sich
4. mich
5. mich
6. sich
7. dir
8. dich

Exercise 86

1. Mr. Clark gets up early every working day.
2. He washes and shaves very quickly.
3. He dresses quickly.
4. Mr. Clark and his wife have breakfast together.
5. He rides to the station in his car.
6. The train arrives soon.
7. Mr. Clark boards the train with many other people.
8. The train leaves in a few minutes.
9. The train arrives in New York in half an hour.
10. All the passengers get off.
11. Mr. Clark walks to his office.
12. He works hard all day.

Exercise 87

3. —dass er sich schnell anzieht.
4. —dass Herr C. und seine Frau zusammen frühstücken.
5. —dass er mit dem Auto zu der U-Bahnstation fährt.
6. —dass der Zug bald ankommt.
7. —dass Herr C. mit . . . einsteigt.
8. —dass der Zug in einigen Minute abfährt.
9. —dass der Zug in einer halben . . . ankommt.
10. —dass alle Passagiere aussteigen.
11. — dass Herr C. in sein Büro zu Fuß geht.
12. —dass er den ganzen Tag tüchtig arbeitet.

Exercise 88

1. Er muss um sechs Uhr aufstehen.
2. Er braucht eine halbe Stunde dazu.
3. Gegen sieben Uhr setzt er sich zum Frühstück.
4. Er frühstückt mit seiner Frau.
5. Sie unterhalten sich über die Kinder.
6. Gewöhnlich hat er Orangensaft, Semmel, Eier und Kaffee.
7. Er fährt mit dem Auto
8. Er liest die Post.
9. Er telephoniert mit verschiedenen Kunden.
10. Zum Mittagessen braucht er nur zwanzig Minuten.
11. Um fünf Uhr verlässt er sein Büro.
12. Um Viertel nach sechs kommt er nach Hause.
13. Am Ende des Tages fühlt er sich müde.
14. Er freut sich, zu Hause zu sein.

Exercise 90

2. Was sagte der Junge?
3. Was antwortete . . .
4. Sein Vater wartete . . .
5. Sie redeten . . .
6. Ich machte . . .
7. Ich lernte . . .
8. Wir setzten uns . . .
9. Sie kaufte . . .
10. Wohntest du . . .
11. Ich wohnte . . .
12. Hattet ihr . . .
13. Wir hatten . . .
14. Was fragte . . .
15. Diese Leute arbeiteten . . .

Exercise 91

2. Die Kinder standen . . . auf.
3. Wann aßen Sie . . .
4. Wir fuhren . . .
5. Es gab . . .
6. Um wie viel Uhr kam . . . an?
7. Um wie viel Uhr fuhr . . . ab?
8. Er trug . . .
9. Viele Leute standen . . .
10. Die Herren saßen . . .
11. In der Deutschstunde sprachen wir . . .
12. Schriebst du . . .

Exercise 92

war, wohnte, sagte, ging, kam, sah, lief, fraß, legte, kam, dachte, fragte, antwortete, sprang, schluckte, legte, schlief, vorbeikam, hörte, trat, sah, schnitt, sprangen, gaben, nähten, fiel, musste

Exercise 93

1d; 2a; 3f; 4h; 5e; 6b; 7g; 8c;

Exercise 94

2. standen
3. kam
4. fuhr
5. fing
6. stiegen aus
7. stiegen ein
8. zogen
9. gab . . . zurück
10. nahm
11. trat . . . ein
12. gingen . . . hinein

Exercise 95

2. . . . Abendessen, sobald Herr Clark nach Hause kam.
3. . . . . müde, weil er den ganzen Tag fleißig arbeitet.
4. Wissen Sie, ob der Zug pünktlich ankommt?
5. . . . Zimmer, als Herr Clark seiner Sekretärin Briefe diktierte.
6. Als Herr Müller Herrn Clarks Wohnung erreichte, regnete es in Strömen.
7. . . . kaufen, weil es zu viel kostet.
8. . . . aus, wenn der Zug in Hamburg ankommt.
9. Wenn Papa nach Hause kommt, freuen sich die Kinder.
10. Während du spielst, muss ich arbeiten.

Exercise 97

1. Der Titel ist „Was für ein schreckliches Wetter."
2. Es regnete in Strömen.
3. Wilhelm öffnete ihm die Tür.
4. Der Lehrer gab dem Jungen Hut und Regenmantel.
5. Herr Clark erschien.
6. Herr Müller sollte Tee mit Rum trinken.

7. Das Wetter war ein passendes Thema für diesen Abend.
8. Sie gingen in das Esszimmer.
9. Frau Clark brachte ihnen den Tee.
10. Sie nahm eine Flasche Rum vom Schrank herunter.
11. Sie stellte den Rum neben die Teekanne.
12. Sie verließ das Esszimmer.
13. Als sie tranken, sprachen die Herren über das Wetter.

Exercise 98

Ich werde / mag
Du wirst / magst
Er wird / mag
Wir werden / mögen
Ihr werdet / mögt
Sie werden / mögen

Exercise 99

2. Er erwartete mich . . .
3. Wir begannen . . .
4. Er verstand mich und ich verstand ihn.
5. Wir besprachen . . .
6. Ich erfuhr, dass . . .
7. Um zwölf Uhr gingen wir . . .
8. Die Rechnung . . . betrug . . .
9. Während wir die Rechnung bezahlten, entstand . . .
10. Wir gingen . . . was los war.

Exercise 100

1. verstand
2. bekam
3. standen . . . auf
4. fährst . . . mit
5. zerriss
6. kaufte . . . ein
7. empfahl
8. erzählte

Exercise 101

1. ihr
2. deinem Vater
3. gehört ihm
4. ihnen
5. Verzeihen Sie mir
6. Ihnen
7. glauben ihm nicht
8. Wem
9. uns
10. meiner Schwester
11. Unser neues Zimmer gefällt uns.
12. ihnen

Exercise 102

. . . möchte Ihnen für Ihr Kommen danken
. . . gefällt mir sehr gut
. . . helfe dir doch immer gern
. . . antwortet ihr ihr nicht?
. . . glaubt ihm alles, was er sagt.

Exercise 103

1. Sie redeten weiter.
2. Er fühlte sich wohl.
3. Es war ihm nicht mehr kalt.
4. Der Winter in New York ist kalt.
5. Oft bekommt man Schnee.
6. Im Frühling wird das Wetter schön.
7. Ein warmer Regen fällt.
8. Er ist kalt.
9. Sie wollen Ski fahren.
10. Es ist warm.
11. In Deutschland ist der Frühling am schönsten.
12. Sie gehen am liebsten spazieren.
13. Die vier Jahreszeiten sind der Frühling, der Sommer, der Herbst und der Winter.

Exercise 104

2. die
3. den (welchen)
4. denen
5. der (welcher)
6. das (welches)
7. die (welche)
8. die
9. dem
10. den

Exercise 105

1. die
2. das
3. die
4. der
5. der
6. dem
7. dessen
8. denen
9. den
10. deren
11. deren
12. die

Exercise 106

1. Meine Kinder bewunderten alle Dinge, die sie im Büro sahen.
2. Die Bilder, von denen wir gestern sprachen, sind sehr teuer.
3. Gefällt dir der Mantel, den ich dir gestern kaufen wollte?
4. Das Auto, das Herr Clark fährt, ist rot.
5. Die Füllfeder, mit der er schreibt, ist grün.

Exercise 107

2. . . . von dem . . .
3. . . . worauf . . .
4. . . . mit dem . . .
5. . . . worüber . . .
6. . . . von denen . . .
7. . . . worauf . . .
8. . . . durch den . . .

Exercise 109

1. Es tut mir leid, zu hören . . .
2. Was fehlt ihm?
3. Kopfschmerzen und Fieber.
4. —aber jetzt fühlt sie sich besser.
5. Vor fünf Jahren . . .
6. —aber ich habe Kaffee lieber.
7. befindet sich.
8. Es machte mir viele Freude . . .
9. den Doktor kommen lassen.
10. zum Abendessen.
11. Es tut uns leid . . .

Exercise 110

1i 2c 3a 4g 5f 6l 7j 8d 9e 10b 11k 12h

Exercise 111

1c 2e 3h 4f 5g 6a 7i 8d 9k 10b 11j

Exercise 112

1. Herr C. muss
2. ich will
3. kann er
4. wir müssen
5. der Zug soll
6. ich mag
7. darf ich
8. er will
9. Können Sie
10. soll ich
11. darf er
12. ich muss
13. wir wollen
14. kannst du
15. soll ich
16. willst du
17. kann ich
18. er mag

Exercise 113

1. ich wollte
2. wir sollten
3. ich konnte
4. wir mochten nicht
5. wir konnten nicht
6. durfte
7. durften nicht
8. ich mochte
9. wollten
10. wir sollten

Exercise 114

2. . . . machen, wenn die Kinder so viel Lärm machen.
3. . . . reden, als wir das Examen machten.
4. . . . warten, bis der Doktor nach Hause kommt.
5. . . . gehen, weil es in Strömen regnete.
6. . . . spielen, weil sie müde ist.

7. . . . gehen, sobald du mit der Arbeit fertig bist.
8. . . . waschen, bevor sie sich an den Tisch setzen.
9. . . . arbeiten, während alle sich amüsierten.
10. . . . aufstehen, als der Lehrer ins Zimmer hereintrat.
11. Ich weiß nicht, ob der Autobus um sieben Uhr abfährt.
12. Weißt du, ob wir für morgen eine Aufgabe haben?

Exercise 115

acc: mich, dich, sich, sich, sich, uns, euch, sich;
dat: mir, dir, sich, sich, sich, uns, euch, sich;

Exercise 116

2. mir
3. euch
4. uns
5. sich
6. dir
7. uns
8. sich

Exercise 117

2. wusch und rasierte
3. zog
4. frühstückten
5. fuhr
6. warteten
7. kam
8. stieg . . . ein
9. fuhr . . . ab
10. versuchten
11. lasen
12. kam, stiegen aus

Exercise 118

Mr. Clark Was Sick

On Thursday, April 20, at eight o'clock in the evening, Mr. Müller arrived at the house of his student. The older son, a boy of twelve years, opened the door and greeted the teacher politely. They went into the living room where Mr. Clark usually awaited his teacher.

But this evening he wasn't there. Mrs. Clark wasn't there either. Mr. Müller was very surprised and asked the boy: "Where is your papa?" The boy answered sadly: "Father is sick. He is in bed, for he has a cold and fever. Mother tried to telephone you in order to tell you that you should not come this evening. But she could not reach you."

The teacher said: "I am very sorry that your father is sick. I wish him a quick recovery. If he is well and cheerful next week we can study two consecutive hours. Well, until next Tuesday. Good-bye, Charles." "The boy answered, "Good-bye, Mr. Müller."

Exercise 120

am siebenundzwanzigsten August
3. am neunzehnten Juni
4. am zwanzigsten Januar
5. am neunten Juli

6. am zehnten Mai
7. am zweiundzwanzigsten März
8. am einundzwanzigsten März
9. der erste Januar
10. das fünfundzwanzigste Kapitel

Exercise 121

2. von fünfzehn vierundsechzig bis sechzehn sechzehn
3. von neunzehn zwei bis neunzehn achtundsechzig
4. von achtzehn siebenundsiebzig bis neunzehn zweiundsechzig
5. von achtzehn zweiundsechzig bis neunzehn einunddreißig
6. von achtzehn vierundsiebzig bis neunzehn neunundzwanzig
7. von neunzehn siebzehn bis neunzehn fünfundachtzig
8. von neunzehn einundzwanzig bis neunzehn neunzig

Exercise 122

1. Die Familie will am Samstag Abend ausgehen.
2. Sie wollen ins Theater gehen.
3. Die Kinder finden das Theater langweilig.
4. Sie wollen ins Kino gehen.
5. Sie suchen einen Film, der für alle passt.
6. Diese Reihe ist besetzt.
7. Sie findet im dritten Saal statt.
8. Sie kaufen Popcorn.
9. Sie sehen Werbung und eine Filmvorschau.
10. Sie klatschen Beifall.
11. Es war ein angenehmer Abend.

Exercise 124

2. gesehen
3. geantwortet
4. gearbeitet
5. geschrieben
6. angesehen
7. gestanden
8. gerechnet
9. geredet
10. gesprochen
11. verkauft
12. gekauft

Exercise 126

2. Wir haben . . . geschenkt.
3. Ich habe . . . getrunken.
4. Ich habe . . . gelesen.
5. Die Kinder haben . . . gesessen.
6. Sie hat . . . geantwortet.
7. Was hat . . . gefragt?
8. Haben Sie . . . gearbeitet?
9. haben wir . . . gehört
10. Was haben . . . gesehen?
11. Ich habe . . . beantwortet.

Exercise 128

2. Er hatte sich . . . gewaschen und angezogen.

3. Unsere Familie hatte . . . gefrühstückt.
4. Der Vater hatte . . . gelesen.
5. Um sieben Uhr hatten wir uns . . . gesetzt.
6. Die Mutter hatte . . . bereitet.
7. Der Geschäftsmann hatte . . . gelesen.
8. Die Kinder hatten sich . . . amüsiert.
9. Wir aber hatten uns . . . gelangweilt.
10. Was hatten . . . getan?

Exercise 130

3. sind
4. Haben
5. haben
6. ist
7. Ist
8. hat
9. sind
10. Haben

Exercise 131

3. waren
4. Hatten
5. hatten
6. war
7. War
8. hatte
9. waren
10. Hatten

Exercise 133

1. Er ist um halb zehn aufgestanden.
2. Sie waren vor ihm aufgestanden.
3. Nein, sie hatten noch nicht gefrühstückt.
4. Um zehn Uhr haben alle sich zum Frühstück gesetzt.
5. Er hat die Sonntagszeitung gelesen.
6. Sie saßen vor dem Fernsehapparat.
7. Die älteren besuchten Freunde.
8. Die Mutter hatte eine schmackhafte Mahlzeit bereitet.
9. Sie wollten ins Kino.
10. Sie mussten also mit ihnen ins Kino.
11. Sie haben sich gelangweilt.
12. Sie sind nach Hause gegangen.
13. Er hat an einen Freund geschrieben.
14. Er hat einige deutsche Kurzgeschichten gelesen.
15. Er ist um elf Uhr zu Bett gegangen.

Exercise 135

2. . . . warum Sie so spät gekommen sind.
3. . . . wieso Sie heute keinen Appetit haben.
4. . . . was Sie essen möchten.
5. . . . wie Ihnen das Bild gefällt.
6. . . . wer mit Ihnen gesprochen hat.
7. . . . wann Sie morgen abreisen.
8. . . . wo Sie Ihre Frau getroffen haben.

Exercise 136

2. , warum Sie. . . verlassen haben?
3. , dass Sie . . . gewesen sind?
4. , wie Sie den Sonntag verbringen.
5. , dass Sie . . . machen.
6. , weil die Kinder gehen wollten.
7. , weil der Film . . . war.
8. , während die Mutter . . . bereitete?
9. , nachdem er . . . gelesen hatte?
10. , dass ich . . . gemacht habe.

Exercise 137

1. Herr Clark hat es erzählt.
2. Herr Müller wollte heute etwas von sich selbst sagen.
3. Er ist in Deutschland geboren.
4. Er ist verheiratet.
5. Er unterrichtet in einer Sekundarschule.
6. Er lehrt Deutsch und Französisch.
7. Er hat diese Sprachen auf dem Gymnasium gelernt.
8. Er hat vier Jahre lang dort gelebt.
9. Er hat bei einer französischen Zeitung gearbeitet.
10. Im Jahre 1983 kam er hier her.
11. Er hat eine Stellung an einer Sekundarschule bekommen.
12. Er hat eine amerikanische Frau geheiratet.

Exercise 138

2. Ich werde
3. werden Sie
4. Wir werden
5. Werden Sie
6. wird er
7. Wirst du
8. Ich werde
9. Wer wird
10. wird diese

Exercise 139

2. Ich werde . . . bleiben.
3. Er wird . . . besuchen.
4. Du wirst . . . mitgehen.
5. Wir werden . . . sein.
6. Ich werde . . . sein.
7. Werden Sie . . . schreiben?
8. Ich werde . . . ankommen.
9. Sie wird . . . sein.
10. Er wird . . . heiraten.

Exercise 140

2. , ob ich . . . vorlesen werde.
3. , dass sie . . . besuchen werden.
4. , ob das Wetter . . . sein wird.
5. , dass unsere Freunde . . . kommen werden.
6. , wo Sie unterrichten werden.
7. , dass niemand . . . kommen wird.
8. , dass du . . . bereiten wirst.

Exercise 142

1. kennen lernen
2. stellen
3. antworten
4. beantwortet
5. kann
6. einen Ausflug
7. belästigt
8. Im Gegenteil. . . gefallen
9. fertig . . . keine Fehler
10. mit Vergnügen

Exercise 143

2. Dort hat sie . . . gemacht.
3. Sie hat . . . bezahlt.
4. Sie hat . . . gebracht.
5. Da hat sie . . . vermisst.
6. Sie ist . . . gelaufen.
7. Gott sei Dank, sie hat . . . gefunden.
8. Der Kassierer hat . . . gereicht.
9. Frau C. hat . . . gedankt.
10. Sie ist . . . eingestiegen.

Exercise 144

2. habe ich Fleisch gegessen
3. habe ich einen Brief geschrieben
4. habe ich nur bis 15 Uhr gearbeitet
5. ist er mit dem Auto gefahren
6. haben Sie ein Buch gelesen
7. hat er eine Pause gemacht
8. seid ihr krank gewesen

Mrs. Clark's Birthday

It was March 22nd, the birthday of Mrs. Clark. On this day she was thirty-five years old. To celebrate her birthday, the Clark family went out to dinner in a German restaurant in the city of New York.

As they entered the restaurant they saw on the table, which was set for Mr. and Mrs. Clark, a beautiful basket full of white roses. Naturally, Mrs. Clark was surprised. She thanked her dear husband, and then the family sat down at the table. A young waitress handed them the menu. All of them ordered their favorite dishes. At the conclusion of the meal each of the four children took out little parcels. In the parcels were presents. They all cried "Happy Birthday," and each child handed Mother his or her present. Marie gave her a silk handkerchief, Charles a pair of gloves, William a woolen scarf, little Anne a drawing.

What a beautiful day, not only for Mother but also for Dad and the children.

As practice in arithmetic, Charles figured out the expenses for this day.

The meal for Mrs. Clark	$19.50
Tip	3.00
Flowers	12.50
Total	$35.00

"The purest coincidence," said Mr. Clark, "thirty-five dollars, thirty-five years."

Exercise 145

A Fantastic Film at the Movies

One evening Mr. and Mrs. Clark went to the movies. The films from Hollywood did not please them, for this evening there were only comedies.

But on this evening there was an extraordinary performance in a movie theater right in the vicinity of their home. The film was a documentary about Germany and actually in the German language.

Mr. and Mrs. Clark arrived at the movie house at 8:30. Almost all the seats were already occupied. So they had to sit in the third row. Mrs. Clark didn't like that, for the movements on the screen hurt her eyes. Fortunately they were able, after a quarter of an hour, to change their seats, and afterwards they sat in the thirteenth row.

The Clark family liked this film very much. Mr. Clark found a great deal of enjoyment in it.

As they were leaving the theater Mr. Clark said to his wife, "Do you know, Helen, I think I shall be able to get along well in Germany. I understood almost everything the actors and actresses were saying in German."

Exercise 146

2. Wir nannten; wir haben . . . genannt.
3. Sandten Sie; haben Sie . . . gesandt?
4. Er dachte; Er hat . . . gedacht.
5. brachtest du; hast du . . . gebracht?
6. verbrachten Sie; haben Sie . . . verbracht?
7. Ich wusste; Ich habe . . . gewusst.
8. Ihr kanntet; Ihr habt . . . gekannt.
9. Ich erkannte; Ich habe . . . erkannt.
10. Wir dachten; wir haben. . . gedacht.

Exercise 147

2. zu bekommen
3. erwarten
4. aufstehen
5. aufzustehen
6. besuchen
7. zu finden
8. spielen
9. zu gehen
10. zu sagen
11. zu reisen
12. sagen

Exercise 149

1. Herr C. hatte einen Brief an seinen Vertreter geschrieben.
2. Er hatte noch nie einen Brief in deutscher Sprache erhalten.
3. Gestern hat er die Antwort bekommen.
4. Der Lehrer hörte aufmerksam zu.
5. Sie fängt an: „Sehr geehrter Herr Clark!"
6. Er wird in München sein.
7. Er wird ihn am Flugplatz erwarten.
8. Er wird sich mit Herrn Clark in deutscher Sprache unterhalten.
9. Er muss Herrn Clark und seinem Lehrer gratulieren.
10. Er hat ihn bis jetzt nur als Geschäftsvertreter gekannt.
11. Er wird erkennen, dass Herr S. auch sehr liebenswürdig ist.
12. Nein, er wird jede Gelegenheit ergreifen, Deutsch zu sprechen.

Exercise 150

2. schöner
3. kälter
4. älter
5. größer
6. jünger
7. interessanter
8. länger
9. mehr
10. besser

Exercise 151

2. der größere Tisch
3. dem längeren Bleistift
4. keine bessere Wohnung
5. einen jüngeren Bruder
6. eine jüngere Schwester
7. eine ältere Bluse
8. die höheren Berge
9. den besseren Platz
10. Ihr jüngerer Bruder

Exercise 152

2. das interessanteste Buch
3. den besten Platz
4. die längsten Tage
5. die kürzesten Tage
6. das wärmste Zimmer
7. den größten Läden
8. seinem ältesten Freund
9. die besten Plätze
10. die höchsten Berge

Exercise 153

1. Der älteste heißt Herr S.
2. Der reichste heißt Herr B.
3. Der größte heißt Herr S.
4. Herr E. ist älter.
5. Herr B. ist kleiner.
6. Herr S. ist weniger reich.
7. Herr B. hat das meiste Geld.
8. Herr S. hat das wenigste.

Exercise 154

2. Deutschland ist größer als Österreich.
3. Die Schweiz ist kleiner als Österreich.
4. Der Großglockner ist höher als die Zugspitze.
5. Herr Müller ist älter als Herr Clark.
6. Wasser ist besser als Wein.
7. Ich habe Äpfel lieber als Orangen.
8. Ich lese öfter als ich fernsehe.

Exercise 155

1. am höchsten
2. am schönsten
3. am kältesten
4. am heißesten
5. am kürzesten
6. am größten
7. am ältesten
8. am besten

Exercise 159

1. Die deutsche Küche bietet dem Touristen viel Abwechslung.
2. Herr C. speist oft mit einem wichtigen Kunden in einem der besten deutschen Restaurants.
3. In Deutschland findet man das Essen nie eintönig.
4. Er wird seiner Frau ein gutes deutsches Kochbuch senden.
5. Das erste Geheimnis der guten deutschen Küche ist, dass man zum Kochen alles von der besten Qualität kaufen muss.
6. Das dritte ist, dass man das Kochen lieben muss.
7. Die Hauptmahlzeit der Deutschen ist das Mittagessen.
8. Sie beginnt mit einer guten Suppe.
9. Dann kommt Fleisch mit Gemüse und Salat.
10. Zum Dessert gibt es Obst oder Obstkuchen.
11. Herr C. hat Strudel am liebsten.
12. Der Strudel ist besonders in Süddeutschland und in Österreich beliebt.
13. Am Ende der Mahlzeit trinkt man Kaffee.
14. Während der Mahlzeit trinkt man Bier oder Wein.

Exercise 162

2. Welche Städte
3. besuchen wird
4. soll
5. alle Sehenswürdigkeiten
6. können
7. wollen
8. viele Ausflüge
9. können
10. erwarten

Exercise 164

1. Herr C. wird sechs Wochen in Deutschland bleiben.
2. Er liest fleißig in Reiseführern.
3. Er wird zwei oder drei Wochen in München bleiben.
4. Man nennt München das moderne Athen.
5. Das „Deutsche Museum" soll das größte sein.

6. Er will im Englischen Garten einen Spaziergang machen.
7. Er möchte einen Ausflug nach Oberammergau machen.
8. Diese Stadt ist Nürnberg.
9. Wagner lebte und komponierte in Bayreuth.
10. Er wird Bonn, Köln und Düsseldorf besuchen.
11. Er wurde in Düsseldorf geboren.
12. Herr C. wird die Heimreise von Hamburg aus unternehmen.
13. Herr Müller möchte ihn begleiten.
14. Nein, er wird ihn nicht begleiten können.

Exercise 165

2. Er liest . . . Deutschland.
3. Er besorgt . . . Reisepass.
4. Er kauft . . . Fahrkarte.
5. Er schreibt . . . Brief.
6. Er bekommt . . . Antwort.
7. Der Vertreter verspricht, ihn abzuholen.
8. Die Kinder schlafen dort viel.
9. Sie waschen sich.
10. Sie ziehen sich an.
11. Die Familie fährt zum Flughafen.
12. Das Flugzeug steigt auf.
13. Herr C. besteigt das Flugzeug.
14. Er reist ab.
15. Er lässt . . . zu Hause.
16. Die Familie verlässt . . . Flughafen.

Exercise 166

2. zu begegnen
3. ausnützen
4. vorzuzeigen
5. wiegen
6. nachprüfen
7. mitzuteilen
8. abzuholen
9. auszunützen
10. mitgehen
11. zu fahren
12. zu besteigen

Exercise 168

1. Herr C. lernt nun seit sechs Monaten Deutsch.
2. Er hat viel Zeit im Gespräch mit seinem Lehrer verbracht.
3. Er hat einige Bücher über Deutschland gelesen.
4. Er kann jetzt Deutsch sprechen.
5. Er hat einen Brief an seinen Geschäftspartner geschrieben.
6. Dieser hat ihm versprochen, ihn am Flughafen abzuholen.
7. Endlich kommt der Tag der Abreise.
8. Das Flugzeug verlässt den Flughafen punkt 19.00 Uhr (sieben Uhr abends).
9. Nein, Frau und Kinder begleiten ihn nicht auf der Reise.
10. Die Kinder müssen das Schuljahr beenden.
11. Sie muss für die Kinder sorgen.
12. Um 5 Uhr nachmittags ist die ganze Familie bereit.
13. Um Viertel nach sechs kommen sie am Flughafen an.

14. Herr C. lässt seine Karte und seinen Reisepass prüfen und sein Gepäck wiegen.
15. Frau und Kinder sehen ihm traurig nach.

Exercise 169

1. aufs Land
2. mit Recht
3. auf dem Lande
4. ergreifen Sie nicht die Gelegenheit
5. Mögen Sie . . . *or* Haben Sie . . . gern?
6. machte er einen Spaziergang
7. reisefertig
8. Ergreifen Sie jede Gelegenheit
9. Seiner Meinung nach
10. Ihrer Meinung nach
11. Wir haben ihn eingeladen

Exercise 170

2. haben wir . . . gegessen
3. schmeckte
4. ich habe . . . eingeladen
5. trank
6. Ich werde . . . zurechtfinden
7. Ergreifen Sie
8. Wir werden . . . beschreiben
9. haben . . . gespeist
10. Er hatte sich bemüht
11. sind . . . aufgestanden
12. bietet
13. mussten
14. bestiegen hatte
15. sind . . . eingestiegen
16. bittet

Exercise 171

positive: groß, dick, schnell, gut, klug, hoch, nahe, gern, wenig;
comparative: größer, dicker, schneller, besser, klüger, höher, näher, lieber, weniger;
superlative: am größten, am dicksten, am schnellsten, am besten, am klügsten, am höchsten, am nächsten, am liebsten, am wenigsten;

Exercise 172

Today Mrs. Clark doesn´t feel like driving to New York to go shopping. Therefore she sits down at her laptop and starts surfing on the internet. First she is looking for the latest fashion. She doesn´t want designer clothes, because they are too expensive. After a short while she finds a pair of jeans which she likes. With a mouse click the jeans end up in her virtual shopping basket. Now she needs a trendy top. She doesn´t have to search for a long time until she finds something suitable. Another mouse click. Then Mrs. Clark starts looking for a CD with the latest hits from the hitparade. Click. Maybe a DVD for today´s evening in front of the VCR? Click. Finally Mrs. Clark wants to buy something to read. She really wants to read the bestseller she has heard about on TV. Click, click. Mrs. Clark can use her credit card to pay. She has bought more than she had really

wanted to but she was able to do everything at home with her computer.

Exercise 175

amerikanischer, verlorenen, lachenden, zwölfjährigen, fleißigen, scurrile, staunenden, kochendes, kauende, kommenden

Exercise 176

2. Das Taxi hat . . . genommen.
3. Ich habe . . . gehabt.
4. Sie haben . . . geplaudert.
5. Mir hat nichts gefehlt.
6. Es hat . . . gefallen.
7. Er hat . . . verbracht.
8. Sein Freund hat versprochen.
9. Er hat . . . gekauft.
10. Haben Sie . . . verlassen?

Exercise 177

2. Er ist . . . geworden.
3. Dann sind sie . . . hinausgegangen.
4. Herr ist . . . entgegengekommen.
5. Sie sind . . . gefahren.
6. Das Taxi ist . . . gerast.
7. Es ist . . . gefahren.
8. Endlich ist der Kaufmann . . . angekommen.
9. Herren sind hineingegangen.
10. bist du . . . gestiegen?

Exercise 178

1. Er ging in den Wartesaal.
2. Ein feinaussehender Herr kam ihm entgegen.
3. Er fragte: „Sind Sie Herr Clark?"
4. Herr Clark erwiderte: „Ja, ich bin's."
5. Sie fuhren zu dem Hotel Königshof.
6. Es fuhr mit grösster Geschwindigkeit.
7. Endlich sind sie am Hotel angekommen.
8. Herr Schiller ging mit ihm hinein.
9. Man hatte für ihn ein feines Zimmer reserviert.
10. Es befand sich im fünften Stock.
11. Der Preis war fünfundsiebzig Euro täglich.
12. Er versprach, ihn anzurufen.

Exercise 181

2. über die Einladung.
3. Ich freue mich auf
4. interessieren sich für
5. Was denken Sie
6. bittet um
7. auf seinen Lehrer
8. auf die Reise
9. an die kommenden Prüfungen
10. Ich denke nicht daran

Exercise 182

1c; 2d; 3f; 4g; 5h; 6b; 7e; 8a;

Exercise 183

1. Herr S. hat ihn eingeladen.
2. Er fuhr mit einem Taxi.
3. Es machte vor einem modernen Miethaus halt.
4. Die Wohnung befand sich in dem vierten Stock.
5. Frau Schiller lud ihn ein, hereinzukommen.
6. Herr S. begrüßte ihn herzlich.
7. Es war im modernen Stil möbliert.
8. Herr S. stellte ihn seiner Frau vor.
9. Sie studieren auf dem Gymnasium.
10. Sie wartete mit einem ausgezeichneten deutschen Essen auf.
11. Zum Dessert gab es Apfelstrudel und Kaffee.
12. Sie unterhielten sich über das Leben in Deutschland, usw.
13. Sie zogen sich auf ihre eigenen Zimmer zurück.
14. Er hatte einen gemütlichen Abend verbracht.

Exercise 184

2. Die Jungen hatten . . . abgeholt.
3. Was hatten Sie . . . getragen?
4. Im Korb hatte sich . . . befunden.
5. Wer hatte . . . zubereitet?
6. Hatte er . . . gewartet?
7. Sie waren . . . vorbeigefahren.
8. Hattest du . . . erkannt?
9. Plötzlich hatte der Lastwagen . . . angehalten.
10. Was war geschehen?
11. Der Fahrer hatte . . . geholfen.
12. Er hatte . . . geliehen.

Exercise 185

2. Die Jungen haben (hatten) helfen wollen.
3. Du hast (hattest) das Zimmer verlassen dürfen.
4. Ich habe (hatte) leider nicht mitgehen können.
5. Wir haben (hatten) nicht spielen mögen.
6. Ich habe (hatte) einen Brief schreiben müssen.
7. Der Mann hat (hatte) nichts annehmen wollen.
8. . . . haben (hatten) wir nicht aufs Land gehen können.
9. . . . haben (hatten) sie in der Stadt bleiben müssen.
10. . . . haben (hatten) sie Fußball spielen wollen.

Exercise 186

2. Die Kinder haben den Ball im Garten liegen lassen.
3. Wir haben sie kommen hören.
4. Wir wollten ein Segelboot mieten.
5. Wir haben ein Segelboot mieten wollen.
6. Wir haben den LKW kommen sehen.
7. Wir haben den LKW gesehen.
8. Die Jungen haben den Reifen wechseln müssen.

Exercise 187

1. Er rief die zwei Söhne des Herrn S. an.
2. Er wollte einen Ausflug an den Ammersee machen.
3. Er lud die Söhne des Herrn Schiller ein.
4. Sie warteten vor seinem Hotel.
5. Ein guter Imbiss war im Korb.
6. Die Mutter hatte ihn zubereitet.
7. Er hörte einen Lärm.

8. Sie hatten eine Reifenpanne.
9. Sie hatten keinen Wagenheber.
10. Ein Lastwagen hielt plötzlich vor ihnen an.
11. Er lieh ihnen einen Wagenheber.
12. In fünf Minuten war alles fertig.

Exercise 188

2. einige interessante Bücher
3. ganz gut Deutsch sprechen?
4. dass er viel fließender Deutsch spricht.
5. von denen wir geredet haben.
6. Gefielen Ihnen
7. seine Musik und seine Küche.
8. was er nicht aus Büchern erlernen konnte.
9. ist nicht ruhiger als in unseren Städten.
10. nicht nur . . . sondern auch
11. rasch erledigen?
12. Ja, und danach konnte ich
13. über das Leben und die Sitten
14. werde ich Sie anrufen.
15. Er hatte Heimweh.
16. wird er die Familie mitnehmen.
17. bei uns zu Abend speisen?
18. den ich schreiben werde.
19. werde ich Ihnen alles erzählen.

Exercise 189

2. Plötzlich ist der LKW stehen geblieben.
3. Leider konnte Herr Clark keinen Wagenheber im Auto finden.
4. In Deutschland hat er viele Sehenswürdigkeiten gesehen.
5. Nun muss er nach NY zurückkehren.

Exercise 190

2. . . . dass er Heimweh hatte.
3. . . . dass er einige Briefe gschrieben hat.
4. . . . dass er das nächste Mal seine Familie mitnehmen wird.
5. . . . dass er nun fließend Deutsch sprechen kann.
6. . . . dass er in NY Herrn Müller anrufen wird.

Exercise 191

1. Herr C. ist im Begriff, Deutschland zu verlassen.
2. Die Sehenswürdigkeiten, die schönen Landschaften, die alten Städte, usw. haben ihm sehr gefallen.
3. Sie war nicht nur eine Geschäftsreise, sondern auch eine Vergnügungsreise.
4. Er konnte seine Geschäfte rasch erledigen.
5. Er hatte Zeit gefunden, nur ein paar Briefe zu schreiben.
6. Im kommenden Jahr möchte er wieder nach Deutschland reisen.
7. Nein, er beabsichtigt, die Familie mitzunehmen.
8. Er hat seine Frau und Kinder vermisst.
9. Er wird Herrn Müller anrufen.
10. Er wird viele Stunden im Gespräch über Deutschland verbringen.

Exercise 192

1. habe . . . geholfen
2. lieh
3. scherzten und lachten
4. verging
5. hat . . . eingeladen
6. haben . . . angenommen
7. schrie
8. hielt
9. betraten
10. begrüßte
11. vorstellen
12. werden . . . machen

Exercise 193

1. ein Geschäftsmann in N.Y.
2. um den Geschäftspartner seiner Firma zu besuchen
3. Er wollte
4. hatte er Deutsch gelernt.
5. Er hatte
6. Deutsch sprechen, lesen und schreiben.
7. über Deutschland
8. Er schrieb
9. bekam er eine Antwort
10. „Ich werde Sie am Flughafen abholen."
11. holte ihn dort ab.
12. fuhren zu dem Hotel
13. glücklicherweise
14. machte er einen Ausflug zum Ammersee
15. gingen mit ihm
16. Er besuchte die Plätze
17. verließ er München und machte eine Rheinreise
18. der längste, der breiteste und der schönste
19. Schließlich fuhr er
20. flog er nach N.Y. zurück
21. wird Herr C. wieder eine Reise nach Deutschland machen
22. wird er seine Familie mitnehmen

Exercise 193

German Television

Just like in the United States most inhabitants of Germany own a television set. Many families have two or more sets. To this VCR or DVD recorders have to be added. Also many children have their own TV set in their rooms.

In Germany there are private and state-owned TV companies. There is an important difference between private and state-owned TV companies. Everyone has already been upset by the advertisements which accompany almost every TV broadcast, whether it be a TV film, on-the-spot reporting, or live sports transmission.

In German state-owned television there are no commercials during films, thus the German TV viewer can enjoy the most interesting television programs without annoying interruptions. Every owner of a television set, however, has to make a monthly payment as a television fee. The state-owned TV companies get this amount. As private TV companies don't get anything from these TV fees, they have to finance themselves just like in the USA: with many interruptions for commercials.

Exercise 195

Mr. Clark's Rhine Journey

After he had settled his business in Munich, Mr. Clark took a pleasure trip through the Rhineland, partly by ship and partly by train.

People assert with reason that the Rhine is one of the most beautiful rivers of Europe. On the stretch from Mainz to Cologne, Mr. Clark admired the dark forests, the terraced vineyards, the small villages with their ancient churches and houses, and the ruins of old castles.

Now the steamer sailed past the Lorelei Rock. Everybody knows the legend of the sorceress who enticed the boatmen to their death with her singing. Heinrich Heine has immortalized this legend in the famous song: "I do not know what it signifies that I am so sad."

The ship stopped at several of the famous Rhine cities. Thus Mr. Clark was able to visit the city of Mainz, the birthplace of Johann Gutenberg, who invented the art of printing.

Soon after, the Dragon Rock appeared, where according to the legend the hero Siegfried killed a dragon. The legend relates that he bathed in the blood of the dragon in order to become invulnerable. In such legends from this region Richard Wagner found the material for some of his well-known operas, as for example *Das Rheingold, Siegfried*, etc.

Then came Bonn, the site of an old university, and after the Second World War the capital of West Germany. Ludwig van Beethoven was born in this city.

The next stop was Cologne. Here the most remarkable thing is the world-famous Cologne cathedral, whose towers reach more than 500 feet high.

The last Rhine city which Mr. Clark visited was Düsseldorf, the birthplace of the great German poet Heinrich Heine.

From Düsseldorf it was on to Hamburg, where Mr. Clark had some business to settle and from where he undertook the home journey by plane.

When Mr. Clark was at home again he often spoke of his interesting and pleasurable Rhine trip.

Exercise 196

3. er hätte
4. wir hätten
5. er schreibe
6. er schriebe
7. ich läse
8. sie läsen
9. er lerne
10. du lerntest
11. du sehest
12. du sähest
13. er komme
14. wir kämen
15. sie gehe
16. sie ginge
17. er fahre
18. er führe
19. ich könne

20. er könnte
21. wir müssen
22. wir müssten
23. ich wisse
24. er wüsste
25. er habe gehabt
26. sie habe studiert
27. ich sei gewesen
28. ich wäre gewesen
29. wir seien gekommen
30. wir wären gekommen
31. du habest gelebt
32. du hättest gelebt

Exercise 197

1. If I had enough money I would take a trip.
2. If the house were larger I would buy it.
3. If I now had a vacation I would travel to Europe.
4. If the weather were nice I would take a walk.
5. If she had time she would write us more often.
6. If he came today we would be happy.
7. If we could play tennis we would accompany you.
8. We would set out if our friends were already there.
9. The child would not fall if he did not run so fast.
10. They could do it if they wanted to do it.
11. If he had had time he would have visited the German Museum.
12. If we had had a jack we would have set to work at once.
13. I would not have believed it if I had not seen it myself.
14. We would have stayed at home if we had known that.
15. If Mr. Clark had not had a representative in Munich, he would not have settled his business matters so quickly.

Exercise 198

1c; 2b; 3e; 4a; 5f; 6d;

Exercise 200

1. He said that he had a representative in Munich.
2. Somebody asked whether Herr Schiller spoke no English.
3. He said that he wanted to speak with him in German.
4. Somebody asked him whether he did not like the city.
5. He answered that he did not like the city. There was too much noise there.
6. He asked when the train for Bonn left.
7. He said one could not get along on a trip without much money.
8. She said little Anne had been sick yesterday.
9. She said the doctor had been here last evening.
10. They said they had gotten up early. They had dressed quickly.
11. They asked whether the children had not yet gone to bed.

12. He said that they had taken a walk after the meal.
13. She said that she would leave on the 1st of May.
14. I asked them whether they would go to the movies this evening.
15. The boy said to me that I should come in.
16. She said to us that we should sit down.

Exercise 201

1. . . . er leider keine Zeit habe.
2. . . . er viel herumgereist sei.
3. . . . sie zuvor intensiv Deutsch gelernt hätten.
4. . . . er wieder nach Deutschland reisen würde.
5. . . . er seine Familie mitnehmen wolle.
6. . . . er Heimweh gehabt habe.
7. . . . Deutschland ein interessants Land sei.
8. . . . er auch Österreich und die Schweiz besuchen wolle.

Exercise 202

1. wurde
2. wird
3. werden wird
4. bin . . . . worden
5. sind . . . . worden
6. wird
7. wurde
8. wird

Exercise 203

1. von
2. durch
3. durch
4. von
5. von

Exercise 204

1. **Das Gepäck wird von dem Gepäckträger hineingetragen.**
2. **Der Gast wird von dem Geschäftsführer begrüßt.**
3. **Der Zimmerschlüssel wird ihm ausgehändigt.**
4. **Indessen wird sein Zimmer vorbereitet.**
5. **Sie werden von dem Zimmermädchen geöffnet.**
6. **Sie werden auf den Tisch gestellt..**
7. **Sie werden von dem Zimmerkellner auf die Kommode gestellt.**
8. **Er wird von dem Hotelboy auf sein Zimmer gebracht.**
9. **Die Jungen wurden plötzlich durch einen lauten Knall erschreckt.**
10. **Die Panne wurde von ihm erkannt.**
11. **Der Reifen wurde gewechselt.**

GERMAN-ENGLISH VOCABULARY

Accent marks are used in the end vocabularies to indicate the stressed syllable of words when the stressed syllable is not the first. The accent mark is simply a pronunciation aid and not part of the spelling.

The cardinal and ordinal numerals are not included in the end vocabularies. The cardinals 1–100 are given in Chapter 14, Grammar Note 1; above 100 in Chapter 15, Grammar Note 1. The ordinals are given in Chapter 25, Grammar Note 1.

A

der **Abend, -s, -e** evening; **am Abend, abends** in the evening

das **Abendessen, -s, -** supper

aber but, however

ab-fahren, er fährt ab, fuhr ab, ist abgefahren to depart, leave, ride off

ab-holen to call for, fetch

die **Abreise, -n** departure

ab-reisen to depart, leave on a trip

abwesend absent

acht-geben (auf) er gibt acht, gab acht, hat achtgegeben to pay attention (to)

alle all, everyone; **alles** everything

allerlei all kinds of

als sub. conj. when, as (in comparisons than)

also so, thus, therefore; well

alt old; **älter** older

das **Amérika** America; der **Amerikáner** American; **amerikánisch** adj. American

sich **amüsíeren** to have a good time, enjoy oneself

an prep. w. dat. or acc. at, on, to, up against

an-bieten, er bietet an, bot an, hat angeboten to offer

ander other; der **andere** the other; die **anderen** the others; etc. **anders** different

der **Anfang, -s, ¨-e** beginning; **anfangs** at first

an-fangen, er fängt an, fing an, hat angefangen to begin

an-geben, er gibt an, gab an, hat angegeben to indicate

die **Angelegenheit, -en** matter, affair

angenehm pleasant, comfortable

an-halten, er hält an, hielt an, hat angehalten to stop

an-kommen, er kommt an, kam an, ist angekommen to arrive

an-nehmen, er nimmt an, nahm an, hat angenommen to take on, accept

an-rufen, er ruft an, rief an, hat angerufen to call up, telephone

an-schauen to look at

an-sehen, er sieht an, sah an, hat angesehen to look at; **etwas ansehen** to look over, view, inspect

anstatt prep. w. gen. instead of

die **Antwort, -en** answer

antworten w. dative to answer

an-ziehen, er zieht an, zog an, hat angezogen to put on, dress; **sich anziehen** to get dressed

der **Anzug, -s, ¨-e** suit (man's)

der **Apfel, -s, ¨-** apple

der **Apparat', -s, -e** apparatus, appliance

der **Appetit', -s** appetite

die **Arbeit, -en** work

arbeiten to work

das **Arbeitszimmer, -s, -** workroom, study

der **Arm, -s, -e** arm

der **Arzt, -es, ¨-e** doctor, physician

der **Aschenbecher, -s, -** ashtray

auch also, too

auf prep. w. dat. or acc. on, upon

auf-bleiben, er bleibt auf, blieb auf, ist aufgeblieben to stay awake, open

der **Aufenthalt** stay, sojourn

die **Aufgabe, -n** task, assignment

aufgeregt excited

sich **auf-halten, er hält sich auf, hielt sich auf, hat sich aufgehalten** stay, sojourn

auf-hören to stop

auf-machen to open

aufmerksam attentive

der **Aufsatz, -es, ¨-e** composition

auf-stehen, er steht auf, stand auf, ist aufgestanden to stand up, get up

auf-warten to wait on, serve

auf-suchen to look up, seek out

das **Auge, -es, -en** eye

aus prep. w. dat. out, out of, from

der **Ausdruck, -es, ¨-e** expression

der **Ausflug, -s, ¨-e** excursion

ausführlich in detail

der **Ausgang, -s, ¨-e** exit

aus-gehen, er geht aus, ging aus, ist ausgegangen to go out

ausgezeichnet excellent

aus-kommen, er kommt aus, kam aus, ist ausgekommen to get along
die **Auskunft, ¨-e** information
aus-nützen to make full use of
aus-packen to unpack
aus-rufen, er ruft aus, rief aus, hat ausgerufen to cry out
aus-sehen, er sieht aus, sah aus, hat ausgesehen to look, appear
außer *prep. w. dat.* outside of, except
außerdem besides, moreover
außergewöhn'lich unusual
außeror'dentlich extraordinary
aus-steigen, er steigt aus, stieg aus, ist ausgestiegen to get out, climb out (of a vehicle)
ausverkauft sold out
das **Auto, -s, -s;** car
der **Autobus, -usses, -usse** bus

B
baden to bathe
das **Badezimmer, -s, -** bathroom
der **Bahnhof, -s, ¨-e** railroad station
der **Bahnsteig, -s, -e** railroad platform
bald soon
der **Balkon', -s, -e** balcony
der **Ball, -es, ¨-e** ball
beabsichtigen to intend
der **Beamte, -n, -n** official
beantworten to answer
bedeúten to mean
die **Bedeútung** meaning
been'den to finish
sich **befin'den** to feel
sich **befin'den** to be located; **Wo befindet sich das Hotel?** Where is the hotel?
begégnen *w. dat.* to meet
begin'nen, er beginnt, begann, hat begonnen to begin
begleíten to accompany
der **Begriff** idea, concept; **im Begriff sein** to be about to
begrüßen to greet
behal'ten, er behält, behielt, hat behalten to retain
behilf'lich helpful
bei *prep. w. dat.* at, with, beside, at the house of; **bei uns** at our house
beide both; **die beiden Herren** both gentlemen
das **Bein, -es, -e** leg
beináhe almost
beitragen to contribute
bekannt' known
bekom'men, er bekommt, bekam, hat bekommen to receive
beläs'tigen to annoy
beliebt' (bei) popular (among, with)
bemer'ken to notice
sich **bemü'hen** to try, endeavor
beneíden to envy
bequem' comfortable
bereit' ready; **bereits** already
bereíten to prepare
der **Berg, -es, -e** mountain
berich'ten to report, inform
der **Beruf, -s, -e** occupation, profession

berühmt' famous
beschäf'tigt busy
beschreíben, er beschreibt, beschrieb, hat beschrieben to describe
besetzt' occupied
besich'tigen to view
besiegen to defeat
beson'ders especially
besor'gen to take care of, to obtain
bespréchen, er bespricht, besprach, hat besprochen to discuss
besser better; **best-, am besten** best
bestéhen, er besteht, bestand, hat bestanden to pass (an examination)
bestéhen (auf) to insist (on)
bestéhen (aus) to consist of
besteígen, er besteigt, bestieg, hat bestiegen to get on, mount
bestel'len to order (goods)
besúchen to visit
betragen, beträgt, betrug, betragen to come to, to amount to
betréten, er betritt, betrat, hat betreten to step into (a place)
das **Bett, -es, -en** bed
bevor' *conj.* before
bewoh'nen to occupy
bewun'dern to admire
bewun'dernswert wonderful, admirable
bezah'len to pay
bezeich'nen to denote
die **Bibliothek', -en** library
das **Bier, -es, -e** beer
bieten, er bietet, bot, hat geboten to offer
das **Bild, -es, -er** picture
bilden to form, shape
bis until
bisher until now
ein **bisschen** a little
bitte please; you are welcome
bitten (um), er bittet, bat, hat gebeten to ask for, to request
blau blue
bleiben, er bleibt, blieb, ist geblieben to remain, stay
der **Bleistift, -s, -e** pencil
die **Blume, -, -n** flower
die **Bluse, -, -n** blouse
das **Blut, -es** blood
böse angry, bad
brauchen to need, use
braun brown
breit broad
der **Brief, -es, -e** letter
bringen, er bringt, brachte, hat gebracht to bring
das **Brot, -es, -e** bread
das **Brötchen, -s, -** roll
der **Bruder, -s, ¨-** brother
das **Buch, -es, ¨-er** book
das **Büfett, -s, -e** sideboard
das **Büró, -s, -s** office
der **Bürger, -s, -** citizen

C
der **Chef** head, manager

D

da *adv.* there, then; *conj.* since, because
dabei at the same time, in connection with that
daher' therefore
die **Dame, -n** lady
damit with it; **damit'** *sub. conj.* so that
danach' after that
der **Dank** gratitude; **vielen Dank!** thanks a lot!
danken *w. dat.* to thank; **danke!** thank you; **danke schön!** thank you kindly!
dann then; **dann und wann** now and then
die **Darstellung, -en** performance
das the, that, that one, who, which
dass *sub. conj.* that
dasselbe the same
das **Datum, -s, die Daten** date
dauern to last
dein, deine, dein, etc. your
denken, er denkt, dachte, hat gedacht to think; **denken an** *w. acc.* to think of
denn *conj.* for, because; *adv.* then
dennoch' nevertheless
der the, that, that one, who, which
dersel'be, dieselbe, dasselbe the same
das **Dessert', -s** dessert
deshalb, deswegen therefore
das **Deutsch** German (language); **auf deutsch** in German
deutsch *adj.* German; der **Deutsche** the German (man)
das **Deutschland, -s** Germany
der **Dezem'ber, -s** December
der **Dichter, -s,** - poet, writer
die the, that, that one, who which
der **Dienstag, -s, -e** Tuesday
das **Dienstmädchen, -s,** - maid, servant girl
dieser, diese, dieses this
diktie'ren to dictate
das **Ding, -es, -e** thing
dividie'ren durch divide by
doch nevertheless
der **Doktor, -s, Dokto'ren** doctor
der **Dollar, -s, -s** dollar
der **Dom, -es, -e** cathedral
der **Donnerstag, -es, -e** Thursday
Donnerwetter! wow!
das **Dorf, es, ¨-er** village
dort there
das **Drama, -s, -en** drama
draußen outside
dunkel dark
dünn thin
durch *prep. w. acc.* through
durch-führen to carry on, carry out, accomplish
durch-kommen, er kommt durch, kam durch, ist durchgekommen to get along, get through
der **Durst, -es** thirst; **Ich habe Durst** I am thirsty
dürfen, er darf, durfte, hat gedurft to be permitted to, allowed to, may
das **Dutzend, -s, -e** dozen
duzen to address with **du**; **sich duzen** to say **du** to each other

E

eben *adv.* just, just now
ebenso just as
die **Ecke, -n** corner
die **Eile** haste
ehe *sub. conj.* before
das **Ei, -es, -er** egg
eigen own
eigentlich really, actually
eilen to hurry
ein, eine, ein *indef. art.* a, an, one
einander each other, one another
das **Einfamilienhaus, -es, ¨-er** private dwelling
der **Eingang, -s, ¨-e** entrance
einige several, some
der **Einkauf, -s, ¨-e** purchase
ein-kaufen to purchase
ein-laden, er lädt ein, lud ein, hat eingeladen to invite
die **Einladung, -en** invitation
ein'mal once; **auf einmal'** all at once
ein-schließen, er schließt ein, schloss ein, hat eingeschlossen include, enclose
die **Eisenbahn, -en** railroad
ein-steigen, er steigt ein, stieg ein, ist eingestiegen to get on (vehicle)
ein-treten, er tritt ein, trat ein, ist eingetreten to step into, enter
die **Eintrittskarte** entrance ticket
ein-wandern to immigrate
der **Einwohner, -s,** - inhabitant
einzig single, sole
das **Eisen, -s** iron; **eisern** *adj.* iron
die **Eltern** parents
empfeh'len, er empfiehlt, empfahl, hat empfohlen to recommend
das **Ende, -s, -n** end; **zu Ende** at an end; **endlich** finally, at last
das **Englisch** English; *adj.* **englisch; auf Englisch** in English
die **Entfer'nung, -en** distance
entfernt' distant
entschul'digen to excuse, pardon
entste'hen, er entsteht, entstand, ist entstanden to arise, originate
entweder . . . oder either . . . or
das **Ereig'nis, -nisses, nisse** event
erfah'ren, er erfährt, erfuhr, hat erfahren to find out
der **Erfolg', -s, -e** success
ergreifen, er ergreift, ergriff, hat ergriffen to seize, take
erhal'ten, er erhält, erhielt, hat erhalten to receive
erin'nern an *w. acc.* to remind (of); **sich erinnern an** *w. acc.* to remember
sich **erkäl'ten** to catch cold
erken'nen, er erkennt, erkannte, hat erkannt to recognize, know, discern
erklä'ren to state, declare
erlau'ben to permit, allow
erle'digen to settle, finish
erler'nen to learn, acquire (knowledge)
ernst earnest
errei'chen to reach
erschei'nen, er erscheint, erschien, ist erschienen to appear
erschre'cken to frighten

erst first; only, not until
erwar'ten to await, expect
erwídern to answer
erzäh'len to relate
die Erzäh'lung, -en story, tale
essen, er isst, aß, hat gegessen to eat
das Essen, -s, - meal
das Esszimmer, -s, - dining room
euer, euere, euer your
etwa approximately, about
etwas something
das Europa Europe; europä'isch European

F
die Fabrik', -en factory
fahren, er fährt, fuhr, ist gefahren to ride
der Fahrer, -s, - driver
die Fahrkarte, -n ticket (for vehicle)
der Fahrplan, -s ¨-e timetable
der Fahrstuhl, -s, ¨-e elevator
fallen, er fällt, fiel, ist gefallen to fall
die Famílie, -n family
die Farbe, -n color
fast almost, nearly
der Februar February
die Feder, -n feather
fehlen w. dat. to be lacking; was fehlt dir? what is the matter
    with you?
der Fehler, -s, - mistake
das Feld, -(e)s, -er field
der Felsen, -s, - rock, cliff
das Fenster, -s, - window
die Ferien (pl. only) vacation
das Fernsehen, -s television
fertig finished, done
fest-setzen to fix, to arrange
das Feuer, -s - fire
das Fieber, -s fever
der Film, -(e)s, -e film, motion picture
finden, er findet, fand, hat gefunden to find
die Firma, -en firm, business
der Fisch, -es, -e fish
die Flasche, -en bottle, flask
das Fleisch, -es meat
fleißig diligent, industrious
fliegen, er fliegt, flog, ist geflogen to fly
fließend fluent(ly)
der Flughafen, -s, ¨- airport
das Flugzeug, -s, -e airplane
dar Fluss, Flusses, Flüsse river
folgen w. dat. to follow
der Fortschritt, -s, -e progress
die Frage, -n question; Fragen stellen to ask (put) questions
fragen to ask
das Franzö'sisch French; auf Französisch in French
das Frankreich France
die Frau, -en woman, wife, Mrs.
das Fräulein, -s, - young lady. Miss
frei free, unoccupied
der Freitag Friday

die Freude, -en joy, pleasure; Es macht mir Freude It gives me
    pleasure
freuen to please; sich freuen über w. acc. to be happy about; sich
    freuen auf w. acc. to look forward to
der Freund, -es, -e friend
frisch fresh
froh happy, glad
fröhlich cheerful, happy, gay
früh early
der Früh'ling, -s spring
das Früh'stück, -s, -e breakfast
früh'stücken to have breakfast
fühlen to feel (something)
sich fühlen to feel (well, sick, etc.): Ich fühle mich wohl. I feel
    well.
führen to lead, to guide
der Füller, -n fountain pen
für prep. w. acc. for
der Fuß, -es, ¨-e foot

G
die Gabel, -n fork
ganz whole, quite, entire
gar nicht not at all
gar nichts nothing at all
der Garten, -s, ¨-n garden
der Gast, -es, ¨-e guest
das Gebäude, -s, - building
geben, er gibt, gab, hat gegeben to give
das Gebir'ge, -s, - mountain range
gebóren born; ich bin geboren I was born; er wurde geboren he
    was born (now dead)
der Gebrauch, -s, ¨-e use, custom
gebrauchen to use, make use of
die Geburt', -en birth
der Geburts'tag, -s, -e birthday
gedul'dig patient
gefal'len w. dat. er gefällt, gefiel, hat gefallen to please; es hat
    mir gefallen it pleased me, I liked it
gegen prep. w. acc. toward, against
die Gegend, -en neighborhood, region
das Gegenteil, -s, -e opposite
das Geheim'nis, -nisses, -nisse secret
gehen, er geht, ging, ist gegangen to go
gehören w. dat. to belong to
gelb yellow
das Geld, -es, -er money
die Geldtasche, -n wallet
geling'en, es gelingt, gelang, ist gelungen to be successful; es
    gelang mir I succeeded
die Gelégenheit, -en opportunity
das Gemü'se, -s - vegetable, vegetables
gemüt'lich sociable, cozy, comfortable
die Gemüt'lichkeit comfort, sociability
genießen, er genießt, genoss, hat genossen to enjoy
genug' enough
die Geographié geography
das Gepäck', -s baggage
geráde just now; straight
das Gericht', -s, -e food, dish

gern gladly; **er spielt gern** he likes to play

das **Geschäft'**, **-s**, **-e** business

der **Geschäfts'mann**, **-s**, businessman; **Geschäftsleute** business-people

die **Geschäfts'sache**, **-n**, business matter

geschéhen, es geschieht, geschah, ist geschehen to happen

das **Geschenk'**, **-s**, **-e** gift

die **Geschich'te**, **-n** history, story

geschmack'voll tasty

das **Gespräch'**, **-s**, **-e** conversation

gestéhen, er gesteht, gestand, hat gestanden to confess

gestern yesterday

die **Gesund'heit** health

das **Gewicht'**, **-s** weight

gewin'nen, er gewinnt, gewann, hat gewonnen to win

gewiss' certain, certainly

gewöhn'lich usual, usually

gießen, er gießt, goss, hat gegossen to spill, pour

der **Gipfel**, **-s**, **-** peak

das **Glas**; **-es**, **¨-er** glass

glauben to believe, think

glücklich happy, fortunate

glücklicherweise luckily

der **Gott**, **-es**, **¨-er** god

das **Gras**, **-es**, **¨-er** grass

gratuliéren *w. dat.* to congratulate

grau gray

groß (größer, am größten) big, great

großartig splendid

grün green

gründlich thoroughly

der **Gruß**, **-es**, **¨-e** greeting

grüßen to greet

gut (besser, am besten) good

das **Gymnásium**, **-s**, **-ien** German secondary school

H

das **Haar**, **-es**, **-e** hair

haben, er hat, hatte, hat gehabt to have

der **Hafen**, **-s**, **-** harbor

halb half; **halb fünf (Uhr)** half past four

der **Hals**, **-es**, **¨-e** neck; **Halsschmerzen** sore throat

das **Halstuch**, **-s**, **¨-er** scarf, neckerchief

halten, er hält, hielt, hat gehalten to hold

halt-machen to stop

die **Hand**, **¨-e** hand; **sie geben sich die Hand** they shake hands

handeln to deal

der **Handschuh**, **-s**, **-e** glove

die **Handtasche**, **-n** handbag

hängen to hang

das **Haupt**, **-es**, **¨-er** head, chief

die **Hauptstadt**, **¨-e** capital

das **Haus**, **-es**, **¨-er** house; **zu Hause** at home, **nach Hause** (to-ward) home

die **Hausaufgabe**, **-n** homework

die **Hausfrau**, **-en** housewife

das **Heft**, **-es**, **-e** notebook

die **Heimat** native place or country

heim-kommen to come home

das **Heimweh** homesickness; **er hat Heimweh** he is homesick

heißen, er heißt, hieß, hat geheißen to be called: **wie heißen Sie?** what is your name?

helfen *w. dat.*, er hilft, half, hat geholfen to help

hell bright

der **Held**, **-en**, **-en** hero

das **Hemd**, **-(e)s**, **-en** shirt

her *shows direction* (hither)

der **Herbst** autumn

herein'-kommen to come in

der **Herr**, **-n**, **-en** gentleman, Mr., Lord

her-reisen to travel here (hither)

herrlich splendid

herun'ter-nehmen, er nimmt herunter, nahm herunter, hat heruntergenommen to take down

herzlich sincere, sincerely, hearty, cordial

heute today; **heute früh** this morning

hier here

die **Hilfe** help

der **Himmel**, **-s** heaven, sky

hin *shows direction away*; **hin und her** back and forth

hinauf-tragen, er trägt hinauf, trug hinauf, hat hinaufgetragen to carry up

hinaus-schauen to look out

sich hingeben, er gibt sich hin, gab sich hin, hat sich hingegeben to devote oneself

hinten in back

hinter *prep. w. dat. or acc.* behind, in back of

hinzú-fügen to add, say further

die **Hitze** heat

hoch (hoh- *before -e*) höher, am höchsten high

hoffen to hope

hoffentlich I hope, it is to be hoped

die **Hoffnung**, **-en** hope

hören to hear

das **Hotel**, **-s**, **-s** hotel

hübsch, pretty

der **Hunger**, **-s** hunger; **ich habe Hunger** I am hungry

der **Hut**, **-es** **¨-e** hat

I

ich I

ihr *pers. pron. fam. plu.* you; **ihr** *poss. adj.* her. their: **Ihr** *poss. adj. pol. form* your

illustriéren to illustrate

der **Imbiss**, **-isses**, **-isse** lunch, snack

immer always; **immer wieder** again and again

importiéren to import

der **Importeur'**, **-s**, **-e** importer

in *prep. w. dat. or acc.* in, into

indem' *subj. conj.* while

indes'sen *adv.* meanwhile

intelligent' intelligent

interessant' interesting

das **Interes'se**, **-s**, **-en** interest

interessiéren to interest; **sich interessiéren für** to be interested in

irgendein, irgendwelcher any (whatsoever)

das **Itálien** Italy

das **Italiénisch** Italian (language)

italiénisch *adj.* Italian

J

ja yes
die **Jacke, -n** jacket
das **Jahr, -es, -e** year
die **Jahreszeit, -en** season
jährlich yearly, annual
der **Januar, -s** January
ja yes, indeed
jeder, -e, -es that, each, every
jedermann everybody
jedesmal every time
jemand somebody
jetzt now
der **Juli** July
jung young
der **Junge, -n, -n** boy, youth
der **Juni** June

K

der **Kaffeé, -s, -s** coffee
der **Kaiser, -s, -** emperor
der **Kalen'der, -s, -** calendar
kalt cold
die **Kälte** cold
das **Kapítel, -s, -** chapter
die **Karte, -n** ticket
der **Kartenschalter, -s, -** ticket office
kaufen to buy
der **Käufer, -s, -** the buyer
der **Kaufmann, -s,** *pl.* **Kaufleute** merchant
kaum scarcely
kein, keine, kein no, not a
keiner nobody
der **Kellner, -s, -** waiter
kennen, er kennt, kannte, hat gekannt to know, be acquainted
   with; **kennen lernen** to get to know, make the acquaintance of
die **Kenntnis, -nisse** knowledge, information
die **Kerámik** ceramics
der **Kessel, -s, -** kettle
das **Kilo, -s, -s** kilogram
der **Kilométer, -s, -** kilometer
das **Kind, -es, -er** child
das **Kino** cinema, movies; **ins Kino gehen** to go to the movies
die **Kirche, -n** church
klar clear
die **Klasse, -n** class
das **Klavier', -s, -e** piano
das **Kleid, -(e)s, -er** dress; *pl.* clothes
klein small
das **Klima, -s, -s** climate
klingeln to ring
klug clever, wise
der **Knabe, -n, -n** boy
kochen to cook
kommen, er kommt, kam, ist gekommen to come
die **Kommode, -n** dresser
komponiéren to compose
der **König, -s, -e** king
können, er kann, konnte, hat gekonnt to be able, can; **er kann
   Deutsch** he knows German

das **Konzert', -s, -e** concert; **ins Konzert gehen** to go to the concert
der **Kopf, -es, ¨-e** head
der **Korb, -es, ¨-e** basket
kostbar dear, expensive
köstlich delicious
kräftig strong, powerful
der **Kraftwagen, -s, -** automobile
krank sick, ill
die **Krankheit, -en** sickness
die **Krawat'te, -en** necktie
der **Krieg, -(e)s, -e** war
die **Küche, -n** kitchen, cuisine
der **Kuchen, -s, -** cake
kühl cool
die **Kultur', -en** culture
der **Kunde, -n, -n** customer
die **Kunst, ¨-e** art
der **Kurs, des Kurses, die Kurse** course
kurz short
küssen to kiss
die **Kuss, Kusses, Küsse** kiss

L

lachen to laugh
der **Laden, -s, ¨-** shop, store
die **Lage, -n** situation, location
die **Lampe, -n** lamp
das **Land, -es, ¨-er** land, country; **auf dem Lande** in the country;
   aufs Land to the country
die **Lankarte, -n** map
die **Landschaft, -en** landscape
lang long
langsam slowly
sich **langweilen** to be bored
der **Lärm, -(e)s** noise
lassen, er lässt, ließ, hat gelassen to let, allow, have something
   done
der **Lastwagen, -s, -** truck
laut loud
das **Leben, -s, -** life
leben to live, be alive
lebhaft lively
legen to put, place, lay
die **Legende, -n** legend
der **Lehnstuhl, -(e)s, ¨-e** easy chair
lehren to teach
der **Lehrer, -s, -** teacher
leicht easy, light
das **Leid** sorrow; **es tut mir leid** I am sorry
leider unfortunately
leihen, er leiht, lieh, hat geliehen to lend
leisten to perform, achieve; **Dienste leisten** to render services
die **Lektion', -en** lesson
lernen to learn
lesen, er liest, las, hat gelesen to read
das **Lesebuch, -(e)s, ¨-er** reader, reading book
letzt last
die **Leute** people
lieb (lieber, am liebsten) dear, agreeable; **ich gehe lieber** I prefer to go; **ich spiele am liebsten** I like best of all to play

liebenswürdig likable, charming
das Lied, -es, -er song
liegen, er liegt, lag, hat gelegen to lie, be situated
die Liste, -n list
loben to praise
der Löffel, -s, - spoon
die Luft, ¨-e air
das Lustspiel, -s, -e comedy
der Lyriker, -s, - lyric poet

M
machen to make, do
das Mädchen, -s, - girl
die Mahlzeit, -en meal
das Mal, -es, -e time; einmal, zweimal, usw. once, twice, three times, etc.; manchmal sometimes; das erste Mal the first time
der Mai, -s May
malerisch picturesque
man indef. pron. one, people, they
mancher, -e, -es many a; pl. many, some
der Mann, es, ¨-er man, husband
der Mantel, -s, ¨- coat
die Mark mark (old unit of German currency, before the Euro)
der Markt, -es, ¨-e market
der März March
die Masse, -n mass
die Mathematik' mathematics
die Medizin' medicine
mehr more
mehrere several
die Meile, -n mile
mein, meine, mein my
meinen to mean, to believe
die Meinung, -en opinion, meaning; meiner Meinung nach in my opinion
meist most; meistens for the most part
der Meister, -s, - master
der Mensch, -en, -en human being, man
das Messer, -s, - knife
mieten to rent
das Miethaus apartment house
die Milch milk
mild mild
mildern to moderate, soften
die Minute, -n minute
mit prep, w dat. with
der Mittag, -s, -e noon
das Mittagessen, -s, - noon meal
die Mitte middle
mit-teilen to inform, impart
der Mittwoch Wednesday
möbliert' furnished
modern' modern
mögen, er mag, mochte, hat gemocht to like, care to, may
möglich possible
die Möglichkeit, -en possibility
möglichst bald as soon as possible
der Monat, -s, -e month
der Montag, -s Monday

der Morgen, -s, - morning; guten Morgen good morning; morgen tomorrow; morgen früh tomorrow morning
müde tired
multipliziéren to multiply
munter cheerful
das Museum, -s, Muséen museum
die Musik' music
müssen, er muss, musste, hat gemusst to have to, must
die Mutter, ¨- mother

N
nach prep. w. dat. after, to, according to
die Nachbarschaft, -en neighborhood
nachdem sub. conj. after
nach-prüfen to check
die Nachricht, -en report, news
nach-schauen to look after
die Nacht, -e night
nah (näher, nächst) near
die Nähe vicinity
nahrhaft nutritious
die Nahrungsmittel pl. foods, groceries
der Name, -ns, -n name
nämlich namely, that is
nass wet
die Natur nature
natür'lich naturally, of course
neben prep. w. dat. or acc. beside, next to
nehmen, er nimmt, nahm, hat genommen to take
nein no (opposite of ja)
nennen, er nennt, nannte, hat genannt to name, call
nett nice
neu new
neugierig curious
die Neuigkeit, -en piece of news; pl. news
neulich recently
nicht not; nicht wahr? isn't that so?
nichts nothing
nie never; niemals never
nieder down
niedrig low
niemand nobody
nimmer never
noch still, yet; noch ein one more; noch nicht not yet
der Norden, -s north
das Notenheft, -s, -e music book
die Nummer, -n number
nun well, now; nun also well then
nur only; nicht nur . . . sondern auch not only . . . but also

O
ob whether, if
obwohl' sub. conj. although
das Obst, -es fruit
oder or; entweder . . . oder either . . . or
offen open
öffnen to open
oft often
ohne prep. w. acc. without
der Onkel, -s, - uncle

die **Oper, -n** opera
die **Operet'te, -n** musical comedy
die **Oran'ge, -n** orange; der **Orangensaft** orange juice
der **Osten** east

P

das **Paar, -(e)s, -e** pair; **ein Paar (Schuhe)** a pair (of shoes); **ein Paar** a couple
packen to pack
paar a few
das **Papier', -s, -e** paper
der **Park, -es, -e** park
das **Parkett', -s, -e** orchestra (part of theater)
der **Passagier', -s, -e** passenger
die **Person', -en** person
persön'lich personally
das **Pfund, -es, -e** pound
die **Photographié, -n** photograph
plagen to pester, annoy
das **Plakat', -(e)s, -e** placard, poster
die **Platte, -n** record, disc
der **Platz, -es, ¨-e** place, seat
plaudern to chat
plötzlich sudden(ly)
die **Polizeíwache, -n** police station
das **Porträt', -s, -e** portrait
die **Post** mail
das **Postamt, -s, ¨-er** post office
der **Preis, -es, -e** price, prize
das **Problem', -s, -e** problem
der **Profes'sor, -s, Professóren** professor
das **Programm', -s, -e** program
das **Prozent', -s, -e** percent
der **Prozent'satz** percentage
prüfen to test, examine
die **Prüfung, -en** the test, examination; **eine Prüfung bestehen** to pass an examination
der **Punkt, -es, -e** period; **Punkt neun Uhr** nine o'clock sharp
pünktlich punctual(ly), on time

Q

die **Qualität', -en** quality
die **Quantität', -en** quantity

R

das **Radio, -s** radio; **im Radio** on the radio
rasch quickly
rasen to rage, rush madly, speed
raten w. dat., **er rät, riet, hat geraten** to guess; **ich rate Ihnen** I advise you
der **Rauch, -es** smoke
rauchen to smoke
sich **rasiéren** to shave oneself
rechnen to figure, reckon
die **Rechnung, -en** bill, sum
das **Recht, -es, -e** right; **mit Recht** correctly, rightly; **sie haben Recht** you are right
reden to talk
die **Regel, -n** rule
der **Regen, -s** rain

der **Regenmantel, -s, ¨-** raincoat
der **Regenschirm, -s, -e** umbrella
regnen to rain
reich rich
reichen to hand, to pass
die **Reihe, -en** row
die **Reise, -n** trip
reisen to travel
der **Reiseführer, -s, -** guide book
reisefertig finished, ready to travel
der **Reisende, -n, -n** traveller
der **Reisepass, -es, -pässe** passport
das **Restaurant, -s, -s** restaurant
reserviéren to reserve
richtig correct, right
die **Rolle, -n** role
rot red
die **Rückreise, -n** trip back
die **Rückfahrkarte, -n** return ticket
die **Rückfahrt** trip back
rufen, er ruft, rief, hat gerufen to call
ruhen to rest
die **Ruhepause, -n** rest period
ruhig quiet
rund round

S

der **Saal, -es, Säle** hall, large room
die **Sache, -n** thing
sagen to say, tell
der **Salat', -s, -e** salad
die **Sammlung, -en** collection
der **Samstag** Saturday
sanft softly, gently
der **Sänger, -s, -** singer
der **Satz, -es, ¨-e** sentence
die **Schachtel, -n** box
scharf sharp
schätzen to estimate
das **Schauspiel, -s, -e** play
der **Schauspieler, -s, -** actor
der **Scheck, -s, -e** check
scheinen, er scheint, schien, hat geschienen to seem, to shine
schenken to present
scherzen to joke
schicken to send
schlafen, er schläft, schlief, hat geschlafen to sleep
das **Schlafzimmer, -s, -** bedroom
schlagen, er schlägt, schlug, hat geschlagen to hit, defeat
schlecht bad(ly)
schließen, er schließt, schloss, hat geschlossen to close
schließlich finally
schlimm bad
das **Schloss, Schlosses, Schlösser** castle
schmecken to taste
der **Schnee, -s** snow
schneiden, er schneidet, schnitt, hat geschnitten to cut
schnell quick(ly), fast
schneien to snow
der **Schnellzug, -(e)s, ¨-e** express

schon already
schön beautiful, fine
der **Schrank, -es, ¨-e** closet; der **Kleiderschrank** wardrobe
schrecklich terrible
schreiben, er schreibt, schrieb, hat geschrieben to write
die **Schreibmaschine, -n** typewriter
der **Schreibtisch, -es, -e** desk
der **Schuh, -es, -e** shoe
schulden to owe
die **Schule, -n** school
der **Schüler, -s, -** schoolboy, pupil
schwach weak
schwärmen to be enthusiastic
schwarz black
schwer heavy, difficult
die **Schwester, -n** sister
schwierig difficult, hard
der **See, -s, -n** lake
die **See, -n** ocean, sea
sehen, er sieht, sah, hat gesehen to see
die **Sehenswürdigkeit, -en,** sight, object of interest
sehr very
seiden *adj.* silk, silken
die **Seife, -n** soap
sein, er ist, war, ist gewesen to be
sein, -e, sein his
seit prep. w. dat. since; **seit einer Woche** for a week
seitdem sub. conj. since; adv. since then
die **Seite, -n** page
die **Sekun'de, -n** second
selber self; **ich selber** I myself, etc
selbst self; **ich selbst** I myself, etc.
selbstverständlich obviously, it goes without saying
die **Semmel, -n** roll
senden, er sendet, sandte, hat gesandt to send
der **September, -s** September
das **Servier'brett, -(e)s, -er** tray
setzen to place, put
sich setzen to sit down, seat oneself
sicher sure
sicherlich surely
sie she, they; **Sie** you
singen, er singt, sang, hat gesungen to sing
die **Sitte, -n** custom
sitzen, er sitzt, saß, hat gessessen to sit
so so, thus; **so groß wie** as large as
sobald sub. conj, as soon as; adv. immediately
soeben just, just now
das **Sofa, -s, -s** sofa
sofort' at once, immediately
sogar' even
sogleich' = sofort' immediately
der **Sohn, -(e)s, ¨-e** son
solcher, -e, -es such; **solch ein** such a
sollen, er soll, sollte, hat gesollt shall, to be supposed to, ought to, should
der **Sommer, -s, -** summer
sondern but, but on the contrary; **nicht nur . . . sondern auch** not only . . . but also
der **Sonntag, -s, -e** Sunday

sonst otherwise
sorgen für to care for, to take care of
die **Sorte, -n** kind
sowie as well as
sowohl als as well as
das **Spanien, -s** Spain
spanisch Spanish
spät late
spaziéren to walk, stroll
spaziéren gehen, er geht spazieren, ging spazieren, ist spazieren gegangen to go for a walk
der **Spazier'gang, -s, ¨-e** walk
die **Speise, -n** food
die **Speisekarte, -n** menu
speisen to dine
spielen to play
der **Sport, -(e)s, -e** sport
die **Sprache, -n** language, speech
sprechen, er spricht, sprach, hat gesprochen to speak
das **Sprichwort, -(e)s, ¨-er** proverb
der **Staat, -es, -en** state
der **Staatsmann, -s ¨-er** statesman
die **Stadt, ¨-e** city
der **Stamm, -es, ¨-e** trunk; tribe
stark strong
die **Station', -en** station
statt prep. w. gen. instead of
statt-finden, er findet statt, fand statt, hat stattgefunden to take place
stehen, er steht, stand, hat gestanden to stand
stellen to place, put; **Fragen stellen** to ask questions
die **Stellung, -en** position, job
sterben, er stirbt, starb, ist gestorben to die
stets always
still still, quiet
stimmt! that's correct
der **Stock, -es, ¨-e** stick, story (of house)
der **Stoff, -es, -e** stuff, material
stolz proud
die **Straße, -en** street
die **Strecke, -n** stretch, distance
strecken to stretch
streiten, er streitet, stritt, hat gestritten to quarrel, fight
der **Strudel, -s, -** strudel
das **Stück, -(e)s, -e** piece
der **Student', -en, -en** student
studiéren to study
das **Studium, -s, Studien** study
der **Stuhl, -es, ¨-e** chair
die **Stunde, -n** hour, lesson
stürmisch stormy
suchen to look for, seek
der **Süden, -s** south
die **Summe, -n** sum
die **Suppe, -n** soup

T
der **Tag, -es, -e** day
täglich daily
tanken to buy gasoline, fill up

die **Tante**, -n aunt
tanzen to dance
das **Taschentuch**, -(e)s, ¨-er handkerchief
die **Tasse**, -n cup; **eine Tasse Kaffee** a cup of coffee
tatsäch'lich in fact
tauschen to change
das **Taxi**, -s, -s taxi
der **Tee**, -s tea
der **Teil**, -(e)s, -e part; **zum Teil** in part
teilen to divide; **geteilt durch** divided by
das **Telefon**, -s, -e telephone
telefoniéren mit to carry on a telephone conversation with a person
der **Teller**, -s, - plate
die **Temperatur'** temperature
teuer dear, expensive
das **Theáter**, -s, - theater; **ins Theater gehen** to go to the theater
das **Thema**, -s, **Themen** theme, topic
die **Tinte**, -n ink
das **Tier**, -(e)s, -e animal
der **Titel**, -s, - title
die **Tochter**, ¨- daughter
der **Tod**, -es, -e death
die **Torte**, -n tart, cake
die **Toilet'te** ladies' or men's room
der **Tourist'**, -en, -en tourist
tragen, er **trägt, trug, hat getragen** to carry
traurig sad
trennen to separate
trinken, er **trinkt, trank, hat getrunken** to drink
das **Trinkgeld**, (e)s, -er tip, gratuity
trotz prep. w. gen. in spite of
das **Tuch**, -es, ¨-er cloth
tüchtig capable
tun, er **tut, tat, hat getan** to do
die **Tür**, -en door

U
üben to practice
über prep. w. dat. or acc. over, across, about
überall' everywhere
überhaupt' at all
übermorgen day after tomorrow
überráschen to surprise
die **Überráschung**, -en surprise
überset'zen to translate
die **Überset'zung**, -en translation
der **Überzieher**, -s, - overcoat
die **Übung**, -en exercise
das **Ufer**, -s, - shore
die **Uhr**, -en watch, clock; **wie viel Uhr ist es?** what time is it? **um wie viel Uhr?** at what time?
um prep. w. acc. around; **um . . . zu** in order to
die **Umgébung**, -en surroundings
umher-reisen to travel around
sich umkleiden to change clothes
um-schauen to look around
und and; **und so weiter (usw.)** and so forth (etc.)
der **Unfall**, -s, ¨-e mishap
ungefähr' about, approximately

die **Universität'**, -en university
unter prep. w. dat. or acc. under, among
unterhal'ten, er **unterhält, unterhielt, hat unterhalten** to entertain; **sich unterhalten (über)** to converse (about)
unterneh'men, er **unternimmt, unternahm, hat unternommen** to undertake
der **Unterricht**, -s instruction **unterrich'ten** to teach, instruct
der **Unterschied**, -s, -e difference
die **Untersuch'ung**, -en inspection
die **Untertasse**, -n saucer
unterwegs' on the way

V
der **Vater**, -s, ¨- father
die **Verab'redung**, -en appointment
das **Verb**, -(e)s, -en verb
die **Verän'derung**, -en change
verbrin'gen, er **verbringt, verbrachte, hat verbracht** to spend (time)
verdiénen to earn
die **Vereínigten Staaten** United States
verges'sen, er **vergisst, vergaß, hat vergessen** to forget
das **Vergnü'gen**, -s, - pleasure
vergnü'gungsvoll pleasurable
verheíratet married
verkaúfen to sell
verlas'sen, er **verlässt, verließ, hat verlassen** to leave, desert
verliéren, er **verliert, verlor, hat verloren** to lose
der **Vers**, -es, -e verse
verschiéden different, varied
verschreíben, er **verschreibt, verschrieb, hat verschrieben** to prescribe
versich'ern to assure, to insure
verspréchen, er **verspricht, versprach, hat versprochen** to promise
die **Verspä'tung**, -en lateness, delay; **der Zug hat Verspätung** the train is late
verstéhen, er **versteht, verstand, hat verstanden** to understand; **das versteht sich** that goes without saying
versúchen to try, taste
der **Vertréter**, s, - representative, agent
der **Verwand'te**, -n, -n relative
verzeíhen, er **verzeiht, verzieh, hat verziehen** to pardon
die **Verzeíhung** pardon; **ich bitte um Verzeihung** I beg your pardon
viel (mehr, meist-) much, many
vielleicht perhaps
vielmals often, many times
voll full
vollkom'men fully, completely
von prep. w. dat. from, of
vor prep. w. dot. or acc. before, in front of; **vor einer Woche** a week ago
voraus ahead; **im voraus** in advance
vorbeífahren, er **fährt vorbei, fuhr vorbei, ist vorbeigefahren** to ride past
sich vorbereiten (auf) w. acc. to prepare for
vorgestern day before yesterday
vorig former, last; **voriges Jahr** last year
vor-legen to place before

vorne in front
der **Vorort, -es, -e** suburb
vor-stellen to introduce
die **Vorstellung, -en** performance, introduction
vorteilhaft advantageous
vor-ziehen, er zieht vor, zog vor, hat vorgezogen to prefer
vorzüg'lich excellent

W

der **Wagen, -s, ¨-** wagon, car
wählen to choose
wahr true; **nicht wahr?** isn't it true?
die **Wahrheit, -en** truth
während *prep. w. gen.* during; *sub. conj.* while
wahrschein'lich probable, probably
der **Wald, -es, ¨-er** forest
die **Wand, ¨-e** wall
die **Wanduhr, -en** wall clock
wann? when?
die **Ware, -n** goods, ware
das **Warenhaus, ¨-er** department store
warm warm
sich **wärmen** to warm oneself
warten auf *w. acc.* to wait for
der **Wartesaal, -es, -säle** waiting room
warum'? why?
was what; **was für** what kind of; **was für ein Tag!** what a day!
sich **waschen, er wäscht sich, wusch sich, hat sich gewaschen** to wash (oneself); **sie waschen sich die Hände** they are washing their hands
das **Wasser, -s** water
wechseln to change; **er wechselt Dollar in Euro** he changes dollars into euros
weder. . . noch neither . . . nor
der **Weg, -es, -e** way; **weg** away
wegen *prep. w. gen.* on account of
weg-gehen to go away
weh-tun, es tut weh, tat weh, hat wehgetan to hurt; **es tut mir weh** it hurts me
die **Weihnachten** Christmas; **zu Weihnachten** for Christmas
weil *sub. conj.* because
die **Weile** while
der **Wein, -es, -e** wine
die **Weise** manner, way; **auf diese Weise** in this way
weiß white
weit far
weiter further, farther; **lesen Sie weiter!** read on, continue reading
weiter-fahren, er fährt weiter, fuhr weiter, ist weitergefahren to ride, drive on
weiter-sprechen, er spricht weiter, sprach weiter, hat weitergesprochen to go on speaking
welcher, -e, -es *interrog. adj. & pron.* which, what; *rel. pron.* who, which, that
die **Welt, -en** world
wenig little, few; **weniger** less, minus; **ein wenig** a little
wenigstens at least
wenn *sub. conj.* if, when, whenever
wer? who? he who
werden, er wird, wurde, ist geworden to become, get; **er wird alt** he is getting old

wert worth
wertvoll useful, worthwhile
der **Westen, -s** west
das **Wetter, -s** weather
wichtig important
wie? how? **so groß wie** as large as
wieder again
wiederhólen to repeat
Wiedersehen; auf Wiedersehen! good-by, au revoir
wiegen, er wiegt, wog, hat gewogen to weigh
wie viel'? wie viele? how much? how many?
der **Wind, -es, -e** wind
winken to beckon
der **Winter, -s** winter
wir we
wirklich really
wissen, er weiß, wusste, hat gewusst to know (a fact)
die **Wissenschaft, -en** science
wo? where? (at what place?)
die **Woche, -n** week
die **Wochenschau** newsreel
woher? from where?
wohin? where? (to what place?)
wohl well, indeed (*used for emphasis:* **ich bin wohl müde** I am indeed tired)
wohnen to dwell, live
die **Wohnung, -en** dwelling, home
das **Wohnzimmer, -s, -** living room
die **Wolke, -n** cloud
der **Wolkenkratzer, -s, -** skyscraper
wolkenlos cloudless
wollen, er will, wollte, hat gewollt to want to, wish to, intend to
das **Wort, -(e)s, die Worte** (*words in phrases and sentences*), die **Wörter** (*words not connected in sense*)
das **Wörterbuch, -s, ¨-er** dictionary
wunderbar wonderful
sich **wundern** (**über** *w. acc.*) to be surprised (at)
wünschen to wish

Z

die **Zahl, -en** number
zahlen to pay
zählen to count
zeigen to show
die **Zeit, -en** time
zeitig early
die **Zeitschrift, -en** magazine
die **Zeitung, -en** newspaper
zerbrechen, er zerbricht, zerbrach, hat zerbrochen to break to pieces
ziehen, er zieht, zog, hat gezogen to pull
das **Ziel, -(e)s, -e** goal
ziemlich rather, fairly
die **Zigaret'te, -n** cigarette
das **Zimmer, -s, -** room
das **Zimmermädchen, -s -** chambermaid
zitieren to cite
die **Zivilisation'** civilization
zu *prep. w. dat.* to, toward; *adv.* too
zu-bereiten to prepare

die **Zuckerdose** sugar bowl
zuerst first, at first
zufriéden satisfied
der **Zug, -(e)s, ¨-e** train
zugleich at the same time
zu-hören to listen to
sich **zurecht'-finden, er findet sich zurecht, fand sich zurecht, hat sich zurechtgefunden** to find one's way
sich **zurück-ziehen, er zieht sich zurück, zog sich zurück, hat sich zurückgezogen** to withdraw

zurück-geben, er gibt zurück, gab zurück, hat zurückgegeben to give back, to return
zurück-legen to put back, to cover a distance
die **Zuversicht** confidence, faith
zuvor'kommend obliging
zusam'men together
zwar it is true
der **Zweifel, -s, -** doubt
zweifel'los doubtless
zwischen *prep. w. dat. or acc.* between

Accent marks are used in the end vocabularies to indicate the stressed syllable of words when the stressed syllable is not the first. The accent mark is simply a pronunciation aid and not part of the spelling.

The cardinal and ordinal numerals are not included in the end vocabularies. The cardinals 1–100 are given in Chapter 13, Grammar Note 1; above 100 in Chapter 14, Grammar Note 1. The ordinals are given in Chapter 24, Grammar Note 1.

A

able (to be) können, er kann, konnte, hat gekonnt
actor der Schauspieler, -s, -
advantageous vorteilhaft
affair die Angelegenheit, -en
after nach *prep. w. dat.;* nachdem *sub. conj.*
again wieder, **again and again** immer wieder
against gegen *prep. w. dat.*
air die Luft, -, -e
airport der Flughafen, -s, ¨-
all aller, -e, -es; **all kinds of** allerlei; **not at all** gar nicht
almost fast, beináhe
already schon
also auch; **not only . . . but also** nicht nur . . . sondern auch
although obgleich' *sub. conj.*
always immer, stets
and und; **and so forth, etc.** und so weiter, usw.
another (one more) noch ein
answer die Antwort, -, -en
answer (to) *(a person)* antworten *w. dat.;* **(a question)** antworten auf *w. acc.* **or** beant'worten *w. acc.*
apartment house das Miethaus, -es, ¨-er
appetite der Appetít; **I have an appetite** ich habe Appetít
arm der Arm, -es, -e
around um *prep. w. acc.*
arrive (to) ankommen
art die Kunst, ¨-e
as . . . as so . . . wie; **as soon as** sobald *sub. conj.*
ashtray der Aschenbecher, -s, -
ask (to) fragen: **to ask for** bitten um; **to ask questions** Fragen stellen
assignment die Aufgabe, -en
at an *prep. w. acc.*
attentive aufmerksam
automobile das Automobíl, -s, -e; das Auto, -s, -s; der Kraftwagen, -s, -
aunt die Tante, -n
autumn der Herbst, -es, -e
await (to) erwárten

B

bad schlecht
balcony der Balkon, -es, -e
basket der Korb, -es, ¨-e
bathroom das Badezimmer, -s, -
be (to) sein, er ist, war, ist gewesen; **to be located** sich befinden
beautiful schön
because weil *sub. conj.;* denn *coord. conj.*
become (to) werden, er wird, wurde, ist geworden
bed das Bett, -es, -en
bedroom das Schlafzimmer, -s, -
beer das Bier, -es, -e
before vor *prep. w. dat. or acc.;* ehe (bevor) *sub. conj.*
begin (to) beginnen, er beginnt, begann, hat begonnen; anfangen, er fängt an, fing an, hat angefangen
beginning der Anfang, -s, ¨-e
behind hinter *prep. w. dat. or acc.*
believe (to) glauben *(w. dat. of persons)*
belong to (to) gehören *w. dat.*
beside neben *prep. w. dat. or acc.;* bei *prep. w. dat.*
besides außerdem
better besser
between zwischen *prep. w. dat. or acc.*
big groß
bill die Rechnung, -en
birthday der Géburtstag, -es, -e
black schwarz
blue blau
book das Buch, -es, ¨-er
bored (to be) sich langweilen
both beide
bottle die Flasche, -n
boy der Junge, -n, -n
bread das Brot, -es, -e
breakfast das Frühstück, -(e)s, -e
breakfast (to) frühstücken
bright hell
bring (to) bringen, er bringt, brachte, hat gebracht
broad breit

brother der Bruder, -s ¨-
brown braun
building das Gebäúde, -s, -
business das Geschäft', -es, -e
busy beschäf'tigt
but aber; **but (on the contrary)** sondern; **not only
. . . but also** nicht nur . . . sondern auch
buy (to) kaufen
buyer der Käufer, -s, -

C

cake der Kuchen, -s, -
calendar der Kalen'der, -s, -
call (to) rufen, er ruft, rief, hat gerufen; **to call for** abholen; **to
call up** anrufen
called (to be) heißen, er heißt, hieß, hat geheißen
capable tüchtig
capital die Haupstadt, ¨-e
car der Wagen, -s, -; das Auto, -s, -s;
carry (to) tragen, er trägt, trug, hat getragen; **to carry up** hinauf-
tragen
certain(ly) gewiss', sicher
chair der Stuhl, -es, ¨-
change (to) wechseln
chat (to) plaudern
cheerful munter, fröhlich
child das Kind, -es, -er
cigarette die Zigaret'te, -n
citizen der Bürger, -s,-
city die Stadt, ¨-e
class die Klasse, -n
clear klar
clever klug
climate das Klima, -s, -s
clock die Uhr, -en; **what time is it?** wie viel Uhr ist es?
close (to) schließen, er schließt, schloss, hat geschlossen
clothes die Kleider *pl.*
coat der Mantel, -s, ¨-
coffee der Kaffeé, -s
cold kalt; **to catch cold** sich erkälten
color die Farbe, -n
come (to) kommen, er kommt, kam, ist gekommen; **to come in**
herein'-kommen
comfortable angenehm, bequem
concert das Konzert', -s, -e; **to go to a concert** ins Konzert gehen
congratulate (to) gratulíeren *w. dat.*
conversation das Gespräch', -s, -e
cook (to) kochen
cool kühl
correct richtig
cost (to) kosten
count (to) zählen
country das Land, -es, ¨-er; **to the country** aufs Land; **in the
country** auf dem Lande
cup die Tasse, -n
curious neugierig
customer der Kunde, -n, -n
cut (to) schneiden, er schneidet, schnitt, hat geschnitten

D

daily täglich
dance (to) tanzen
dark dunkel
date das Datum, -s, Daten
daughter die Tochter, ¨-
day der Tag, -es, -e; **day after tomorrow** übermorgen; **day before
yesterday** vorgestern
dear teuer **(expensive)**, lieb
depart (to) ab-reisen, ab-fahren
departure die Abreise, -n
describe (to) beschreíben, er beschreibt, beschrieb, hat
beschrieben
desk der Schreibtisch, -es, -e; das Pult, -es, -e
dictionary das Wörterbuch, es, ¨-er
different anders, verschiéden
difficult schwer
diligent fleißig
dine (to) speisen
dining room das Esszimmer, -s, -
dinner (*midday*) das Mittagessen, -s, -
dish der Teller, -s, -; die Platte, -n
divide (to) dividíeren, teilen
do (to) tun, machen
doctor der Doktor, -s, Doktóren; der Arzt **(physician)**, -es, ¨-e
door die Tür, -en
doubt der Zweifel, -s, -; **doubtless** zweifellos, ohne Zweifel
dozen das Dutzend, -s, -e
drama das Drama, -s, Dramen
dress das Kleid, -er, ¨-er
dress oneself sich an-ziehen
drink (to) trinken, er trinkt, trank, hat getrunken
driver der Fahrer, -s, -
during während *prep. w. gen.*
dwell (to) wohnen

E

each jeder, -e, -es
early früh
earn verdiénen
earnest ernst
easy leicht
eat (to) essen, er isst, aß, hat gegessen
egg das Ei, -es, -er
either . . . or entweder . . . oder
end das Ende, -s, -en; **at an end** zu Ende
English das Englisch *noun*; englisch *adj.*; **in English** auf Englisch
enjoy (to) genießen, er genießt, genoss, hat genossen; **to enjoy
oneself** sich amüsíeren
enough genug
enter (to) ein-treten
entrance der Eingang, -s, ¨-e
even sogar
evening der Abend, -s, -e; **in the evening** am Abend; **evenings**
abends
event das Ereig'nis, -ses, -se
everybody jedermann
everywhere überall

examination die Prüfung, -en
excellent vorzüg'lich, ausgezeich'net
except außer *prep. w. dat.*
excited aufgeregt
excursion der Ausflug, -s, ˝-e
exercise die Übung, -en
exit der Ausgang, es, ˝-e
expensive teuer, kostbar
explain (to) erklären
express (train) der Schnellzug, -s, ˝-e
extraordinary außeror'dentlich
eye das Auge, -s, -n

F
factory die Fabrik, -en
fall (to) fallen, er fällt, fiel, ist gefallen
family die Famílie, -n
famous berühmt'
far weit, fern
fast schnell, rasch
father der Vater, -s, ˝-
feel (to) fühlen; **to feel well, sick, etc.** sich fühlen; **I feel well** ich fühle mich wohl
fever das Fieber, -s, -
finally schließlich, endlich
foot der Fuß, -es, ˝-e
French das Franzö'sisch; französisch *adj.;* **in French** auf Französisch
friend der Freund, -es, -e
from von *prep. w. dat.*
fruit das Obst, -es; die Frucht, ˝-e
full voll
further weiter; **read further** lesen Sie weiter!

G
garden der Garten, -s, ˝-
German das Deutsch; deutsch *adj.;* **in German** auf Deutsch
get (to) bekom'men, erhal'ten; **to get along** sich zurecht'-kommen; **to get on** *(mount)* besteígen, ein-steigen; **to get out** *(of vehicle)* aus-steigen; **to get up** auf-stehen
gift das Geschenk', -s, -e
girl das Mädchen, -s, -
give (to) er gibt, gab, hat gegeben; **to give back** zurück-geben
glad froh
gladly gern; **he likes to play** er spielt gern
glass das Glas, -es, ˝-er
glove der Handschuh, -s, -e
go (to) gehen, er geht, ging, ist gegangen
goal das Ziel, -es, -e
good gut
goods die Ware, -n
gray grau
green grün
greet (to) grüßen
greeting der Gruß, -es, ˝-e
guest der Gast, -es, ˝-e

H
hand die Hand, ˝-e
hand (to) reichen
handbag die Handtasche, -n
handkerchief das Taschentuch, -s, ˝-er
hang (to) *(something)* hängen
happen (to) geschéhen, es geschieht, geschah, ist geschehen
happy glücklich
hat der Hut, -es, ˝-e
have (to) haben; **to have to** müssen, er muss, musste, hat gemusst
head der Kopf, -es, ˝-e
hear (to) hören
heavy schwer
help die Hilfe
help (to) helfen *w. dat.,* er hilft, half, hat geholfen
here hier
high hoch; **higher** höher; **highest** der, die, das höchste
hold (to) halten, er hält, hielt, hat gehalten
home die Wohnung, -en, das Heim, **home country** die Heimat; **I am going home** ich gehe nach Hause; **I am at home** ich bin zu Hause; **homesickness** das Heimweh; **he was homesick** er hatte Heimweh
homework die Hausaufgabe, -n
hope (to) hoffen
hot heiß
hotel das Hotel, -s, -s
hour die Stunde, -n
house das Haus, -es, ˝-er
how? wie? **how many?** wie viel'(e); **how much?** wie viel?
human being der Mensch, -en, -en
hunger der Hunger; **I am hungry** ich habe Hunger
hurry eilen
hurt (to) weh-tun *w. dat.;* **it hurts me** es tut mir weh

I
if wenn *sub. conj.*
immediately sofort', sobald', sogleich'
import (to) importiéren
important wichtig
in, into in *prep. w. dat. or acc.*
industrious fleißig
information die Auskunft, ˝-e
inhabitant der Einwohner, -s, -
ink die Tinte, -n
intelligent intelligent'
interested; to be interested in sich interessiéren für
interesting interessant'
introduce vor-stellen
introduction die Vorstellung, -en
invitation die Einladung, -en
invite (to) ein-laden, er lädt ein, lud ein, hat ein-geladen

J
job die Stellung, -en
joke (to) scherzen
joy die Freude; **it gives me pleasure** es macht mir Freude
just: just now soében

K

kilogram das Kilogramm', -s, -e; das Kilo, -s, -s
kilometer der Kilométer, -s, -
kind die Sorte, -n
kiss (to) küssen
kitchen die Küche, -n
knife das Messer, -s, -
know (to): to know facts wissen; **to know, be acquainted with** kennen; **to get to know** kennen lernen
known bekannt'

L

lady die Dame, -n
lake der See, -s, -n
lamp die Lampe, -n
land das Land, -es, ¨-er
language die Sprache, -, -n
last letzt
last (to) dauern
late spät
laugh (to) lachen
lead (to) führen
leave (to) on a trip ab-reisen, ab-fahren; **to leave a person or place** verlassen
lend (to) leihen, er leiht, lieh, hat geliehen
less weniger
lesson die Stunde, -, die Lektion', -en; **assignment** die Aufgabe, -n
let (to) lassen, er lässt, ließ, hat gelassen
letter der Brief, -es, -e
library die Bibliothek', -en
lie (to) liegen, er liegt, lag, hat gelegen
life das Leben, -s, -
like (to) mögen, er mag, mochte, hat gemocht; *verb* + gern **I like to read** ich lese gern
listen (to) zu-hören
little klein; **a little** ein wenig, ein bisschen
live (to) leben; **(dwell)** wohnen
living room das Wohnzimmer, -s, -
long lang
look sehen, er sieht, sah, hat gesehen; schauen; **to look at** an-schauen; **to look for** suchen
lose (to) verliéren, er verliert, verlor, hat verloren
loud laut
love (to) lieben
luckily glücklicherweise

M

magazine die Zeitschrift, -en
maid (servant) das Dienstmädchen, -s, -
mail die Post
make (to) machen
man der Mann, -es, ¨-er
manager (head) der Chef, -s, -s
many viel, viele
map die Landkarte, -n
mark *(old unit of German currency)* die Mark
market der Markt, -es, ¨-e
married verheíratet
may *(to be permitted to)* dürfen, er darf, durfte, hat gedurft

meal die Mahlzeit, -en
mean (to) bedeúten, meinen
meat das Fleisch, -es
medicine die Medizin'
meet (to) begeg'nen *w. dat.;* **to get acquainted with** kennen lernen
menu die Speisekarte, -n
merchant der Kaufmann, -s, die Kaufleute
milk die Milch
minute die Minúte, -en
Miss das Fräulein, -s, -
mistake der Fehler, -s, -
money das Geld, -es, -er
month der Monat, -s, -e
more mehr
morning der Morgen, -s, -; **good morning!** guten Morgen; **tomorrow morning** morgen früh; **this morning** heute Morgen
most der, die, das meiste; **for the most part** meistens
mother die Mutter, ¨-
mount (to) *(a vehicle)* einsteigen
movies das Kino; **I am going to the movies** ich gehe ins Kino
Mr. der Herr, -n, -en
museum das Muséum, -s, die Muséen
music die Musik'
must müssen, er muss, musste, hat gemusst

N

name (to) nennen, er nennt, nannte, hat genannt
named (to be) heißen, hieß, hat geheißen
naturally natür'lich
near nah(e); **nearer** näher
nearly fast, beináhe
need (to) brauchen
neither . . . nor weder . . . noch
never nie, niemals, nimmer
nevertheless doch
new neu
news die Nachricht, -en
newspaper die Zeitung, -en
next der, die, das nächste
nice nett
night die Nacht, ¨-e
no nein; **no, not a, not any** kein, keine, kein
nobody keiner, niemand
not nicht; **not at all** gar nicht
notebook das Heft, -es, -e
nothing nichts
now jetzt, nun
number die Zahl, -en; die Nummer, -n

O

occupation der Beruf', -s, -e
occupied besetzt'
occupy (to) bewoh'nen
of von *prep. w. dat.*
offer (to) bieten, er bietet, bot, hat geboten; an-bieten
office das Büró, -s, -s
often oft, vielmals
old alt; **older** älter

on (on top of) auf *prep. w. dat. or acc.;* **on (at, up against)** an *prep. w. dat. or acc.*
once einmal; **all at once** auf einmal
one (people, they) man *indef. pron.;* **one says (people say, it is said)** man sagt
only nur
open offen
open (to) öffnen, auf-machen
opportunity die Gelégenheit, -en
or oder; **either . . . or** entweder . . . oder
order: in order to um . . . zu
other der, die, das andere
otherwise sonst
ought sollen, er soll, sollte, hat gesollt
out of aus *prep. w. dat.*
outside draußen
outside of außer *prep. w. dat.*
over über *prep. w. dat. or acc.*

P
pack (to) packen
page die Seite, -n
pair das Paar, -es, -e
paper das Papier', -s, -e; **newspaper** die Zeitung, -en
pardon (to) entschul'digen *w. acc.;* verzeíhen *w. dat.,* er verzeiht, verzieh, hat verziehen
parents die Eltern
part der Teil, -es, -e; **in part** zum Teil
parking lot der Parkplatz,-es, ¨-e
pass (to) *(an examination)* bestehen
passenger der Passagier', -s, -e
passport der Reisepass, -passes, -pässe
pay (to) (be)zahlen
pay attention (to) acht-geben
pen der Stift, -e
pencil der Bleistift, -s, -e
people die Leute
percent das Prozent, -s, -e
performance die Vorstellung, -en
perhaps vielleicht'
permit (to) erlaúben
permitted (to be) dürfen, er darf, durfte, hat gedurft
person die Person', -en
photograph die Photographié, -n, das Foto
piano das Klavier', -s, -e
picture das Bild, -es, -er
piece das Stück, -es, -e
place der Platz, -es, ¨-e
place (to) setzen; **to place before** vor-legen
plate der Teller, -s, -
play das Schauspiel, -s, -e
play (to) spielen
pleasant angenehm
please bitte!
please (to) gefal'len *w .dat.,* er gefällt, gefiel, hat gefallen
pleasure das Vergnü'gen, -s, -
popular (with) beliebt' (bei)
portrait das Porträt', -s, -e
position die Stellung, -en
possible möglich

post office das Postamt, -s, ¨-er
pound das Pfund, -es, -e
practice üben
praise loben
prefer (to) vor-ziehen; lieber + *verb:* **I prefer spring** ich habe den Frühling lieber
prepare (to) bereíten
present (to) schenken
present das Geschenk', -s, -e
pretty hübsch
price der Preis, -es, -e
probably wahrschein'lich
problem das Problem', -s, -e
profession der Beruf', -s, -e
professor der Profes'sor, -s, Professóren
program das Programm', -s, -e
progress der Fortschritt, -s, -e
promise (to) verspréchen
proud (of) stolz auf *w .acc.*
pupil der Schüler, -s, -
purchase der Einkauf, -s, ¨-e
purchase (to) kaufen, einkaufen
put (to) stellen

Q
question die Frage, -n
quickly schnell, rasch
quiet ruhig, still
quite ganz, recht

R
radio das Radio, -s; **on the radio** im Radio
rain der Regen, -s
rain (to) regnen
raincoat der Regenmantel, -s, ¨-
rather ziemlich
reach (to) erreíchen
read (to) lesen, er liest, las, hat gelesen
really eigentlich, wirklich
receive (to) bekom'men; erhal'ten
recently neulich
recognize (to) erken'nen
record die Schallplatte, -n
red rot
relate (to) erzäh'len
remain (to) bleiben, er bleibt, blieb, ist geblieben
remember (to) sich erin'nern an *w. acc.*
rent (to) mieten
report (to) berich'ten
representative der Vertréter, -s, -
rest (to) ruhen
restaurant das Restaurant', -s, -s
rich reich
ride fahren, er fährt, fuhr, ist gefahren; **to ride past** vorbei-fahren
right das Recht; **rightly** mit Recht; **you are right** Sie haben Recht
ring up (to) an-rufen
role die Rolle, -, -n
room das Zimmer, -s, -
round rund

row die Reihe, -n
run (to) laufen, er läuft, lief, ist gelaufen

S
sad traurig
satisfied zufriéden
saucer die Untertasse, -n
say (to) sagen
scarcely kaum
school die Schule, -n
sea die See, -n
season die Jahreszeit, -en
seat der Platz, -es, ¨-e; der Sitz, -es, -e
see (to) sehen, er sieht, sah, hat gesehen
sell (to) verkaúfen
send (to) senden, schicken
several einige, mehrere
sharp scharf; **5 o'clock sharp** Punkt 5 Uhr
shirt das Hemd, -es, -en
shoe der Schuh, -es, -e
shop der Laden, -s, ¨-
shop (to) ein-kaufen, Einkäufe machen
short kurz
should sollen, er soll, sollte, hat gesollt
show (to) zeigen
sick krank
side die Seite, -n
since seit *prep. w. dat.;* seitdem' *sub. conj.*
sincerely herzlich
sing (to) singen, er singt, sang, hat gesungen
single *(sole)* einzig
sister die Schwester, -n
sit (to) sitzen, er sitzt, saß, hat gesessen; **to sit down** sich setzen
sleep schlafen, er schläft, schlief, hat geschlafen
slow langsam
small klein
smoke (to) rauchen
snow (to) schneien
so so, also
sofa das Sofa, -s, -s
some etwas, einige, mehrere
somebody jemand
something etwas
son der Sohn, -es, ¨-e
soon bald; **as soon as** sobald' *sub. conj.*
sorry: I am sorry es tut mir leid
soup die Suppe, -n
speak (to) sprechen, er spricht, sprach, hat gesprochen
spend (to) *(time)* verbrin'gen; *(money)* ausgeben
spite: in spite of trotz *prep. w. gen.*
splendid herrlich, großartig
spoon der Löffel, -s, -
spring der Frühling, -s
stand (to) stehen, er steht, stand, hat gestanden; **to stand up** auf-stehen
station die Station', -en; der Bahnhof, -s, ¨-e
stay (to) bleiben, er bleibt, blieb, ist geblieben
still ruhig, still
stop (to) halt-machen; **(cease)** auf-hören
store der Laden, -s, ¨-

story die Geschich'te, -, -n
street die Straße, -n
student der Student', -en, -en
study *(workroom)* das Arbeitszimmer, -s, -
suburb der Vorort, -s, -e
succeed (to) gelin'gen *w .dat.,* es gelingt, gelang, ist gelungen; **I succeed** es gelingt mir
such solcher, -e, -es; **such a** solch ein
suddenly plötzlich
suit *(man's)* der Anzug, -s, ¨-e; *(woman's)* das Kostüm', -s, -e
suitcase der Koffer, -s, -
sum die Summe, -n
summer der Sommer, -s
supper das Abendessen, -s, -
supposed: to be supposed to sollen, er soll, sollte, hat gesollt
surely sicherlich, gewiss
surprise die Überráschung, -en

T
take (to) er nimmt, nahm, hat genommen; **to take place** statt-finden
talk (to) reden, sprechen
taste (to) *w .obj.* versúchen; **it tastes good** es schmeckt gut
taxi das Taxi, -s, -s
tea der Tee, -s
teach (to) lehren, unterrich'ten
teacher der Lehrer, -s, -
telephone das Telefon', -s, -e
telephone (to) an-rufen
television das Fernsehen; **(set)** der Fernsehapparat
test (to) prüfen
thank danken *w. dat.;* **thanks** danke!, danke schön; **many thanks** vielen Dank!
that jener, -e, -es; dass *sub. conj.;* das **(pointing out) that is a book, etc.** das ist ein Buch, usw.
theater das Theáter, -s, -; **to the theater** ins Theater
their ihr, ihre, ihr
then dann, denn; **now and then** dann und wann
there dort, da
therefore deshalb, deswegen, daher
thing die Sache, -n; das Ding, -es, -e
think (to) denken, er denkt, dachte, hat gedacht; **to think of** denken an *w. acc.*
thirst der Durst; **I am thirsty** ich habe Durst
through durch *prep. w. acc.*
ticket die Karte, -n; **(of admission)** die Eintrittskarte; *(for vehicle)* die Fahrkarte
time die Zeit, -en; **once, twice, three times, etc.** einmal, zweimal, dreimal, usw., **at the same time** zugleich'
tip das Trinkgeld, -s, -er
tired müde
to zu *prep. w. dat.;* **up to** bis
today heute
together zusam'men
too zu; *(also)* auch
tourist der Tourist', -en, -en
train der Zug, -es, ¨-e
travel (to) reisen
traveler der Reisende, -n, -n
trip die Reise, -n

true wahr; **isn't it true** nicht wahr?
truth die Wahrheit, -en
try (to) versúchen
typewriter die Schreibmaschine, -n

U

uncle der Onkel, -s, -
under unter *prep. w. dat. or acc.*
understand (to) versteh'en, er versteht, verstand, hat verstanden
unfortunately leider
university die Universität', -en
until bis
use (to) gebraúchen
usual gewöhn'lich

V

vacation die Ferien *(plur.)*
vegetable das Gemü'se, -s, -
very sehr
village das Dorf, -es, ¨-er
visit (to) besúchen

W

wait (to) warten; **to wait for** warten auf *w. acc.*
waiter der Kellner, -s, -
waiting room der Wartesaal, -s, -säle
walk gehen, er geht, ging, ist gegangen; **to take a walk** spaziéren gehen, einen Spazier'gang machen
wall die Wand, ¨-e
want wollen, er will, wollte, hat gewollt
warm warm; **warmer** wärmer
wash (to) waschen, er wäscht, wusch, hat gewaschen; **to wash oneself** sich waschen
watch die Uhr, -en
water das Wasser, -s
weather das Wetter, -s
week die Woche, -n

well gut, wohl; **well-known** bekannt
wet nass
what? was? welcher, -e, -es? **what kind of?** was für ein?
when, whenever wenn *sub. conj.;* wann *interr.*
where? wo? **(at what place?)**; wohin? **(to what place?)**
whether ob *sub. conj.*
which welcher, -e, -es
while während *sub. conj.*
white weiß
who? wer?
whole ganz
why? warum?
win (to) gewin'nen, er gewinnt, gewann, hat gewonnen
window das Fenster, -s, -
wine der Wein, -es, -e
winter der Winter, -s, -
wish (to) wünschen
with mit *prep. w. dat.*
without ohne *prep. w. acc.*
woman die Frau, -en
wonderful wunderbar
word (in phrases and sentences) das Wort, -es, -e; **(not connected in sense)** das Wort, -es, ¨-er
work die Arbeit, -en
work (to) arbeiten
world die Welt
write schreiben, er schreibt, schrieb, hat geschríeben

Y

year das Jahr, -es, -e
yesterday gestern
yet noch; **not yet** noch nicht
you du, ihr, Sie; **your** dein, deine, dein; euer, euere, euer, Ihr, Ihre, Ihr
young jung

COMMUNICATION GAMES

1. GETTING TO KNOW EACH OTHER

Find classmates, German students, etc. who have something in common with you.

a. Fill out the chart with information about yourself (in German, of course!)

b. Move around the classroom and talk to different classmates asking for the information needed.

c. Whenever you find someone who has something in common with you, write that person's name in the corresponding square.

d. Report to the class if there are some striking similarities.

Geburtsmonat	Lieblingsessen	Wohnort
Ich: _____	Ich: _____	IIch: _____
Freund: _____	Freund: _____	Freund: _____
Geschwister	Hobby	Alter
Ich: _____	Ich: _____	Ich: _____
Freund: _____	Freund: _____	Freund: _____
Lieblingsgetränk	Beruf	Nationalität
Ich: _____	Ich: _____	Ich: _____
Freund: _____	Freund: _____	Freund: _____

Wichtige Redemittel:

Wie alt bist du / sind Sie?
Wie viele Geschwister hast du / haben Sie?
Wann bist du / sind Sie geboren?
Wo wohnst du / wohnen Sie?
Wo kommst du / kommen Sie her?
Was isst oder trinkst du / essen oder trinken Sie am liebsten?
Was ist dein / Ihr Beruf?
Was machst du / machen Sie in deiner / Ihrer Freizeit?

Idea: Maria Zaorob and Elizabeth Chin: *Games for Grammar Practice*, Cambridge: CUP 2003.

2. WHAT IS YOUR PROFESSION?

a. Pick one profession from the list below.

b. The others ask questions in order to find the profession chosen. You may answer only with **ja** *or* **nein**.

Lehrer	Polizist	Fußballspieler	Mechaniker
Bäcker	Anwalt	Pilot	Verkäuferin
Sängerin	Krankenschwester	Taxifahrer	Pfarrer
Frisör	Schauspieler	Koch	Sekretärin
Arzt	Tischler	Feuerwehrmann	Fotograf

Wichtige Redemittel

Arbeitest du / Arbeiten Sie am Tage?

in der Nacht?
allein?
mit Kollegen?
im Freien?
im Büro?
im Sitzen?
im Stehen?
mit Werkzeug?
vor Publikum?

Idea: Sanchez, Sanz, Dreke: *Spielend Deutsch lernen*, Berlin: Langenscheidt 1998.

3. MY NEIGHBORS

Use the clues below to find out about the people in your neighborhood.

Hausnummer	2	4	6	8	10
Name					
Alter					
Beruf					
Haustier					
Lieblingsgetränk					

a. Der Mann in Haus 2 ist 48 Jahre alt.

b. Frau Braun wohnt nicht neben Fräulein Meier.

c. Eine Bewohnerin trinkt am liebsten Tee.

d. Frau Schiller wohnt mit ihrem Hund in Haus 4.

e. Der jüngste Bewohner ist erst 22 Jahre alt.

f. Die Verkäuferin trinkt am liebsten Wein.

g. Der Herr in Haus 8 hat kein Haustier.

h. Die Pensionistin füttert manchmal Fische in einer fremden Wohnung.

i. Herr Clark hat sich schon oft wegen des Hundegebells mit seiner Nachbarin bestritten.

k. Frau Meier hat nur einen Nachbarn.

l. Herr Müller ist Student.

m. Die Frisörin schneidet dem befreundeten Geschäftsmann manchmal gratis die Haare.

n. Frau Braun ist schon 79 Jahre alt.

o. Die 25 jährige trinkt am liebsten Kaffee.

p. Ein entflogener Wellensittich landete bei einem Bewohner, der am liebsten Wasser trinkt.

q. Die Katze vom Bierliebhaber läuft manchmal zur 36 jährigen Nachbarin.

4. TIC TAC TOE

Play to the rules of Tic Tac Toe. (The player who manages to have three symbols in a row—horizontally, vertically, diagonally—wins.) In this game, however, you can only place your symbol if you have answered the question before. If your answer is incorrect you are not allowed to place your symbol and it is your opponent's turn.

a. Gegenteile (opposites)

reich	warm	gut
schnell	traurig	dünn
alt	klein	dunkel

b. Komparativ, Superlativ (comparative, superlative)

reich	warm	gut
schnell	traurig	dünn
alt	klein	dunkel

c. Bilden Sie das Präteritum (put into the "präteritum")

können	sprechen	haben
laufen	fahren	kommen
rufen	sagen	sollen

d. Bilden Sie das korrekte Partizip II (find the past participle)

können	sprechen	haben
laufen	fahren	kommen
rufen	sagen	sollen

Idea: Mario Rinvolucri: *Grammar Games*, Cambridge: CUP 1984.